DK TRAVEL GUIDES

BERLIN

DORLING KINDERSLEY *TRAVEL GUIDES*

BERLIN

Main Contributor: MAŁGORZATA OMILANOWSKA

DORLING KINDERSLEY PUBLISHING, INC.
LONDON • NEW YORK • SYDNEY • DELHI
PARIS • MUNICH • JOHANNESBURG
www.dk.com

A DORLING KINDERSLEY BOOK

www.dk.com

Produced by Wydawnictwo Wiedza i Życie, Warsaw

MANAGING EDITOR Ewa Szwagrzyk
SERIES EDITOR Joanna Egert
DTP DESIGNER Pawel Pasternak
CONSULTANT Nils Meyer
ILLUSTRATIONS Andrzej Wielgosz,
Lena Maminajszwili, Dorota Jarymowicz
PHOTOGRAPHY Dorota and Mariusz Jarymowicz
CORRECTION Bożena Leszkowicz
PRODUCTION Anna Kożurno-Królikowska, Ewa Roguska

Dorling Kindersley Limited
EDITORS Nancy Jones, Esther Labi, Hugh Thompson
SENIOR EDITOR Helen Townsend

CONTRIBUTORS Małgorzata Omilanowska, Christian Tempel
MAPS Maria Wojciechowska, Dariusz Osuch
(D. Osuch i spółka)

Reproduced by Colourscan, Singapore
Printed and bound by Sun Fung Offset Binding Co., Ltd., China

First American Edition, 2000
4 6 8 10 9 7 5 3
Published in the United States by
Dorling Kindersley Publishing, Inc.
95 Madison Avenue, New York 10016

Copyright © 2000 Dorling Kindersley Limited, London

Library of Congress Cataloging-in-Publication Data

Omilanowska, Małgorzata.
Berlin/main contributor, Małgorzata Omilanowska.
p. cm. -- (Dorling Kindersley travel guides)
Includes index.
ISBN 0-7894-5168-9 (alk. paper)
1. Berlin (Germany) -- Guidebooks. I. Title. II. Series.

DD859.045 1999
914.3'15504879 -- dc21   99-056183

**The information in every
Dorling Kindersley Travel Guide is checked annually**.
Every effort has been made to ensure that this book is as
up-to-date as possible at the time of going to press. Some details,
however, such as telephone numbers, opening hours, prices,
gallery hanging arrangements and travel information are liable
to change. As a result of the return of the German government to
Berlin, and the large amount of construction work under way,
whole areas of the city are in a constant state of change. The
publishers cannot accept responsibility for any consequences
arising from the use of this book. We value the views and
suggestions of our readers very highly. Please write to:
Senior Managing Editor, Dorling Kindersley Travel Guides,
9 Henrietta Street, London WC2E 8PS.

CONTENTS

A child's drawing of Berlin's Fernsehturm (Television Tower), Siegessäule and Funkturm (Radio Tower)

Bomb-damaged Kaiser-Wilhelm-
Gedächtniskirche (see pp146–7)

The Spree river passing by the Nikolaiviertel *(see pp88–9)*

Chicken fricassée with crayfish *(see p231)*

Modern architecture by the former Checkpoint Charlie *(see p136)*

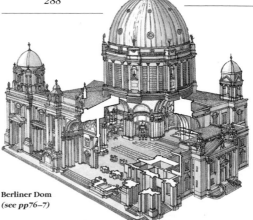

Berliner Dom *(see pp76–7)*

HOW TO USE THIS GUIDE

THIS DORLING KINDERSLEY travel guide helps you to get the most from your visit to Berlin. It provides detailed practical information and expert recommendations. *Introducing Berlin* maps the city and the region, and sets it in its historical and cultural context, and describes events through the entire year. *Berlin at a Glance* is an overview of the city's main attractions. *Berlin Area by Area* starts on page 52. This is the main sightseeing section, which covers all of the important sights, with photographs, maps and illustrations. *Greater Berlin* covers the nearby historic city of Potsdam, as well as three walking tours. Information about hotels, restaurants, shops and markets, entertainment and sports is found in *Travellers' Needs*. The *Survival Guide* has advice on everything from using Berlin's medical services, telephones and post offices to the public transport system.

FINDING YOUR WAY AROUND THE SIGHTSEEING SECTION

Each of eight sightseeing areas in Berlin is colour-coded for easy reference. Every chapter opens with an introduction to the area of the city it covers, describing its history and character, and has a *Street-by-Street* map illustrating typical parts of that area. Finding your way around the chapter is made simple by the numbering system used throughout. The most important sights are covered in detail in two or more full pages.

Each area has colour-coded thumb tabs.

1 Introduction to the area
For easy reference, the sights in each area are numbered and plotted on an area map. To help the visitor, this map also shows U- and S-Bahn stations, main bus and tram stops and parking areas. The area's key sights are listed by category, such as Museums.

Locator map

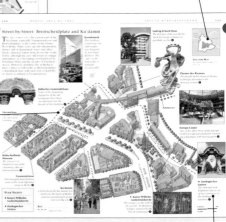

A locator map shows where you are in relation to other areas in the city centre.

A suggested route takes in some of the most interesting and attractive streets in the area.

2 Street-by-Street map
This gives a bird's-eye view of interesting and important parts of each sightseeing area. The numbering of the sights ties up with the area map and the fuller description of the entries on the pages that follow.

Stars indicate the features that no visitor should miss.

BERLIN AREA MAP

The coloured areas shown on this map *(see inside front cover)* are the eight main sightseeing areas used in this guide. Each is covered in a full chapter in *Berlin Area by Area (see pp52–205)*. They are highlighted on other maps throughout the book. In *Berlin at a Glance*, for example, they help you locate the top sights. They are also used to help you find the position of three walks *(see pp198–205)*.

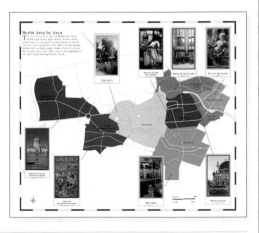

Numbers refer to each sight's position on the area map and its place in the chapter.

Practical information provides everything you need to know to visit each sight. Map references pinpoint the sight's location on the *Street Finder* map *(see pp300–323)*.

3 Detailed information

All the important sights in Berlin are described individually. They are listed in order following the numbering on the area map at the start of the section. Practical information includes a map reference, opening hours and telephone numbers. The key to the symbols is on the back flap.

The visitors' checklist gives all the practical information needed to plan your visit.

Story boxes provide information about historical or cultural topics relating to the sights.

4 Berlin's major sights

Historic buildings are dissected to reveal their interiors; museums and galleries have colour-coded floorplans to help you find the most important exhibits.

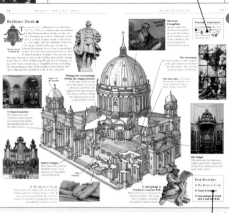

The list of star sights recommends the places that no visitor should miss.

INTRODUCING
BERLIN

Putting Berlin on the Map

Berlin, THE CAPITAL OF the Federal Republic of Germany, has a population of approximately 3.5 million and covers 889 sq km (343 sq miles). Situated in the eastern part of the country, in the middle of the Brandenburg region, Berlin occupies the flatlands on the banks of the Havel and Spree rivers, which merge in the Spandau district. The whole city is criss-crossed with numerous canals.

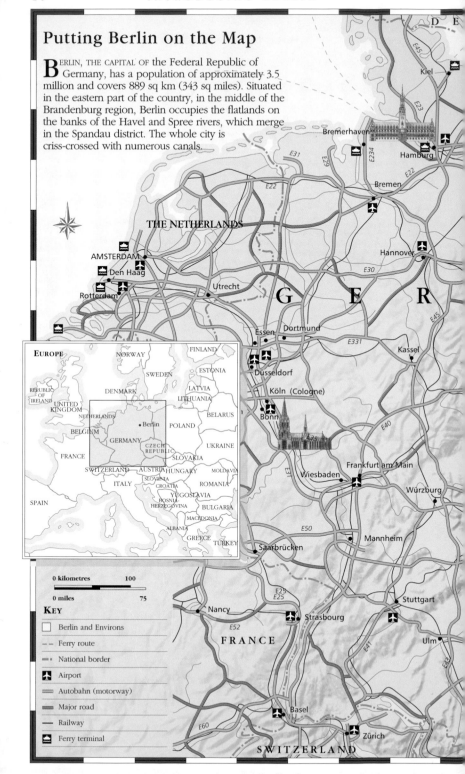

EUROPE

NORWAY
FINLAND
SWEDEN
ESTONIA
REPUBLIC OF IRELAND
UNITED KINGDOM
DENMARK
LATVIA
LITHUANIA
NETHERLANDS
• Berlin
BELARUS
BELGIUM
POLAND
GERMANY
CZECH REPUBLIC
UKRAINE
FRANCE
SLOVAKIA
SWITZERLAND
AUSTRIA
HUNGARY
MOLDAVIA
SLOVENIA
ITALY
CROATIA
ROMANIA
SPAIN
BOSNIA-HERZEGOVINA
YUGOSLAVIA
BULGARIA
MACEDONIA
ALBANIA
GREECE
TURKEY

KEY

☐	Berlin and Environs
- - -	Ferry route
∙■∙	National border
✈	Airport
═══	Autobahn (motorway)
━━━	Major road
—	Railway
⚓	Ferry terminal

0 kilometres   100
0 miles   75

THE NETHERLANDS

AMSTERDAM
Den Haag
Rotterdam
Utrecht

D   E

Kiel

Bremerhaven

Hamburg

Bremen

Hannover

G   E   R

Essen   Dortmund

Düsseldorf

Kassel

Köln (Cologne)

Bonn

Frankfurt am Main

Wiesbaden

Würzburg

Mannheim

Saarbrücken

Nancy

Strasbourg

Stuttgart

Ulm

FRANCE

Basel

Zürich

SWITZERLAND

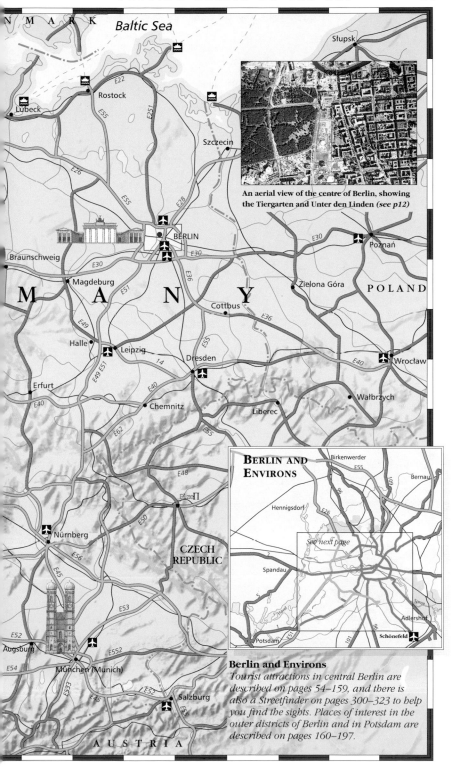

Baltic Sea

Słupsk

Rostock

Lübeck

Szczecin

An aerial view of the centre of Berlin, showing
the Tiergarten and Unter den Linden *(see p12)*

Braunschweig

BERLIN

E30

Poznań

M   A   N   Y

Magdeburg

Zielona Góra

POLAND

Cottbus

Halle   Leipzig

Dresden

Wrocław

Erfurt

Chemnitz

Liberec

Wałbrzych

**BERLIN AND
ENVIRONS**

Birkenwerder

Bernau

Hennigsdorf

See next page

Nürnberg

CZECH
REPUBLIC

Spandau

Augsburg

Adlershof

München (Munich)

Potsdam

Schönefeld

Salzburg

Berlin and Environs
*Tourist attractions in central Berlin are
described on pages 54–159, and there is
also a Streetfinder on pages 300–323 to help
you find the sights. Places of interest in the
outer districts of Berlin and in Potsdam are
described on pages 160–197.*

A   U   S   T   R   I   A

Greater Berlin

Berlin in its present form was created in 1920, through an amalgamation of several towns and villages surrounding the historic centre. It now consists of 23 administrative districts (becoming 12 in 2001), some of which, like Spandau and Köpenick, were formerly separate municipalities. The city is surrounded by recreational areas, including lakes and woodlands. To the southwest lies the city of Potsdam with its splendid palaces, which can be reached easily by public transport.

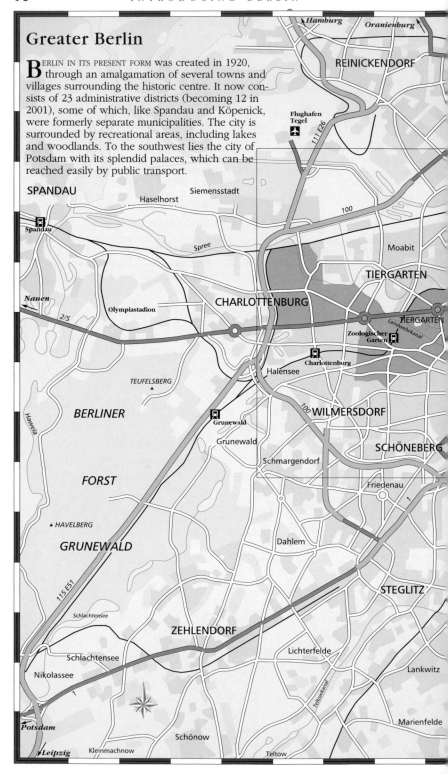

Hamburg *Oranienburg*

REINICKENDORF

Flughafen Tegel

111 E26

100

SPANDAU

Siemensstadt

Haselhorst

Moabit

Spandau

Spree

TIERGARTEN

Nauen

2/5

Olympiastadion

CHARLOTTENBURG

Landwehrkanal

TIERGARTEN

Zoologischer Garten

Charlottenburg

Halensee

100

WILMERSDORF

TEUFELSBERG

BERLINER

Grunewald

Grunewald

SCHÖNEBERG

Schmargendorf

Havela

Friedenau

1

FORST

▲ *HAVELBERG*

Dahlem

GRUNEWALD

115 E51

STEGLITZ

Schlachtensee

ZEHLENDORF

Lichterfelde

Schlachtensee

Lankwitz

Nikolassee

1

Potsdam

Schönow

Marienfelde

Leipzig   Kleinmachnow

Teltow

Teltokanal

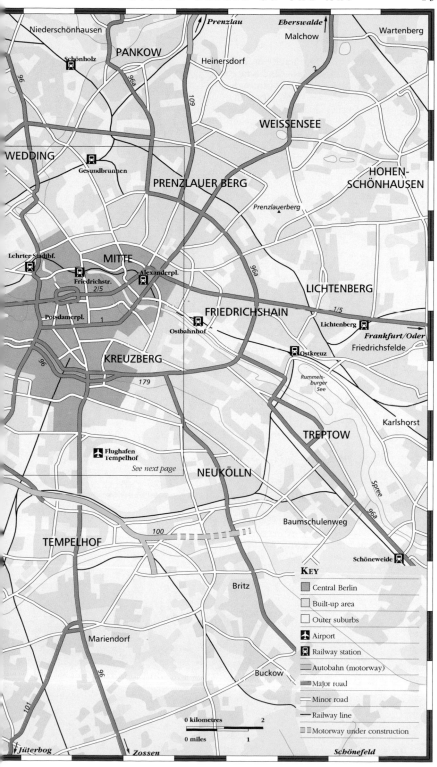

Niederschönhausen

Schönholz

PANKOW

Prenzlau

Eberswalde

Malchow

Wartenberg

Heinersdorf

WEISSENSEE

WEDDING

Gesundbrunnen

PRENZLAUER BERG

Prenzlauerberg

**HOHEN-
SCHÖNHAUSEN**

Lehrter Stadtbf.

MITTE

Friedrichstr.
2/5

Alexanderpl.

LICHTENBERG

FRIEDRICHSHAIN

1/5

Potsdamerpl.
1

Ostbahnhof

Lichtenberg

Friedrichsfelde

Frankfurt/Oder

KREUZBERG

Ostkreuz

179

Rummels-
burger
See

Karlshorst

Flughafen
Tempelhof

See next page

TREPTOW

NEUKÖLLN

Spree

Baumschulenweg

TEMPELHOF

100

Schöneweide

Britz

KEY

Central Berlin

Built-up area

Outer suburbs

Airport

Railway station

Autobahn (motorway)

Major road

Minor road

Railway line

Motorway under construction

Mariendorf

Buckow

0 kilometres   2

0 miles   1

Jüterbog

Zossen

Schönefeld

Central Berlin

CENTRAL BERLIN is divided into eight colour-coded sightseeing areas. The historic core is located along the eastern and northern banks of the Spree river, around the grand boulevard Unter den Linden and on Museum Island. West of the centre is the sprawling green Tiergarten. To the south is Kreuzberg, an area renowned for its alternative lifestyle. Further west is Kurfürstendamm, the centre of former West Berlin. Finally, at the edge of the city centre is the summer residence of the Prussian kings, the Schloss Charlottenburg.

Around Schloss Charlottenburg

The Baroque Charlottenburg Palace, named after Sophie Charlotte (wife of Friedrich III), is one of Berlin's greatest tourist attractions. Its magnificent rooms contain many beautiful objects (see pp150–59).

Kulturforum, Tiergarten

The Kulturforum is a cluster of interesting museums and libraries. It is also the home of the Berlin Philharmonic (see pp112–31).

KEY

▮	Major sight
▮	Other sight
🚉	Railway station
U	U-Bahn
S	S-Bahn
P	Parking
✝	Church
✡	Synagogue

Around Kurfürstendamm

The Kurfürstendamm, or Ku'damm as it is often called, is the main thoroughfare of western Berlin. This area contains numerous shops, restaurants, bars and cinemas (see pp140–49).

Berliner Dom, Museum Island
*On this island are Berlin's Protestant
cathedral, with its Neo-Baroque interior
and massive dome, and
a museum complex
(see pp70–85).*

**Rotes Rathaus,
East of the Centre**
*This monumental
town hall, which
replaces the former
medieval Rathaus,
dates from the 1860s.
It is decorated with
terracotta bas-reliefs,
(see pp86–97).*

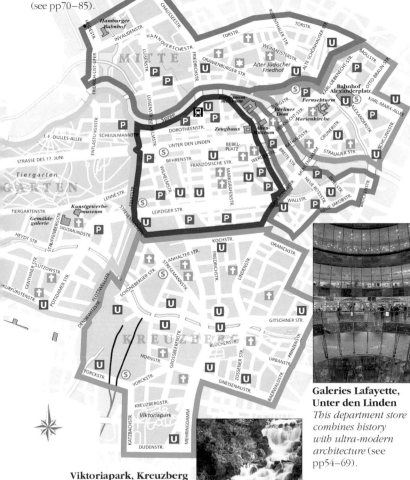

**Galeries Lafayette,
Unter den Linden**
*This department store
combines history
with ultra-modern
architecture (see
pp54–69).*

Viktoriapark, Kreuzberg
*This park is situated on a hill in the
Kreuzberg district, whose inhabitants include many Turks and
eccentric artists (see pp132–9).*

| 0 metres | 500 |
| 0 yards | 500 |

THE HISTORY OF BERLIN

Berlin is one of the younger *European capitals. The first written reference to the small fishing settlement of Cölln appeared in the year 1237. Together with the equally insignificant settlement of Berlin on the opposite bank of the Spree river, it was to become first a successful trading city under the control of the Margraves of Brandenburg, then capital of Prussia, and finally, the capital of Germany. Following World War II and the 1949 armistice, Berlin became a central arena for the Cold War. In 1991, after the fall of the Berlin wall, the city became the capital of the newly-united Federal Republic of Germany.*

EARLY SETTLEMENTS

During the first centuries AD the banks of the Spree and Havel rivers were inhabited by various tribes, most notably the Germanic Semnones. By the end of the 6th century the Semnones were competing for land with Slavic tribes, who built forts at what are now the Berlin suburbs of Köpenick *(see p167)* and Spandau *(see p177)*. Five hundred years later the Slavic tribes were finally defeated following the arrival of the warlike Saxon, Albrecht the Bear of the House of the Ascanians, who became the first *Markgraf* (Margrave, or Count) of Brandenburg. The banks of the Spree river were now resettled with immigrants from areas to the west including the Harz mountains, the Rhine valley and Franconia.

Statue of Albrecht the Bear

BEGINNINGS OF THE MODERN CITY

Berlin's written history began in the early 13th century, when the twin settlements of Berlin and Cölln grew up on opposite banks of the Spree river, around what is now the Nikolaiviertel *(see p90)*. Trading in fish, rye and timber, the towns formed an alliance in 1307, becoming Berlin-Cölln, a deal celebrated by the construction of a joint town hall.

Following the death of the last Ascanian ruler in 1319, Brandenburg became the object of a long and bloody feud between the houses of Luxemburg and Wittelsbach, with devastating effects for the area's inhabitants. In 1411 the desperate townspeople appealed to the Holy Roman Emperor for help, receiving in response Friedrich von Hohenzollern as the town's special protector. Then in 1415 Rome duly rewarded Friedrich by naming him Elector of Brandenburg, a fateful appointment that marked the beginning of the 500-year rule of the House of Hohenzollern.

TIMELINE

1100	1150	1200	1250	1300	1350	1400
1134 Investiture of Albrecht the Bear	**1197** First mention of Spandau	**1237** First written reference to Cölln	**1307** Signing of the treaty between Cölln and Berlin	**1359** Berlin and Cölln join Hanseatic League	**1415** Friedrich von Hohenzollern appointed Elector of Brandenburg	
1157 Albrecht the Bear defeats Slavic tribes and is crowned Margrave of Brandenburg	**1209** First documented mention of Köpenick		**1244** First written reference to the settlement of Berlin	**c.1260** Berlin is enlarged		

Silver denarius of 1369

◁ **Adolf von Menzel's symbolic painting *Borussia*, or *Prussia* (1868), at the Ephraim-Palais**

Deposition from the Cross (c.1520), a pane of a
Gothic polyptych from the time of the Reformation

THE EARLY HOHENZOLLERNS

In 1432 Berlin and Cölln were formally
unified. By 1443 Elector Friedrich II,
son of Friedrich I, had begun
construction of the town's first castle,
the future Stadtschloss *(see p71)*. This
was part of his plan to make Berlin-
Cölln the capital of Brandenburg and
to reduce the powers and privileges
of its citizens. Despite fierce opposition from the local population,
the castle was built. By 1448 all
opposition had been violently
crushed, and in 1451 the castle
became the Elector's official
residence. To symbolize the
consolidation of Hohenzollern
power, he added an iron chain
and padlock around the neck
of the city's heraldic bear.

By the time Friedrich's
nephew Johann Cicero became

**A falconer on a
16th-century tile**

Elector in 1486, Berlin-Cölln was formally established as the capital of the
March of Brandenburg.

REFORMATION AND
THE THIRTY YEARS' WAR

During the first half of the 16th
century, the radical religious ideas
of Martin Luther (1483–1546) spread
quickly throughout the whole of
Brandenburg. In 1539 the new
Protestantism was adopted by the
Elector, Joachim II Hector, and most
of the town's aldermen.

For a time the city grew fast, boosted
by the arrival of religious refugees
from the Netherlands, as well as Italian
artists invited by the subsequent elector, Joachim Georg. However, successive epidemics of the bubonic
plague occurred in 1576, 1598 and
1600, checking the town's growth. The
effect was compounded by the advent
of the Thirty Years' War which raged
from 1618 to 1648, turning the whole
of the Holy Roman Empire into a
bloody battlefield. In 1627 the Elector
of Brandenburg had fled, relocating
his court to the less exposed town of
Königsberg. By 1648 the population
of Berlin-Cölln had fallen to just 6,000,
its population being decimated by
famine and disease.

BERLIN UNDER
THE GREAT ELECTOR

The fortunes of Berlin were
turned by the arrival of
Friedrich Wilhelm von Hohenzollern, who ascended the
Brandenburg throne in 1640.
Under the rule of this man,
later known as the Great
Elector, Berlin experienced a
period of an unprecedented
growth. The city's population

TIMELINE

1415	1465	1515	1565

1432 Unification of
Cölln and Berlin

1486 Elector Johann
Cicero makes Berlin his
permanent residence

1539 Elector Joachim II
converts to the
Protestant faith

1447–8 Berlin rebellion
against the Elector

1594 Building of the
Spandau citadel completed

1442 Construction begins on
the royal castle in Cölln

*Tankard in the shape of
Berlin's heraldic bear (1562)*

The former Stadtschloss (Berlin Castle), with Lange Brücke in the foreground, c.1685

rose to 20,000 by 1688 at the end of Friedrich Wilhelm's long reign.

In 1648 work started on the modern fortification of the city. The Lustgarten *(see p74)* was established opposite the Stadtschloss and the road later to become known as Unter den Linden *(see p60)* was planted with lime trees. The city's economic power increased following the building of the canal linking the Spree and Oder rivers, which turned Berlin into the hub of all Brandenburg trade.

Berlin began to expand in all directions with the creation of new satellite towns: Friedrichswerder was founded in 1658, Dorotheenstadt, in 1668, and Friedrichstadt in 1688. They would all be absorbed into a unified city of Berlin in 1709.

In 1671 several wealthy Jewish families expelled from Vienna settled in Berlin, while following the 1685 Edict of Potsdam, large numbers of French Huguenots flocked to Brandenburg, forced out of their homeland after Louis XIV repealed the Edict of Nantes. Both these events came to play a major role in the future development of the city.

THE CAPITAL OF PRUSSIA

The successor to the Great Elector, Friedrich III inherited the title in 1688. Thirteen years later he raised Brandenburg's status to that of a kingdom, and was crowned King Friedrich I of Prussia. Ambitious and with a taste for luxury, Friedrich became a powerful patron of the arts. Under his rule Berlin acquired its Academies of Fine Arts and Science. Artists transformed the castle into a Baroque palace. The Zeughaus *(see pp58–9)* and the summer palace or Schloss in Lietzenburg, later renamed Charlottenburg *(see pp154–5)*, were built at this time.

The next ruler of Prussia, Friedrich Wilhelm I (1713–40), was unlike his father and soon became known as the "Soldier-King". His initiatives were practical: Berlin was further expanded and encircled with a new wall, not for defence but as a measure against the desertion of conscripted citizens. Pariser Platz *(see p67)*, Leipziger Platz *(see p126)* and Mehringplatz *(see p138)* were all built at that time, and the population reached 90,000.

The next king was Friedrich II (1740–1786), otherwise known as Frederick the Great or "Alter Fritz" (Old Fritz). An educated man who appreciated art, he oversaw the city's transformation into a sophisticated cultural centre. He was also an aggressive empire builder, sparking the Seven Years' War of 1756–63 with his invasion of Silesia, during which Berlin was briefly occupied by Austrian and Russian troops. The city's development continued, however, and at the time of Friedrich II's death in 1786, its population numbered 150,000.

Friedrich II (1740–86)

1618–48 Thirty Years' War	**1688** Establishment of the new town of Friedrichstadt	**1751–2** Friedrich II introduces conscription
1668 Opening of the Spree-Oder canal	**1701** Coronation of Friedrich III as the first king of Prussia	**1756–63** Seven Years' War
1615	**1665**	**1715**	**1765**
1685 Edict of Potsdam allows large numbers of French Huguenot refugees to settle in Berlin	**1709** Unification of Berlin	**1740** Coronation of Frederick the Great
	1696 Opening of the Academy of Fine Arts (Akademie der Künste)	

Silver chalice (1695)

The Baroque Period

BERLIN'S BAROQUE PERIOD lasted from the second half of the 17th century to the end of the 18th, and saw the expansion of Berlin-Cölln from a small town, devastated by successive epidemics of bubonic plague and the ravages of the Thirty Years' War, into a rich and cosmopolitan metropolis. Population growth was rapid, aided by the official amalgamation of Berlin-Cölln with the previously independent communities of Dorotheenstadt, Friedrichstadt and Friedrichswerder. New city walls were built, as were many substantial buildings, including the Akademie der Künste, the Charité and Schloss Charlottenburg.

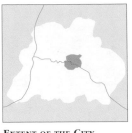

EXTENT OF THE CITY

| ■ 1734 | □ Today |

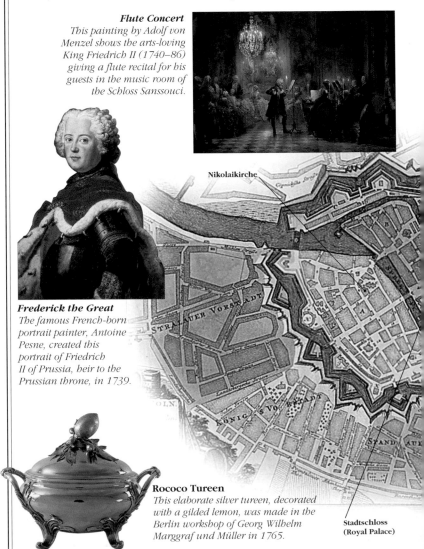

Flute Concert
This painting by Adolf von Menzel shows the arts-loving King Friedrich II (1740–86) giving a flute recital for his guests in the music room of the Schloss Sanssouci.

Nikolaikirche

Frederick the Great
The famous French-born portrait painter, Antoine Pesne, created this portrait of Friedrich II of Prussia, heir to the Prussian throne, in 1739.

Rococo Tureen
This elaborate silver tureen, decorated with a gilded lemon, was made in the Berlin workshop of Georg Wilhelm Marggraf und Müller in 1765.

Stadtschloss (Royal Palace)

Love in the Italian Theatre (1714)
French painter Jean-Antoine Watteau (1684–1721) was a favourite with King Friedrich II, and as a result many of his works can still be seen in Berlin.

Zeughaus (Former Arsenal)
The splendid Baroque Zeughaus was completed in 1730. Used to store weapons until 1875, it will house the Deutsches Historisches Museum. This view of it was painted in 1786 by Carl Traugott Fechhelm.

Rondell (now Mehringplatz)

Oktogon (now Leipziger Platz)

King Friedrich I
This medallion bears the likeness of the first King of Prussia (1688–1713). The work of sculptor and architect Andreas Schlüter (1660–1714), it adorns the king's tomb.

Quarré (now Pariser Platz)

BERLIN IN 1740

This map shows the layout of the city's 18th-century fortifications, with various landmark buildings. Contrary to today's convention, this map was drawn with the north pointing down, rather than up.

BAROQUE ARCHITECTURE IN BERLIN

Many of Berlin's Baroque buildings have been destroyed, but in the city centre some fine examples still exist. Don't miss the Zeughaus *(see pp58–9)*, two fine churches in Gendarmenmarkt – the Deutscher Dom and the Französischer Dom *(see pp64–5)* – the Parochialkirche *(see p97)* and Sophienkirche *(see p104)*. Another Baroque highlight, even though it is largely a reconstruction, is Schloss Charlottenburg *(see pp152–3)* with its delightful park.

Schloss Charlottenburg

Unter den Linden

Antique scroll depicting the grand boulevard of Unter den Linden, 1821

BEGINNINGS OF THE MODERN ERA

By the time Friedrich Wilhelm II (1786–97) ascended the throne of Prussia, the country's era of absolute rulers was nearing an end. New trends associated with Romanticism were gaining popularity, and there was an explosion of ideas from outstanding personalities such as writers Gotthold Ephraim Lessing (1729–81) and Friedrich and August-Wilhelm von Schlegel.

Throughout Europe, French Emperor Napoleon Bonaparte (1769–1821) was waging war, defeating the Prussians in 1806 at the battles of Jena and Austerlitz. As French troops moved in to occupy Berlin, Friedrich Wilhelm took his court to Königsberg, while Berlin's pride, the horse-drawn chariot (*Quadriga*) crowning the Brandenburg Gate, was dismantled and taken to Paris.

By the end of 1809 the royal court had returned to Berlin, and, having received huge reparations, Napoleon and his troops finally left the city. In 1814 the *Quadriga* was returned to Berlin, and a year later Napoleon was defeated at Waterloo. Granted the mineral-rich lands of the Rhineland and Westphalia at the subsequent Congress of Vienna, Prussia enjoyed rapid industrialization during the next 30 years, particularly in Berlin. By 1837 August

Borsig had opened his locomotive factory in the city, and in 1838 the first train ran on the Berlin–Potsdam railway. Many outstanding buildings were designed at this time by Karl Friedrich Schinkel *(see p179)*, including the Neue Wache *(see p60)* and the Schauspielhaus, renamed the Konzerthaus *(see p64)*. Berlin University (now Humboldt Universität) was established in 1810 and became a major seat of learning, attracting famous lecturers such as philosophers Georg Hegel (1770–1831) and Arthur Schopenhauer (1788–1860).

In 1844, however, recession hit Europe, leaving a quarter of all Prussians in poverty. Hunger riots rocked the city in April 1847 and by 1848 Berlin saw a people's uprising in which over 250 demonstrators were shot dead by the Prussian army.

BUILDING AN EMPIRE

In 1861 Friedrich Wilhelm IV (1840–1861) was forced by madness to cede the throne to his brother, Wilhelm (1861–1888). Otto von Bismarck was soon appointed Chancellor, with a foreign policy to install Prussia in Austria's place at the head of all German-speaking states. In 1864 Prussia declared war on Denmark, and successfully acquired Schleswig-Holstein.

Portrait of Friedrich
Wilhelm IV

TIMELINE

1791 Building of the Brandenburg Gate completed	**1799** Foundation of the Bauakademie	**1810** Berlin University established	**1831** Cholera epidemic breaks out	**1844** Opening of the Berlin zoo (Zoologischer Garten)
1785	**1800**	**1815**	**1830**	**1845**
Enamelled box, mid-18th century		**1806** Beginning of the 2-year French occupation of Berlin	**1830** Opening of the Altes Museum	
			1838 Opening of the Berlin–Potsdam railway line	

In 1866, following war with Austria, Prussia established dominance over the North German Confederation, an association of 22 states and free towns. In 1870 Prussia went to war with France, annexing the provinces of Alsace and Lorraine. Bismarck's next move was the proclamation of a German Empire on 18 January 1871, with Berlin as its capital and King Wilhelm I as Kaiser (Emperor). Thanks to the colossal reparations paid by France, and the abolition of trade barriers, Berlin now entered another period of rapid industrial growth, accompanied by a population explosion. By 1877 Berlin's population had grown to one million; by 1905 it was two million.

Poster advertising the Berlin Secession Exhibition of 1900, by Wilhelm Schulz

Berlin's original Reichstag (parliament) building, constructed in 1894

TRIUMPH AND DISASTER

The late 19th century saw an explosion of scientific and cultural achievement in the city, including the completion of a new sewage system in 1876, dramatically improving public health. By 1879 electric lamps lit the streets and in 1881 the first telephones were installed. A year later the first urban train line, the S-Bahn, was opened. Berlin's cultural and scientific life flourished, headed by such outstanding personalities as writer Theodor Fontane, painter Adolf von Menzel and bacteriologist Robert Koch. In 1898 Max Liebermann (see p67) founded the hugely influential Berlin Secessionist movement, with members including Käthe Kollwitz and Max Slevogt.

As the city prospered, political developments in Germany and throughout Europe were moving towards the stalemate of 1914. Initially, the outbreak of World War I had little effect on the life of Berlin, but the subsequent famine, strikes and total German defeat led to the November Revolution in 1918, and the abdication of Kaiser Wilhelm II.

The Berlin Congress of 1878 by Anton von Werner

Mosaic by Martin-Gropius-Bau

Capital of the German Empire

O N 18 JANUARY 1871, Berlin became the capital of the newly-established German Empire, fulfilling the expansionist ambitions of the Prussian Chancellor Otto von Bismarck. Bringing together many previously independent German-speaking regions, the new Empire stretched beyond the borders of present-day Germany, into what are now France, Poland, Russia and Denmark. Massive reparations paid by France after her defeat in the Franco-German war of 1870 stimulated the rapid growth of a fast-industrializing Berlin, accompanied by an explosion of scientific and artistic invention. Standing at just 300,000 in 1850, by 1900 the city's population had reached 1.9 million.

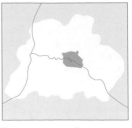

EXTENT OF THE CITY
▓ 1800   ☐ Today

House of Hohenzollern
Mosaics depicting the Hohenzollern rulers decorate the bombed remains of the Kaiser-Wilhelm-Gedächtnis-kirche (see pp146–7), completed in 1895.

The Stadtschloss
The Stadtschloss was the royal residence at the declaration of the Prussian Empire in 1871. Decorating the Rathausbrücke, in the foreground, was the magnificent statue of the Great Elector, now in the courtyard of Schloss Charlottenburg (see pp154–5).

Prussian nobles

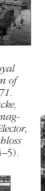

Members of parliament

Riehmers Hofgarten
In the late 19th century a huge number of buildings were erected, from tenement blocks to grand public buildings like this one.

Neptunbrunnen
This exuberant fountain (see p92) created by sculptor Reinhold Begas in 1891 was a present to Wilhelm II from the Berlin town council.

Hackescher Markt Station
Formerly called Bahnhof Börse, this is one of Berlin's first S-Bahn stations, built to a design by Johannes Vollmer and opened in 1902.

Vase with Portrait of Wilhelm II
Designed by Alexander Kips and bearing a portrait of Kaiser Wilhelm II, this vase was mass-produced at the Berlin Königliche-Porzellan-Manufaktur. Pieces were often presented to visiting heads of state.

Empress Augusta Victoria

Heir to the throne, Wilhelm

Black mourning clothes for women and black armbands for men were obligatory after the deaths of the two Kaisers, Wilhelm I and Friedrich III, in 1888.

Diplomatic corps

Prussian Chancellor Otto von Bismarck

Kaiser Wilhelm II

Opening of the Reichstag
This enormous canvas, painted by Anton von Werner in 1893, portrays Kaiser Wilhelm II giving a speech to the Members of Parliament, nobles and other dignitaries at the official opening of the Reichstag. This important event took place only 11 days after the coronation of the new Kaiser.

Charlotte Berend
The arts flourished in the years before World War I. This 1902 portrait of an actress is by Berlin artist, Lovis Corinth.

The burning of one of the thousands of buildings belonging to Jews on Kristallnacht, November 1938

THE WEIMAR REPUBLIC

On 9 November 1918 two politicians simultaneously proclaimed the birth of two German Republics. Social democrat Philipp Scheidemann announced the founding of a Democratic Republic, while hours later Karl Liebknecht, founder of the German communist movement, declared the Free Socialist Republic of Germany. Rivalries between the two groups erupted in January 1919 in a week of rioting, crushed by the Freikorps army who also brutally murdered communist leaders Karl Liebknecht and Rosa Luxemburg.

In February 1919 the National Assembly elected Social Democrat Friedrich Ebert President of the German Republic. In 1920 urban reform dramatically increased the size of Berlin, causing the population to swell to 3.8 million. Berlin, like the rest of the country, fell on hard times, with rising unemployment and rampant hyper-inflation.

At the same time, the city became the centre of a lively cultural life. Leading figures in theatre included Max Reinhardt and Bertolt Brecht, while from the UFA film studio came such classics as *The Cabinet of Dr Cagliari* and *Metropolis*. Jazz was popular, and the Berlin Philharmonic gained worldwide fame. Architecture flourished with Walter Gropius and Bruno Taut, while Berlin scientists Albert Einstein, Carl Bosch and Werner Heisenberg were all awarded the Nobel Prize.

THE THIRD REICH

The world stock-market crash of October 1929 and the ensuing Depression put the fragile German democracy under great pressure, paving the way for extremist politicians. On 30 January 1933 Adolf Hitler was appointed Chancellor. The Reichstag fire in February was used as a pretext to arrest communist and liberal opponents, and by March 1933 Hitler's Nazi (National Socialist Workers) Party was in control of the Reichstag. Books by "un-German" authors were burned in front of the Alte Bibliothek, and works of art deemed to be "degenerate" were removed from libraries.

Inferno (1946),
Fritz Koelle

The 1936 Olympic Games in Berlin were intended to be a showcase for Aryan supremacy. Although Germany won 33 gold medals, the real hero was the black American athlete Jesse Owens, with four gold medals.

The effects of the Nazi regime were felt particularly by Jews and intellectuals, many of whom were

Ein Volk, ein Reich, ein Führer!

Nazi propoganda poster of
Hitler, printed in 1938

TIMELINE

1919 Proclamation of the Weimar Republic	**1926** The Funkturm (radio tower) is opened		**1938** Kristallnacht on the night of 9–10 November	**1945** Germany surrenders on 8 May
		1930 Opening of the Pergamonmuseum		**24 June 1948–12 May 1949** Soviet blockade of Berlin
1920	**1930**		**1940**	**1950**	**1960**
1928 Premiere of the *Threepenny Opera* by Bertolt Brecht		**1933** Hitler accedes to power	**1942** Wannsee Conference	
1920 Urban reform creates Greater Berlin		**1939** Outbreak of World War II on 1 September	*Poster depicting the German race*	

forced to emigrate. On the night of 9–10 November 1938, known as *Kristallnacht* (Night of the Broken Glass), thousands of synagogues, cemeteries, Jewish homes and shops throughout Germany were looted and burned.

WORLD WAR II

Hitler's invasion of Poland on 1 September 1939 signalled the start of World War II. For the citizens of Berlin, food shortages were followed in August 1940 by British air raids. By 1941 the government policy of the mass deportation of Jews to concentration camps had begun. Other groups targeted included homosexuals, priests and Romany gypsies. In January 1942, at a conference held in a villa in Wannsee *(see p173)* it was decided to embark on a systematic extermination of all European Jews. The unsuccessful attempt to assassinate Hitler in 1944 ended up with Nazis murdering many members of the German resistance.

After nearly four years of bitter warfare, the tide began to turn against the Germans. In April 1945 more than 1.5 million Soviet soldiers invaded Berlin. On 30 April Hitler committed suicide, and Germany conceded defeat.

BERLIN DIVIDED

The Potsdam Conference of 1945 *(see p191)* divided Berlin into four sectors, occupied respectively by Soviet, US, British and French troops. This put the devastated city at the centre of the Communist-Capitalist Cold War. On 24 June 1948 the Soviet authorities in their attempt to annex the whole city introduced a blockade of its Western sectors. The Allies responded with the Berlin Airlift, which thwarted the Soviet plans. On 12 May 1949 the blockade was lifted.

Historic buildings at the Gendarmenmarkt destroyed by British and American bombs, 1945–6

The same year saw the birth of the Federal Republic of Germany, with its capital in Bonn, and the German Democratic Republic (GDR), with the capital in East Berlin. West Berlin remained as a separate enclave. On 17 June 1953 workers' strikes in the GDR and East Berlin turned into an uprising which was bloodily crushed by the authorities. In their attempt to staunch the ever-rising flood of refugees, the GDR authorities decided in 1961 to surround West Berlin with a wall, and shoot at anyone attempting to cross it.

The political changes which occurred all over Eastern Europe in 1989 led to the fall of the Berlin Wall and the opening of the frontiers between the two republics. On 3 October 1990, Germany was officially reunified and Berlin once again became the capital. The government moved here on 20 June 1991.

Celebrations as the Berlin Wall falls, 9 November 1989

			1990 Official reunification of Germany, 3 October	
1961 Construction of the Berlin Wall on 13 August	**1971** "Basic Treaty" allows travel from West to East Berlin	**1987** Celebratoin of Berlin's 750th anniversary		**1994** Allies leave Berlin
	1970	**1980**	**1990**	**2000**
			1991 Berlin becomes the German captial, 20 June	**1999** Presidential election held in the rebuilt Reichstag in May

Trabant – the most popular car in the GDR

1989 Fall of the Berlin Wall, 9 November

BERLIN AT A GLANCE

MORE THAN 150 PLACES of interest are described in the *Area byArea* section of this book. These include a range of sights from historic monuments, such as the Nikolaikirche *(see p90)*, to modern landmarks like the ambitious showcase architecture of the new Potsdamer Platz district *(see p126);* from the peace of the Botanical Garden *(see p169)* to the noisier charms of Berlin's long-established zoo *(see p144).* To help you make the most of your stay, the following 16 pages provide a time-saving guide to the very best that Berlin has to offer. Museums and galleries, historic buildings, parks and gardens, modern architecture, the legacy of the divided city and famous Berliners all feature in this section. Below is a top ten selection of attractions that no visitor should miss.

BERLIN'S TOP TEN ATTRACTIONS

Pergamonmuseum
See pp80–83.

Schloss Charlottenburg
See pp154–5.

**Kungstgewerbe-
museum**
See pp118–21.

Gemäldegalerie
See pp122–5.

Nikolaiviertel
See pp88–9.

Zoologischer Garten
See p144.

Fernsehturm
See p93.

Brandenburger Tor
See p67.

Reichstag
See p130.

**Kaiser Wilhelm Gedächt-
niskirche** *See pp146–7.*

◁ Interior of the Reichstag *(see p130)*, with its new dome designed by Lord Norman Foster

Berlin's Best: Museums and Galleries

Ancient Greek vase

BERLIN BOASTS SOME of the finest museum collections in the world. Since 1990 many of the collections previously split between East and West Berlin have been brought together in new venues. One example is the Gemäldegalerie collection, a magnificent collection of Old Master paintings. Berlin's major museum complexes are located on Museum Island, around Schloss Charlottenburg, at the Kulturforum and at Dahlem.

Kunstgewerbemuseum
The arts and crafts collection at the Kunstgewerbemuseum (see pp118–21) is among the most interesting in Europe. One of its many treasures is this 17th-century gold elephant-shaped vessel.

Around Schloss Charlottenburg

Tiergarten

Around Kurfürstendamm

Gemäldegalerie
This world-famous collection illustrates the history of European painting from the 13th to the 18th centuries. Originally part of a triptych, The Adoration of the Magi (1470) was painted by Hugo van der Goes (see pp122–5).

Museumszentrum Dahlem
This huge complex houses several museums devoted to ethnography and non-European art (see p170).

| 0 metres | 750 |
| 0 yards | 750 |

Hamburger Bahnhof
Featuring artists such as Joseph Beuys and Andy Warhol, this collection of modern art has occupied the former Hamburger railway station since 1993 (see pp110–11).

Deutches Historisches Museum
Once building works are finished, the Baroque Zeughaus will contain the Museum of German History. Everyday objects as well as works of art will be used to illustrate historical events (see pp58–9).

North of the Centre

East of the Centre

Pergamonmuseum
This museum owes its name to the reconstructed Pergamon Zeus altar, which stands in its main hall (see pp80–83).

Around Unter den Linden

Museum Island

Altes Museum
The ground floor of Friedrich Schinkel's Neo-Classical building has been used since 1998 to exhibit a collection of Greek and Roman antiquities (see p75).

Kreuzberg

Deutsches Technikmuseum
The development of a range of industrial technologies, from locomotive-building to brewing, is illustrated in this entertaining museum (see pp138–9).

Jüdisches Museum
Berlin's Jewish museum was designed by Daniel Libeskind, an American architect of Jewish descent. The form of the building is based on the Star of David (see p137).

...ing Berlin's Museums

Majolica plate, Kunstgewerbemuseum

DESPITE BEING DAMAGED DURING World War II, Berlin's numerous museums are still among the finest, and the most heavily subsidized, in the world. Many collections were split up when the city was partitioned in 1946, and although the process of bringing them together again is under way, some collections are still scattered around different sites, and many of the older museums are undergoing refurbishment.

Picasso's *Head of the Faun* (1937) in the Sammlung Berggruen

ANCIENT ART

THE ART OF ANCIENT Egypt is shown at the **Ägyptisches Museum** (Egyptian Museum). The jewel of this museum is the bust of Queen Nefertiti. Works of art from Ancient Greece and Rome are kept in the 19th-century **Altes Museum** (Old Museum). Another large collection of antiquities can be found in the **Pergamonmuseum**, where visitors can see several reconstructed architectural wonders, including the Pergamon Zeus altar and the Market Gate from Miletus. The museum also holds an impressive collection of Middle Eastern art, including a reconstruction of the Babylonian Ishtar Gate.

Bust of Nefertiti, Ägyptisches Museum

German and Italian sculpture will be housed in the **Bodemuseum**, due to open in 2004 following refurbishment. The **Alte Nationalgalerie** (Old National Gallery), also undergoing refurbishment and due to open in 2002, will display 18th- and 19th-century art. Highlights from its collection can be seen at the nearby Altes Museum building.

Galerie der Romantik (Romantics' Gallery) in Charlottenburg boasts a collection of paintings by the German Romantics, including famous landscapes by Caspar David Friedrich. A collection of sculpture from the late-16th to the mid-19th centuries can be seen in the **Schinkel-Museum**. The **Neue Nationalgalerie** (New National Gallery) is filled with late 19th- and early 20th-century paintings and sculpture. Art Nouveau and Art Deco works are featured at the **Bröhan-Museum**, while works by modern greats, such as Pablo Picasso, Paul Klee and Georges Braque, are on show at the **Sammlung Berggruen** (Berggruen Collection).

The **Brücke-Museum** displays the works of German Expressionists, and contemporary art is exhibited in the **Hamburger Bahnhof**.

Arts and crafts, from the Middle Ages to the present, are displayed at the **Kunstgewerbemuseum** (Museum of Applied Arts). The **Bauhaus-Archiv** displays applied arts by members of the influential inter-war Bauhaus movement.

FINE ART AND DESIGN

BERLIN'S LARGEST collection of 13th- to 18th-century European painting is displayed in the **Gemäldegalerie** (Picture Gallery). Here are works by old masters including Dürer, Rembrandt, Titian, Botticelli and Caravaggio. In the same museum complex is the **Kupferstichkabinett**, with drawings and prints from the Middle Ages to the present.

Old masters can also be seen in the **Jagdschloss Grunewald**, a Renaissance palace home to German and Dutch paintings from the 14th to 19th centuries. A large collection of predominantly 17th-century paintings is exhibited in the **Bildergalerie** (Gallery of Paintings) in Potsdam.

***Étienne Chevalier with St Stephen* by Jean Fouquet, Gemäldegalerie**

NON-EUROPEAN ART

THOSE INTERESTED in Asian art should visit the **Museums-zentrum Dahlem**. This complex houses three large collections: the Museum für Ostasiatische Kunst (Museum of East Asian Art), the Museum für Indische Kunst (Museum of Indian Art) and the Museum für Völkerkunde (Museum of Ethnography), which explores the heritage of non-European nations.

The **Museum für Islamische Kunst** (Museum of Islamic Art) is located in the same building as the Pergamonmuseum.

Totem pole, Museum für Völkerkunde

HISTORY

THE COLLECTION of the **Deutsches Historisches Museum** (Museum of German History) traces German history from the Middle Ages to the present. The **Hugenotten-museum** (Huguenot Museum), located in the tower of the Französischer Dom, charts the history of the city's Huguenots.

The **Centrum Judaicum** (Jewish Centre) in the Neue Synagoge (New Synagogue), and the **Jüdisches Museum** (Jewish Museum), in a new building by architect Daniel Libeskind and scheduled to open in late 2001, are devoted to the history and cultural heritage of the Jewish people.

Berlin has several museums associated with World War II. The **Topographie des Terrors** (Topography of Terror) exhibition is displayed at the site of the former Gestapo and SS headquarters. A deeply shocking collection of documents concerning the Holocaust is kept at the **Haus der Wannsee-Konferenz**. The tools of terror used on the citizens of the German Democratic Republic can be seen at the **Stasimuseum**, while the **Haus am Check-point Charlie** (House at Checkpoint Charlie) museum tells the stories of citizens who crossed the Berlin Wall.

TECHNOLOGY AND NATURAL HISTORY

THE **Museum für Natur-kunde** (Museum of Natural History) contains the world's biggest dinosaur skeleton. Also popular with visitors is the **Deutsches Technik-museum**, (German Technology Museum), in a large site around a former railway station. It features railway cars, locomotives and a range of machinery. Those interested in technology should also visit the the **Deutsches Rundfunk Museum** (German Museum of Radio and Broadcasting) with its array of old broadcasting equipment, and the **Museum für Post und Kommunikation** (Museum of Post and Communications).

SPECIALIST SUBJECTS

BERLIN IS NOT SHORT OF specialist museums. There are museums devoted to laundry, sugar, hemp and even teddy bears. Lovers of theatre and literature can visit the one-time home of Bertolt Brecht (1898–1956), now the **Brecht-Weigel Gedenkstätte** (Brecht-Weigel Memorial). Worth a visit to see the magnificent Wurlitzer organ alone is the **Musikinstrumenten-Museum** (Musical Instruments Museum). The outdoor **Domäne Dahlem** (Dahlem Farm Museum) shows 300 years of local farm life and exhibits old-fashioned tools.

A wide array of exhibits in the Musikinstrumenten-Museum

Berlin's Best: Historic Architecture

Berlin is a relatively new city. It expanded slowly until the first half of the 19th century, and then grew with increasing rapidity from around 1850 onwards. Although many of the city's finest architectural treasures were destroyed by World War II bombing, it is still possible to discover many interesting historic buildings (for more information, *see pp36–7*). In nearby Potsdam *(see pp180–195)* you can visit the splendid Schloss Sanssouci. Set in magnificent parkland, the palace was built for Friedrich II (1740–1786) and extended by subsequent rulers.

Schloss Charlottenburg
The construction of this Baroque royal palace at Potsdam was begun in 1695. Subsequent extension works took place throughout the 18th century (see pp154–5).

Around Schloss Charlottenburg

Tiergarten

Around Kurfürstendamm

Schloss Bellevue
This Rococo palace by Philipp Daniel Boumann is now the official residence of the President of the Federal Republic of Germany.

The Reichstag
This massive Neo-Renaissance building was designed in 1884 by Paul Wallot. Its elegant new dome is the work of British architect Norman Foster (see p130).

Schloss Sanssouci
This small palace was the favourite residence of Friedrich II.

Neues Palais
The Neues Palais combines elements of Baroque and Neo-Classical style.

POTSDAM PALACES

The summer palace of Schloss Sanssouci gives its name to Potsdam's Park Sanssouci, a royal complex with highlights including the grand 18th-century Neues Palais and the small but charming Schloss Charlottenhof.

0 metres	750
0 yards	750

Brandenburger Tor
This Neo-Classical gate stands at the end of Unter den Linden. Crowned by a Quadriga (chariot) driven by the Goddess of Victory, it is the symbol of Berlin (see p67).

Zeughaus
Upon completion of re-building, this Baroque armoury will house the Deutsches Historisches Museum (see pp58–9). Its courtyard will contain masks of dying warriors by sculptor Andreas Schlüter (1660–1714).

Marienkirche
This Gothic church, founded in the 13th century, contains a striking 15th-century mural. It is one of the city's oldest buildings (see pp94–5).

North of the Centre

East of the Centre

Around Unter den Linden

Museum Island

Kreuzberg

Rotes Rathaus
Berlin's main Town Hall is named "red" after the colour of its brick exterior, not the political persuasion of the Mayor (see p90).

Berliner Dom
This enormous cathedral, built between 1894 and 1905, is an example of the Neo-Renaissance style in Berlin (see pp76–7).

Schauspielhaus
Built in 1820 to replace a theatre destroyed by fire, this beautiful building on the Gendarmenmarkt was designed by Karl Friedrich Schinkel (see pp64–5).

Exploring Berlin's Historic Architecture

UNTIL THE INDUSTRIAL REVOLUTION of the late 19th century, Berlin was little more than a small town surrounded by villages. As a result, the city's oldest buildings are concentrated in the central core around Unter den Linden and along the Spree river, an area which suffered heavy damage during World War II. Older country residences, however, as well as some important newer buildings, can be seen in former villages such as Wedding and Charlottenburg, which now form part of Greater Berlin.

14th-century Gothic doorway of the Nikolaikirche in the Nikolaiviertel

MIDDLE AGES AND RENAISSANCE

THE **Nikolaikirche** is the oldest building in central Berlin. The base of its massive front tower is Romanesque and dates back to about 1230, although the church itself is Gothic and was built between 1380 and 1450. The second Gothic church in the city centre is the **Marienkirche**. Nearby are the ruins of a **Franciscan friary**, and the **Heiliggeistkapelle**. Many medieval churches outside the city centre have survived the war. Among the most beautiful is the late-Gothic **Nikolai-kirche** in Spandau, dating

from the early 15th century. A further ten village churches, most dating from the 13th century, can be found hidden among high-rise apartment buildings. **St Annen-Kirche** in Dahlem, however, still enjoys an almost rural setting.

The few surviving secular structures include fragments of the **city walls** in the city centre, and the **Julius-turm** in Spandau, a huge, early 13th-century tower which stands in the grounds of the Spandau Citadel. Berlin's only surviving Renaissance buildings are the **Ribbeckhaus** with its four picturesque gables, the **Jagdschloss-Grunewald**, a modest hunting lodge designed by Casper Theyss in 1542, and the **Spandau Citadel** (or fortress), a well-preserved example of Italian-style military defence architecture. Finished in 1592, the construction of the Citadel was begun in 1560 by Christoph Römer using plans by Italian architect Francesco Chiaramella da Gandino. It was brought to completion by Rochus Guerrini Graf zu Lynar (the Count of Lynar).

Detail of the Zeughaus

BAROQUE EXPANSION

THE THIRTY YEARS' WAR (1618–48) put a temporary stop to the town's development, and it was not until the Peace of 1648 that new building work in the Baroque style began. One of the first of the city's Baroque buildings is the late 17th-century **Schloss Köpenick**. More buildings followed, many of which survive today. They include the **Parochialkirche**, the **Deutscher Dom** and the **Französischer Dom**, as well as the magnificent **Zeughaus**, or arsenal, built between 1695 and 1730. During this period Andreas Schlüter (1664–1714) designed the now-demolished Stadtschloss (Royal Palace), while Johann Arnold Nering (1659–95) designed **Schloss Char-lottenburg**. Other surviving Baroque palaces include **Schloss Podewils**, **Schloss Friedrichs-felde** and **Schloss Niederschönhausen**.

One of the few buildings dating from the reign of Friedrich Wilhelm I (1713–40) is the **Kollegienhaus** at Lindenstrasse No. 14 , designed by Philipp Gerlach and built in 1733. During the reign of Friedrich II (1740–86), many buildings were erected in the late Baroque and Rococo styles. These include **Schloss Sanssouci** in Potsdam and the **Alte Bibliothek** building on Unter den Linden, which completed the Forum Friedericianum project, now better known as Bebelplatz (*see pp56–7*).

NEO-CLASSICISM AND ROMANTICISM

THE NEO-CLASSICAL architecture of the late-18th and early-19th centuries has given Berlin much of its basic form. One dominant figure of this period was Carl Gotthard Langhans (1732–1808), creator of the **Brandenburg Gate** and of **Schloss Bellevue**. Even more influential, however, was the

Renaissance-style defence, the Citadel building at Spandau

prolific Karl Friedrich Schinkel *(see p179).* His work includes some of Berlin's most important public buildings, among them the **Neue Wache**, the **Altes Museum** and the **Schauspielhaus**. Many of Schinkel's residential commissions are also still standing, with some such as **Schloss Klein Glienicke** and **Schloss Tegel** open to the public. Schinkel's Neo-Gothic work includes **Schloss Babelsberg** and the **Friedrichswerdersche Kirche**.

Elegant Neo-Classicism at Karl Friedrich Schinkel's Schloss Klein Glienicke

INDUSTRIALIZATION AND THE MODERN AGE

THE SECOND HALF of the 19th century was a time of rapid development for Berlin. After Schinkel's death, his work was continued by his students, Ludwig Persius (1803–45) and Friedrich August Stüler (1800–65). Stüler designed the Neo-Classical **Alte Nationalgalerie** between 1866 and 1876. Some splendid Neo-Romanesque and Neo-Gothic churches and several notable public buildings in various styles were also produced at this time. The spirit of the Italian Neo-Renaissance is seen in the **Rotes Rathaus** designed by Hermann Friedrich Waesemann, and in the **Martin-Gropius-Bau**, by Martin Gropius in 1877. Late Neo-Renaissance features are used in Paul Wallot's **Reichstag** building and in Ernst von

Decorative frieze on the Martin-Gropius-Bau

Ihne's **Statsbibliothek** building. Julius Raschdorff's **Berliner Dom** shows Neo-Baroque influences. Much of the religious architecture of the period continued in the Neo-Gothic style, while Franz Schwechten designed the **Kaiser-Wilhelm-Gedächtniskirche** in the Neo-Romanesque style. Many structures of this period are built in the modernist style inspired by the industrial revolution, the textbook example being the huge electronics factory, **AEG-Turbinenhalle**, designed by Peter Behrens in the 1890s.

BETWEEN THE TWO WORLD WARS

THE GREATEST architectural achievements of this period include a number of splendid housing estates, such as the **Hufeisensiedlung** designed by Bruno Taut and Martin Wagner in 1924, and **Onkel-Toms-Hütte** in Zehlendorf. An interesting example of the Expressionist style is Erich Mendelsohn's **Einstein Turm** in Potsdam. Art Deco is represented by Hans Poelzig's **Haus des Rundfunks**, the country's first Broadcasting House. Hitler's rise to power in the 1930s marked a return to the classical forms which dominated German architecture of the Fascist period. Representatives of this period include the **Tempelhof Airport** Terminal building and the **Olympia-Stadion**, built for the 1936 Olympic Games.

20th-century Neo-Renaissance detail of the massive **Berliner Dom**

Reminders of the Divided City

IN 1945, AS PART OF THE post-war peace, Berlin was divided into four zones of occupation: Soviet, American, British and French. Hostilities erupted in June 1948, when the Soviets blockaded West Berlin in an attempt to bring the area under their control. The ensuing year-long standoff marked the start of the Cold War. By the 1950s, economic problems in the East had led to bloodily-suppressed riots and a mass exodus to the West. In 1961 the East German government constructed the infamous Berlin Wall *(die Mauer)* to contain its citizens. Between this time and reunification at the end of 1989, more than 180 people were shot trying to cross the Wall.

Berlin Wall
Protected to the east by land mines, the Wall, known by the East German authorities as the "Anti-Fascist Protection Wall", surrounded West Berlin and was 155 km (95 miles) long (see p162).

Memorial to Soviet Soldiers
Part of West Berlin, the area around this monument to Red Army troops killed in the 1945 Battle of Berlin was closed for many years due to attacks on its Soviet guards (see p131).

Around Schloss Charlottenburg

Tiergarten

0 metres   1000

0 yards   1000

Around Kurfürstendamm

KEY

— Berlin Wall

BERLIN BEFORE REUNIFICATION

The Wall cut the city in half, severing its main transport arteries, the S-Bahn and U-Bahn lines. West Berliners were excluded from the centre of the city. Running along the Wall was a no-man's-land, now Berlin's biggest building site.

KEY

— Berlin Wall

— Sector boundaries

✈ Airport

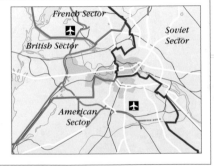

French Sector

British Sector

Soviet Sector

American Sector

Tränenpalast (Palace of Tears)
Until 1989 the Tränenpalast, next to the final S-Bahn station in East Berlin, was a border checkpoint for S-Bahn passengers heading west.

Checkpoint Charlie
This border crossing between the American and Soviet sectors was used by foreign citizens and diplomats. It was here that the American and Soviet authorities exchanged arrested spies.

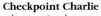

North of the Centre

East of the Centre

Around Unter den Linden

Museum Island

East Side Gallery
The longest remaining section of the Berlin Wall became an open-air gallery in 1990, covered with an eclectic mixture of paintings by 118 artists (see p165).

Kreuzberg

Luftbrücke
This striking memorial commemorates those who died during the Berlin Airlift of 1948–9. Allied planes delivered 2.5 million tons of supplies to West Berlin in the face of the year-long Soviet blockade (see p139).

Haus am Checkpoint Charlie
This museum holds photos and other Wall memorabilia, including a selection of escape vehicles (see p136).

Berlin's Best: Modern Architecture

FOLLOWING BERLIN'S DEVASTATION in World War II,
intense post-war reconstruction turned the
city into a giant building site. With the help of
architects from several countries the city
acquired many modern structures and estates,
ranked among the best in the world. The city's
reunification in 1990 and the reinstatement of
Berlin as the main seat of government gave
rise to a second wave of building activity,
carried out on a scale unprecedented in Europe.
The architectural elite are participating in the
design of the new Berlin, and the sites in the
city centre that stood empty until 1990 are being
filled with new buildings at an incredible rate.

Bauhaus-Archiv
*This cubist structure was completed
in 1978 to house the Bauhaus
museum. It was designed much
earlier by Walter Gropius (1883–
1969), director of the Bauhaus
art school from 1919 to 1928.*

*Around Schloss
Charlottenburg*

Tiergarten

*Around
Kurfürstendamm*

Kant-Dreieck
*This building, with
its pure forms and
the eccentric sail-like
structure mounted on
the roof, is the work of
Josef Paul Kleihues.*

Ludwig-Erhard-Haus
*Reminiscent of a giant
battleship, this building was
designed by the prolific English
architect Nicholas Grimshaw.
Completed in autumn 1998,
it houses the Berlin Stock
Exchange and the Chamber
of Trade and Industry.*

0 metres   750

0 yards   750

Kammermusiksaal

Both the Berliner Philharmonie building (1961) and the adjacent Kammermusik-saal, or chamber music hall (1987), were designed by Hans Scharoun. The latter was built posthumously by Edgar Wisniewski, Scharoun's pupil.

Galeries Lafayette

This gigantic department store in Friedrichstrasse, designed by Jean Nouvel, brings Parisian chic to the heart of Berlin.

North of the Centre

East of the Centre

Around Unter den Linden

Museum Island

Kreuzberg

Quartier Schützenstrasse

This part of the city features the work of Italian architect Aldo Rossi. With high-rise blocks and bold colour schemes, the area shows modernity and classical forms standing side by side.

Philip-Johnson-Haus

This postmodernist office block near Checkpoint Charlie was named after the elder statesman of American architecture, Philip Johnson, who designed it when he was 91 years old.

Gemäldegalerie

The new Gemäldegalerie, designed by the Hilmer and Sattler Partnership, was opened in June 1998. The main hall is particularly elegant.

Exploring Berlin's Modern Architecture

AROUND THE WORLD architects are forever designing buildings with innovative and interesting structures, but in Berlin this creative process is happening on an unprecedented scale. The city is a vast melting pot of trends and styles, where the world's greatest architects scramble for new commissions and where the buildings compete with each other in the originality of their form and in their use of the latest technology.

Haus der Kulturen der Welt in the Tiergarten

FROM 1945 TO 1970

WORLD WAR II exacted a heavy price from Berlin. The centre was reduced to rubble and the partitioning of the city made it impossible to carry out any co-ordinated reconstruction. In 1952, East Berlin decided to develop **Karl-Marx-Allee** in the Socialist-Realist style. In reply, West Berlin employed the world's greatest architects to create the **Hansaviertel** estate. Le Corbusier built one of his *unités d'habitation*, while the American architect, Hugh A Stubbins, built the Kongress-halle (now the **Haus der Kulturen der Welt**). The West's response to the cultural venues inherited by the East Berliners, including the opera, the library and the museums, was the **Kulturforum** complex. The complex included such magnificent buildings as the **Philharmonie**, designed by Hans Scharoun, and the **Neue Nationalgalerie**, designed by Mies van der Rohe. While West Berlin acquired its huge "trade temple" – the **Europa-Center**, constructed in 1965, East Berlin boasted its **Fernsehturm** (television tower), built in 1969.

FROM 1970 TO 1990

THE CONTINUING rivalry, as each part of the city tried to outdo the other, resulted in the construction of East Berlin's **Palast der Republic** in 1976. The West replied with the ultramodern **Internationales Congress Centrum** in 1979. The Kulturforum complex was further extended with designs by Scharoun, including the **Kammermusiksaal** and the **Staatsbibliothek** (library). The impressive **Bauhaus-Archiv** was developed from a design by Walter Gropius. In 1987 Berlin celebrated its 750th anniversary, which in the East saw the completion of the huge **Nikolaiviertel** development, with its pre-War allusions. In the West, the IBA's 1987 scheme gave town its enormous new post-modernist housing estates in Kreuzberg and also in the **Tegel** area.

POST-REUNIFICATION ARCHITECTURE

THE GOVERNMENT district is under construction within the bend of the Spree river. Its designers include Charlotte Frank and Axel Schultes. The **Reichstag** building has been famously remodelled by Norman Foster. **Pariser Platz** has been filled with new designs by Günther Behnisch, Frank O Gehry, Josef Paul Kleihues and others. The magnificent **Friedrichstadtpassagen** complex became the scene of rivalry between Jean Nouvel and Oswald M Ungers. Many interesting office buildings have sprung up around town, including **Ludwig-Erhard-Haus** by Nicholas Grimshaw and the nearby **Kantdreieck** by Josef Paul Kleihues. Housing has also been transformed, with perhaps the most original example being Aldo Rossi's **Quartier Schützen-strasse**. The city has also acquired some fine museums, including the new **Gemälde-galerie** designed by the Hilmer and Sattler Partnership, and the Deconstructivist style **Jüdisches Museum**, designed by Daniel Libeskind.

MODERN ARCHITECTURE

Neue Nationalgalerie at Kulturforum designed by Mies van der Rohe

Potsdamer Platz

IN THE SHORT space of a few years a new financial and business district has sprung up on the vast empty wasteland surrounding the Potsdamer Platz. It boasts splendid constructions designed by Renzo Piano, Arata Isozaki and Helmut Jahn. As well as office blocks, the area has many public buildings, including cinemas and a theatre, as well as a huge shopping centre – the Arkaden, plus a luxury hotel, restaurants and several bars.

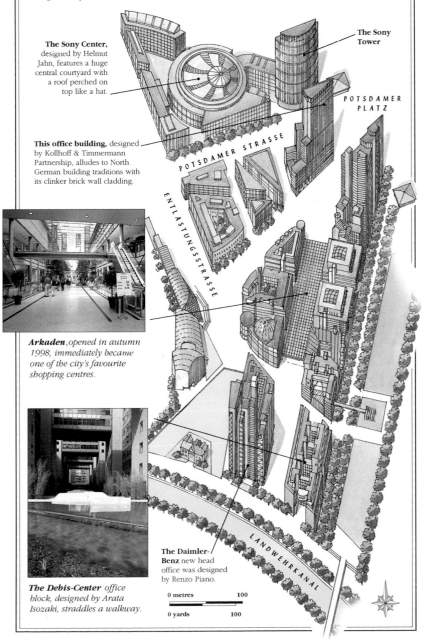

The Sony Center, designed by Helmut Jahn, features a huge central courtyard with a roof perched on top like a hat.

The Sony Tower

POTSDAMER PLATZ

POTSDAMER STRASSE

This office building, designed by Kollhoff & Timmermann Partnership, alludes to North German building traditions with its clinker brick wall cladding.

ENTLASTUNGSSTRASSE

Arkaden, opened in autumn 1998, immediately became one of the city's favourite shopping centres.

LANDWEHRKANAL

The Daimler-Benz new head office was designed by Renzo Piano.

The Debis-Center office block, designed by Arata Isozaki, straddles a walkway.

0 metres 100

0 yards 100

Berlin's Best: Parks and Gardens

BERLIN IS UNDOUBTEDLY one of Europe's greenest capital cities, with the sprawling Tiergarten at its centre. However, most of Berlin's districts have their own smaller parks and gardens, too, some of them with children's play areas and nature trails. To the west of the city is the vast Grunewald, a beautiful area of forest which contains mountain bike trails and scenic paths for walkers and cyclists. In summer, numerous lakes, rivers and canals provide excellent facilities for water sports.

Zoologischer Garten
Popular with children, Berlin's zoo has some 14,000 animals, representing 1,400 different species. It is the oldest zoo in Germany (see p144).

Schloss Charlottenburg
The well-maintained grounds of this royal palace were designed in the French Baroque style (see pp154–5).

Around Schloss Charlottenburg

Around Kurfürstendamm

Botanischer Garten
Established from 1899 to 1910 in Dahlem, this botanical garden is one of the biggest in the world (see p169).

Park Babelsberg
This vast landscaped park was designed by Peter Joseph Lenné, and now lies within the Potsdam city limits. It surrounds the picturesque Schloss Babelsberg (see pp202–203).

Tiergarten
Once a royal zoological garden, this was converted into a park after 1818 by landscape designer Peter Joseph Lenné (see p128).

Monbijoupark
The park once surrounded Monbijou Palace, which was destroyed during World War II (see p103).

North of
the Centre

East of
the Centre

Around Unter
den Linden

Museum
Island

Tiergarten

Kreuzberg

Tierpark Friedrichsfelde
In 1954 the park at Schloss Friedrichsfelde was converted into the East Berlin Zoological Garden (see p166).

Britzer Garten
The landscaped park with its beautiful lime-tree avenue, surrounds the early 18th-century Schloss Britz (see p168).

Viktoriapark
This large park winds around a hill with good views of Kreuzberg. At its peak stands a memorial to the wars of liberation fought against Napoleon (see p139).

| 0 metres | | 1000 |
| 0 yards | | 1000 |

Famous Berliners

M ANY OF BERLIN'S FAMOUS CITIZENS include
artists and scientists who made notable
contributions to the world's cultural heritage.
Berlin universities were home to the most
eminent German philosophers and scientists,
and the thriving theatrical life of the city
attracted Germany's finest writers, actors
and directors. During the 1920s Berlin was
also an important centre of the movie
industry, attracting film stars and directors
from all over Europe.

Bertolt Brecht (1898–1956)
The author of the Three-
*penny Opera, Brecht
founded the Berliner
Ensemble in 1949* (see
p108). *His apartment
has been turned into a
museum* (see p109).

Robert Koch (1843–1910)
*This noted scientist won a
Nobel Prize in medicine in
1905 for his discoveries in the
field of bacteriology. He
became director of the Institute
of Microbiology, where there is
a small memorial museum.*

*Around Schloss
Charlottenburg*

Tiergarten

*Around
Kurfürstendamm*

Herbert von Karajan
(1908–89)
*This famous Austrian conduc-
ted the Berlin Philharmonic
from 1954 to 1989.*

Marlene Dietrich
(1901–92)
*Hollywood's all-time
great star began her
career in Berlin.
She is buried in the
Friedenau Cemetery.*

Albert Einstein (1879–1955)
*Einstein was the director of the Berlin
Institute of Physics from 1914 until
1933, when repressive Nazi policies
forced him to leave Germany.*

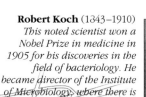

Jacob Grimm (1785–1863) **and Wilhelm Grimm** (1786–1859)
Best known for their children's fairy-tales, including "Little Red Riding Hood" and "Hänsel and Gretel", the Brothers Grimm also began work on the definitive German language dictionary, Das Deutsche Wörterbuch.

Käthe Kollwitz (1867–1945)
Sculptor and graphic artist Käthe Kollwitz spent much of her life in Prenzlauer Berg. She recorded the lives of the poor of the district, where a monument to her now stands.

Georg Wilhelm Friedrich Hegel (1770–1831)
Hegel was one of the most influential philosophers of the early 19th century. He taught at Berlin University from 1818 until his death in 1831.

North of the Centre

East of the Centre

Museum Island

Around Unter den Linden

Kreuzberg

Theodor Fontane (1819–98)
Of Huguenot ancestry, Fontane was one of the greatest German novelists of the 19th century. He also wrote theatrical reviews for 20 years.

Felix Mendelssohn-Bartholdy (1809–47)
Composer of the "Wedding March" and grandson of philosopher Moses Mendelssohn, Felix Mendelssohn-Bartholdy is buried in Kreuzberg's Friedhöfe vor dem Halleschen Tor (see p138).

Richard Strauss (1864–1949)
Now best known as a composer, Strauss directed the Berlin Court Opera from 1898 to 1917.

| 0 metres | 750 |
| 0 yards | 750 |

BERLIN THROUGH THE YEAR

LIKE ALL MAJOR European capitals, Berlin offers a wide range of activities throughout the year. The best seasons for cultural and sporting events are spring and autumn, when the city hosts many spectacular fairs and exhibitions. During summer the city's population shrinks, as many locals head for their holiday destinations. But the weather is often pleasant, and rarely

Karneval der Kulturen

very hot, so this is a good time for serious sightseeing. In winter, although it can get quite cold, it is possible to spend time visiting museums or simply walking around the city. The streets teem with shoppers during the run up to Christmas. A more detailed programme of events can be obtained from tourist information offices (see p278) or on the internet at www.berlinonline.de/kultur.

The Whitsun Karneval der Kulturen in the streets of Kreuzberg

SPRING

IN SPRINGTIME, Berlin holds many interesting fairs and cultural events in its squares, parks and gardens, allowing the visitor to appreciate fully the beauty of the city as the trees and flowers burst into life. With the arrival of the warmer weather, another natural resource springs to life as cruise and rowing boats start operating on the Spree river and the city's canals.

MARCH

ITB-Internationale Tourismus-Börse (early Mar). The biggest European fair devoted to tourism where representatives from all parts of the world try to attract visitors to their countries.
Music-Biennale Berlin (2nd week in Mar) is a busy festival of experimental, electronic and contemporary music held on odd-number years.

Rassehunde-Zuchtschau (weekend mid-Mar) is a huge show for pedigree dogs and pedigree dog lovers.
Berliner Motorradtage (end Mar). Motorcyclists from all over Germany converge on Berlin for this specialist event.

APRIL

Festtage (Apr). A series of popular concerts and operas performed by world class musicians in the Philharmonie and at the Staatsoper.
Easter (exact date varies). Huge markets open around the Kaiser-Wilhelm-Gedächtniskirche, Alexanderplatz and other central locations as the city prepares for the feast.
Britzer Baumblüte (all of Apr) is a month-long spring festival organized in Britz, a suburb in the south of the city famous for its windmills.
Neuköllner Frühlingsfest (all of Apr) Hasenheide. Traditional springtime festival celebrating the new season.

MAY

German Women's Tennis Open (3rd week in May). Each year this tournament attracts the world's top women players. The current strength of German tennis ensures huge crowds turn up eager to cheer on the home players.
Theatertreffen Berlin (May). This important Berlin theatre festival has been running since 1963, and provides a platform for theatre productions from German-speaking regions worldwide.
Karneval der Kulturen (around Whitsun). For three days, the streets of Kreuzberg district are brought to life by singing and dancing in this colourful display celebrating multicultural Berlin.
Theatertreffen der Jungend (end May–early June). This is a festival of amateur youth theatre, providing a showcase for talented young thespians from all over Germany.

Street recitation of poetry during the Theatertreffen Berlin in May

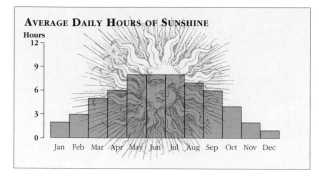

AVERAGE DAILY HOURS OF SUNSHINE

Hours

Jan Feb Mar Apr May Jun Jul Aug Sep Oct Nov Dec

Sunshine Chart
In Berlin, the highest number of sunny days occurs in May, but June, July and August also enjoy good weather. The cloudiest month is December, followed by January and November.

SUMMER

SUMMERTIME in Berlin is marked by many open-air events. There are concerts of classical music and opera performances, as well as open-air concerts and festivals for the young, including the famous Love Parade. It is also possible to take advantage of the good weather by taking a walk or bicycle ride in the Grunewald, or even swimming in the nearby lakes of Wannsee or Müggelsee.

An outdoor artist at work in the Potsdamer Platz

JUNE

Deutsch-Französisches Volksfest *(early Jun–mid-Jul)*. This German-French folk festival takes place near Kurt-Schumacher-Damm.
Jazz Across the Border *(throughout Jun)*. This jazz festival is organized by the Haus der Kulturen der Welt.
Konzertsommer im Englischen Garten *(mid-Jun–end Jul)* is a schedule of open-air concerts.
Christopher Street Day *(end Jun)* features a gay and lesbian parade with revellers in extravagant outfits, held around Ku'damm.

Berliner Theatermarkt an der Deutschen Oper *(end Jun)* is a programme of open days at the opera.
Open-Air-Saison *(end Jun–early Jul)*. Series of operas in Waldbühne with a gala finale in Gendarmenmarkt.

JULY

Bach Tage Berlin *(1st week in Jul)* features concerts of Johann Sebastian Bach's music, performed in concert halls throughout the city.
Love Parade *(2nd Sun in Jul)*. This huge techno-beat parade attracts youth from all over the world intent on dancing late into the night.
Heimatklänge *(mid-Jul–end Aug)*. A spectacular array of groups give open-air concerts in this world music festival; every Wednesday to Sunday.

AUGUST

Deutsch-Amerikanisches Volksfest *(30 Jul–22 Aug)*. A programme of entertainment

Berlin's world famous Love Parade techno event

with an American theme that always draws the crowds.
Kreuzberger Festliche Tage *(end Aug–early Sep)*. This is a large multi-event festival of traditional classical music held in Kreuzberg.
Berliner Gauklerfest *(Aug)*. Stalls set up on Unter den Linden to sell speciality foods, while crowds are entertained by acrobats and musicians.

Prokofiev's *The Love of Three Oranges* performed in the Komische Oper

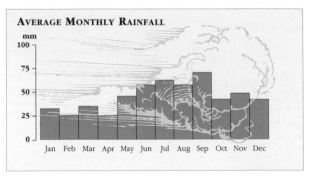

AVERAGE MONTHLY RAINFALL

mm
100
75
50
25
0

Jan Feb Mar Apr May Jun Jul Aug Sep Oct Nov Dec

Rainfall Chart
*The lowest amount
of rainfall occurs in
February and again
in April, as the tem-
perature begins to rise.
The amount of rain in
September can dampen
the enthusiasm of the
unprepared visitor.
Unexpectedly heavy
cloudbursts can also
occur during the
summer months.*

AUTUMN

AUTUMN IN Berlin is marked
by major cultural events.
In September the city's hotels
fill with visitors arriving for
the Berliner Festwochen, to
hear concerts given by some
of the world's top artists and
to make the most of the wide
range of culture on offer.
Autumn is also a time for
major sports events, including
the Berlin Marathon, the third
biggest in the world after
New York and London.

SEPTEMBER

**Internationales Stadionfest
(ISTAF)** *(first week Sep)*.
International track and field
event in the Olympiastadion.
Berliner Festwochen
(throughout Sep). The whole
city is involved in this major
festival staging concerts,
theatre performances,
exhibitions and meetings.

Berlin-Marathon
*(2nd or 3rd Sun in
Sep)*. This enormous
international running
event brings the
city's traffic to a halt
for several hours.
Art Forum in Berlin
(end Sep). Artists and
art collectors from
all over Europe
gather for this five-
day modern art fair.
Jazztreff Berlin
(end Sep–early Oct).
This festival of jazz
music is held in the
Musikinstrumenten-
museum in Tiergar-
tenstrasse *(see p116)*.

OCTOBER

Tag der Deutschen Einheit
(3 Oct). Berlin celebrates the
reunification of Germany by
staging an annual grand
parade through the streets.
Oktoberfest *(early Oct)*.
Held around Möckernstrasse,

Participants in the September Berlin-Marathon

this is a slightly scaled down
version of the Bavarian
Festival, a celebration of beer
drinking and traditional food.
AAA Exhibition *(early Oct)*
Internationales Congress Centrum *(see p172)* plays host to
the Berlin Motor Show.

NOVEMBER

Jazz Fest Berlin *(early Nov)*.
Held annually since 1964, this
respected jazz festival kicks
off in the Haus der Kulturen
der Welt *(see p130)*.
Treffen Junge Musik-Szene
(early Nov). Music for the
younger generation.
Jüdische Kulturtage
(throughout Nov). A festival
devoted to Jewish arts and
culture with films, plays,
concerts and lectures.
Internationales Reitturnier
(3rd week in Nov).
International horse-jumping.
**KinderMusik Theater
Wochen** *(Nov)*. This is a
great feast of theatre and
music for the very young,
and the young at heart.

Marching through the Brandenburg Gate during Deutschland Fest

AVERAGE MONTHLY TEMPERATURE

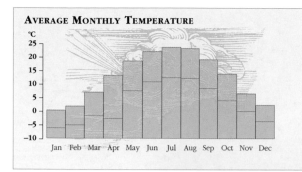

°C
25
20
15
10
5
0
-5
-10

Jan Feb Mar Apr May Jun Jul Aug Sep Oct Nov Dec

Temperature Chart
*Average maximum
and minimum tem-
peratures are shown
here. The warmest
months are June, July
and August when the
temperature exceeds
20°C. Winters are cold
and temperatures can
drop below –5°C in
January, with the
chance of heavy snow-
falls or extreme frost.*

WINTER

BERLIN'S WINTERS are usually
cold and the temperature
can sometimes drop to below
zero, with a carpet of snow
lining the streets. During
December, the city prepares
for Christmas with many
traditional markets. January
brings numerous Carnival
balls, while the major event in
February is the great cinema
gala – the Berlin Film Festival.

DECEMBER

Weihnachtsmärkte
(throughout Dec). In the
month before Christmas the
city is dotted with picturesque
fairs and festive stalls selling
Christmas gifts and regional
culinary specialities.
Christmas (Weihnachten)
(25–26 Dec). As in many
other European cities, Berlin's
traditional celebrations include
Christmas trees, present-giving,
family gatherings and
communal feasts.
New Year's Eve (Silvester)
(31 Dec) is celebrated in
hotels, restaurants, discos,
clubs and in private homes;
another traditional activity is
the popping of champagne
corks at the Brandenburg Gate.

JANUARY

Berliner Neujahrslauf
(1 Jan). For those unaffected
by the previous night's revelry,
this 4-km (2.4-mile) run along
the city streets starts off at the
Brandenburg Gate.
Sechs-Tage-Rennen *(early
Jan).* This meeting in the
Velodrome features a six-day
bicycle-race and other events.

Berlinale – the grand festival of world cinema

Berliner Team-Marathon
(22 Jan). Race organized by
Sport Klub Charlottenburg.
Lange Nacht der Museen
(end of Jan) A series of events
organized by Berlin's
museums which stay open
until midnight or later.
Internationale Grüne Woche
(last week of Jan). This giant
fair is devoted to agriculture
and food; it provides an ideal
opportunity to sample delicacies from all over the world.

Christmas shopping in the
KaDeWe department store

FEBRUARY

**Berlinale – Internationale
Filmfestspiele** *(2nd and 3rd
week in Feb).* This gala of
cinematography in Potsdamer
Platz attracts big movie stars
and features the best films of
the season. It is held in tandem
with the **Internationales
Forum des Jungen Films**
which features remarkable
low-budget movies in the
Palais Podewils *(see p97).*
**Berliner Rosenmontags-
konzerte** is a series of
classical music concerts.

PUBLIC HOLIDAYS

Neujahr New Year (1 Jan)
Karfreitag Good Friday
Ostermontag Easter Mon
Tag der Arbeit Labour
  Day (1 May)
Christi Himmelfahrt
  Ascension Day
Pfingsten Whitsun
Nationalfeiertag (3 Oct)
Weihnachten Christmas
  (25–26 Dec)

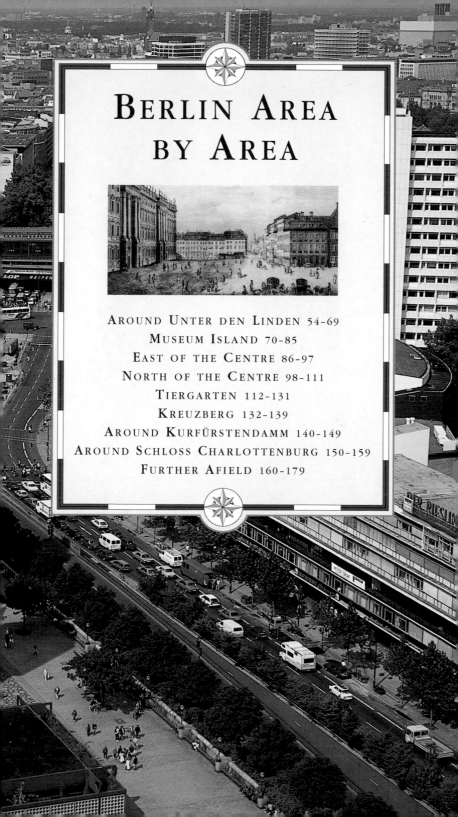

BERLIN AREA
BY AREA

AROUND UNTER DEN LINDEN

T HE AREA around the grand avenue Unter den Linden is among the most attractive in Berlin. Its development started during the Baroque period with the establishment of Dorotheenstadt to the north and Friedrichstadt to the south. From the early 18th century, prestigious buildings began to appear here, and work started on the

**Bas-relief from the Schadow-Haus,
located on Schadowstrasse**

Forum Friedericianum (later Bebelplatz). Over the following two centuries Unter den Linden became one of the city's most imposing avenues. World War II bombing took a heavy toll, but despite only partial reconstruction by the East German government, the area is still home to the highest concentration of historic buildings in Berlin.

SIGHTS AT A GLANCE

Churches
Deutscher Dom ⑱
Französischer Dom ⑯
Friedrichswerdersche Kirche ⑭
St-Hedwigs-Kathedrale ⑪

Museums and Galleries
Deutsche Guggenheim ❼
Zeughaus (Deutsches Historisches Museum) (pp58–59) ❶
Museum für Post und Kommunikation ㉒

Streets and Squares
Bebelplatz ⑩
Gendarmenmarkt ⑮
Pariser Platz ㉔
Unter den Linden ❷

Theatres
Admiralspalast ㉚
Komische Oper ㉘

Konzerthaus ⑰
Maxim Gorki Theater ㉛
Staatsoper Unter den Linden ⑫

Historic Buildings and Sites
Alte Bibliothek ❾
Altes Palais ❽
Brandenburger Tor ㉕
Humboldt Universität ❹
Kronprinzenpalais ⑬
Mohrenkolonnaden ⑳
Neue Wache ❸
Palais am Festungsgraben ㉜
Reiterdenkmal Friedrichs des Grossen ❺
Spittelkolonnaden ㉑
Staatsbibliothek ❻

Others
S-Bahnhof Friedrichstrasse ㉙
Ehemaliges Regierungsviertel ㉓
Friedrichstadtpassagen ⑲
Hotel Adlon ㉖
Russische Botschaft ㉗

KEY

▨	Street-by-Street map *See pp56–57*
🚉	Railway station
Ⓢ	S-Bahn station
Ⓤ	U-Bahn station
🅿	Parking

GETTING THERE
This area is served by S-Bahn 1, 3, 5, 7, 9 and 75; U-Bahn 6 and 9; and buses 100 and 348.

0 metres 400
0 yards 400

◁ **Sculpture of the personification of History on the plinth of Schiller's monument, Gendarmenmarkt**

Street-by-Street: Around Bebelplatz

THE SECTION OF UNTER DEN LINDEN between Schlossbrücke and Friedrichstrasse is one of the most attractive places in central Berlin. There are some magnificent Baroque and Neo-Classical buildings, many of them designed by famous architects. There are also some restored palaces that are now used as public buildings. Of particular interest is the beautiful Baroque building of the Zeughaus (the former Arsenal), which now houses the German History Museum.

Staatsbibliothek
This Neo-Baroque building, designed by Ernst von Ihne, was built between 1903 and 1914. It houses a collection that dates from the 17th century **6**

Humboldt Universität
The entrance to the courtyard is framed by two guardroom pavilions and is crowned with the allegorical figures of Dawn and Dusk **4**

Equestrian Statue of Frederick the Great
The impressive statue dates from 1851 and is the work of Christian Daniel Rauch **5**

Deutsche Guggenheim
The building, which was rebuilt after World War II, provides exhibition space for the fifth branch of the famous Guggenheim museum **7**

KEY

– – – Suggested route

Altes Palais
This Neo-Classical palace was built between 1834 and 1837 for the future Kaiser Wilhelm I. It was reconstructed after World War II **8**

Alte Bibliothek
The west side of Bebelplatz features a Baroque building with an unusual concave façade. Locals have nick-named it the "chest of drawers" **9**

★ Zeughaus (Deutsches Historisches Museum)
One of the most beautiful Baroque buildings in northern Germany, the pediment of the Zeughaus shows Minerva, the Roman goddess of wisdom **1**

LOCATOR MAP
See Street Finder, maps 6, 7, 15 &16

| 0 metres | 100 |
| 0 yards | 100 |

★ Neue Wache
Since 1993, this monument has served as a memorial to all victims of war and dictatorship **3**

Unter den Linden
This magnificent avenue was replanted with four rows of lime trees in 1946 **2**

Kronprinzenpalais
The rear elevation of the palace pavilion features a magnificent portal from the dismantled Bauakademie building **13**

★ Friedrichswerdersche Kirche
In this Neo-Gothic church, designed by Karl Friedrich Schinkel, is a museum devoted to this great architect **14**

Staatsoper Unter den Linden
Unter den Linden's opera house is Germany's oldest theatre building not attached to a palace residence **12**

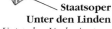

St-Hedwigs-Kathedrale
Bas-reliefs (1837) by Theodore Wilhelm Achtermann adorn the cathedral's supports **11**

Bebelplatz
Designed in the 18th century as the Forum Friedericianum, this square was renamed in 1947 in honour of social activist, August Bebel. The Nazis burned books here in 1933 **10**

STAR SIGHTS

★ **Zeughaus (Deutsches Historisches Museum)**

★ **Neue Wache**

★ **Friedrichswerdersche Kirche**

Zeughaus (Deutsches Historisches Museum) ❶

THIS FORMER ARSENAL was built in the Baroque style in 1706 under the guidance of Johann Arnold Nering, Martin Grünberg, Andreas Schlüter and Jean de Bodt. It is a magnificent structure, its wings surrounding an inner courtyard. Its exterior is decorated with Schlüter's sculptures, including masks of

Warrior's mask, courtyard arcade

dying warriors on the headstones in the inner courtyard arcades. Since 1952 it has housed the German History Museum. The museum is currently closed for major refurbishment, and until it reopens the collection can be seen in the Kronprinzenpalais (see p63).

Europe and Asia
This group of Meissen porcelain figurines, depicting the continents, was designed by Johann Joachim Kändler.

Soldiers Plundering a House
This painting by Sebastian Vrancx dates from around 1600 and depicts a scene from the religious wars which ravaged the Netherlands during the 16th century.

GALLERY GUIDE
When the extension and refurbishment of the museum is completed, the first floor will be devoted to a new exhibition "Bilder und Zeugnisse der Deutschen Geschichte" or "Pictures and Evidence from German History" which will trace the course of German history.

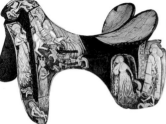

Saddle
This valuable mid-15th-century saddle is decorated with graphic carved plaques made of ivory.

★ Martin Luther
This portrait, painted by Lucas Cranach the Elder in 1529, will be the focal point of an exhibition devoted to the Reformation.

STAR EXHIBITS

★ Martin Luther

★ Gloria Victis

VISITORS' CHECKLIST

Unter den Linden 2.
Map 7 A3, 16 E2. 📞 20 30 40.
Ⓢ Hackescher Markt. 🚌 100,
157, 348. ⬤ until 2004.

Unter den Linden
Carl Traugott Fechhelm's painting shows Berlin's grandest avenue, Unter den Linden, at the end of the 18th century.

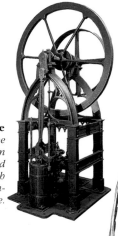

Steam Engine
The history of the Industrial Revolution will be illustrated with exhibits such as this 1847 steam-powered engine.

★ Gloria Victis
The death of a friend in the final days of the Franco-Prussian War (1870–71) inspired French artist Antonin Mercié to create this moving allegory.

The inner courtyard
will be covered with a glass roof by IM Pei.

KEY

- ☐ From the Middle Ages to the Thirty Years' War
- ☐ Baroque
- ☐ Enlightment to Unification
- ☐ Weimar Empire and Republic
- ☐ The Third Reich and World War II
- ☐ Post-1945 Era
- ☐ Non-exhibition rooms

Prisoner's Jacket
This jacket, which once belonged to a concentration camp prisoner, will be used to illustrate the horrors of the Nazi regime.

Unter den Linden as depicted in Franz Krüger's *Opernplatz Parade* (1824–30)

Unter den Linden ❷

Map 6 E3, 6 F3,15 A3, and 16 D3.
Ⓢ *Unter den Linden.* 🚌 *100,
157, 348.*

ONE OF THE MOST FAMOUS
streets in Berlin, Unter
den Linden starts at Schlossplatz and runs down to Pariser
Platz and the Brandenburg
Gate. It was once the route to
the royal hunting grounds that
were later transformed into the
Tiergarten. In the 17th century
the street was planted with
lime trees, to which it owes
its name. Although removed
around 1658, they were
replanted in four rows in 1820.
    During the 18th century,
Unter den Linden became the
main street of the westward-
growing city. It was gradually
filled with prestigious buildings
that were restored after World
War II. Following the reunification of Germany, Unter den
Linden has acquired several
cafés and restaurants, as well
as many smart new shops.
This street is also the venue
for many interesting outdoor
events; it is usually crowded
with tourists and students
browsing the bookstalls around
the Humboldt Universität and
the Staatsbibliothek.

Neue Wache ❸

Unter den Linden 4. **Map** 7 A3, 16 E2.
Ⓢ *Hackescher Markt.* 🚌 *100, 157,
348.* 🕐 *10am–6pm daily.*

THIS WAR MEMORIAL, designed
by Karl Friedrich Schinkel
and built between 1816 and
1818, is considered to be one

of the finest examples of Neo-
Classical architecture in Berlin.
The front of the monument is
dominated by a huge Doric
portico with a frieze made up
of bas-reliefs depicting goddesses of victory. The triangular tympanum above the
pediment shows allegorical
representations of Battle,
Victory, Flight and Defeat.
    The building was originally
used as a royal guardhouse,
but during 1930 and 1931 it
was turned it into a monument
to the soldiers killed in World
War I. In 1960, following its
restoration, Neue Wache became the Memorial to the Victims of Fascism and Militarism.
Then, in 1993 it was rededi-
cated once again, this time to
the memory of all victims of
war and dictatorship.
    Inside the building is an
eternal flame and a granite slab
over the ashes of an unknown
soldier, a resistance fighter and
a concentration camp prisoner.
Under the circular opening in
the roof is a copy of the 20th

century sculpture *Mother with
her Dead Son,* by Berlin artist
Käthe Kollwitz, who lost her
own son in World War I.

Humboldt Universität ❹
HUMBOLDT UNIVERSITY

Unter den Linden 6. **Map** 7 A3, 16 D2.
Ⓢ & Ⓤ *Friedrichstrasse.* 🚌 *100,
157, 348.*

THE UNIVERSITY BUILDING was
constructed in 1753, for
Prince Heinrich of Prussia, the
brother of Frederick the Great.
The university was founded
in 1810 on the initiative of
Wilhelm von Humboldt. It
became the Berlin University
but was renamed in von
Humboldt's honour in 1949.
    The overall design of the
palace, with its main block
and the courtyard enclosed
within a pair of wings, has
been extended many times.
Two marble statues (1883)
by Paul Otto stand at the

WILHELM AND ALEXANDER VON HUMBOLDT

The Humboldt brothers rank among the most
distinguished Berlin citizens. Wilhelm (1767–
1835) was a lawyer and politician, occupying
various government posts. It was on his
initiative that the Berlin University (later
renamed Humboldt University) was
founded, and he conducted studies in
comparative and historical linguistics
there. Alexander (1769–1859),
a professor at the University,
researched natural science,
including meteorology, ocean-
ography and agricultural science.

Statue of Alexander von Humboldt

entrance gate and represent Wilhelm von Humboldt (holding a book) and his brother Alexander (sitting on a globe), who was a famous explorer. The entrance gate leads to the courtyard, which was designed by Reinhold Begas.

Many famous scientists have worked at the University, including philosophers Fichte and Hegel, physicians Rudolf Virchow and Robert Koch and physicists Max Planck and Albert Einstein. Among its graduates are Heinrich Heine, Karl Marx and Friedrich Engels.

After World War II, the University was in the Russian sector of the divided city and the difficulties encountered by the students of the western zone led to the establishment of a new university in 1948 – the Freie Universität (see p171).

Humboldt University courtyard
with statue of Hermann Helmholtz

Reiterdenkmal Friedrichs des Grossen ❺

EQUESTRIAN STATUE OF FREDERICK THE GREAT

Unter den Linden. **Map** 7 A3. Ⓢ & Ⓤ Friedrichstrasse. 🚌 100, 157, 348.

THIS IS ONE OF the most famous monuments in Berlin, featuring a massive bronze statue 5.6 m (18.5 ft) in height and standing on the centre lane of Unter den Linden. It was designed by Christian Daniel Rauch and created between 1839 and 1851. It depicts Frederick the Great on horseback, wearing a uniform and a royal cloak. The base of the high plinth is surrounded

by statues of famous military leaders, politicians, scientists and artists. The top tier of the plinth is decorated with bas-reliefs depicting scenes from the life of Frederick the Great. Out of line with GDR ideology, the monument was removed to Potsdam, where until 1980 it stood by the Hippodrome in Park Sanssouci.

Staatsbibliothek ❻

STATE LIBRARY

Unter den Linden 8. **Map** 7 A3, 16 D2. 📞 266 23 03. Ⓢ & Ⓤ Friedrichstrasse. 🚌 100, 157, 348.

THE NUCLEUS OF the State Library collection was the library belonging to the Great Elector – Friedrich Wilhelm – founded in 1661 and situated in the Stadtschloss. At the end of the 18th century it was moved to the Alte Bibliothek building. Its current home was designed by Ernst von Ihne and constructed between 1903 and 1914 on the site of the Academy of Science and the Academy of Fine Arts. This impressive building was severely damaged during

World War II and underwent extensive restoration. The collection, numbering 3 million books and periodicals, was scattered during the war, including a collection of priceless music manuscripts, which ended up in the Jagiellonian Library in Cracow, Poland.

After the war only part of the collection was returned to the building in Unter den Linden, and the remaining part was held in West Berlin. Following reunification, both the collections are now under the same administration.

Deutsche Guggenheim ❼

Unter den Linden 13–15. **Map** 7 A3, 16 D3. 📞 202 09 30. ◯ 11am–8pm during exhibitions. Ⓢ & Ⓤ Friedrichstrasse. 🚌 100, 157, 348.

THE DEUTSCHE GUGGENHEIM building is home to the German branch of the New York-based Guggenheim Foundation. The museum does not have its own permanent collection, but is regularly used to display a variety of temporary exhibitions.

The ivy-clad Staatsbibliothek building on Unter den Linden

A window with a heraldic shield on the Altes Palais

Altes Palais ❽
THE OLD PALACE

Unter den Linden 9. **Map** 7 A3, 16 D3.
Ⓢ & Ⓤ *Friedrichstrasse.*
🚌 *100, 157, 348.* ● *to the public.*

Tᴴɪꜱ ɴᴇᴏ-ᴄʟᴀꜱꜱɪᴄᴀʟ palace,
near the former Opernplatz
(Bebelplatz), was built for the
heir to the throne – Prince
Wilhelm (later Kaiser Wilhelm
I). The Kaiser lived here all his
life. He was able to watch the
changing of the guards every
day from the ground-floor
window on the far left.

The palace, built from 1834
to 1837, was designed by Carl
Ferdinand Langhans but its
splendid furnishings were
destroyed during World War II.
The palace was subsequently
restored, and is now used by
Humboldt Universität.

Alte Bibliothek ❾
THE OLD LIBRARY

Bebelplatz. **Map** 7 A3, 16 D3. Ⓢ &
Ⓤ *Friedrichstrasse.* 🚌 *100, 157,
348.* ● *10am–5pm Mon–Sat,
1–5pm Sun.*

Tʜᴇ ᴏʟᴅ ʟɪʙʀᴀʀʏ, known by
locals as the *Kommode* or
"chest of drawers" after its
curved façade, is actually one
of the city's most beautiful
Baroque buildings. It was
designed by Georg Christian
Unger and built around 1775
to house the royal library collection. In fact, Unger based
his design on an unrealized
plan for an extension to the
Hofburg complex in Vienna,
prepared by the famous architect Josef Emanuel Fischer
von Erlach in 1725. The concave façade of the building is
accentuated by three breaks,

surrounded at the top by a
row of massive Corinthian
pilasters and groupings of
heraldic shields.

Bebelplatz ❿

Map 7 A3, 16 D3. Ⓢ & Ⓤ
Friedrichstrasse. 🚌 *100, 157, 348.*

Oɴᴄᴇ ɴᴀᴍᴇᴅ Opernplatz
(Opera Square), Bebelplatz
was to be the focal point of
the intended Forum Frideric-
ianum, an area designed by
Georg Wenzeslaus von
Knobelsdorff to mirror the
grandeur of ancient Rome.
Although the initial plans were
only partly implemented, many
important buildings rose
around the square with the
passage of time.

On 10 May 1933 Opernplatz
was the scene of the infamous
book burning act organized by
the Nazi propaganda machine.
Some 25,000 books written by
authors considered to be
enemies of the Third Reich

were burned. These included
works by Thomas and Hein-
rich Mann, Robert Musil and
Lion Feuchtwanger.

Today, a monument at the
centre of the square, designed
by Micha Ullman in 1995,
commemorates this dramatic
event. A translucent panel
inserted into the road surface
provides a glimpse of a room
filled with empty bookshelves.
Next to it is a plaque bearing
the tragically prophetic words
of the poet Heinrich Heine,
written in 1820: "Where books
are burned, in the end people
will burn."

St-Hedwigs-Kathedrale ⓫
ST HEDWIG'S CATHEDRAL

Bebelplatz. **Map** 7 A4, 16 D3, E3.
Ⓢ & Ⓤ *Friedrichstrasse.* 🚌 *100,
157, 348.* ● *9am–9pm Mon–Fri,
9am–5pm Sat.*

Tʜɪꜱ ʜᴜɢᴇ ᴄʜᴜʀᴄʜ, set back
from the road and crowned
with a dome, is the Catholic
Cathedral of the Roman Arch-
diocese of Berlin. It was built
to serve the Catholics of Silesia
(part of present-day Poland),
which became part of the
Kingdom of Prussia in 1742
following defeat in the
Silesian Wars of 1740–63.

The initial design, by Georg
Wenzeslaus von Knobelsdorff,
was similar to the Roman Pantheon. Construction began in
1747 and the cathedral was
consecrated in 1773, although

The façade of St Hedwig's Cathedral features beautiful bas-relief sculptures

work continued on and off until 1778. Its design was modified repeatedly. Later, additional work was carried out from 1886 to 1887.

The cathedral was damaged during World War II, and subsequently rebuilt between 1952 and 1963. The building received a reinforced concrete dome and its interior was refurbished in a modern style.

The crypt holds the tombs of many of the bishops of Berlin. It also contains a 16th-century Madonna and a Pietà dating from 1420.

The imposing façade of the Kronprinzenpalais

Bas-relief of Apollo and Mars on the façade of the Staatsoper

Staatsoper Unter den Linden ⑫

STATE OPERA HOUSE

Unter den Linden 7. **Map** 7 A3, 16 D3. **C** 20 82 861. **S** & **U** Friedrichstrasse. 🚌 100, 157, 348.

THE EARLY Neo-Classical façade of the State Opera House is one of the most beautiful sights along Unter den Linden. It was built by Georg Wenzeslaus von Knobelsdorff in 1741–3 as the first building of the intended Forum Friedericianum. Following a fire, the opera house was restored from 1843 to 1844 under the direction of Carl Ferdinand Langhans, who altered only its interior.

Following wartime destruction, the opera house was rebuilt from 1952 to 1955, almost from the ground up. It has played host to famous singers, musicians and artists; one of its directors and conductors was Richard Strauss, and its stage designers included Karl Friedrich Schinkel.

Kronprinzenpalais

⑬ CROWN PRINCE'S PALACE

Unter den Linden 3. **Map** 7 A3, B3, 16 E3. **S** & **U** Friedrichstrasse. 🚌 100, 157, 348. ⏱ 10am–6pm Thu-Tue.

THIS STRIKING late-Neo-Classical palace is home to the Deutsches Historiches Museum collection while the Zeughaus (see pp58–9) is undergoing restoration. The palace takes its name from its original inhabitants – the heirs to the royal, and later to the imperial, throne. Its form is the outcome of numerous alterations made to what was originally a modest house dating from 1663–9. The first extensions, in the late-Baroque style, were conducted by Philipp Gerlach in 1732 and 1733. Between 1856 and 1857 Johann Heinrich Strack added the second floor. These extensions were rebuilt following World War II.

The palace served the royal family until the abolition of the monarchy. From 1919 to 1937, it was used as a branch of the Nationalgalerie. Under Communist rule it was renamed Palais Unter den Linden and became a residence for official government guests. Here, on 31 August 1990, the pact was signed paving the way for German reunification.

A restaurant pavilion has been added to the rear of the palace. Its walls feature the portal and terracotta slabs from the Bauakademie building,

designed by Karl Friedrich Schinkel and dismantled after World War II.

Joined to the main palace by an overhanging passageway is the smaller Prinzessinnenpalais (Princesses' Palace), built for the daughters of Friedrich Wilhelm III.

Friedrichswerdersche Kirche (Schinkel-Museum) ⑭

Werderstrasse. **Map** 7 B4, 16 E3. **C** 208 13 23. **U** Hausvogteiplatz. 🚌 100, 147, 157, 257, 348. ⏱ 10am–6pm Tue-Sun. 📷 ♿

THIS PICTURESQUE church, designed by Karl Friedrich Schinkel and constructed between 1824 and 1830, was the first Neo-Gothic church to be built in Berlin. The small single-nave structure, with its twin-tower façade, resembles an English college chapel.

Schinkel's original interior of the church was largely destroyed in World War II.

Following its reconstruction, the church was converted to a museum. It is currently used by the Nationalgalerie to house its permanent exhibition of sculptures from the late 16th to the mid 19th century. Highlights include a model of the famous group sculpture by Johann Gottfried Schadow, depicting the princesses Friederike and Luise (later Queen of Prussia).

Princesses Luise and Friederike in the Schinkel-Museum

Gendarmenmarkt ⑮

THIS IS one of Berlin's most beautiful squares, created at the end of 17th century as a market square for the newly established Friedrichstadt. It is named after the Regiment Gens d'Armes who had their stables here. In 1950 it was renamed Platz der Akademie; after reunification the square reverted to its original name.

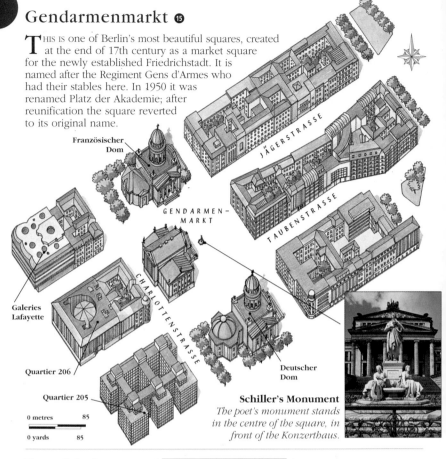

Französischer Dom

JÄGERSTRASSE

GENDARMEN-MARKT

TAUBENSTRASSE

Galeries Lafayette

CHARLOTTENSTRASSE

Quartier 206

Deutscher Dom

Quartier 205

0 metres   85

0 yards   85

Schiller's Monument
The poet's monument stands in the centre of the square, in front of the Konzerthaus.

Französischer Dom ⑲

FRENCH CATHEDRAL

Gendarmenmarkt 6. **Map** 7 A4, 16 D4.
📞 229 17 60. Ⓤ *Stadtmitte or Französische Strasse.* **Museum**
🕐 *noon–5pm Tue–Sat, 11am–5pm Sun.* 🎦 **Viewing Platform** 🕐 *9am–7pm daily* 🎫 **Church** 🕐 *noon–5pm Tue–Sun.* 🕐 *Sun 10am.*

ALTHOUGH THE TWO churches standing on the opposite sides of Schauspielhaus seem to be identical, they differ from each other quite considerably. Their only common feature is the identical front towers. The French cathedral was built for the Huguenot community, who found refuge in protestant Berlin following their expulsion from France after the revocation of the Edict of Nantes.

Side elevation of the Französischer Dom, built for Huguenot refugees

The modest church, built between 1701 and 1705 by Louis Cayart and Abraham Quesnay, was modelled on the Huguenot church in Charenton, France, which was destroyed in 1688. The main entrance, on the west elevation

(facing Charlottenstrasse), leads to an uncomplicated interior with a rectangular nave and semicircular sections on both sides. It features a late-Baroque organ from 1754.

The structure is dominated by a massive, cylindrical tower which is encircled by Corinthian porticos at its base. The tower and porticos were designed by Carl von Gontard and added around 1785, some 80 years after the church was built. It houses the Huguenot Museum, which details the history of the Huguenot community in France and Brandenburg.

There is a smart restaurant on the upper floor, and on the top is a viewing platform offering a magnificent view. The 60-bell carillon in the tower can be heard every day at noon, 3pm and 7pm.

The interior of the Konzerthaus, formerly the Schauspielhaus

Konzerthaus ⑰
CONCERT HALL

Gendarmenmarkt 2. **Map** 7 A4, 16 D4. 🄲 20 30 921 01. Ⓤ Stadtmitte.

A LATE NEO-CLASSICAL jewel, this magnificent theatre building, known until recently as the Schauspielhaus, is one of the greatest achievements of Berlin's best-known architect, Karl Friedrich Schinkel. It was built between 1818 and 1821 around the ruins of Langhan's National Theatre, destroyed by fire in 1817. The portico columns were retained in the new design. Schinkel was responsible not only for the architectural structure but also for the interior design, right down to the door handles. Following bomb damage in World War II, it was reconstructed as a concert hall with a different interior layout. The exterior was restored to its former glory. The Konzerthaus is now home to the Berlin Symphony Orchestra.

The theatre façade includes a huge Ionic portico with a set of stairs that was only used by the middle classes (the upper classes entered via a separate entrance where they could leave their horse-drawn carriages). The whole building is richly decorated with sculptures

alluding to drama and music. These include statues of musical geniuses mounted on lions and panthers, as well as figures representing the Muses and a Bacchanal procession. The façade is crowned with the sculpture of Apollo riding a chariot pulled by griffins.

In front of the theatre stands a shining, white marble statue of Friedrich Schiller. It was sculpted by Reinhold Begas, and erected in 1869. Removed by the Nazis during the 1930s, the monument was finally returned to its rightful place in 1988. Schiller's head was copied by the sculptor from a bust of the poet created in 1794 by Johann Heinrich Dannecker. The statue is mounted on a high pedestal surrounded by allegorical figures representing Lyric Poetry, Drama, Philosophy and History.

Deutscher Dom ⑱
GERMAN CATHEDRAL

Gendarmenmarkt 1. **Map** 7 A4, 16 D4. Ⓤ Stadtmitte or Französische Strasse. 🄲 22 73 04 31. **Exhibition** ⊙ 10am–6pm Tue–Sun.

T HE CATHEDRAL at the southern end of the square, to the left of Konzerthaus, is an old German Protestant-Reformed church. It was designed by Martin Grünberg and built in 1708 by Giovanni Simonetti. The design was based on a five-petal shape, and in 1785 it acquired a dome-covered tower identical to that of the French cathedral.

Burned down in 1945, the church was finally rebuilt in 1993. Its exterior was painstakingly reconstructed, including its sculpted decorations. The interior is now modern and has been adapted as an exhibition space. On display is the popular "Fragen an die Deutsche Geschichte" ("Questions on German History"), which was formerly on show in the Reichstag building.

Sculpture from the Deutscher Dom

Friedrichstadt-passagen ⑲
FRIEDRICHSTADT PASSAGES

Friedrichstrasse 205, 206, 207. **Map** 6 F4, 15 C4. Ⓤ Französische Strasse or Stadtmitte.

T HIS GROUP of passages is part of a huge development of luxury shops, offices, restaurants and apartments built in recent years along Friedrichstrasse.

Quartier 207 is the famous Galeries Lafayette, a branch of the French department store occupying a charming building designed by Jean Nouvel and constructed almost entirely of glass. The building's axis is formed by an inner courtyard, which is defined by two glass cones with their bases facing each other. The highly reflective glass panes, together with the multicoloured stands that are clustered around the structure, make an extraordinary impression on the visitor.

The next passage, Quartier 206, has offices and smart luxury boutiques, and is the work of the American design team Pei, Cobb, Freed & Partners. The building owes its alluring, but somewhat nouveau-riche appearance to the use of forms inspired by Art Deco architecture, including sophisticated details and expensive stone cladding.

The southernmost building in the complex, and the largest passage, is Quartier 205, which is the work of Oswald Mathias Ungers.

The dazzling Art Deco-style hall in Quartier 206

Mohren-kolonnaden ②⓪

Mohrenstrasse 37b and 40/41.
Map 6 F5, 15 B5. **U** *Mohrenstrasse.*

DESIGNED BY Carl Gotthard Langhans, these Neo-Classical arcades resting on twin columns were constructed in 1787. They originally surrounded a bridge that spanned the moat around the city of Berlin. The bridge has since been demolished, and the arcades have been incorporated into buildings of a much later architectural style located on Mohrenstrasse.

One of the original arcades known as the Mohrenkolonnaden

Spittelkolonnaden ②①

Leipziger Strasse. **Map** 7 B5, 16 E5.
U *Spittelmarkt.*

IN THE VICINITY of Spittelmarkt is a picturesque Baroque-Neo-Classical colonnade squeezed between several 20-storey tower blocks. These tower blocks were erected to obscure the view of the Axel Springer Publishers' building, which stood on the opposite side of the Berlin Wall.

A pair of such semicircular colonnades, designed by Carl von Gontard and built in 1776, originally surrounded Spittelmarkt. The southern one was demolished in 1929, and the northern one was destroyed during World War II.

A copy of one of the original Spittelkolonnaden in Leipziger Strasse

In 1979, a copy of the colonnades was erected in Leipziger Strasse, using elements from the original.

Museum für Post und Kommunika-tion ②②

MUSEUM OF POST AND TELECOMMUNICATIONS

Leipziger Strasse 16. **Map** 6 F5, 15 C5.
U *Stadtmitte* ▦ *142.* **C** *20 29 40.*
◯ *9am–5pm Tue–Fri, 11am–7pm
Sat–Sun.* ● *Mon.*

THE POST OFFICE museum, founded in 1872, is the world's oldest establishment of its kind. A dozen or so years after it was founded, it moved into the corner of the huge building constructed for the main post office. The office wings, with their modest Neo-Renaissance elevations, contrast with the museum premises, which has a grand Neo-Baroque façade that is richly decorated with sculptures. The museum's rooms house exhibits that illustrate the history of postal and telecommunication services.

Ehemaliges Regierungsviertel ②③

Leipzigerilhelmstrasse, Leipziger
Strasse, Voss Strasse. **Map** 6 E5. **U**
Potsdamer Platz, Mohrenstrasse.

WILHELMSTRASSE, and the area situated to the west of it up to Leipziger Platz, was the former German government district, where the main departments had offices from the mid-19th century until 1945. The building at Voss Strasse No. 77 was once the Reich's Chancellery and Otto von Bismarck's office. From 1933, it served as the office of Adolf Hitler, for whom the building was specially extended by Albert Speer.

In the spring of 1945 the square was the scene of fierce fighting, and after World War II most of the buildings had to be demolished. Among those that survived are the former Prussian Landtag offices – the huge complex occupying the site between Leipziger and Niederkirchner Strasse. This building in the Italian Renaissance-style was designed by Friedrich Schulz, and constructed from 1892 to 1904. It consists of two segments: the one on the side of Leipziger Strasse (No. 3–4) once housed the upper chamber of the National Assembly (the Herrenhaus) and is now used by the Bundesrat. The building on the side of Niederkirchner Strasse (No. 5) was once the seat of the Landtag's lower chamber, and is now the Berliner Abgeordnetenhaus (House of Representatives).

The second surviving complex is the former Ministry of Aviation (Reichsluftfahrtminis-terium), at Leipziger Strasse No. 5, built for Hermann Göring in 1936 by Ernst Sagebiel. This awesome building is typical of architecture of the Third Reich.

Pariser Platz ❷

Map 6 E3, 15 A3.
Ⓢ Unter den Linden. 🚍 100.

THIS SQUARE, situated at the end of Unter den Linden, was created in 1734 as part of the urban development scheme involving the enlarged Friedrich- and Dorotheenstadt. Originally called Quarrée, it was renamed Pariser Platz after 1814 when the *Quadriga* sculpture from the Branden-burg Gate was returned to Berlin from Paris.

The square, enclosed on the west by the Brandenburg Gate, was densely built-up until World War II. Almost all the buildings, including the Academy of Fine Arts and the house of the painter Max Liebermann, were destroyed in 1945 and subsequently demolished. The empty area, intersected by the Berlin Wall, featured only a single restored gate, originally part of the Academy of Fine Arts.

Following reunification, the square was redeveloped. Twin houses designed by Josef Paul Kleihues, named Sommer and Liebermann, now flank the Brandenburg gate. On the north side of the square stands the Dresdner Bank building. Next to it is the French Embassy building. On the south side will be the United States Embassy, the DG Bank head office and the Akademie der Künste (Academy of Fine Arts). The east end of the square is closed by the huge bulk of the Adlon Hotel and an office building.

MAX LIEBERMANN (1849–1935)

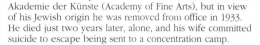

One of the greatest German painters, Max Liebermann was also one of the most interesting and controversial figures of Berlin's élite circles at the turn of the 20th century. A sensitive observer as well as an outstanding portraitist, Liebermann was famously stubborn – he could stand up even to the Kaiser himself. From 1920 he was president of the Akademie der Künste (Academy of Fine Arts), but in view of his Jewish origin he was removed from office in 1933. He died just two years later, alone, and his wife committed suicide to escape being sent to a concentration camp.

A frieze from the Brandenburg Gate

Brandenburger Tor ❷

BRANDENBURG GATE

Pariser Platz. Map 6 E3, 15 A3.
Ⓢ Unter den Linden. 🚍 100.

THE BRANDENBURG GATE is the quintessential symbol of Berlin. This magnificent Neo-Classical structure was designed by Carl Gotthard Langhans and modelled on the Athenian Propylaea (the entrance to the Acropolis). It was erected from 1778 to 1791, but it took until 1795 to complete its sculptured decorations. A pair of pavilions, once used by guards and customs officers, frames its powerful Doric colonnade, crowned with an entablature. The bas-reliefs depict scenes from Greek mythology, and the whole structure is crowned by the famous sculpture, *Quadriga*, designed by Johann Gottfried Schadow. The *Quadriga* was originally regarded as a symbol of peace. In 1806, during the French occupation, it was dismantled on Napoleon's orders and taken to Paris. On its triumphal return in 1814, it was declared a symbol of victory, and the goddess received the staff bearing the Prussian eagle and the iron cross adorned with a laurel wreath.

The Brandenburg Gate has borne witness to many of Berlin's important events. Both military parades and demonstrating workers have marched under its arches, and it saw celebrations marking the birth of the Second Reich as well as Hitler's ascent to power. It was here, too, that the Russian flag was raised in May 1945, and on 17 June 1953 that 25 workers demonstrating for better conditions were killed.

The gate, located in East Berlin, was restored between 1956 and 1958, when the damaged *Quadriga* was rebuilt in West Berlin. Over the next 40 years it stood watch over the divided city, until 1989, when the first section of the Berlin Wall came down.

Oskar Kokoschka's *Pariser Platz in Berlin* (1925–6), Nationalgalerie

The luxurious interior of the Adlon Hotel

Hotel Adlon ㉖

Unter den Linden 77. **Map** 6 E3,
6 E4, 15 A3, 15 B3. ☏ *226 10.*
Ⓢ *Unter den Linden.* ▦ *100.*

CONSIDERED TO BE the most
important society venue
in Berlin, the original Hotel
Adlon opened its doors to the
public in 1907. Its luxurious
suites were once used by the
world's celebrities, including
Greta Garbo, Enrico Caruso
and Charlie Chaplin. The
hotel suffered bomb damage
in World War II, and was
demolished in 1945. A new
building bearing the same
name was opened in a blaze
of publicity on 23 August 1997.

Today, it is once again the
best address in town. Comfort,
discretion and lavish interiors
featuring exotic timber, marble
and heavy silk, still tempt
visitors despite high prices.
Those who cannot afford to
stop for a night should at
least drop in for a cup of
coffee in the main hall. In this
hall stands the only authentic
remnant of the former Adlon
Hotel, an elegant black
marble fountain decorated
with elephants, which once
stood in the orangery.

Russische Botschaft ㉗
RUSSIAN EMBASSY

Unter den Linden 63/65. **Map** 6 F3,
15 B3. Ⓢ *Unter den Linden.* ▦ *100.*

THE MONUMENTAL, white
Russian Embassy building
is an example of the Stalinist
"wedding cake" style, or

Zuckerbäckerstil. Built between 1948 and 1953, it was
the first post-war building
erected on Unter den Linden.
It is built on the site of a
former palace that had
housed the Russian
(originally Tsarist)
embassy from 1837.

The building is the
work of the Russian
architect Anatoli
Strizhevsky. This
structure, with its
strictly symmetrical
layout, resembles the
old Berlin palaces of
the Neo-Classical period.
The sculptures that
adorn it, however,
belong to an altogether
different era: the gods
of ancient Greece
and Rome have been
replaced by working-
class heroes.

**Statue of a worker
on the Russian
Embassy building**

Komische Oper ㉘
COMIC OPERA

Behrenstr. 55/57. **Map** 6 F4, 15 C3.
☏ *47 99 74 00.* Ⓤ *Französische-
strasse.* Ⓢ *Unter den Linden.*
▦ *100, 147, 348.*

LOOKING AT the modern
façade of this theatre it is
hard to believe that it hides
one of Berlin's most im-
pressive interiors. Originally
called the Theater Unter den
Linden, the theatre was built
in 1892 by the internationally
famous Viennese architectural
practice of Ferdinand Fellner
and Hermann Helmer. It has
served as a variety theatre
and as the German National
Theatre in the past, and has
only housed the Komische
Oper since World War II.
The post-war reconstruction
deprived the building of its
former façades but the
beautiful Viennese
Neo-Baroque interior
remained, full of
stuccoes and gilded
ornaments. Parti-
cularly interesting are
the expressive and
dynamically posed
statues on the pilasters
of the top balcony – the
work of Theodor Friedel.
The Komische Oper is
one of Berlin's three
leading opera comp-
anies. Its repertoire
consists mainly of
light opera.

Crowded balconies and the plush interior of the Komische Oper

S-Bahnhof Friedrichstrasse ㉙

Map 6 F2, 6 F3 & 15 C2.

ONE OF THE CITY'S most famous urban railway stations, Bahnhof Friedrichstrasse used to be the border station between East and West Berlin. It was built in 1882 to a design by Johannes Vollmer. In 1925 a roof was added, covering the hall and the platforms.

The original labyrinth of passages, staircases and checkpoints no longer exists but it is possible to see a model of the station at the Stasi-Museum (see p166). Now used as a theatre, the only remaining structure from the original station is the special pavilion once used as a waiting room by those waiting for emigration clearance. It earned the nickname Tränenpalast, the "Palace of Tears", as it is here that Berliners from different sides of the city would say goodbye to each other after a visit.

Admiralspalast ㉚

Friedrichstr. 101–102. **Map** 6 F2, 15 C1. 🅄 and Ⓢ Friedrichstrasse.

THE ADMIRALSPALAST was built in 1911 to house an indoor swimming pool and an ice-rink. Designed by Heinrich Schweitzer, the main façade is punctuated by Doric half-columns and inlaid with bas-relief slabs made of Istrian marble. Quite different in style, the façade on Planckstrasse is also interesting. It was designed by Ernst Westphal and includes various exotic overlapping motifs.

The area around Friedrichstrasse was once well known for its excellent theatres, and in 1922 part of the Admiralspalast was converted to house the Metropol-Theater. Through this and subsequent remodelling works the building has retained its original façade. The Metropol-Theater specialized in variety and musical productions until it was declared bankrupt in 1997.

Part of the building, which is in urgent need of refurbishment, is now used by one of

A window of the Admiralspalast decorated with marble slabs

the best political cabarets in Berlin, Die Diestel, which hails from East Berlin.

Maxim Gorki Theater ㉛

Am Festungsgraben 2. **Map** 7 A3, 16 E2. 📞 20 22 11 29. 🅄 & Ⓢ Friedrichstrasse. 🚌 100, 157, 348.

THE MAXIM GORKI theatre was once a singing school or Sing-Akademie. Berlin's oldest concert hall, it was built in 1827 by Karl Theodor Ottmer, who based his design on drawings by Karl Friedrich Schinkel. This modest Neo-Classical building, with its attractive façade resembling a Greco-Roman temple, was well known for the excellent acoustic qualities of its concert hall.

Many famous composer-musicians performed at the Maxim Gorki Theater, including violinist Niccolò Paganini and pianist Franz Liszt. In 1829, Felix Mendelssohn-Bartholdy conducted a performance of the St Matthew

Maxim Gorki Theater occupying the oldest concert hall in Berlin

Passion by Johann Sebastian Bach, the first since the composer's death in 1750. Following reconstruction after World War II, the building is now used as a theatre.

Palais am Festungsgraben (Museum Mitte) ㉜

PALACE AM FESTUNGSGRABEN (MITTE MUSEUM)

Am Festungsgraben 1. **Map** 7 A3, 16 E2. 📞 20 84 000. Ⓢ Friedrichstrasse. 🚌 100, 157, 348. 🕐 1–5pm Wed and Thu, Fri 1–8pm, Sat 11am–8pm, Sun 11am–5pm.

THE PALACE IN Festungsgraben is one of the few structures in this part of town that has maintained its original interior decor. Built as a small Baroque palace in 1753, it owes its present form to major extension work, carried out in 1864 in the style of Karl Friedrich Schinkel, by Heinrich Bürde and Hermann von der Hude.

The late Neo-Classical style of the building is reminiscent of Schinkel's later designs. The interior includes a magnificent double-height marble hall in the Neo-Renaissance style and modelled on the White Room in the former Stadtschloss (see p71). In 1934 one of the ground-floor rooms was turned into a music salon, and many musical instruments were brought here from the 19th-century house (now demolished) of wealthy merchant and manufacturer Johann Weydinger (1773–1837).

MUSEUM ISLAND

THE LONG ISLAND that nestles in the tributaries of the Spree river is the cradle of Berlin's history. It was here that the first settlements appeared at the beginning of the 13th century – Cölln is mentioned in documents dating back to 1237 and its twin settlement, Berlin, is mentioned a few years later (1244). Not a trace of Gothic and Renaissance Cölln is left now: the island's character was transformed by the construction of the Brandenburg

Bas-relief from the façade of the Berliner Dom

Electors' palace, which served as their residence from 1470. Over the following centuries, the palace was converted first into a royal and later into an imperial palace – the huge Stadtschloss. Although it was razed to the ground in 1950, some interesting buildings on the island's north side have survived, including the huge Berliner Dom (cathedral) and the impressive collection of museums that give the island its name – Museumsinsel.

SIGHTS AT A GLANCE

Museums and Galleries
Alte Nationalgalerie **7**
Altes Museum p75 **6**
Bodemuseum **10**
Galgenhaus **19**
Historischer Hafen Berlin **13**
Märkisches Museum **14**
Neues Museum **8**
Pergamonmuseum pp80–83 **9**

Streets, Squares and Parks
Lustgarten **5**
Märkisches Ufer **15**
Schlossplatz **1**

Historic Buildings
Berliner Dom pp76–7 **4**
Ermeler-Haus **16**
Gertraudenbrücke **17**
Marstall **11**
Nicolai-Haus **18**
Ribbeckhaus **12**
Schlossbrücke **3**

Other Buildings
Palast der Republik **2**

KEY

	Street-by-Street map *See pp72–73*
U	U-Bahn Station
	Bus terminus
P	Parking

GETTING THERE
The easiest way to get to Museum Island and Schlossplatz is to walk from Hackescher Markt S-Bahn station, or to take a bus, either the 100, 157 or the 348. The Breite Strasse district is served by buses 147 and 257, while the south end of the island can be reached by U-Bahn line 2, going to Spittelmarkt, and by buses 142 and 147 to Märkisches Ufer.

0 metres   400
0 yards   400

◁ **The elegant Bodemuseum, with the Fernsehturm (Television Tower) in the background**

Street-by-Street: Museum Island

O N THIS ISLAND ARE the pretty Lustgarten and the Berliner Dom (Berlin Cathedral). It is also where you will find some of the most important museums in the east of the city. These include the Bodemuseum, the Altes Museum, the Alte National-galerie and the splendid Pergamonmuseum, famous for its collection of antiquities and visited by crowds of art-lovers from around the world.

Bodemuseum
The dome-covered rounded corner of the building provides a prominent landmark at the tip of the island ❿

Railway bridge, also used by the S-Bahn.

★ Pergamonmuseum
The museum is famous for its reconstruction of fragments of ancient towns, as well as the original friezes from the Pergamon altar ❾

AM KUPFER-GRABEN

Alte Nationalgalerie
The equestrian statue of King Friedrich Wilhelm IV in front of the building is the work of Alexander Calandrelli ❼

BODESTRASSE

Schlossbrücke
Under the GDR regime this unusual bridge was called Marx-Engels-Brücke ❸

0 metres		100
0 yards		100

Neues Museum
The building, which once housed a col-lection of Egyptian antiquities, is currently in the early stages of reconstruction ❽

STAR SIGHTS

★ Altes Museum

★ Berliner Dom

★ Pergamonmuseum

KEY

▬ ▬ ▬   Suggested route

★ Altes Museum
The corners of the central building feature figures of Castor and Pollux, heroes of Greek myth also known as the Dioscuri **6**

LOCATOR MAP
See Street Finder, maps 7 &16

★ Berliner Dom
The Neo-Baroque interior of the Berlin Cathedral features some extravagant late 19th-century furnishings **4**

Lustgarten
The 70-ton granite bowl was the biggest in the world when it was placed in the garden in 1828 **5**

Palast der Republik
The fate of this contro-versial building is uncertain; it may be restored or pulled down to make way for the rebuilding of the Stadtschloss **2**

Schlossplatz
Excavations con-ducted here have unearthed the cellars of the demolished Stadtschloss **1**

Schlossplatz ❶

Map 7 B3, 16 F3. Ⓢ *Hackescher Markt.* 🚌 *100, 157, 348.*

THIS SQUARE was once the site of a gigantic residential complex known as Stadtschloss (City Castle). Built in 1451, it served as the main residence of the Brandenburg Electors. It was transformed from a castle to a palace in the mid-16th century when Elector Friedrich III (later King Friedrich I) ordered its reconstruction in the Baroque style. The building works, which lasted from 1698 until 1716, were overseen initially by Andreas Schlüter and then by Johann von Göthe and Martin Heinrich Böhme.

The three-storey residence, designed around two courtyards, was the main seat of the Hohenzollern family for almost 500 years until the end of the monarchy. The palace was partly burned during World War II, but after 1945 it was provisionally restored and used as a museum. In 1950–51, despite protests, the palace was demolished and the square was renamed Marx-Engels-Platz under the GDR.

Now all that remains of the palace is the triumphal-arch portal that once adorned the façade on the Lustgarten side. This is now incorporated into the wall of the government building, the Staatsratgebäude, erected in 1964 on the square's south side. The building's

The surviving Stadtschloss portal fronting a government building

décor features the remaining original sculptures, including the magnificent atlantes by the famous Dresden sculptor, Balthasar Permoser. Their inclusion was not due to appreciation of their artistic merit, but rather to their propaganda value: it was from the balcony of the portal that in 1918 Karl Liebknecht proclaimed the birth of the Socialist Republic.

In 1989 the square reverted to its original name. There have been ongoing discussions about rebuilding the palace, but no final decision has yet been reached. In 1993, however, a spectacular model was built out of cloth stretched over a scaffolding frame.

Palast der Republik ❷

PALACE OF THE REPUBLIC

Map 7 B3, 16 F2. Ⓢ *Hackescher Markt.* 🚌 *100, 157, 348.*

BUILT ON THE SITE of the Stadtschloss in 1976, the Palast der Republik was once considered to be one of East Berlin's most prestigious buildings. Although it housed the GDR parliament, it was also accessible to the public. It boasted restaurants, a theatre, a discotheque, sports facilities and a large hall that could hold up to 5,000 people. In 1990 the discovery that asbestos had been used in its construction led to its immediate closure. The site is currently being cleaned but, despite much debate, its future remains unresolved – whether to restore the Palast der Republik or to rebuild the Stadtschloss.

Schlossbrücke ❸

Map 7 B3, 16 E2. Ⓢ *Hackescher Markt.* 🚌 *100, 157, 348.*

THIS IS ONE of the town's most beautiful bridges, connecting Schlossplatz with Unter den Linden. It was built in 1824 to a design by Karl Friedrich Schinkel. Statues were

Sculptures on the Schlossbrücke

added to the top of the bridge's sparkling red-granite pillars in 1853. These figures were also created by Schinkel and made of white Carrara marble. The statues depict tableaux from Greek mythology, such as Iris, Nike and Athena training and looking after their favourite young warriors. The elaborate wrought-iron balustrade is decorated with intertwined sea creatures.

Berliner Dom ❹

BERLIN CATHEDRAL

See pp76–7.

Lustgarten ❺

Map 7 B3, 16 E2. Ⓢ *Hackescher Markt.* 🚌 *100, 157, 348.*

THE ENCHANTING garden in front of the Altes Museum looks as though it has always been there, but in its present form it was established as recently as 1998 to 1999.

Used to grow vegetables and herbs for the Stadtschloss until the late-16th century, it became a real *Lustgarten* (pleasure garden) in the reign of the Great Elector (1620–88). However, its statues, grottoes, fountains and exotic vegetation were removed when Friedrich Wilhelm I (1688–1740), known for his love of military pursuits, turned the garden into an army drill ground.

Following the construction of the Altes Museum, the ground became a park, designed by Peter Joseph Lenné. In 1831 it was adorned with a monolithic granite bowl by Christian Gottlieb Cantian, to a design by Schinkel. The 70-ton bowl, measuring nearly 7 m (23 ft) in diameter, was intended for the museum rotunda, but was too heavy to carry inside.

After 1933, the Lustgarten was paved over and turned into a parade ground, remaining as such until 1989. Its current restoration is based on Lenné's designs.

Altes Museum ❻

THE MUSEUM BUILDING, designed by Karl Friedrich Schinkel, is undoubtedly one of the world's most beautiful Neo-Classical structures, with an impressive 87-m (285-ft) high portico supported by 18 Ionic columns. Officially opened in 1830, this was one of the first purpose-built museums in Europe, built to house the royal collection of paintings and antiquities. Following World War II, the building was only used to display temporary exhibitions. Since 1998 the Altes Museum has housed the Antikensammlung, a magnificent collection of Greek and Roman antiquities.

VISITORS' CHECKLIST

Am Lustgarten (Bodestr. 1–3). **Map** 7 B3. 20 90 55 55. Ⓢ Hackescher Markt. 100, 157, 348. 10am–6pm Tue–Thu & Sun, 10am– 8pm Fri & Sat.

Pericles' Head
This is a Roman copy of the sculpture by Kresilas that stood at the entrance to the Acropolis in Athens.

Andochides' Amphora
The amphora is decorated with the figures of wrestlers, a common motif.

Staircase

The monumental colonnade at the front of the building dominates the façade.

Main entrance

The stately rotunda is decorated with sculptures and ringed by a colonnade. Its design is based on the ancient Pantheon.

Mosaic from Hadrian's Villa
(c.117–138)
This colourful mosaic depicts a battle scene between centaurs and a tiger and lion. The mosaic comes from a floor of Hadrian's Villa, near Tivoli on the outskirts of Rome.

GALLERY GUIDE
The ground floor galleries house Greek and Roman antiquities; the first floor is currently used for 19th-century paintings from the Nationalgalerie.

KEY

☐ Greek and Roman antiquities

☐ Temporary exhibitions

Berliner Dom ❹

Royal crest of Friedrich III

THIS PROTESTANT cathedral was built from 1747 to 1750 as a church and mausoleum for the Hohenzollern family on the site of a Dominican church. Although it now has a central copper dome some 85 m (279 ft) high, the first Berliner Dom was a far more modest Baroque design by Johann Boumann. It was later remodelled in the Neo-Classical style from 1816 to 1821 by Karl Friedrich Schinkel. The present Neo-Baroque structure is the work of Julius Raschdorff, dating from 1894 to 1905. Following World War II damage, it has now been restored in a simplified form, including the dismantling of the Hohenzollern mausoleum that once adjoined the northern wall of the cathedral.

Figures of the apostles

Philipp der Grossmütige (Philip the Magnanimous)
At the base of the arcade stand the statues of church reformers and those who supported the Reformation. The statue of Prince Philip the Magnanimous is the work of Walter Schott.

★ **Church Interior**
The impressive and richly-decorated interior was designed by Julius Raschdorff at the turn of the 20th century.

Sauer's Organ
The organ, the work of Wilhelm Sauer, is set against an exquisitely carved backdrop.

Main entrance

★ **The Elector's Tomb**
This tomb is the oldest relic to be found in the cathedral, dating from c.1530. It was commissioned from the Vischer's studio in Nürnberg by Joachim I for his grandfather, Johann Cicero.

The Four Evangelists

Mosaics depicting the Four Evangelists decorate the ceilings of the smaller niches in the cathedral. They were designed by Woldemar Friedrich.

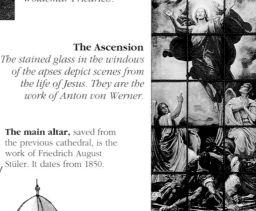

The Ascension

The stained glass in the windows of the apses depict scenes from the life of Jesus. They are the work of Anton von Werner.

The main altar, saved from the previous cathedral, is the work of Friedrich August Stüler. It dates from 1850.

The Pulpit

This elaborate Neo-Baroque pulpit is part of the cathedral's ornate decor dating from the early 20th century.

★ Sarcophagi of Friedrich I and his Wife

Both of these were designed by Andreas Schlüter. The sculpture on Sophie Charlotte's sarcophagus depicts death.

STAR FEATURES

★ The Elector's Tomb

★ Church Interior

★ Sarcophagi of Friedrich I and his Wife

Arnold Böcklin's *The Island of the Dead*, 1883, Alte Nationalgalerie

Alte Nationalgalerie **❼**

OLD NATIONAL GALLERY

Bodestrasse 1–3. **Map** 7 B2, 16 E1. **🄲** *20 90 55 55.* **Ⓢ** *Hackescher Markt or Friedrichstrasse.* **🚌** *100, 147, 257, 348.* **🚋** *1, 2, 3, 4, 5, 13, 53, 58.* **◗** *until Oct 2001.*

THE NATIONALGALERIE building was erected between 1866 and 1876 and designed by Friedrich August Stüler, who took into account the sketches made by Friedrich Wilhelm IV. The building is situated on a high platform reached via a double staircase. On the top stands an equestrian statue of Friedrich Wilhelm IV, the work of Alexander Calandrelli in 1886. The façade of the building is preceded by a magnificent colonnade, which becomes a row of half-columns higher up. The decorations are in keeping with the purpose of the building – the tympanum features Germania as patroness of art, while the top is crowned with the personification of the arts.

The museum was originally intended to house the collection of modern art that had been on display since 1861 in the Akademie der Künst *(see p67).* After World War II the collection was split up. Part of it was shown in West Berlin, where the Neue Nationalgalerie

was erected for this purpose *(see p126).* This building was then renamed Alte (meaning Old) Nationalgalerie.

Following the reunification of Germany, the modern art collections were merged again. The more recent paintings are now shown in the Neue Nationalgalerie, and the 19th-century works are shown here. The current collection includes works of masters such as Adolf von Menzel, Wilhelm Leibl, Max Liebermann and Arnold Böcklin. Other works include paintings by the Nazarene Brotherhood and the French Impressionists. There is also no shortage of sculptures, including works by Christian Daniel Rauch, Johann Gottfried Schadow and Reinhold Begas. The building has been undergoing renovation since 1998, so the collection is awaiting its permanent home.

Neues Museum **❽**

NEW MUSEUM

Bodestrasse 1–3. **Map** 7 B2, 16 E2. **Ⓢ** *Hackescher Markt or Friedrichstrasse.* **🚌** *100, 147, 257, 348.* **🚋** *1, 2, 3, 4, 5, 13, 53, 58.* **◗** *until 2005.*

THE NEUES MUSEUM was built on Museum Island in order to relieve the Altes Museum, which was already very

crowded. The building was erected between 1841 and 1855 to a design by Friedrich August Stüler. Until World War II it housed a collection of antiquities, mainly ancient Egyptian art. The monumental building's beautiful rooms were decorated to complement the exhibitions they contained. Wall paintings by Wilhelm von Kaulbach depicted key events in world history.

Façade statue, Neues Museum

In 1945 the building was badly damaged and it took a long time to decide if it would be feasible to rebuild it. Reconstruction work has only recently started, based on designs by David Chipperfield.

When the reconstruction is complete it will once again house the collection of Egyptian art, although the exact interior decor will not be restored. The building will serve not only as a venue for exhibitions, but it will also contain an information centre for the whole Museum Island (Museumsinsel) complex.

Pergamonmuseum **❾**

See pp80–81.

Bodemuseum ⑩

Monbijoubrücke. (Bodestrasse 1–3).
Map 7 A2, 16 D1. E1. 〖 *20 90 57
01.* ⑤ *Hackescher Markt or Friedrichstrasse.* 🚌 *100, 147, 257, 348.* 🚃 *1,
2, 3, 4, 5, 13, 53, 58.* ⦿ *until 2004.*

THE FOURTH MUSEUM building
on the island was erected
between 1897 and 1904. It was
designed by Ernst von Ihne to
fit in the wedge-shaped end
of the island. The interior was
designed with the help of an
art historian, Wilhelm von
Bode, who was the director
of the Berlin state museums
at the time. The museum
displayed a rather mixed
collection that included some
old masters. Its original name,
Kaiser Friedrich Museum, was
changed after World War II.
Following the reassembling of
the Berlin collections, all of
the paintings were put in
Kulturforum *(see pp122–3)*,
while the Egyptian art and the
papyrus collection were
moved to the Ägyptisches
Museum (Egyptian Museum)
at Charlottenburg *(see p158)*.
  Following its refurbishment
the building will once again
house its collection of coins,
medals and Byzantine art. It
will also have the reassembled
collection of sculptures, which
include the works of Tilman
Riemenschneider, Donatello,
Gianlorenzo Bernini and
Antonio Canova. A copy of
the magnificent equestrian
statue of the Great Elector,
Friedrich Wilhelm, by Andreas
Schlüter will once again take
its place in the old hall.

Marstall ⑪

THE ROYAL STABLES

Schlossplatz/Breite Strasse 36/37.
Map 7 B3, C3, C4, 16 F3.
Ⓤ *Spittelmarkt.* 🚌 *147, 257.*

THIS HUGE COMPLEX, occupying the area between the
Spree and Breitestrasse, south
of Schlossplatz, is the old
Royal Stables' block. The
wing on the side of Breite
Strasse is a fragment of the
old structure built in 1669. It
was designed by Michael
Matthias Smids and is the
only surviving early Baroque
building in Berlin. The wings
running along Schlossplatz
and the Spree river were built
much later, between 1898 and
1901. Although they were
designed by Ernst von Ihne,
these buildings are reminiscent
of the Berlin Baroque style –
probably because von Ihne
modelled them on designs by
Jean de Bodt from 1700.

Ribbeckhaus ⑫

RIBBECK'S HOUSE

Breite Strasse 35. **Map** 7 C4.
Ⓤ *Spittelmarkt.* 🚌 *147, 257.*

FOUR IDENTICAL, picturesque
gables crown central Berlin's
only surviving Renaissance
building. The house was built
c.1624 for Hans Georg von
Ribbeck, a court counsellor,
who sold it shortly afterwards
to Anna Sophie of Brunswick.
The architect Balthasar Benzelt
converted the house for her
in 1629. After her death in

**The Ribbeckhaus, central Berlin's
only surviving Renaissance building**

1659, the house passed to her
nephew Elector Friedrich
Wilhelm. As crown property,
the building later housed
various state administrative
offices. When another storey
was added, the row of gables
was retained by royal decree.
  The house also has an
interesting late-Renaissance
portal, ornamented with the
date and coat of arms of the
first owners – von Ribbeck
and Katharina von Brösicke
his wife. This was replaced ˙
in 1960 with a copy. Original
features of interest include the
beautiful wrought-iron grilles
in the ground-floor windows.

Historischer Hafen Berlin ⑬

HISTORIC PORT OF BERLIN

Märkisches Ufer. **Map** 8 D4.
〖 *21 47 32 57.* Ⓤ *Märkisches
Ufer.* ⑤ *Jannowitzbrücke.* 🚌 *265.*
◯ *1 Apr–31 Oct: Tue–Fri 2–6pm,
Sat–Sun 11am–6pm.* 🈁

MOORED ON THE south shore
of Museum Island, in an
area called Fischerinsel, and
opposite the Märkisches Ufer
are several examples of boats,
barges and tug-boats which
operated on the Spree river at
the end of the 19th century.
These craft constitute an open-
air museum which was once
located in the Humboldt Port.
One of the boats is now used
as a summer café, while
another, the *Renate Angelika*,
houses a small exhibition
illustrating the history of
inland waterway transport.

The Bodemuseum designed by Ernst von Ihne

Pergamonmuseum ❾

THE PERGAMONMUSEUM WAS BUILT between 1912 and 1930 to a design by Alfred Messel and Ludwig Hoffmann. It houses one of the most famous collections of antiquities in Europe, and owes its name to the famous Pergamon Altar which takes pride of place in the main hall. The three independent collections – the Museum of Antiquities (Greek and Roman), the Museum of Near Eastern Antiquities and the Museum of Islamic Art – are the result of intensive archaeological excavations by German expeditions to the Near and Middle East at the end of the 19th and beginning of the 20th century.

★ **Pergamon Altar** *(160 BC)*
This scene, featuring the goddess Athena, appears on the large frieze illustrating a battle between the gods and the giants.

Roman Mosaic (*2nd or 3rd century BC*)
This ancient mosaic was found at Jerash, Jordan. A second part of it is in the collection of the Stark Museum of Art, Texas.

Non-exhibition rooms

First floor

The Goddesss Athena
This enchanting Hellenistic sculpture of the goddess Athena is one of many displayed in the museum.

Ground floor

Main entrance

Assyrian Palace
Parts of this beautifully reconstructed palace interior, from the ancient kingdom of Assyria, date from the 12th century BC.

Aleppo Zimmer
(c.1603)
This magnificent panelled room comes from a merchant's house in the Syrian city of Aleppo.

GALLERY LAYOUT
The central section of the ground floor houses reconstructions of ancient monumental structures, and the left wing is devoted to the Antiquities of Greece and Rome. The right wing houses the Museum of Near Eastern Antiquities; the first floor of the right wing houses the Museum of Islamic Art.

Façade of the Mshatta Palace *(744 AD)*
This fragment is from the southern façade of the Jordanian Mshatta Palace, presented to Wilhelm II by Sultan Abdul Hamid of Turkey in 1903.

★ Market Gate from Miletus *(c. 120 AD)*
This gate, measuring over 16 m (52 ft) in height, opened on to the southern market of Miletus, a Roman town in Asia Minor.

★ Ishtar Gate from Babylon
(6th century BC)
Original glazed bricks decorate both the huge Ishtar gate and the impressive Processional Way that leads up to it.

STAR EXHIBITS

- ★ **Pergamon Altar**
- ★ **Ishtar Gate from Babylon**
- ★ **Market Gate from Miletus**

KEY

- Antiquities (Antikensammlung)
- Near Eastern Antiquities (Vorderasiatisches Museum)
- Islamic Art (Museum für Islamische Kunst)
- Non-exhibition rooms

Exploring the Pergamonmuseum

O PENED IN 1930, the Pergamonmuseum
is the newest museum in the Museum
Island complex and is one of Berlin's major
attractions. The building was one of the first
in Europe designed specifically to house big
architectural exhibits. The richness of its collections is the result of large-scale excavations by
German archaeologists at the turn of the
20th century. The proposed transfer here
of the Ägyptisches Museum collection from
Schloss Charlottenburg *(see p158)* will be a great
addition to the museum's collection of antiquities.

Bird from Mesopotamia

The Greek goddess Persephone, from Tarentum, 5th century BC

Restored entrance hall of the Nikephoros Athena temple, 2nd century BC

COLLECTION OF ANTIQUITIES

B ERLIN'S COLLECTION OF Greek
and Roman antiquities
(Antikensammlung) came into
existence during the 17th
century. Growing steadily in
size, the collection was opened
for public viewing in 1830,
initially in the Altes Museum
(see p75), and from 1930 in
the new, purpose-built
Pergamonmuseum. The high-

light of the collection is the
huge Pergamon Altar from the
acropolis of the ancient city of
Pergamon in Asia Minor (now
Bergama, Turkey). It formed
part of a larger architectural
complex, a model of which is
also on display in the museum.
The magnificently restored
altar is thought to have been
built to celebrate victory in war
and to have been commis-
sioned by King Eumenes in
160 BC. Probably dedicated to
the god Zeus and the goddess
Athena, this artistic masterpiece was discovered in a
decrepit state by German
archeologist Carl Humann
who, after long negotiations,
was allowed to transport the
surviving portions of the altar
to Berlin. The front section of
the building was restored at
the museum, together with the
so-called small frieze, which
once adorned the inside of
the building, and fragments of
the large frieze, which originally encircled the base of the
colonnade. The large frieze
has now been reconstructed
around the interior walls of the
museum and its theme is the
Gigantomachy (the battle of
the gods against the giants).
The small frieze tells the story

of Telephos, supposed founder
of the city and son of the hero
Heracles. The frieze is an
attempt to claim an illustrious
ancestry for Pergamon's rulers.
   The collection also contains
fragments of other Pergamon
structures from the same
period, including part of the
Nikephoros Athena temple.
Also featured here are some
excellent examples of Greek
sculpture, both originals and
Roman copies, as well as many
statues of the Greek gods
unearthed at Miletus, Samos
and Nakosos, and various
examples of Greek ceramic art.
   Roman architecture is represented by the striking market
gate from the Roman city of
Miletus, on the west coast of
Asia Minor. The gate dates
from the 2nd century BC, and
shows strong Hellenistic
influences. Discovered by a
German archaeological
expedition, it was transported
to Berlin where it was
restored in 1903. Also on
display are a number of magnificent Roman mosaics. A
huge and impressive marble

Roman marble sarcophagus depicting the story of Medea, 2nd century AD

sarcophagus dates from the 2nd century AD and is decorated with delicate bas-relief carvings depicting the story of the Greek heroine Medea.

Glazed-brick wall cladding from the palace of Artaxerxes II in Susa, capital of the Persian Empire

MUSEUM OF NEAR EASTERN ANTIQUITIES

THE COLLECTION NOW on display in the Museum of Near Eastern Antiquities (Vorderasiatisches Museum) was made up initially of donations from individual collectors. However, hugely successful excavations, begun during the 1820s, formed the basis of a royal collection that is one of the richest in the world. It features architecture, sculpture and jewellery from Babylon, Iran and Assyria.

One striking exhibit is the magnificent Ishtar Gate and the Processional Way that leads to it. They were built during the reign of Nebuchadnezzar II (604–562 BC) in the ancient city of Babylon. The original avenue was about 180 m (590 ft) long. Many of the bricks used in its reconstruction are new, but the lions – sacred animals of the goddess Ishtar (mistress of the sky, goddess of love and patron of the army) – are all originals. Although impressive in size, the Ishtar Gate has in fact not been reconstructed in full and a model of the whole structure shows the scale of

the original complex. Only the inner gate is on display, framed by two towers. Dragons and bulls decorate the gate, emblems of the Babylonian gods, Marduk, patron of the city, and Adad, god of storms.

The collection also includes pieces from the neighbouring regions of Persia, Syria and Palestine including a gigantic basalt sculpture of a bird from Tel Halaf and a glazed wall relief of a spear bearer from Artaxerxes II's palace in Susa. Other Mesopotamian peoples, including the Assyrians and the Cassians, are represented here too, as are the inhabitants of Sumer in the southern part of the Babylonian Empire with pieces dating from the 4th century BC.

MUSEUM OF ISLAMIC ART

THE HISTORY OF the Museum of Islamic Art (Museum für Islamische Künst) begins in 1904 when Wilhelm von Bode launched the collection by donating his own extensive selection of carpets. He also brought to Berlin a 45-m (150-ft) long section of the façade of a Jordanian desert palace. The façade, covered with exquisitely carved limestone cladding, was presented to Kaiser Wilhelm II in 1903 by Sultan Abdul Hamid of Turkey. The palace was part of a group of defence fortresses and residential buildings dating from the Omayyad period (AD661–750). These were probably built for the Caliph al-Walid II.

Another fascinating exhibit is a beautiful 13th-century *mihrab*, the niche in a

Brilliantly-glazed *mihrab* from a Kashan mosque built in 1226

mosque that shows the direction of Mecca. Made in the Iranian town of Kashan renowned for its ceramics, the *mihrab* is covered in lustrous metallic glazes that make it sparkle as if studded with sapphires and gold.

The collection's many vivid carpets come from as far afield as Iran, Asia Minor, Egypt and the Caucasus. Highlights include an early 15th-century carpet from Anatolia decorated with an unusual dragon and phoenix motif and, dating from the 14th century, one of the earliest Spanish carpets in existence.

Other rooms hold collections of miniature paintings and various objects for daily use. An interesting example of provincial Ottoman architecture is an exquisitely-panelled early 17th-century reception room, known as the Aleppo Zimmer, which was once part of a Christian merchant's house in the Syrian city of Aleppo.

17th-century carpet with flower motif from western Anatolia

The exterior of the Märkisches Museum, echoing a medieval monastery

Märkisches Museum ⑭

Am Köllnischen Park 5. **Map** 8 D4.
C 308 660. **U** Märkisches Museum.
S Jannowitzbrücke. 147, 240,
265. ⬜ 10am–6pm Tue-Sun.
Presentation of mechanical musical
instruments 3pm Wed, 11am Sun.

THIS ARCHITECTURAL pastiche is a complex of red brick buildings that most resembles a medieval monastery. It was built between 1901 and 1907 to house a collection relating to the history of Berlin and the Brandenburg region, from the time of the earliest settlers to the present. Inspired by the brick-Gothic style popular in the Brandenburg region, architect Ludwig Hoffmann has also included references to Wittstock Castle near Potsdam and to St Catherine's Church in Brandenburg. In the entrance hall, a statue of the hero Roland stands guard, a copy of the 15th-century monument in the city of Brandenburg. The main hall features the original Gothic portal from the Berlin residence of the Margraves of Brandenburg (see pp17–27), demolished in 1931. Also featured is a horse's head from the Schadow Quadriga, which once crowned the Brandenburg Gate (see p67). A further collection in the same building is devoted to the Berlin theatre during the period 1730 to 1933, including many posters, old programmes and stage sets. One of the galleries houses some charming old-time mechanical musical instruments, which can be heard playing during special shows.

The Märkisches Museum is a branch of the Stadtmuseum Berlin organization, and those who wish to find out more

about the history of the city can visit other affiliated museums and monuments such as the Nikolaikirche (see pp90–91), the Ephraim-Palais (see p91) and the Knoblauchhaus (see p91). Surrounding the museum is the Köllnischer Park, home to three brown bears, the official city mascots, and an unusual statue of Berlin artist Heinrich Zille.

Märkisches Ufer ⑮

Map 8 D4. **U** Märkisches Museum.
S Jannowitzbrücke. 265.

ONCE CALLED Neukölln am Wasser, this street, which runs along the Spree river, is one of the few corners of Berlin where it is still possible to see the town much as it must have looked in the 18th and 19th centuries. Eight picturesque houses have been meticulously conserved here.

Two Neo-Baroque houses at No. 16 and No. 18, known as Otto-Nagel Haus, used to contain a small museum displaying paintings by Otto Nagel, a great favourite with the communist authorities. The building now houses the photographic archives for the

state museums of Berlin. A number of picturesque garden cafés and fashionable restaurants make this attractive area very popular with tourists.

The Baroque interior of the Ermeler-Haus restaurant

Ermeler-Haus ⑯

ERMELER HOUSE

Märkisches Ufer 10. **Map** 7 C4.
U Märkisches Museum.
S Jannowitzbrücke. 265.

WITH ITS HARMONIOUS Neo-Classical façade, Märkisches Ufer No. 12 stands out as one of the most handsome villas in Berlin. This house was once the town residence of Wilhelm Ferdinand Ermeler, a wealthy merchant and shopkeeper, who made his money trading in tobacco. It originally stood on Fischerinsel on the opposite bank of the river, at Breite Strasse No. 11, but in 1968 the house was dismantled and reconstructed on this new site. The house was remodelled in 1825 to Ermeler's specifications, with a decor

Barges moored alongside Märkisches Ufer

that includes a frieze alluding to aspects of the tobacco business. Restorers have recreated much of the original façade. The Rococo furniture dates from about 1760 and the notable 18th-century staircase has also been rebuilt.

A modern hotel has been built to the rear of the house facing Wallstrasse, using Ermeler-Haus as its kitchens while the elegant first floor rooms house a restaurant.

Gertrauden-brücke ⑰

St Gertrude's Bridge

Map 7 B4, 16 F4.
Ⓤ *Spittelmarkt.* 🚌 *142.*

ONE OF Berlin's more interesting bridges, this connects Fischer Island with Spittelmarkt at the point where St Gertrude's Hospital once stood. The Gertrauden-brücke was designed by Otto Stahn and built in 1894.

Standing in the middle of the bridge is a bronze statue of the hospital's patron saint, St Gertrude, by Rudolf Siemering. A 13th-century Christian mystic, St Gertrude is shown here as a Benedictine abbess. Leaning over a poor youth she hands him a lily (symbol of virginity), a distaff (care for the poor), and a vessel filled with wine (love). The pedestal is surrounded by mice, a reference to the fact that Gertrude is patron saint of farmland and graves – both popular environments for mice.

Statue of St Gertrude

Nicolai-Haus ⑱

Brüderstr. 13. **Map** 7 B4, 16 F4.
Ⓤ *Spittelmarkt.* 🚌 *142, 147, 257.*
⬤ *until Jun 2001.*

BUILT AROUND 1710, the Nicolai-Haus is a fine example of Baroque architecture with the original, magnificent oak staircase still in place.

The house owes its fame, however, to its time as the home and bookshop of the publisher, writer and critic Christoph Friedrich Nicolai (1733–1811). Nicolai acquired the house around 1788 when he had it rebuilt to a Neo-Classical design by Karl Friedrich Zelter to become a bookshop and major German cultural centre.

One of the outstanding personalities of the Berlin Enlightenment, Nicolai was a great supporter of such revolutionary talents as the Jewish philosopher Moses Mendelssohn (*see p102*) and the playwright Gotthold Ephraim Lessing (1729–81). Other regular literary visitors to the Nicolai-Haus at this period included Johann Gottfried Schadow, Karl Wilhelm Ramler and Daniel Chodowiecki, all of whom are commemorated with a wall plaque.

Between 1905 and 1935 the building housed a museum devoted to Gotthold Ephraim Lessing. Today the rear wing features a fine staircase from the Weydinger-Haus, demolished in 1935. Installed in the Nicolai-Haus in the late 1970s, the staircase previously stood in the nearby Ermeler Haus (*see p84*).

Part of the Galgenhaus collection

Galgenhaus ⑲

Gallows House

Brüderstrasse 10. **Map** 7 B4, 16 F4.
Ⓒ *201 12 08.* Ⓤ *Spittelmarkt.*
🚌 *142, 147, 257.* ⭘ *by appointment.*

LOCAL LEGEND HAS IT that an innocent girl was once hanged in front of this building, which dates from 1700. It was originally built as the presbytery of the now vanished church of St Peter. Redesigned in the Neo-Classical style around 1805, the front portal and one of the rooms on the ground floor are all that remain of the original Baroque structure.

Today the Galgenhaus shows how Berlin has changed over the years with photographs of buildings and monuments. There is also a collection of clothes which provides an insight into the fashions of East Germany.

Cölln

An ancient settlement in the area called Fischerinsel at the southern end of Museum Island, the village of Cölln has now been razed almost to the ground. Not even a trace remains of the medieval St Peter's parish church. Until 1939, however, this working-class area with its tangle of narrow streets maintained a historic character and unique identity of its own. This vanished completely in the 1960s when most of the buildings were demolished, to be replaced with prefabricated tower blocks. A few historic houses, including Ermeler-Haus (*see p84*), were reconstructed elsewhere, but the atmosphere of this part of town has changed forever.

An engraving of old Cölln

EAST OF THE CENTRE

THIS PART of Berlin, belonging to the Mitte district, is the historic centre. A settlement called Berlin was first established on the eastern bank of the Spree river in the 13th century. Together with its twin settlement, Cölln, it grew into a town. This district contains traces of Berlin's earliest history, including the oldest surviving church (Marienkirche). In later centuries, it became a trade and residential district, but the Old Town (the Nikolaiviertel)

The organ-grinder at Gerichtslaube

survived until World War II. The GDR regime replaced the huge apartment buildings and department stores just to the north with a square, Marx-Engels-Forum, and built the Fernsehturm (television tower). Their redevelopment of the Nikolaiviertel was controversial – buildings were faithfully rebuilt but were grouped rather than being placed in their original locations. The area still offers cosy mews and alleys, which are surrounded by post-war high-rise blocks.

SIGHTS AT A GLANCE

Churches
Franziskaner Klosterkirche ⓯
Heiliggeistkapelle ❿
Nikolaikirche ❸
Marienkirche ⓫
Parochialkirche ⓱

Historic Buildings
Ephraim-Palais ❻
Gaststätte "Zur letzten Instanz" ⓲
Gerichtslaube ❼
Knoblauchhaus ❹
Palais Podewils ⓰
Palais Schwerin and Münze ❺
Rotes Rathaus ❶
Stadtgericht ⓮
Stadtmauer ⓳

Others
Alexanderplatz ⓭
Fernsehturm p93 ⓬

Neptunbrunnen ❾
Nikolaiviertel ❷
Marx-Engels-Forum ❽

KEY

▨	Street-by-Street map *See pp88–89*
Ⓡ	Railway station
Ⓢ	S-Bahn station
Ⓤ	U-Bahn station
Ⓟ	Parking

0 metres   400
0 yards   400

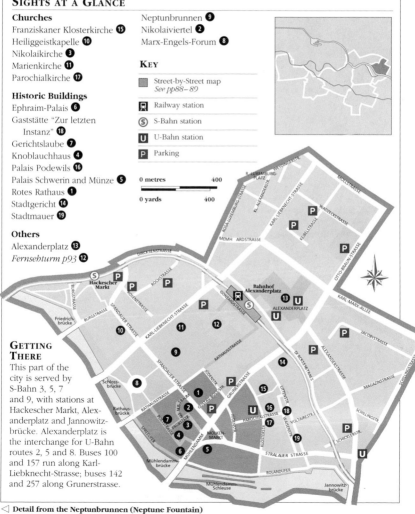

GETTING THERE
This part of the city is served by S-Bahn 3, 5, 7 and 9, with stations at Hackescher Markt, Alexanderplatz and Jannowitzbrücke. Alexanderplatz is the interchange for U-Bahn routes 2, 5 and 8. Buses 100 and 157 run along Karl-Liebknecht-Strasse; buses 142 and 257 along Grunerstrasse.

◁ **Detail from the Neptunbrunnen (Neptune Fountain)**

Street-by-Street: Nikolaiviertel

S T NICHOLAS' QUARTER, or the Nikolaiviertel, owes its name to the parish church whose spires rise above the small buildings in this part of town. The Nikolaiviertel is full of narrow alleys crammed with popular restaurants, tiny souvenir shops and small museums. The district was once inhabited by artists and writers, but now it is usually filled with tourists looking for a place to rest after an exhausting day of sightseeing – particularly in the summer. Almost every other house is occupied by a restaurant, inn, pub or café, so the area is quite lively until late at night.

Bear on façade of the Rathaus

Nikolaikirche
The church is now a museum, with its original furnishings incorporated into the exhibition ❸

Gerichtslaube
The replica arcades and medieval court-house now contain restaurants ❼

St George Slaying the Dragon
This statue once graced a courtyard of the Stadtschloss.

0 metres   75
0 yards   75

Knoblauchhaus
This Biedermeirer-style room is on the first floor of the building, which is one of the few to survive World War II damage ❹

★ Ephraim-Palais
A feature of this palace is the elegant façade. Inside there is also an impressive spiral staircase and balustrade ❻

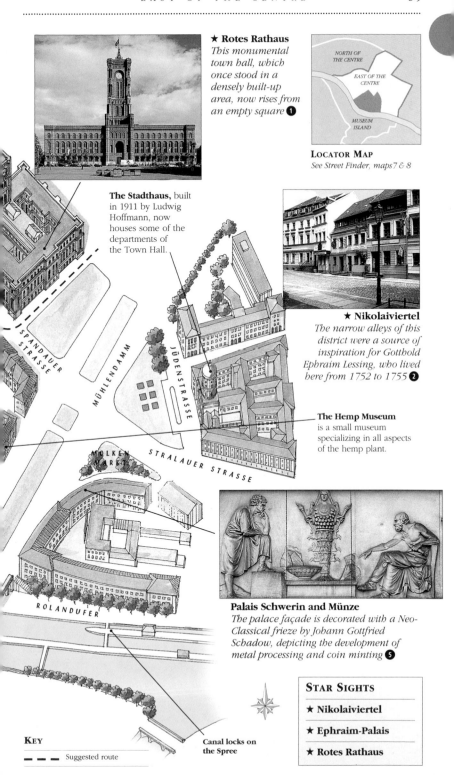

★ **Rotes Rathaus**
This monumental town hall, which once stood in a densely built-up area, now rises from an empty square ❶

LOCATOR MAP
See Street Finder, maps 7 & 8

The Stadthaus, built in 1911 by Ludwig Hoffmann, now houses some of the departments of the Town Hall.

★ **Nikolaiviertel**
The narrow alleys of this district were a source of inspiration for Gotthold Ephraim Lessing, who lived here from 1752 to 1755 ❷

The Hemp Museum
is a small museum specializing in all aspects of the hemp plant.

Palais Schwerin and Münze
The palace façade is decorated with a Neo-Classical frieze by Johann Gottfried Schadow, depicting the development of metal processing and coin minting ❺

STAR SIGHTS

★ **Nikolaiviertel**

★ **Ephraim-Palais**

★ **Rotes Rathaus**

KEY
- - - Suggested route

Canal locks on the Spree

Red-brick walls giving the the Red Town Hall its name

Rotes Rathaus ❶

RED TOWN HALL

Rathausstr. 15. **Map** 7 C3. **U** & **S** *Alexanderplatz.* **U** *Klosterstrasse.* 🚌 *100, 142, 157, 257, 348.*

THIS IMPRESSIVE structure is Berlin's main town hall. Its predecessor was a much more modest structure and by the end of the 19th century, it was insufficient to the needs of the growing metropolis.

The present building was designed by Hermann Friedrich Waesemann, and the construction works went on from 1861 until 1869. The architect took his main inspiration from Italian Renaissance municipal buildings, but the tower is reminiscent of Laon cathedral in France. The walls are made from red brick and it was this, rather than the political orientation of the mayors, that gave the town hall its name. The whole building has a continuous frieze known as the "stone chronicle", which was added in 1879. It features scenes and figures from the city's history and the development of its economy and science.

The Rotes Rathaus was severely damaged during World War II and following its reconstruction between 1951 and 1958, it became the seat of the East Berlin authorities. The West Berlin magistrate was housed in the Schöneberg town hall *(see p169)*. After the reunification of Germany, the Rotes Rathaus became the centre of authority, housing the

offices of the mayor and the Berlin cabinet. The forecourt sculptures were added in 1958. These are by Fritz Kremer and depict Berliners helping to rebuild the city.

Nikolaiviertel ❷

Map 7 C3, C4. **U** & **S** *Alexanderplatz.* **U** *Klosterstrasse.* 🚌 *100, 142, 157, 257, 348.*

THIS SMALL AREA on the bank of the Spree, known as the Nikolaiviertel (St Nicholas Quarter), is a favourite place for strolling, for both Berliners and tourists. Some of Berlin's oldest houses stood here until they were destroyed in World War II. The redevelopment of the whole area, carried out by the GDR government between 1979 and 1987, was an interesting, if somewhat controversial, attempt at recreating a medieval village. With the exception of one or two restored buildings, the Nikolaiviertel consists of newly built replicas of historic buildings.

The narrow streets of the Nikolaiviertel tempt the visitor with their small shops, as well as many cafés, bars and restaurants. One of the most popular is Zum Nussbaum, a historical inn that was once located on Fischer Island. The original building, dating from 1507, was destroyed but was subsequently reconstructed at the junction of Am Nussbaum and Propststrasse.

The interior of the Nikolaikirche, one of Berlin's oldest churches

Nikolaikirche ❸

Nikolaikirchplatz. **Map** 7 C3. 🕻 *24 00 20.* **U** & **S** *Alexanderplatz.* **U** *Klosterstrasse.* 🚌 *100, 142, 157, 257, 348.* 🕐 *10am–6pm Tue–Sat.* 🎫 *(free Wed).* ♿

THE NIKOLAIKIRCHE is the oldest sacred building of historic Berlin. The original structure erected on this site was started probably around 1230, when the town was granted its municipal rights. What remains now of this stone building is the massive base of the two-tower façade of the present church, which dates from c.1300. The presbytery was completed around 1402, but the construction of the main building went on until the mid-15th century. The result was a magnificent Gothic brick hall church, featuring a chancel with an

Riverside buildings of the Nikolaiviertel

ambulatory and a row of low chapels. In 1877 Hermann Blankenstein, who conducted the church restoration works, removed most of its Baroque modifications and reconstructed the front towers.

Destroyed by bombing in 1945, the Nikolaikirche was eventually rebuilt in 1987. Today it houses an exhibition covering the history of Berlin, featuring items that escaped the ravages of war. The west wall of the southern nave contains Andreas Schlüter's monument to the goldsmith Daniel Mannlich and his wife, which features a gilded relief portrait of the couple above a mock doorway.

A fine example of German Baroque architecture, the Ephraim-Palais

Knoblauchhaus ❹

Poststr. 23. **Map** 7 C3. ☎ 24 00 20. Ⓤ & Ⓢ *Alexanderplatz,* Ⓤ *Klosterstrasse.* 🚌 *100, 142, 157, 257, 348.* ◯ *10am–6pm Tue–Sat.* 🎫 *(free Wed).*

THIS SMALL TOWNHOUSE in Poststrasse is the only Baroque building in Nikolaiviertel that escaped damage during World War II. It was built in 1759 for the Knoblauch family which includes the famous architect, Eduard Knoblauch. His works include, among others, the Neue Synagoge (*see p102*).

The current appearance of the building is the result of work carried out in 1835, when the façade was given a Neo-Classical look. The ground floor houses a popular wine bar, while the upper floors belong to a museum. On the first floor it is possible to see the interior of an early 19th-century middle-class home, including a beautiful Biedermeier-style room.

Palais Schwerin and Münze ❺

Molkenmarkt 1–3. **Map** 7 C4. Ⓤ & Ⓢ *Alexanderplatz.* Ⓤ *Klosterstrasse.* 🚌 *100, 142, 157, 257, 348.*

THESE TWO ADJOINING houses have quite different histories. The older one, at No 2, is Palais Schwerin, which was built by Jean de

Bodt in 1704 for a government minister, Otto von Schwerin. Despite subsequent remodelling, the palace retained its beautiful sculptured window cornices, the interior wooden staircase, and the magnificent cartouche featuring the von Schwerin family crest.

The adjoining house is the mint which was built in 1936. Its façade is decorated with a copy of the frieze that once adorned the previous Neo-Classical mint building in Werderscher Markt. The antique style of the frieze was designed by Friedrich Gilly and produced in the workshop of JG Schadow.

Ephraim-Palais ❻

Poststr. 16, **Map** 7 C3 ☎ 24 00 20. Ⓤ & Ⓢ *Alexanderplatz.* Ⓤ *Klosterstrasse.* 🚌 *100, 142, 157, 257, 348.* ◯ *10am–6pm Tue–Sat.* 🎫 *(free Wed).*

THE CORNER ENTRANCE of the Ephraim-Palais, standing at the junction of Poststrasse and Mühlendamm, used to be called "die schönste Ecke Berlins", meaning "Berlin's most beautiful corner". This

Baroque palace was built by Friedrich Wilhelm Diterichs in 1766 for Nathan Veitel Heinrich Ephraim, Frederick the Great's mint master and court jeweller. During the widening of the Mühlendamm bridge in 1935 the palace was demolished, which may have been due in some part to the Jewish origin of its owner. Parts of the façade, saved from demolition, were stored in a warehouse in the western part of the city. In 1983 they were sent to East Berlin and used in the reconstruction of the palace, which was erected a few metres from its original site. One of the first floor rooms features a restored Baroque ceiling, designed by Andreas Schlüter. The ceiling previously adorned Palais Wartenberg, which was dismantled in 1889.

Currently Ephraim-Palais houses a branch of the Stadtmuseum Berlin (Berlin City Museum). The ground floor features ceramics from Königliche Porzellan-Manufaktur Berlin, while the first and the second floor rooms house a collection of paintings by Berlin artists.

Frieze from the façade of the Münze (the Mint)

Gerichtslaube ●

Poststrasse. 28. **Map** 7 C3.
U & **S** Alexanderplatz. **U** Klosterstrasse. ▥ 100, 142, 157, 257, 348.

THIS SMALL BUILDING, with its sharply angled arcades, has had a turbulent history. It was built around 1280 as part of Berlin's town hall in Spandauer Strasse. The original building was a single storey arcaded construction with vaults supported by a central pillar. It was open on three sides and adjoined the shorter wall of the town hall. A further storey was added in 1485 to provide a hall to which the magnificent lattice vaults were added a few decades later, in 1555.

In 1692, Johann Arnold Nering refurbished the town hall in a Baroque style, but left the arcades unaltered. Then, in 1868, the whole structure was dismantled to provide space for the new town hall, the Rotes Rathaus (see p90). The Baroque part was lost forever, but the Gothic arcades and the first floor hall were moved to the palace gardens in Babelsberg, where they were reassembled as a building in their own right (see pp202–3). When the Nikolaiviertel was undergoing restoration it was decided to restore the court of justice as well. The present building in Poststrasse is only a copy of a part of the former town hall, erected on a different site from the original one. Inside is a restaurant specializing in local cuisine.

Marx-Engels-Forum ●

Map 7 C3, 16 F2. **S** Hackescher Markt or Alexanderplatz.
▥ 100, 157.

THIS VAST, eerily empty square, stretching from the Fernsehturm (television tower) to the Spree river in the west, was given the inappropriate name Marx-Engels-Forum (it is not really a forum). Devoid of any surroundings, the only features in this green square are the statues of Karl Marx

Statue of Karl Marx and Friedrich Engels in Marx-Engels-Forum

and Friedrich Engels. Marx sits and Engels stands, seemingly staring at the Fernsehturm. The statues, added in 1986, are by Ludwig Engelhart. The base is decorated with bas-reliefs showing the "old order" at the rear, the "world revolution from Marx-Engels to the present day" at the front, and the "dignity and beauty of free men" on the sides.

Neptunbrunnen ●
NEPTUNE FOUNTAIN

Spandauer Str. (Rathausvorplatz).
Map 7 C3. **S** Hackescher Markt or Alexanderplatz. ▥ 100, 157.

THIS MAGNIFICENT fountain, sparkling with cascades of running water, provides a splendid feature on the main axis of the town hall building. It was created in 1886 by Reinhold Begas, to stand in front of the southern wall of the former Stadtschloss (Berlin Castle). It was moved to its present site in 1969.

Begas, who designed it in the Neo-Baroque style, was undoubtedly inspired by the

Neptune surrounded by goddesses personifying Germany's rivers

famous Roman fountains by Bernini and the Latony fountain in Versailles. The statue of Neptune, in a dynamic pose and occupying the centre of the fountain, is surrounded by four figures representing Germany's greatest rivers of the time: the Rhine, the Vistula, the Oder and the Elbe. The naturalism of the composition and the attention to detail, such as the beautiful bronze fish, crayfish, snails and fishing nets, are noteworthy.

The Gothic Chapel of the Holy Spirit, seen from Spandauer Strasse

Heiliggeistkapelle ●
CHAPEL OF THE HOLY SPIRIT

Spandauer Strasse 1. **Map** 7 B2, 16 F2. **S** Hackescher Markt.
▥ 100, 157, 348.

THIS MODEST Gothic structure is the only surviving hospital chapel in Berlin. It was built as part of a hospital complex in the second half of the 13th century, but was subsequently rebuilt in the 15th century. The hospital itself was demolished in 1825, but the chapel was retained. In 1906, it was incorporated into a newly erected College of Trade, designed by Cremer and Wolffenstein.

The chapel is a fine example of Gothic brick construction. Its rather modest interior features a 15th century star-shaped vault. The supports under the vault, or consoles, are decorated with half-statues of prophets and saints.

Marienkirche ●

See pp94–95.

Fernsehturm ⑫

THE TELEVISION TOWER, called by the locals *Telespargel*, or toothpick, remains to this day the city's tallest structure at 365 m (1,197 ft). It is also the second-tallest structure in Europe – only Warsaw's Palace of Culture is taller. The tower was built in 1969 to a design by a team of architects including Fritz Dieter and Günter Franke, with the help of Swedish experts. However, the idea for this colossal tower originated much earlier from Hermann Henselmann (creator of the Karl-Marx-Allee development) in the Socialist-Realist style.

VISITORS' CHECKLIST

Panoramastrasse **Map** 7 C2. Ⓢ & Ⓤ *Alexanderplatz.* 🚌 100, 157. ○ May–Sep: 9am–1am daily; Oct–Apr: 10am–midnight daily. **Café** ○ 10am–1am daily.

The television antenna is visible all over Berlin.

Viewing Platform
Situated inside a steel-clad giant sphere, the viewing platform is 203 m (666 ft) above the ground.

Television Tower
The slim silhouette of the Fernsehturm is visible from almost any point in Berlin. The ticket office and elevator entrance are located at the base of the tower.

Trans-mitter aerials

The metal sphere is covered with steel cladding.

Concrete structure rising to 250 m (820 ft)

The concrete shaft contains two elevators that carry passengers to the café and viewing platform.

The elevators are small, resulting in long queues at the base of the tower.

Tele-Café
One of the attractions of the tower is the revolving café. A full rotation takes about half an hour, so it is possible to get a bird's-eye-view of the whole city while sipping a cup of coffee.

View from the Tower
On a clear day the viewing platform offers a full view of Berlin. Visibility can reach up to 40 km (25 miles).

Marienkirche ⓫

ST MARY'S CHURCH, or the Marienkirche, was first established as a parish church in the second half of the 13th century. Construction started around 1280 and was completed early in the 14th century. During reconstruction works in 1380, following a fire, the church was altered slightly but its overall shape changed only in the 15th century when it acquired the front tower. In 1790, the tower was crowned with a dome designed by Carl Gotthard Langhans. The church was once hemmed in by buildings, but today it stands alone in the shadow of the Fernsehturm (Television Tower). The early-Gothic hall design and the lavish decorative touches make this church one of the most interesting in Berlin.

The Tower
The dome that crowns the tower includes both Baroque and Neo-Gothic elements.

Crucifixion (1562)
This image of Christ, flanked by Moses and St John the Baptist, was painted in the Mannerist style by Michael Ribestein.

Totentanz, meaning "dance of death", is the name of a 22-m (72-ft) long Gothic wall fresco, dating from 1485.

Retable
The central part of the Gothic altar, dating from 1510, features figures of three unknown monks.

STAR FEATURES

★ **Pulpit**

★ **Baptismal Font**

Main entrance

★ Pulpit
Carved from alabaster, this masterpiece by Andreas Schlüter, completed in 1703, is placed by the fourth pillar. The pulpit is decorated with bas-reliefs of St John the Baptist and the personi-fications of the Virtues.

Von Röbel Family Tomb
This richly decorated Mannerist-Baroque tomb of Ehrentreich and Anna von Röbel was probably built after 1630.

Main Altar
The Baroque altar was designed by Andreas Krüger c.1762. The paintings, including Deposition from the Cross in the centre; Christ on the Mount of Olives and Doubting Thomas on the sides, are the works of Christian Bernhard Rode.

★ Baptismal Font
This Gothic font dating from 1437 is supported by three black dragons and decorated with the figures of Jesus Christ, Mary and the Apostles.

The magnificent interior of the Stadtgericht

Alexanderplatz ⑬

Map 8 D2. **U** & **S** *Alexanderplatz.*
🚊 *100, 142, 157, 257.*

ALEXANDERPLATZ, or "Alex" as it is locally called, has a long history, although it would be difficult now to find any visible traces of the past. Once called Ochsenmarkt (oxen market), it was the site of a cattle and wool market. It was later renamed after Tsar Alexander I, who visited Berlin in 1805. At the time, the square boasted a magnificent monumental colonnade, which was designed by Carl von Gontard *(see pp168–9)*.

With the passage of time, many houses and shops sprung up around the square, and a market hall and an urban train line were built nearby. "Alex" had become one of the town's busiest spots. Its frenzied atmosphere was captured by Alfred Döblin (1878-1957) in his novel, *Berlin Alexanderplatz*.

In 1929, attempts were made to develop the square, though only two office buildings were added – the Alexanderhaus and the Berolinahaus. These two, both by Peter Behrens, are still standing today.

World War II erased most of the square's buildings. It is now surrounded by characterless 1960s edifices, including the Forum Hotel (formerly Hotel Stadt Berlin) and the Fernsehturm *(see p93)*. Alexanderplatz awaits its next transformation, which will happen soon: a winning design has been chosen from a competition for the square's redevelopment.

Stadtgericht ⑭

COURTS OF JUSTICE

Littenstrasse 13–17. **Map** 8 D3.
U & **S** *Alexanderplatz or*
U *Klosterstrasse.* 🚊 *142, 257.*

THIS GIGANTIC building, situated on a long stretch of Littenstrasse, does not seem particularly inviting, but its interior hides a true masterpiece of the Viennese Secession style of architecture. At the time of its construction, the building was the largest in Berlin after the Stadtschloss *(see p74)*. The Neo-Baroque structure, built between 1896 and 1905, was designed by Paul Thomer and Rudolf Mönnich, but its final shape is the work of Otto Schmalz.

This maze-like complex, with its 11 inner courtyards, was partly demolished in 1969. What remains, however, is still worth seeing, especially the magnificent staircase in the form of overlying ellipses. The staircase is an example of Secession architecture at its boldest. The slim Neo-Gothic pillars and the Neo-Baroque balustrades further enhance the fairytale interior.

Franziskaner Klosterkirche ⑮

FRANCISCAN FRIARY CHURCH

Klosterstrasse 74. **Map** 8 D3.
U *Klosterstrasse.* 🚊 *142, 257.*

THESE PICTURESQUE ruins surrounded by greenery are the remains of an early-Gothic Franciscan church. The Franciscan friars settled in Berlin in the early 13th century. Between 1250 and 1265 they built a church and a friary, which survived almost unchanged until 1945. The church was a triple-nave basilica with an elongated presbytery, widening into a heptagonal section that was added to the structure in c.1300. Protestants took over the church after the Reformation and the friary became a famous grammar school, whose graduates included Otto von Bismarck and Karl Friedrich Schinkel.

The friary was so damaged in World War II that it was subsequently demolished, while the church ruins were

Ruins of the Franziskaner Kloster-kirche (Franciscan Friary Church)

made safe and turned into a modern art centre. The giant Corinthian capitals, emerging from the grass near the ruins, are from a portal from the Stadtschloss (Berlin Castle).

Façade of the twice-restored Palais Podewils

Palais Podewils ⑯

PODEWILS PALACE

Klosterstrasse 68–70. **Map** 8 D3.
Ⓤ *Klosterstrasse.* 142, 257.

THIS CHARMING Baroque palace, set back from the street, was built between 1701 and 1704 for the Royal Court's counsellor, Caspar Jean de Bodt. Its owes its present name to its subsequent owner, a minister of state called von Podewils, who bought the palace in 1732.

After World War II, the palace was restored twice: in 1954 and then again in 1966 after it had been damaged by fire. The carefully reconstructed building did not lose much of its austere beauty, but the interior completely changed to suit its current needs. Today, the palace serves as a cultural centre that organizes concerts and theatre performances, including ballet.

Parochialkirche ⑰

PARISH CHURCH

Klosterstr. 67. **Map** 8 D3. Ⓤ *Klosterstrasse.* 142, 257. ◯ *May-end Sep: 11am–7pm daily; Oct-Apr: 11am–5pm daily.* ⑃ *Sunday 10am.*

THIS BUILDING was, at one time, one of most beautiful Baroque churches in Berlin.

Johann Arnold Nering prepared the initial design, with four chapels framing a central tower. Unfortunately, Nering died as construction started in 1695. The work was continued by Martin Grünberg, but the collapse of the nearly completed vaults forced a change in the design. Instead of the intended tower over the main structure, a vestibule with a front tower was built. The church was completed in 1703, but then, in 1714, its tower was enlarged by Jean de Bodt in order to accommodate a carillon.

World War II had a devastating effect on the Parochialkirche. The interior was completely destroyed, and the tower collapsed. Recently, the main structure was stabilized. The interior, however, is still waiting to be restored. At the moment it is covered in bare bricks, and displays temporary exhibitions. During the summer, mass is held in the church.

Medallion from a headstone in the Parochialkirche

Gaststätte Zur letzten Instanz ⑱

INN OF THE LAST INSTANCE

Waisenstrasse 14–16. **Map** 8 D3.
Ⓤ *Klosterstrasse.* 142, 257.

THE SMALL STREET at the rear of the Parochialkirche leads directly to one of the oldest inns in Berlin, Zur letzten Instanz, which translates as the Inn of the Last Instance. The inn occupies one of the four picturesque houses on Waisenstrasse – the only survivors of the whole row of houses that

once adjoined the town wall. Their history goes back to medieval times, but their present form dates from the 18th century. The houses are actually the result of an almost total reconstruction carried out after World War II. This was when one of the houses acquired its spiral Rococo staircase, which came from a dismantled house on the Fischerinsel.

The Zur letzten Instanz was first established in 1621 and initially specialized in serving alcoholic beverages. Interestingly, it was frequently patronized by lawyers. Today, however, the Zur letzten Instanz is one of Berlin's finest historic pub-restaurants frequented by all types of people, not just lawyers. Its interior is full of interesting old memorabilia.

Stadtmauer ⑲

TOWN WALL

Waisenstrasse **Map** 8 D3.
Ⓤ & Ⓢ *Alexanderplatz or* Ⓤ *Klosterstrasse.* 142, 257.

THE TOWN WALL that once surrounded the settlements of Berlin and Cölln were erected in the second half of the 13th century. The ring of fortifications, built from fieldstone and brick, was made taller in the 14th century. Having finally lost its military significance by the 17th century, the wall was almost entirely dismantled. Today, some small sections survive around Waisenstrasse, because they were incorporated into other buildings.

Remains of the Berlin's Stadtmauer (old town wall)

NORTH OF THE CENTRE

THE AREA NORTHWEST of Alexanderplatz, bounded by Friedrichstrasse and Karl-Liebknecht-Strasse, is the former Spandauer Vorstadt, so called because one of its main streets, Oranienburger Strasse, led to Spandau. The eastern part of the area is known as Scheunenviertel (Barn Quarter). In 1672, the Great Elector moved the hay barns – a fire hazard – out of the city limits. From that time it became a refuge for Jews fleeing Russia and Eastern Europe, and by the 19th century it had become the well-established centre for Berlin's Jewish community. The area also

Detail from Postfuhramt

attracted artists, writers and political activists in the 1920s. Shops, hospitals, small factories and narrow streets of houses inhabited by workers and merchants gave the district its unique, lively character. After World War II the area gradually fell into decay. However, it has recently become fashionable again. Today, its newly restored houses, grand buildings and trendy restaurants stand side by side with dilapidated tenement blocks, shabby courtyards and buildings engulfed in scaffolding. The area is popular with tourists and Berliners alike, especially in the evenings.

SIGHTS AT A GLANCE

Streets and Parks
Alte and Neue Schönhauser Strasse ⑩
Monbijoupark ④
Oranienburger Strasse ③
Sophienstrasse ⑨

Churches and Synagogues
Neue Synagoge ①
Sophienkirche ⑧

Theatres
Berliner Ensemble ⑬
Deutsches Theater ⑭
Friedrichstadtpalast ⑫
Volksbühne ⑪

Museums
Brecht-Weigel-Gedenkstätte ⑰
Centrum Judaicum ②

Hamburger Bahnhof pp110–11 ⑲
Museum für Naturkunde ⑱

Cemeteries
Alter Jüdischer Friedhof ⑦
Dorotheenstädtischer Friedhof pp106–7 ⑯

Others
Charité ⑮
Gedenkstätte Grosse Hamburger Strasse ⑥
Hackesche Höfe ⑤

GETTING THERE
S-Bahn lines 3, 5, 7 and 9 run along the south of the area, with stops at Lehrter Stadtbahnhof, Friedrichstrasse and Hackescher Markt. S-Bahn lines 1 and 2 stop at Oranienburger Strasse. U-Bahn line 6 goes to Oranienburger Tor station, line 8 to Weinmeisterstrasse and line 2 to Rosa-Luxemburg-Platz.

KEY

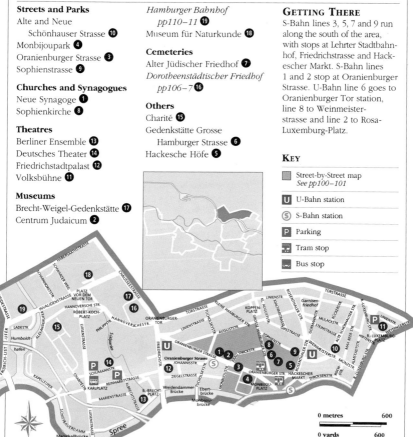

◻ Street-by-Street map
See pp100–101

Ⓤ U-Bahn station

Ⓢ S-Bahn station

Ⓟ Parking

🚊 Tram stop

🚌 Bus stop

0 metres 600
0 yards 600

◁ **The first courtyard in Hackesche Höfe**

Street-by-Street: Scheunenviertel

UNTIL WORLD WAR II Scheunenviertel lay at the heart of Berlin's large Jewish district. During the 19th century the community flourished, its prosperity reflected in grand buildings such as the Neue Synagoge, which opened in 1866 in the presence of Chancellor Otto von Bismarck. Left to crumble for nearly 50 years after the double devastations of the Nazis and Allied bombing, the district has enjoyed a huge revival since the fall of the Wall. Recently cafés and bars have opened and visitors can expect to find some of the liveliest nightlife in East Berlin.

★ **Neue Synagoge**
Sparkling with gold, the recently-restored New Synagogue is now used again for services ❶

The Postfuhramt
was used originally as stables for the horses that delivered the post. Its ceramic-clad façade resembles a palace more than a post office.

Centrum Judaicum
Standing next to the Neue Synagoge, the Jewish Centre houses documents relating to the history and cultural heritage of the Berlin Jews ❷

Oranienburger Strasse
Filled with unusual furniture made from scrap metal, Café Silberstein is one of Oranienburger Strasse's many popular bars and cafés ❸

KEY

– – – Suggested route

STAR SIGHTS

★ **Neue Synagoge**

★ **Hackesche Höfe**

S-Bahn line

Sophienkirche
*This small Protestant church
was founded in 1712 by
Princess Sophie Luisa* **8**

LOCATOR MAP
See Street Finder maps 1 & 6

Gedenkstätte Grosse Hamburger Strasse
*This modest memorial to the
Berlin Jews stands on the site
of the city's first Jewish old
people's home* **6**

Dorotheen-
städtischerfriedhof

GROSSE HAMBURGER STRASSE

HACKESCHER MARKT

★ **Hackesche Höfe**
*This attractive series of
interconnected courtyards
is home to many popular
entertainment venues* **5**

0 metres   50

0 yards   50

Alter Jüdischer Friedhof
*Now a tree-filled park, the
city's oldest Jewish cemetery
was systematically destroyed
by the Gestapo in 1943* **7**

**Fernsehturm
(television
tower)**

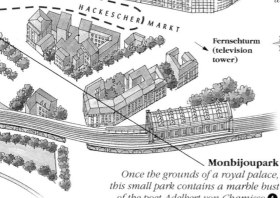

Monbijoupark
*Once the grounds of a royal palace,
this small park contains a marble bust
of the poet Adelbert von Chamisso* **4**

Neue Synagoge ❶

NEW SYNAGOGUE

Oranienburger Strasse 30. **Map** 7 A1.
Ⓢ *Oranienburger Strasse.*
🚋 *1, 13.* 🚌 *157.* ⭕ *10am–6pm
Sun–Thu, 10am–2pm Fri.* 📷
⬤ *Jewish festivals.* 🚫

The Centrum Judaicum, centre for research into Jewish heritage

THE BUILDING OF the New Synagogue was started in 1859 by architect Eduard Knoblauch, and completed in 1866. The design was a highly sophisticated response to the asymmetrical shape of the plot of land, with a narrow façade flanked by a pair of towers and crowned with a dome containing a round vestibule. A series of small rooms opened off the vestibule, including an ante-room and two prayer rooms – one large and one small. The two towers opened onto a staircase leading to the galleries, and the main hall had space for around 3,000 worshippers. An innovative use of iron in the construction of the roof and galleries put the synagogue at the forefront of 19th-century civil engineering.

With its gilded dome, this fascinating structure was Berlin's largest synagogue, until 9 November 1938, when it was partially destroyed during the infamous *"Kristallnacht" (see pp26–7)*. The building was damaged further by Allied bombing in 1943 and was finally demolished in 1958 by government authorities.

Reconstruction started in 1988 and was completed with due ceremony in 1995. The front of the building is now used for public exhibitions by the Centrum Judaicum.

Centrum Judaicum ❷

JEWISH CENTRE

Oranienburger Strasse 29. **Map** 7 A1.
📞 *28 40 13 16.* Ⓢ *Oranienburger
Strasse.* 🚋 *1, 13.* 🚌 *157.*
⭕ *10am–6pm Sun–Thu, 10am–2pm
Fri.* 📷 ⬤ *Jewish festivals.* 🚫

THE ENTRANCE TO the Jewish Centre is easy to recognize thanks to the policemen permanently stationed there. All visitors must undergo a strict security check involving the use of a metal detector, which is conducted by guards who are polite but firm. The Centrum Judaicum occupies the former premises of the Jewish community council, and contains a library and archives and a research centre devoted to the history and cultural heritage of the Berlin Jews. Next door to the Centrum, the restored rooms of the Neue Synagoge are used to exhibit material relating to the local Jewish community, including one of the greatest of all Jewish thinkers and social activists, Moses Mendelssohn. Next to the Centrum is the well-known restaurant Oren, which serves Jewish and Middle Eastern cuisine.

Oranienburger Strasse ❸

Map 6 F1, 7 A1 & 7 B2.
Ⓢ *Oranienburger Strasse or
Hackescher Markt.* 🚋 *1, 2, 3, 4,
5, 13, 15, 53.* 🚌 *157.*

ORANIENBURGER STRASSE is home to many of Berlin's most popular nightspots. People of all ages flock here, spending pleasant hours in the area's numerous cafés, restaurants and bars. The district has traditionally been a centre for alternative culture, home to the famous state-sponsored Tacheles centre for the arts. The life of the Tacheles centre may now be coming to an end, but many good art galleries remain in this area. As you stroll around the district it is worth looking out for a

**The Neue Synagoge with its
splendidly reconstructed dome**

MOSES MENDELSSOHN (1729–1786)

One of the greatest German philosophers of the 18th century, Moses Mendelssohn arrived in Berlin in 1743 and was a central figure in the Jewish struggle for citizenship rights. About 50 years later the first Jewish family was granted full civic rights, however, it wasn't until the Emancipation Edict of 1812 that Jewish men finally became full citizens. The grandfather of composer Felix Mendelssohn-Bartholdy, he is immortalized in the drama "Nathan der Weise" (Nathan the Wise) by his friend Gotthold Ephraim Lessing.

number of interesting buildings, such as the one at Oranienburger Strasse No. 71–2, which was built by Christian Friedrich Becherer in 1789 for the Great National Masonic Lodge of Germany.

Monbijoupark ④

MONBIJOU PARK

Oranienburger Strasse. **Map** 7 B2. Ⓢ *Oranienburger Strasse or Hackescher Markt.* 🚊 *1, 2, 3, 4, 5, 13, 15, 53.* 🚌 *157.*

THIS SMALL PARK, situated between Oranienburger Strasse and the Spree river, was once the grounds of the Monbijou Palace. Damaged by bombing during World War II, the palace was finally dismantled in 1960. A rare green space in this part of town, the well-kept park makes a pleasant place to sit. It features a marble bust of the poet Adelbert von Chamisso, and a swimming pool for children.

Hackesche Höfe ⑤

Rosenthaler Strasse 40–41. **Map** 7 B1 7 B2. Ⓢ *Hackescher Markt.* 🚊 *1, 2, 3, 4, 5, 13, 15, 53.*

RUNNING FROM Oranienburger Strasse and Rosenthaler up as far as Sophienstrasse, the Hackesche Höfe (*Höfe* means yard) is a huge, early 19th-century complex. It is made up of an intricate series of nine interconnecting

One of the striking inner courtyards at the Hackesche Höfe

courtyards surrounded by tall and beautifully proportioned buildings. The development dates from 1906, and was designed by Kurt Berendt and August Endell, both of whom were outstanding exponents of the German Secession style.

Damaged during World War II, Hackesche Höfe has been restored recently to its original splendour. The first courtyard is especially attractive, featuring glazed facings with geometric designs decorated in fabulous colours. A whole range of restaurants, bars, art galleries, shops and restaurants can be found here, as well as offices and apartments on the upper floors. The complex also has its own theatre, the Hackesche Hoftheater, specializing in mime. For many Berliners the Hackesche Höfe has became something of a cult spot, and for visitors it is definitely a sight not to be missed.

Gedenkstätte Grosse Hamburger Strasse ⑥

GROSSE HAMBURGER STRASSE MEMORIAL

Grosse Hamburger Strasse. **Map** 7 B1. Ⓢ *Hackescher Markt.* 🚊 *1, 2, 3, 4, 5, 13, 15, 53.*

UNTIL THE YEARS leading up to World War II, Grosse Hamburger Strasse was one of the main streets of Berlin's Jewish quarter. It was home to several Jewish schools, an old people's home and the city's oldest Jewish cemetery, established in 1672. The home was used during World War II as a detention centre for many thousands of Berlin Jews condemned to death in the camps at Auschwitz and Theresienstadt. The building was later destroyed, and in its place now stands a small monument representing a group of Jews being led to their deaths. A modest commemorative plaque is displayed nearby.

Nearby, at Grosse Hamburger Strasse No. 27, stands a Jewish school, originally founded in 1778 by Moses Mendelssohn. Rebuilt in 1906, the building was reopened as a Jewish secondary school in 1993. The empty space once filled by house No. 15–16, destroyed by World War II bombing, is now an installation, *"The Missing House"* by Christian Boltanski, with plaques recording the names and professions of the former inhabitants of the house.

The Gedenkstätte Grosse Hamburger Strasse commemorating Berlin Jews murdered in the Holocaust

Alter Jüdischer Friedhof ●

OLD JEWISH CEMETERY

Grosse Hamburger Strasse. **Map** 7 B2.
Ⓢ *Hackescher Markt.* 🚋 *1, 2, 3, 4, 5, 13, 15, 53.*

THE OLD JEWISH CEMETERY was established in 1672 and, until 1827 when it was finally declared full, it provided the resting place for over 12,000 Berliners. After this date Jews were buried in cemeteries in Schönhauser Allee and in Herbert-Baum-Strasse. The Alter Jüdische Friedhof was destroyed by the Nazis in 1943, and in 1945 the site was turned into a park. Embedded in the original cemetery wall, a handful of Baroque *masebas* (or tombstones) provide a poignant reminder of the past. A new *maseba* stands on the grave of the philosopher Moses Mendelssohn *(see p102)*, erected in 1990 by members of the Jewish community.

Tombstone of Moses Mendelssohn

Sophienkirche ●

Grosse Hamburger Str. 29. **Map** 7 B1.
Ⓢ *Hackescher Markt.*
Ⓤ *Weinmeisterstrasse.* 🚋 *1, 2, 3, 4, 5, 13, 15, 53.*

A NARROW PASSAGEWAY and a picturesque gate take you through to this small Baroque church. Founded in 1712 by Princess Sophie Luisa, the Sophienkirche was the first

Interior of the Sophienkirche with its original 18th-century pulpit

Eighteenth-century buildings around Sophienstrasse

parish church of the newly-developed Spandauer Vorstadt area *(see p99)*. Between 1729 and 1735 the church acquired its tower, designed by Johann Friedrich Grael.

In 1892 the building was extended to include a new presbytery, though the church still retains its original Baroque character. A modest, rectangular structure, the Sophienkirche is typical of its period, with the tower adjoining the narrower, side elevation. The interior still contains a number of its original 18th-century furnishings, including the pulpit and the font.

Several gravestones have survived in the small cemetery surrounding the church, the earliest dating from the 18th century.

Sophienstrasse ●

Map 7 B1. **Sammlung Hoffmann**
Sophienstrasse 21. ☎ *284 99 121.*
Ⓢ *Hackescher Markt.* Ⓤ *Weinmeisterstrasse.* 🚋 *1, 2, 3, 4, 5, 13, 15, 53.* ⏰ *11am–5pm daily.* 📷

THE AREA AROUND Sophienstrasse and Gipsstrasse was first settled at the end of the 17th century. In fact, Sophienstrasse was once the main street of Spandauer Vorstadt. The area underwent extensive restoration during the 1980s. It was one of the first parts of East Berlin in which renovation was chosen in favour of large-scale demolition and redevelopment. Now these modest but charming 18th-century Neo-Classical buildings are home to a number of different arts and crafts workshops, cosy bars, unusual boutiques and interesting art galleries.

One building with a particularly eventful history is Sophienstrasse No. 18. The house was erected in 1852, although its striking and picturesque, terracotta double doorway dates from the time of its extensive restoration. This was undertaken in 1904 by Joseph Franckel and Theodor Kampfmeyer on behalf of the Crafts Society. Founded in 1844, the Crafts Society moved its headquarters to Sophienstrasse in 1905. On 14 November 1918 the very same house was used as the venue for the first meeting of the Spartacus League *(see pp24–5)*, which was later to become the Communist Party of Germany.

The main door of the house at Sophienstrasse No. 21 leads into a long row of interior courtyards running up as far as Gipsstrasse. In one of these courtyards is a private modern art gallery, the **Sammlung Hoffmann**, which can be reached by passing through a brightly-lit tunnel.

Alte and Neue Schönhauser Strasse ❿

Map 7 B1, 7 C1. Ⓢ *Hackescher Markt.* Ⓤ *Weinmeisterstrasse.*
🚊 *1, 2, 3, 4, 5, 15.*

Alte Schönhauser Strasse is one of the oldest streets in the Spandauer Vorstadt district, running from the centre of Berlin to Pankow and Schönhausen. In the 18th and 19th centuries this was a popular residential area among wealthy merchants. The proximity of the neighbouring slum area of the Scheunenviertel *(see pp100–103)* to the west, however, lowered the tone of the neighbourhood quite considerably.

For a long time, bars, small factories, workshops and retail shops were the hallmark of the neighbourhood around Alte Schönhauser Strasse. Small private shops survived longer here than in most other parts of Berlin, and until recently the largely original houses maintained much of their pre-1939 atmosphere.

Much has changed, however, since the fall of the Berlin Wall. Some of the houses have now been restored, and many old businesses have been replaced by fashionable new shops, restaurants and bars. Throughout the district, the old and the new now stand side by side. One poignant example is at Neue

The *Schwarzen Raben* restaurant on Neue Schönhauser Strasse

Schönhauser Strasse No. 14. This interesting old house in the German Neo-Renaissance style was built in 1891 to a design by Alfred Messel. The first-floor rooms were home to the first public reading-room in Berlin, while on the ground floor was a *Volkskaffeehaus*, a soup-kitchen with separate rooms for men and women. Here the poor of the neighbourhood could get a free bowl of soup and a cup of ersatz (imitation) coffee.

Today, ironically, the building is home to one of Berlin's most fashionable restaurants, the Schwarzen Raben *(see p239)*.

Volksbühne ⓫

PEOPLE'S THEATRE

Rosa-Luxemburg-Platz. **Map** 8 D1.
【 *247 67 72.* Ⓤ *Rosa-Luxemburg-Platz.* 🚌 *100, 157.* 🚊 *1, 2, 3, 4, 5, 15.*

Founded during the early years of the 20th century, this theatre owes its existence to the efforts of the 100,000 members of the Freie Volksbühne (Free People's Theatre Society). The original theatre was built to a design by Oskar Kaufmann in 1913, a time when the Scheunenviertel district was undergoing rapid redevelopment. During the 1920s the theatre became famous thanks to the director Erwin Piscator (1893–1966), who later achieved great acclaim at the Metropol-Theater on Nollendorfplatz.

Destroyed during World War II, the theatre was eventually rebuilt during the early 1950s to a new design by Hans Richter.

The eye-catching façade of the Friedrichstadtpalast theatre complex

Friedrichstadtpalast ⓬

FRIEDRICHSTADT PALACE

Friedrichstrasse 107. **Map** 6 F2.
【 *23 26 23 26.* Ⓤ *Oranienburger Tor.* Ⓢ *Oranienburger Strasse or Friedrichstrasse.* 🚌 *147.*

Multi-coloured glass tiles and a pink, plume-shaped neon sign make up the gaudy but eye-catching façade of the Friedrichstadtpalast. Built in the early 1980s, this gigantic theatre complex specializes in revues and variety shows. Nearly 2,000 seats are arranged around a huge podium, used by turns as a circus arena, a swimming pool and an ice-rink. In addition, a further huge stage is equipped with every technical facility. There is also a small cabaret theatre with seats for 240 spectators.

The original and much-loved Friedrichstadtpalast suffered bomb damage during World War II, and was later condemned and replaced with the existing version. Built as a market hall, the earlier building was later used as a circus ring. In 1918 it became the Grosse Schauspielhaus, or Grand Playhouse, opening on 28 November 1919 with a memorable production of Aeschylus' *The Oresteia* directed by the extraordinary Max Reinhardt (1873–1943).

The building itself was legendary, its central dome supported by a forest of columns and topped with an Expressionist, stalactite-like decoration. An equally fantastical interior provided seating for 5,000 spectators.

Dorotheenstädtischer Friedhof 16

Copy of Schadow's Martin Luther

THIS SMALL CEMETERY, established in 1763, is the final resting place of many famous Berlin citizens. It was enlarged between 1814 and 1826, but in 1899, following the extension of Hannoversche Strasse, the southern section of the cemetery was sold and its graves moved. Many of the monuments are outstanding works of art, coming from the workshops of some of the most prominent Berlin architects, including Karl Friedrich Schinkel *(see p79)* and Johann Gottfried Schadow. A tranquil, tree-filled oasis, the cemetery is reached via a narrow path, leading from the street, between the wall of the French Cemetery and the Brecht-Weigel-Gedenkstätte house *(see p109)*.

★ **Johann Gottfried Schadow** (1764–1850)
Schadow created the famous Quadriga, *which adorns the Brandenburg Gate.*

Friedrich August Stüler (1800–1865)
Damaged during World War II, the grave of this famous architect was rebuilt in a colourful, post-modernist style.

Heinrich Mann (1871–1950)
This famous German novelist died in California but was buried in Berlin. The portrait is the work of Gustav Seitz.

Bertolt Brecht (1898–1956)
The grave of this famous playwright is marked with a rough stone. Beside him rests his wife, the actress Helene Weigel.

Hermann Wentzel (1820–1889)
This architect designed his own tombstone; the bust was carved by Fritz Schaper.

Main entrance

Friedrich Hoffmann
(1818–1900)
The tomb of this engineer, best known as the inventor of the circular brick-firing kiln, takes the form of a colonnade faced with glazed bricks.

VISITORS' CHECKLIST

Chausseestrasse 126. **Map** 6 F1.
461 72 79. 832 51 01.
Zinnowitzerstrasse or Oranienburger Tor. 157.
13. Apr–Sep: 8am–6pm; Nov–Feb: 8am–5pm.

★ Karl Friedrich Schinkel
(1781–1841)
Schinkel was the most prominent German architect of his time, and the creator of many of Berlin's best-loved buildings.

Georg Wilhelm Friedrich Hegel
(1770–1831)
Probably the greatest German philosopher of the Enlightenment era, Hegel worked for many years as a professor at Berlin University.

Luther's statue
is a copy of the monument designed by JG Schadow.

BIRKENALLEE

Johann Gottlieb Fichte
(1762–1814)
A well-known philosopher of the Enlightenment era, Fichte was also the first Rector of Berlin University.

Chapel

STAR FEATURES

★ JG Schadow

★ KF Schinkel

0 metres   20

0 yards   20

Bertolt Brecht's monument in front of the Berliner Ensemble

Berliner Ensemble ⓭

Bertolt-Brecht-Platz 1. **Map** 6 F2.
(282 31 60. **(S)** & **U**
Friedrichstrasse.

D ESIGNED BY Heinrich
Seeling in a Neo-Baroque
style and built from 1891 to
1892, this theatre has been
witness to many important
changes in Berlin's cultural
life. First known as the Neues
Theater am Schiffbauerdamm,
it soon became famous for
staging important premieres.
In 1895 it put on the first
performance of *The Weavers*,
by Gerhart Hauptmann. Later
on, the theatre was acclaimed
for its memorable productions
by Max Reinhardt. These
included Shakespeare's *A
Midsummer Night's Dream* in
1905 which, for the first time,
used a revolving stage and
real trees as part of the set. In
1928 the theatre presented the
world premiere of Bertolt

Brecht's *The Threepenny
Opera*. The building was
destroyed during World War
II and subsequently restored
with a much simpler exterior,
but its Neo-Baroque interior,
including Ernst Westphal's
decorations, survived intact.
After 1954 the theatre returned
to prominence with the arrival
of the Berliner Ensemble under
the directorship of Bertolt
Brecht and his wife, the actress
Helene Weigel. The move from
its former home, the Deutsches
Theater, to the new venue
was celebrated in November
1954, by staging the world
premiere of *The Caucasian
Chalk Circle*, written by Brecht
in 1947. After Brecht's death
his wife took over running the
theatre, maintaining its innovative tradition.

Deutsches Theater ⓮

Schumannstrasse 13. **Map** 6 E2.
(28 44 12 22. **Kammerspiele**
U *Oranienburger Tor.* 🚌 *147, 157.*

T HE BUILDING currently used
by the theatre was designed
by Eduard Titz and built
between 1849 and 1850 to
house the Friedrich-Wilhelm
Städtisches Theater. In 1883,
following substantial reconstruction, it was renamed
Deutsches Theater and opened
with Friedrich Schiller's *Intrigue
and Love*. The theatre became
famous under its next director,
Otto Brahm, and it was here
that Max Reinhardt began his
career as an actor, before

eventually becoming director
from 1905 until 1933. On
Reinhardt's initiative the
theatre's façade was altered
and in 1906 the adjacent casino
was converted into a compact
theatre – **Kammerspiele**. At
the time, the first-floor auditorium was decorated with a
frieze by Edvard Munch (now
in the Neue Nationalgalerie).
Another famous figure
associated with the Deutsches
Theater was Bertolt Brecht
who, until 1933, wrote plays
for it; after World War II he
became the director of the
Berliner Ensemble, whose
first venue was the Deutsches
Theater. Brecht's debut as
director was his play, *Mother
Courage and Her Children*.

Elegant 19th-century façade of the Deutsches Theater

Charité ⓯

Schumannstrasse 20/21. **Map** 6 E1, E2.
(28 02 25 42. **U** *Oranienburger
Tor.* 🚌 *147.* ⌚ *1–4pm Mon–Tue,
1–7pm Wed, 1–4pm Thu–Fri.*

T HIS HUGE BUILDING complex
near Luisenstrasse contains
the Charité hospital. Germany's
oldest teaching hospital, it
was first established in 1726
and has been attached to the
Humboldt University *(see p60)*
since its foundation in 1810.
The oldest buildings of the
current complex date back to
the 1830s. Over the years,
Charité has been associated
with many famous German
doctors and scientists who
worked here, including Rudolf
Virchow and Robert Koch.
In 1899 Virchow founded
the Museum of Pathology,
which occupied purpose-built
premises next to the Institute
of Pathology. Its collection
consisted of some 23,000
specimens, which were also
available for public viewing.

MAX REINHARDT (1873–1943)

This actor and director became famous as one of the 20th
century's greatest theatre reformers. He worked in Berlin,
first as an actor in the Deutsches Theater, and then from
1905 as its director. As well as setting up the
Kammerspiele, he produced plays for the
Neues Theater am Schiffbauerdamm
(renamed the Berliner Ensemble) and the
Schumann Circus (later to become the
Friedrichstadtpalast), which was
converted specially for him by Hans
Poelzig. His experimental productions
of classic and modern works brought
him world-wide fame. Forced to emigrate
because of his Jewish origins, he left
Germany in 1933 and settled in the
United States, where he died in 1943.

Although many artifacts were destroyed in World War II, the museum itself has survived and was reopened in 1999.

Dorotheenstädtischer Friedhof ⑯

See pp106–107.

Brecht-Weigel-Gedenkstätte ⑰
BRECHT-WEIGEL MEMORIAL

Chausseestrasse 125. ☎ 283 057 044.
Map 6 E1. Ⓤ *Zinnowitzer Strasse or Oranienburger Tor.* 🚋 *157.* 🚊 *13.*
⭕ *10am–noon Tue–Fri, also 5–6:30pm Thu, 9:30am–1:30pm Sat , 11am–6pm Sun.* ⬛ *compulsory. Every half hour (every hour on Sun).* ● *Mon, public hols.*

Brachiosaurus skeleton in the Museum für Naturkunde

BERTOLT BRECHT, one of the greatest playwrights of the 20th century, was associated with Berlin from 1920, but emigrated in 1933. After the war, his left-wing views made him an attractive potential resident of the newly created German socialist state. Lured by the promise of his own theatre he returned to Berlin in 1948, with his wife, actress Helene Weigel. Working as the director of the Berliner Ensemble until his death, he concentrated mainly on the production of his plays.

In 1953 he moved into the first-floor at Chausseestrasse 125 and lived there until his death in 1956. He is buried in Dorotheenstädtischer Friedhof *(see pp106–107)*. His wife lived in the second-floor apartment, and after Brecht's death moved to the ground floor. She also founded an archive of Brecht's works which is located on the second floor of the building.

Museum für Naturkunde ⑱
NATURAL HISTORY MUSEUM

Invalidenstrasse 43. **Map** 6 E1.
☎ *20 93 85 91.* Ⓤ *Zinnowitzer strasse.* 🚋 *157, 245, 340.*
⭕ *Tue–Sun 9:30am–5pm.*

ONE OF THE BIGGEST natural history museums in the world, the collection here contains over 60 million exhibits. Occupying a purpose-built Neo-Renaissance building, constructed between 1883 and 1889, the museum has been operating for over a century, and although it has undergone several periods of extension and renovation, it has maintained its unique old-fashioned atmosphere.

The highlight of the museum is the world's largest original dinosaur skeleton which is housed in the glass-covered courtyard. This colossal 23-m (75-ft) long and 12-m (39-ft) high brachiosaurus was discovered in Tanzania in 1909 by a German fossil-hunting expedition. Six other smaller reconstructed dinosaur skeletons and a replica of the fossilized remains of an archaeopteryx, thought to be the prehistoric link between reptiles and birds, complete this fascinating display.

The adjacent rooms feature extensive collections of colourful shells and butterflies, as well as stuffed birds and mammals. Particularly popular are the dioramas – scenes of stuffed animals set against the background of their natural habitat. A favourite with young children is Bobby the Gorilla, who was brought to Berlin Zoo in 1928 as a 2-year old and lived there until 1935. The museum also boasts an impressive collection of minerals and meteorites.

Bertolt Brecht's study in his former apartment

Hamburger Bahnhof ⑲

THIS MUSEUM is situated in a specially adapted Neo-Renaissance building that was formerly the Hamburg Railway station, which dates from 1847. The building stood vacant after World War II, but following extensive refurbishment by Josef Paul Kleihues, it was opened to the public in 1996. The neon installation surrounding the façade is the work of Dan Flavin. The museum houses a magnificent collection of works by Erich Marx, with additional works of contemporary art contributed by the Neue Nationalgalerie and other museums. The result is one of the best modern art museums in Europe, which features not only representative art, but also film, video, music and design.

★ **Richtkräfte** (1974–77)
Joseph Beuys' work – often a record of his thoughts – created an archive of the artist's vision.

Untitled (1983)
This is a fine example of Anselm Kiefer's work, which often attempts to come to terms with Germany's past.

First floor

GALLERY GUIDE
The gallery has over 10,000 sq m (108,000 sq ft) of exhibition space. The west wing contains works by Beuys and the main hall is used for special installations.

Ground floor

Genova (1980)
In this painting, Sandro Chia contrasts a finely-drawn Renaissance palace with a colourful sky full of movement and two mysteriously floating figures.

Main entrance

Untitled (1983)
Keith Haring uses a simple means of expression, one that is reminiscent of graffiti, comic book art and woodblock prints.

Untitled (1990)
This painting is a fine example of Cy Twombly's distinctive style, characterized by apparently random scrawls and scribbles, rejecting traditional composition.

Bourgeois Bust – Jeff and Ilona (1991)
The Rococo-style marble bust by Jeff Koons depicts himself with his wife at the time, Ilona, better known as La Cicciolina. The sculpture is deliberately pretentious and tawdry.

Second floor

Not Wanting to Say Anything About Marcel (1969)
John Cage created this work after the death of his friend, the famous artist Marcel Duchamp.

★ Mao (1973)
This well-known portrait by Andy Warhol initially elevated the Chinese communist leader to the rank of pop icon.

First Time Painting (1961)
This work by American artist Robert Rauschenberg was created while he worked with John Cage at Black Mountain College.

KEY
⬜ Exhibitions

STAR EXHIBITS

★ **Mao**

★ **Richtkräfte**

TIERGARTEN

Once a royal hunting estate, the Tiergarten became a park in the 18th century. In the 19th century a series of buildings, mostly department stores and banks, was erected at Potsdamer Platz. During World War II many of these buildings were destroyed. The division of Berlin changed the character of the area. The Tiergarten area ended up on the west side of the Wall, and later regained its glory with the creation of the Kulturforum and the Hansaviertel. The area around Potsdamer Platz fell in East Berlin, and became a wasteland. Since reunification, however, this area has witnessed exciting development. Together with the new government offices near the Reichstag, this ensures that the Tiergarten area is at the centre of Berlin's political and financial district.

The Caller, on Strasse des 17 Juni

SIGHTS AT A GLANCE

Museums and Galleries
Bauhaus-Archiv ⑭
Bendlerblock (Gedenkstätte Deutscher Widerstand) ⑫
Gemäldegalerie pp122–5 ⑧
Kunstbibliothek ⑥
Kunstgewerbemuseum pp118–21 ④
Kupferstichkabinett ⑤
Musikinstrumenten-Museum ②
Neue Nationalgalerie ⑨

Districts, Squares and Parks
Diplomatenviertel ⑮
Grosser Stern ⑰
Hansaviertel ⑲

Potsdamer Platz ⑩
Regierungsviertel ㉒
Tiergarten ⑯

Historic Buildings
Haus der Kulturen der Welt ㉑

Philharmonie und Kammermusiksaal ③
Reichstag ㉓
Shell-Haus ⑪
Schloss Bellevue ⑳
Staatsbibliothek ①
St-Matthäus-Kirche ⑦
Villa von der Heydt ⑬

Monuments
Siegessäule ⑱
Sowjetisches Ehrenmal ㉔

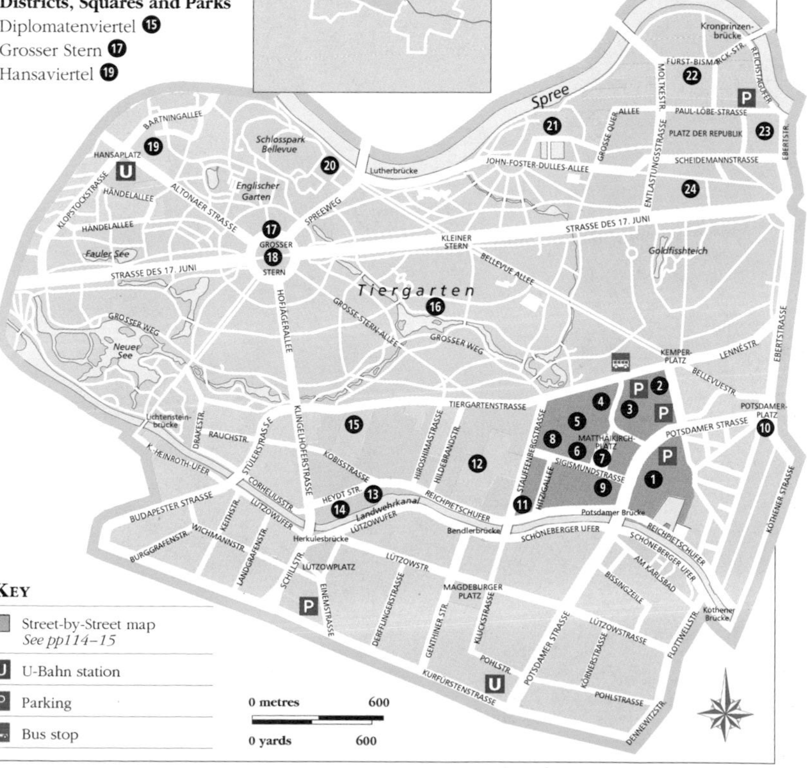

KEY

Street-by-Street map
See pp114–15

Ⓤ U-Bahn station

Ⓟ Parking

Bus stop

0 metres   600
0 yards   600

◁ **One of the many charming stretches of water in the Tiergarten**

Street-by-Street: Around the Kulturforum

Sculpture by Henry Moore

THE IDEA OF CREATING a new cultural centre in West Berlin was first mooted in 1956. The first building to go up was the Berlin Philharmonic concert hall, built to an innovative design by Hans Scharoun in 1961. Most of the plans for the various other components of the Kulturforum were realized between 1961 and 1987, and came from such famous architects as Ludwig Mies van der Rohe. The area is now a major cultural centre which attracts millions of visitors every year.

★ Kunstgewerbe-museum
Among the collection at the Museum of Arts and Crafts you can see this intricately carved silver and ivory tankard, made in an Augsburg workshop in around 1640 ❹

Kupferstichkabinett
The large collection of prints and drawings owned by this gallery includes this portrait of Albrecht Dürer's mother ❺

★ Gemäldegalerie
Among the most important works of the Old Masters exhibited in this gallery of fine art is this Madonna in Church *by Jan van Eyck (circa 1425)* ❽

Kunstbibliothek
The Art Library boasts a rich collection of books, graphic art and drawings, many of which are displayed in its exhibition halls ❻

STAR SIGHTS

★ **Gemäldegalerie**

★ **Kunstgewerbe-museum**

★ **Philharmonie**

KEY

– – – Suggested route

REICHPIETSCHUFE

LANDWEHRKANAL

Neue Nationalgalerie
Sculptures by Henry Moore and Alexander Calder stand outside this streamlined building, designed by Ludwig Mies van der Rohe ❾

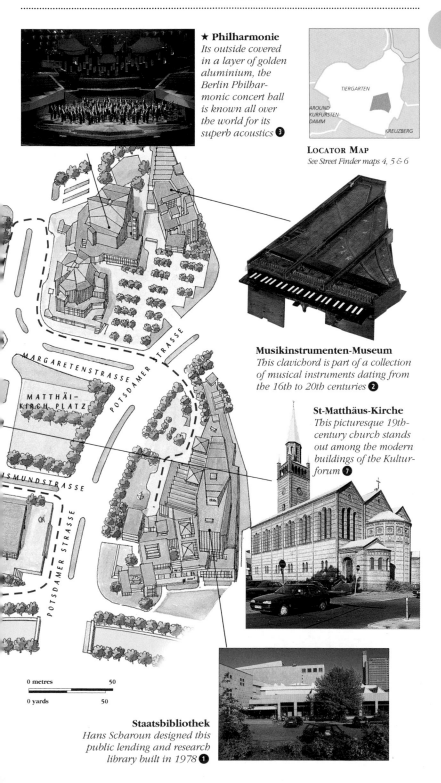

★ **Philharmonie**
Its outside covered in a layer of golden aluminium, the Berlin Philharmonic concert hall is known all over the world for its superb acoustics ❸

LOCATOR MAP
See Street Finder maps 4, 5 & 6

TIERGARTEN

AROUND KURFÜRSTEN-DAMM

KREUZBERG

Musikinstrumenten-Museum
This clavichord is part of a collection of musical instruments dating from the 16th to 20th centuries ❷

St-Matthäus-Kirche
This picturesque 19th-century church stands out among the modern buildings of the Kultur-forum ❼

MARGARETENSTRASSE

POTSDAMER STRASSE

MATTHÄI-KIRCH PLATZ

SIGISMUNDSTRASSE

POTSDAMER STRASSE

0 metres 50

0 yards 50

Staatsbibliothek
Hans Scharoun designed this public lending and research library built in 1978 ❶

The main reading room in the Staatsbibliothek

Staatsbibliothek ❶

STATE LIBRARY

Potsdamer Strasse 33. **Map** 6 D5.
C 266 23 03. **S** & **U** *Potsdamer Platz.* 129, 142, 148, 248, 348.
O *9am–9pm Mon–Fri, 9am–7pm Sat.*

A N UNUSUAL-SHAPED building with an east facing gilded dome, the Staatsbibliothek is home to one of the largest collections of books and manuscripts in Europe and is fondly referred to by Berliners as the Stabi. After World War II, East and West Berlin each inherited part of the pre-war state library collection and the Staatsbibliothek was built to house the part belonging to West Berlin. The building itself was designed by Hans Scharoun and Edgar Wisniewski and constructed between 1967 and 1978.

It is a building where the disciplines of function and efficiency took precedence to that of form. The storerooms hold about five million volumes; the hall of the vast reading room is open plan, with an irregular arrangement of partitions and floor levels; general noise and the sound of footsteps is muffled by fitted carpets, making the interior a very quiet and cosy place in which to work.

The library itself houses more than four million books, and an excellent collection of manuscripts. In recent years the Staatsbibliothek has been formally linked to the Staatsbibliothek on Unter den Linden *(see p61)*.

Musikinstrumen-ten-Museum ❷

MUSEUM OF MUSICAL INSTRUMENTS

Tiergartenstrasse 1. **Map** 6 D5. **C** 20 90 55 55. **S** & **U** *Potsdamer Platz or* **U** *Mendelssohn-Bartholdy-Park.* 129, 142, 148, 248, 348.
O *9am–5pm Tue–Fri, 10am–5pm Sat–Sun.* **Wurlitzer Organ demonstration** *noon, first Sat of the month.*

H IDDEN BEHIND the Philharmonie, in a small building designed by Edgar Wisniewski and Hans Scharoun between 1979 and 1984, the fascinating Museum of Musical Instruments houses over 750 exhibits in a collection dating from 1888. Intriguing displays enable you to trace each instrument's development from the 16th century to the present day. You can marvel at the harpsichord of Jean Marius, once owned by Frederick the Great, and the violins made by Amati and Stradivarius.

Most spectacular of all is the silent-film era cinema organ, a working Wurlitzer dating from 1929. With a range of sounds that extends even to locomotive impressions, the Saturday demonstrations of its powers attract enthusiastic crowds. However, during the the week the sounds of exhibited instruments can be heard on tapes. The museum also has an excellent archive and library open to the public.

Philharmonie und Kammer-musiksaal ❸

PHILHARMONIC AND CHAMBER MUSIC HALL

Herbert-von-Karajan-Str. 1. **Map** 6 D5.
C 25 48 80. **S** & **U** *Potsdamer Platz or* **U** *Mendelssohn-Bartholdy-Park.* 129, 142, 148, 248, 348.

H OME TO ONE of the most renowned orchestras in Europe, this unusual building is among the finest postwar architectural achievements in Europe. The Philharmonie, built between 1960 and 1963 to a design by Hans Scharoun, pioneered a new concept for concert hall interiors. The orchestra's podium occupies the central section of the pentagonal-shaped hall, around which are galleries for the public, designed to blend into the perspective of the five corners. The exterior

The tent-like gilded exterior of the Philharmonie and Kammermusiksaal

reflects the interior and is reminiscent of a circus tent. The gilded exterior was added between 1978 and 1981.

The Berlin orchestra was founded in 1882, and has been directed by such luminaries as Hans von Bülow, Wilhelm Furtwängler and the controversial Herbert von Karajan, who led the orchestra from 1954 until his death in 1989. The current director is Claudio Abbado, though from 2002 Sir Simon Rattle will take over the directorship. The orchestra attained renown not only for the quality of its concerts but also through its prolific symphony recordings.

Between the years 1984 to 1987 the Kammermusiksaal, which was designed by Edgar Wisniewski on the basis of sketches by Scharoun, was added to the Philharmonie. This building consolidates the aesthetics of the earlier structure by featuring a central multi-sided space covered by a fanciful tent-like roof.

Kunstgewerbe-museum ❹

MUSEUM OF ARTS AND CRAFTS

See pp118–121.

Kupferstich-kabinett ❺

PRINT GALLERY

Matthäikirchplatz 6. **Map** 5 C5.
📞 20 90 55 55. Ⓢ & Ⓤ
Potsdamer Platz or Ⓤ *Mendelssohn-Bartoldy-Park.* 🚌 *129, 142, 148, 248, 348.* **Exhibitions** *10am–6pm Tue–Fri, 11am–6pm Sat–Sun.* **Studio gallery** *9am–4pm Tue–Fri.* 📷 ♿
🪑 📷 📷 📷 ∅

T HE PRINT COLLECTIONS of galleries in the former East and West Berlin were united in 1994 in this building located in the Kulturforum. These displays originate from a collection started by the Grand Elector in 1652, which has been open to the public since 1831. Despite wartime losses it has an imposing breadth and can boast around 2,000 engraver's plates, over 520,000 prints and at least 80,000

Edvard Munch's *Girl on a Beach*, a coloured lithograph

drawings and watercolours. Unfortunately, only a small fraction of these treasures can be even briefly exposed to daylight. Therefore the museum does not have a permanent exhibition, only galleries with temporary displays. For those with a special interest, items in storage can be viewed in the studio gallery by prior arrangement.

The collection includes work from every renowned artist from the Middle Ages to contemporary times. Well represented is the work of Botticelli (including illustrations for Dante's *Divine Comedy*), Dürer, Rembrandt and the Dutch Masters, Watteau, Goya, Daumier, and painters of the Brücke art movement.

Kunstbibliothek ❻

ART LIBRARY

Matthäikirchplatz 6. **Map** 5 C5.
📞 20 90 55 55. Ⓢ & Ⓤ *Potsdamer Platz or* Ⓤ *Mendelssohn-Bartoldy-Park.* 🚌 *129, 142, 148, 248, 348.* **Exhibits** *9am–6pm Tue–Sun.* **Library** *2–8pm Mon, 9am–8pm Tue–Fri.* 📷

T HE KUNSTBIBLIOTHEK is not only a library with a wide range of publications about the arts, it is also a museum with a massive collection of posters, advertisements and an array of other practical forms of design. Worth seeing is a display on the history of fashion, as well as a vast collection of items of architectural interest. The latter

includes around 30,000 original plans and drawings by architects such as Johann Balthasar Neumann, Erich Mendelssohn, and Paul Wallot.

The exhibitions can be seen in the reading and studio rooms, although parts of the collection are also exhibited in the library's own galleries.

St-Matthäus-Kirche ❼

ST MATTHEW'S CHURCH

Matthäikirchplatz. **Map** 5 C5. Ⓢ & Ⓤ *Potsdamer Platz or* Ⓤ *Mendelssohn-Bartoldy-Park.* 🚌 *129, 142, 148, 248, 348.* 🕐 *10am–6pm Tue–Fri, 11am–6pm Sat–Sun.*

S T MATTHEW'S CHURCH once stood in the centre of a small square surrounded by buildings. After bomb damage in World War II, the structure was restored, making it the focal point of the Kulturforum. The church was originally built between 1844 and 1846 to a design by Friedrich August Stüler and Herbert Wentzel in a style based on Italian Romanesque temples.

Each of the three naves is covered by a separate two-tier roof, while the eastern end of the church is closed by a semi-circular apse. The exterior of the church is covered in a two-tone brick façade arranged in yellow and red lines. Ironically, this picturesque church with its slender tower now creates quite an exotic element among the many ultramodern and sometimes extravagant buildings of the Kulturforum complex.

The colourful exterior of the St-Matthäus-Kirche

Kunstgewerbemuseum ❹

Meissen porcelain figure

T HE MUSEUM OF Arts and Crafts holds a rich collection embracing many genres of craft and decorative art, from the early Middle Ages to the modern day. Goldwork is especially well represented, as are items made from other metals during the Middle Ages. Among the most valuable exhibits is a collection of medieval goldwork from the church treasuries of Enger near Herford, and the Guelph treasury from Brunswick. The museum also takes great pride in its collection of late Gothic and Renaissance silver from the civic treasury in the town of Lüneberg. There are also fine examples of Italian majolica, and 18th- and 19th-century German, French and Italian glass, porcelain and furniture.

★ **Domed Reliquary** (1175–80)
From the Guelph treasury in Brunswick, the figures in this temple-shaped reliquary are made from walrus ivory.

Main entrance

Minneteppich (c.1430)
The theme of this famous tapestry is courtly love. Amorous couples, accompanied by mythical creatures, converse on topics such as infidelity, their words extending along the banners they hold.

★ **Goblet** (c.1480)
This glass Gothic goblet was made in Venice and is decorated with scenes from the lives of Adam and Eve.

Lüneburg Lion (1540)
From the civic treasury in Lüneburg, this gold-plated silver jug in the form of a lion was crafted in the workshop of Joachim Worm.

Basement

VISITORS' CHECKLIST

Matthäikirchplatz. **Map** 5 C5.
📞 20 90 55 55. Ⓢ Potsdamer
Platz. Ⓤ Potsdamer Platz or
Mendelssohn-Bartholdy-Park.
🚌 129, 142, 148, 248, 341,
348. ◻ 10am–6pm Tue–Fri,
11am–6pm Sat & Sun.
⬤ Tue after Easter, Whitsun,
1 Oct, 24, 25 & 31 Dec. 📷
♿ 🅿 ∅ 🏧 🏠

Candelabra (1900)
*This striking Art
Nouveau candelabra
made from silver,
ivory and onyx is the
work of Belgian artists
Egide Rombaux and
Frans Hoosemans.*

Wedding Dress (c.1780)
*Made from brocade, with a lace
collar and cuffs, this Rococo
wedding dress belonged to
Eleonor Schuster from
Breslau (now Wrocław).*

★ **Cabinet** (early 18th century)
*Made in the Baltic city of Danzig
(now Gdańsk), this amber cabinet is
decorated with bas-reliefs in ivory.
The two drawers have been engraved
on the reverse with games boards.*

Second floor

First floor

Ground floor

KEY

◻ Middle Ages
◻ Renaissance
◻ Baroque
◻ Neo-Classical, Art Nouveau
◻ 20th-century
◻ Temporary exhibitions

GALLERY GUIDE
*The entrance to the museum
is on the first floor, where
there is also an information
gallery. In the basement is an
exhibition of contemporary
art, on the ground floor are
exhibits from the Middle Ages
and the Renaissance, and on
the second floor are handi-
crafts from the Renaissance
through to Art Nouveau.*

STAR EXHIBITS

★ **Domed
  Reliquary**

★ **Goblet**

★ **Cabinet**

Exploring the Kunstgewerbemuseum

Pendant of the suffering of Christ

OPENED IN 1867, the Museum of Arts and Crafts was the first of its kind in Germany. It was housed initially in the Martin-Gropius-Bau *(see p136)*, then, from 1919 to 1939 it occupied the Stadtschloss *(see p74)*, and in 1940 it was moved to Schloss Charlottenburg *(see pp156–7)*. The current building, designed by Rolf Gutbrod especially to house the collection, was built between 1978 and 1985. It provides ideal conditions for conservation and displaying the exhibits.

MIDDLE AGES

A LARGE PART OF this collection is devoted to sacred art, much of it originating from church treasuries. A fine 8th-century reliquary in the shape of a burse (the container used in the Roman Catholic mass to hold the white linen cloth on which the bread and the wine are placed), comes from the treasury of a church in Enger in Westphalia. More reliquaries, many in the form of crosses, date from the 11th and 12th centuries. Two of the most interesting are the Heinrichskreuz, a gift to the cathedral in Basel from the Roman Emperor Heinrich II, and the Welfenkreuz, which comes from the Guelph treasury in Brunswick. Also from the latter comes a beautiful domed reliquary in the form of a small temple, and a portable altarpiece decorated with enamelwork, produced around 1150 by the craftsman Eilbertus of Cologne.

Exhibits from the Gothic period (12th to 16th centuries) include the stunning reliquary of St George of Elbing, made around 1480. Also fascinating are examples of secular art from this period, including caskets, vessels, a mirror, a knight's amulet and the renowned Minneteppich. This tapestry depicts a number of love scenes, and is designed to hang on the wall above a seat as a decorative means of keeping out draughts.

RENAISSANCE

THE ARTS AND CRAFTS of the Renaissance period are well represented here. Especially valuable is a collection of Italian majolica, a type of pottery glazed in bright metallic oxides, imported into Tuscany from Majorca in the 15th century. Majolica workshops flourished during the 16th century, and many, including those of Faenza, Cafaggiolo and Urbino, are on show here.

Other interesting exhibits in this section are the 15th- and 16th-century Venetian glass, porcelain decorated with enamel work from Limoges in central France, and fine furniture and tapestry collections. The highlight of the collection is a set of 32 magnificent, richly decorated goblets, bowls and jugs from the civic treasury at Lüneburg in northern

11th-century reliquary cross

Germany, acquired by the museum in 1874. Made of gold-plated silver, the set is the work of the skilled metalworkers of the town; many take the form of lions. Also notable are the works of the Nürnberg master craftsmen, above all the renowned Wenzel Jamnitzer and his nephew Christoph Jamnitzer.

As a result of the 16th-century fashion for *Kunstkammern*, or art rooms, the collection also includes rare examples of naturalistic and exotic creations from other cultures, as well as some unusual technical equipment. Look out for a few pieces from the Pommersche Kunstschrank (curio cabinet), made for a 16th-century Pomeranian prince, Phillip II, as well as a display of 17th-century clocks and scientific instruments.

BAROQUE

TREASURES FROM the Baroque period include an exquisite collection of German and Czech glass. A few pieces are made from so-called "ruby glass", a style pioneered by Johann Kunckel in the second half of the 17th century.

A rich collection of 18th-century ceramics includes some German faïence work, with amusingly decorated jugs and tankards. The porcelain display begins with a series of Böttger ceramics, the result of some of the first European experiments in porcelain production, undertaken by Johann Friedrich Böttger.

16th-century tapestry entitled *The Triumph of Love*

Baroque cupboard with bas-relief decoration in the Danzig style

Among the finest works from various European factories, porcelain from the Meissen factory is particularly well represented, with several pieces by one of the most famous Meissen modellers, Johann Joachim Kaendler. Also on show is a selection of artifacts from the Königliche Porzellan-Manufaktur (Royal Porcelain Factory) in Berlin *(see p129)*. The collection of porcelain is complemented by a display of silver dishes produced in European workshops at the same period.

A separate exhibition is devoted to the fashion for chinoiserie which swept through Europe in the 18th century. Particularly impressive is the Chinesisches Kabinett (Chinese Room), a completely reconstructed room decorated in the Chinese style, which was originally part of the Palazzo Graneri in Turin.

NEO-CLASSICAL REVIVAL AND ART NOUVEAU

A COMPREHENSIVE collection of late-18th and early-19th century Neo-Classical artifacts includes porcelain from some of the most famous European and Russian factories, French and German silver, as well as comprehensive exhibitions of glassware and furniture.

The Revival movement in central European art and crafts took place during the second half of the 19th century and is well represented here. A high standard of craftsmanship is seen in the sophisticated Viennese glass and jewellery. The collection also includes furniture made from papier-mâché. This interesting technique was first applied to furniture in England around 1850 and involves a wooden or wire frame which is covered in layers of paste and paper. Decorative techniques include painting and inlaying with mother-of-pearl.

Baroque clock by Johann Gottlieb Graupner (1739)

The Secessionist and Art Nouveau movements of the 1890s and 1900s are represented by various artists including Henri van der Velde and Eugène Gaillard. Of note are the frosted glass vases by French artist Emile Gallé, and pieces by the American Louis Comfort Tiffany, creator of the Favrile style of iridescent stained glass. Also displayed are pieces by the legendary René Lalique, including jewellery and glassware.

An interesting diversion is offered by two entertaining pieces of furniture, both dating from 1885, by the Italian designer, Carlo Bugatti. Taking inspiration from Native American, Islamic and Far Eastern art, Bugatti made spectacular use of rare woods and delicate inlays.

THE 20TH CENTURY

T HE YEARS BETWEEN the two World Wars were a time of mixed trends in the decorative arts. On the one hand the traditions of the 19th-century Historical movement were continued, while on the other many artists were developing a completely new perspective on both form and decoration.

Art Nouveau vase, Emile Gallé (1900)

This part of the museum includes pieces that embody both approaches, but the strongest emphasis is placed on the innovative Art Deco style. Notable examples include a small porcelain tea service by Gertrud Kant, and a silver coffee set decorated with inlaid ebony, designed by Jean Puiforcat.

The museum's unique 20th-century collection has been continually updated since 1945, aiming to document developments in 20th- and 21st-century decorative arts. On display are a wide range of ceramics, furniture by well-known designers, and a variety of items in daily use.

Gemäldegalerie ⓼

Woman in a Bonnet by Rogier van der Weyden

THE GEMÄLDEGALERIE collection is exceptional in the consistently high quality of its paintings. Unlike those in many other collections, they were chosen by specialists who, from the end of the 18th century, systematically acquired pictures to ensure that all the major European schools of painting were represented. Originally part of the Altes Museum collection *(see pp74–5)*, the paintings achieved independent status in 1904 when they were moved to what is now the Bodemuseum *(see p79)*. After the division of Berlin in 1945, part of the collection was kept in the Bodemuseum, while the majority ended up in the Dahlem Museum *(see pp170–71)*. Following reunification, with the building of a new home as part of the Kulturforum development, this unique set of paintings has finally been united again.

★Cupid Victorious (1602)
Inspired by Virgil's Omnia vincit Amor, Caravaggio depicted a playful god, trampling over the symbols of Culture, Fame, Knowledge and Power.

Madonna with Child (c.1477)
A frequent subject of Sandro Botticelli, the Madonna and Child depicted here are surrounded by singing angels holding lilies, symbolizing purity.

Circular lobby leading to the galleries

Birth of Christ (c.1480)
This beautiful religious painting is one of the few surviving paintings on panels by Martin Schongauer.

Portrait of Hieronymus Holzschuher (1529)
Albrecht Dürer painted this affectionate portrait of his friend, who was the mayor of Nuremberg.

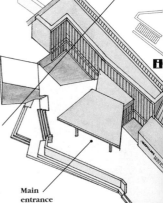

Main entrance

The Glass of Wine
(c.1658–61)
Jan Vermeer's carefully composed picture of a young woman drinking wine with a young man gently hints at the relationship developing between them.

VISITORS' CHECKLIST

Matthäikirchplatz 8.
Map 5 C5. 20 90 55 55.
Ⓢ & Ⓤ *Potsdamer Platz.*
Ⓤ *Mendelssohn-Bartholdy-Park.*
129, 142, 148, 248, 348.
○ *Tue–Sun 10am–6pm.*
● *first Tue after Easter and Whitsun, 1 May, 24, 25 & 31 Dec.*

Love in the French Theatre
This picture has a companion piece called Love in the Italian Theatre *(see p21). Both are the work of French painter, Jean-Antoine Watteau.*

★ Portrait of Hendrickje Stoffels (1656–7)
This portrait of Rembrandt's lover, Hendrickje Stoffels, is typical in that the painter focuses on the subject and ignores the background.

KEY

■ German painting:
13th–17th centuries (I–III & 1–4)
18th c. (XII–XIV & 23–28)
19th c. (20–22)

□ Dutch painting:
14th–17th c. (IV–VI & 5–7)
& Flemish 18th c. (VII–XI & 8–19)

■ French painting:
14th–17th c. (IV–VI & 5–7)
& Spanish 18th c. (XII–XVIII & 23–28)
& English 18th c. (20–22)

□ Italian painting:
14th–17th c. (XV–XVIII & 29–41)
18th–19th c. (XII–XIV & 23–28)

■ Miniatures

GALLERY GUIDE
The main gallery contains over 900 masterpieces grouped according to their country of origin and period. These are complemented by around 400 works in the study gallery on the lower floor, as well as by a computerized digital gallery.

★ Dutch Proverbs (1559)
Pieter Breugel managed to illustrate more than 100 proverbs in this painting.

STAR EXHIBITS

★ **Cupid Victorious**

★ **Portrait of Hendrickje Stoffels**

★ **Dutch Proverbs**

Visiting the Gemäldegalerie

T HE GEMÄLDEGALERIE'S MODERN building was designed by Heinz Hilmer and Christopher Sattler and its exhibition space offers a superb environment in which to view the paintings. The pictures are gently lit by the diffused daylight that streams in from above, while the walls are covered in light-absorbing fabric. The vast hall which occupies the centre of the building allows the visitor to take a break from sightseeing at any time. The hall, with a futuristic sculpture by Walter de Maria set in a water-filled pool, provides an ideal setting for a few moments of quiet contemplation and rest.

Frans Hals' portrait, *Malle Babbe* or *Crazy Babette* (c.1629–30)

Hans Holbein's *Portrait of Georg Gisze* (1532)

GERMAN PAINTING

G ERMAN PAINTINGS are exhibited in several areas of the gallery. The first group comprises art from the 13th–16th centuries. A fine body of religious paintings and altarpieces contains a historic 13th-century rectangular altarpiece from Westphalia. Other religious artifacts include the side panels of the 15th-century *Wurzach Altar*, ascribed to Hans Multscher, which vividly depict the torment of Christ and the life of the Virgin Mary. A real rarity is the *Nativity* by Martin Schongauer. Often thought of primarily as an engraver, he was one of the most significant painters of the late 15th century but few of his paintings have survived.

Another artist known for his engravings as well as paintings, Albrecht Dürer was a major figure in Renaissance art in northern Europe. His works displayed here include *Madonna with the Siskin*, painted in 1506 while he was visiting Italy, and two later portraits of Nürnberg patriarchs. There are also exhibits by Hans Süss von Kulmbach, Hans Baldung Grien and Albrecht Altdorfer. Among the many works by Lucas Cranach the Elder is the delightful *Fountain of Youth*, from which old women emerge young and beautiful, while men regain their youth through amorous liaisons with the women. Another excellent painting in this collection is a portrait of the Danzig merchant Georg Gisze, painted by Hans Holbein the Younger at a time when both men were living in London. 17th- and 18th-century paintings, including the works of Adam Elsheimer and Johann Heinrich Tischbein, are on show elsewhere.

DUTCH AND FLEMISH PAINTING

T HE GALLERY WITH Dutch and Flemish paintings begins with the captivating canvases of Jan van Eyck. In addition to his precise portraits, you can see here the celebrated *Madonna in a Church*. The high quality of paintings is maintained with the works of Petrus Christus and Rogier van der Weyden. Among the pictures by Hugo van der Goes, the most prized is *The Adoration of the Magi*, once the centre panel of a triptych.

The collection has a triptych by Hans Memling, and also the small *Madonna with Child* painted by one of his pupils, Michel Sittow. There is a large group of paintings by Gerard David, Jan Gossaert and Joos van Cleve. Try to keep an eye out for a modest picture by Hieronymus Bosch called *St John on Patmos*. One of the most outstanding paintings of the whole collection is Pieter Bruegel the Elder's *Dutch Proverbs*. However, in order to fully appreciate the mastery and humour in this painting, make sure you use the accompanying board which explains all the one hundred or so proverbs illustrated here.

Within the large collection of excellent Flemish paintings you can marvel at the Baroque vitality and texture evident in the canvases of friends and

Salomon van Ruysdael's *Riders and Cattle* (1656)

sometime collaborators Petrus Paulus Rubens, Jacob Jordaens, Jan Brueghel the Elder and Frans Snyders. The exceptional portraits of Anton van Dyck, who painted complex, psychologically revealing studies, are indicative of the artist at the height of his powers.

The gallery of 17th-century Dutch paintings probably holds the richest collection in the museum. Included among these are the portraits by Frans Hals, which perfectly illustrate his enormous artistic talents. Excellent examples of his varied work are the vigorous *Malle Babbe (c.1629–30)* – a portrait of the "crazy Babette" of Haarlem.

In fact, all the most famous Dutch painters are represented here but, of course, the works of Jan Vermeer and the master, Rembrandt, attract the greatest amount of interest. The works of Rembrandt include the paintings *Samson and Delilah*, *Susanna and the Two Elders*, and *Joseph and the Wife of Potiphar*. It is also worth taking time to view the *Man in the Golden Helmet*, a sad yet noble painting originally attributed to Rembrandt. Carbon dating has shown it to be the work of members of his studio. It is a magnificent tribute to his skill as a teacher.

Jean Baptiste Siméon Chardin's *The Draughtsman* (1737)

FRENCH, ENGLISH AND SPANISH PAINTING

T HE COLLECTION OF French art can be found in various parts of the gallery. Paintings of the 15th and 16th century are exhibited alongside Dutch paintings of that era. The oldest works date from the

Titian's *Venus with the Organ Player* (1550–52)

beginning of the 15th century, and the *Madonna with Child*, dating from c.1410, is one of the oldest preserved works of art painted on a canvas. One of the most valuable French works is by Jean Fouquet, entitled *Étienne Chevalier with Saint Stephen*. Comprising half of the *Diptych of Melun* this is one of Fouquet's few non-miniature paintings.

Nicolas Poussin, the mainspring of the French Classical tradition, and Claude Lorrain, famous for his idealized landscapes, represent 17th-century French painting. Eighteenth-century painting is strongly represented by the canvases of Jean-Antoine Watteau, Jean Baptiste Siméon Chardin and François Boucher.

Two areas in which this collection is less complete are Spanish and English painting. Nevertheless, there is a portrait by Diego Velázquez which is worth seeing, while the English pictures include good portraits by rivals Sir Joshua Reynolds and Thomas Gainsborough.

Sir Joshua Reynolds' *Portrait of Lady Sunderlin* (1786)

ITALIAN PAINTING

T HE COLLECTION of Italian paintings is fairly comprehensive. There are exemplary works by 14th-century masters, including *Laying the Body to Rest in the Grave* and parts of *Scenes from the Life of St Humilitas Pietro Lorenzeti*, attributed to Giotto. Paintings by Piero della Francesca, Fra Angelico, Masaccio, Andrea del Verrocchio, Sandro Botticelli, and Antonio del Pollaiuolo all represent the 15th century. In this collection you will also find later works by Raphael, including the *Madonna di Casa Colonna*, and the *Madonna di Terranuova*, painted after Raphael's arrival in Florence around 1505. There is also a collection of works by the Venetian Renaissance painter, Giovanni Bellini.

Indeed, the Venetian school in general is well represented: *Portrait of a Young Man* by Giorgione is a vibrant and colourful study; there is also Titian's *Venus and the Organ Player* and Tintoretto's *Virgin and the Child Adored by Saints Mark and Luke*. It is worth comparing Caravaggio's *Cupid Victorious*, whose provocative and distinctly human sexuality contrasts with the spiritual orthodoxy of *Heavenly and Earthly Love*, by Giovanni Baglione. Similar in style, the two paintings convey opposing ideologies. Cardinal Giustiani, whose brother owned Caravaggio's controversial canvas, commissioned the latter painting. Works by Giovanni Battista Tiepolo, Francesco Guardi and Antonio Canaletto represent the art of 18th-century Venice.

Karl Schmidt-Rottluff's _Farm in Daugart_ (1910), Neue Nationalgalerie

Neue Nationalgalerie 🟡

Potsdamer Strasse 50. **Map** 5 C5.
🟥 20 90 55 55. 🟦 & Ⓢ _Potsdamer Platz_ or 🟦 _Mendelssohn-Bartholdy-Park._ 🚌 _129, 142, 148, 248, 348._
⬜ _10am–6pm Tue–Fri, 11am–6pm Sat & Sun._ 🎧 ♿

THIS MAGNIFICENT collection of modern art ended up in West Berlin after World War II and required the construction of a suitable building to house it. A commission was given to the elder statesman of modern architecture, the 75-year-old Mies van der Rohe. The result is a striking building with a flat steel roof over a glass hall, barely supported by six slender interior struts.

The collection of the Neue Nationalgalerie comprises largely 20th-century art, but begins with artists of the late 19th century, such as Edvard Munch, Ferdinand Hodler and Oskar Kokoschka. German movements, such as Die Brücke, are well represented, with pieces by Ernst Ludwig Kirchner and Karl Schmidt-Rottluff. As well as the Bauhaus movement, the gallery shows works by exponents of a crass realism, such as Otto Dix and Georg Grosz. The most celebrated artists of other European countries are also included in the collection – Pablo Picasso, Ferdinand Léger, or the Surrealists

Giorgio de Chirico, Salvador Dalí, René Magritte and Max Ernst. Post-World War II art is represented by the works of Barnett Newman and Frank Stella, among others. Following reunification, a number of new works have been added to the collection. The most recent artworks are displayed in the Hamburger Bahnhof branch _(see pp110–11)_, a former train station turned art museum.

Office building designed by Arat Isozaki near Potsdamer Platz

Potsdamer Platz 🔟

Map 6 E5. 🟦 & Ⓢ _Potsdamer Platz._

UNDER CONSTRUCTION since the mid 1990s, the scale of building in Potsdamer Platz has been unprecedented. Now the drab piece of no-man's-land which once divided East and West Berlin has been transformed into an ultramodern city centre for the 21st century.

Until World War II, Potsdamer Platz was one of the busiest and most densely built-up areas of Berlin. Most of the city centre landmarks – hotels such as the Palasthotel and the Fürstenhof, the huge Wertheim department store, and Columbus-Haus (a tower-block designed by Eric Mendelsohn) – ceased to exist after the bombing of 1945. The destruction was completed when the Berlin Wall was built, as the burned-out ruins were finally pulled down.

The huge new Potsdamer Platz complex comprises not only office buildings, but also a concert hall, IMAX theatre and multi-screen cinema complexes, and a Hyatt hotel _(see p219)._ Overseeing the whole project were architects Wilmer and Sattler.

The work was funded mainly by large companies: the first finished structure being the Daimler-Benz-Areal designed by Renzo Piano and Christoph Kohlbecker. To the north lies the Sony-Centre complex, by Helmut Jahn. The latter's futuristic architecture has absorbed part of the now demolished Grandhotel Esplanade. The Neo-Baroque Emperor's Hall was moved 70 m (230 ft) to its new location at a cost of 50 million marks. In other parts of the complex two smaller pre-War structures, the Weinhaus Huth and the Mosse-Palais, have also survived the bombs and the builders.

Shell-Haus 🟤

Reischpietschufer 60. **Map** 5 C5.
🟦 _Mendelssohn-Bartholdy-Park._
🚌 _129._

THIS IS UNDOUBTEDLY a gem for lovers of the architecture developed during the period between World Wars I and II. This modernist office block was designed by Emil Fahrenkamp. Built from 1930 to 1931, it was one of the first buildings in Berlin to use a steel-frame construction. The most eye-catching wing extends along Landwehrkanal with a zig-zag elevation; from a height of five storeys it climbs upwards in a series of steps, finishing up ten storeys high. Beautiful proportions and original design place the structure among the finest of Berlin's buildings of its era.

The German State Naval Office, now part of the Bendlerblock complex

Bendlerblock (Gedenkstätte Deutscher Widerstand) ⑫

Stauffenbergstrasse 13–14. **Map** 5 B5, 5 C5. 📞 *26 54 72 02.* Ⓤ *Mendelssohn-Bartholdy-Park.* 🚌 *129.* ⏰ *9am–6pm Mon–Fri, 9am–1pm Sat & Sun.* 🔴 *1 Jan, 24, 25 & 31 Dec.* 🎧

THE COLLECTION of buildings known as the Bendlerblock was built during the Third Reich as an extension to the German State Naval Offices. During World War II these buildings were the headquarters of the Wehrmacht (German Army). It was here that a group of officers planned their famous and ultimately unsuccessful assassination attempt on Hitler on 20 July 1944. When the attempt led by Claus Schenk von Stauffenberg

failed, he and his fellow conspirators were quickly arrested. The death sentences on these men were passed at the Plötzensee prison *(see p178)*. General Ludwig Beck was forced to commit suicide, while Stauffenberg, Friedrich Olbricht, Werner von Haeten, and Ritter Mertz von Quimheim were shot in the Bendlerblock courtyard.

A monument commemorating this event, designed by Richard Scheibe in 1953, stands where the executions were carried out. On the upper floor of the building there is an exhibition documenting the history of the German anti-Nazi movements.

Villa von der Heydt ⑬

Von-der-Heydt-Strasse 18. **Map** 11 B1. Ⓤ *Nollendorfplatz.* 🚌 *100, 129, 187, 341.*

THIS FINE VILLA, built in a late-Neo-Classical style, is one of the few surviving reminders that the southern side of the Tiergarten was one of the most expensive and beautiful residential areas of Berlin.

Designed by Hermann Ende and GA Linke, the villa was built from 1860 to 1862. The neatly manicured gardens and railings around the villa are adorned with busts of Christian Daniel Rauch and Alexander von Humboldt. The statues, by Reinhold Begas, originally lined the Avenue of Triumph in the Tiergarten. After restoration in 1967, the villa became the headquarters of one of the

most influential cultural bodies, the Stiftung Preussischer Kulturbesitz (Foundaton of Prussian Cultural Heritage).

The captivating, streamlined buildings of the Bauhaus-Archiv

Bauhaus-Archiv ⑭

Klingelhöferstrasse 14. **Map** 11 A1. 📞 *254 00 20.* Ⓤ *Nollendorfplatz.* 🚌 *100, 129, 187, 341.* ⏰ *10am–5pm Wed–Mon.* 🎧 *(free Mon).* 🔵 🚻 🔲 🍽

THE BAUHAUS school of art, started by Walter Gropius in 1919, was one of the most influential art institutions of the 20th century. Originally based in Weimar, and from 1925 in Dessau, this school provided inspiration for numerous artists and architects. Staff and students included Mies van der Rohe, Paul Klee, Wassily Kandinsky, Theo van Doesburg and László Moholy-Nagy. The school moved to Berlin in 1932, but was closed down by the Nazis in 1933.

After the war, the Bauhaus-Archiv was relocated to Darmstadt. In 1964 Walter Gropius designed a building to house the collection, but it was never realized. The archive was moved to Berlin in 1971 and the design had to be adapted to the new site. The maestro was no longer alive, so the project was taken over by Alexander Cvijanovic. The gleaming white building with its distinctive glass-panelled gables was built between 1976 and 1979 and houses the archive, library and exhibition halls for temporary displays.

Neo-Classical façade of the elegant Villa von der Heydt

Diplomaten-viertel ⑮

DIPLOMATIC QUARTER

Map 4 F5, 5 A5, B5, C5.
U *Nollendorfplatz.* 🚌 *100, 129, 187, 341.*

A LTHOUGH A NUMBER of consulates existed in the Tiergarten area as early as 1918, the establishment of a diplomatic district along the southern edge of the Tiergarten, between Stauffenberg-strasse and Lichtensteinallee, did not take place until the period of Hitler's Third Reich between 1933 and 1945. During the years 1938 to 1943 large embassies representing the Axis Powers, Italy and Japan, were built here.

Despite the fact that these monumental buildings were designed by a number of different architects, the Fascist interpretation of Neo-Classicism and the influence of Albert Speer as head architect meant that the group was homogenous, if bleak. Many of the buildings did not survive World War II bombing. A new diplomatic area has now emerged along Tiergartenstrasse. The Austrian embassy designed by Hans Hollein stands at the junction of Stauffenbergstrasse, next door to the embassies of Turkey and the Republic of South Africa. At Tiergartenstrasse Nos. 21–3 the pre-World War II Italian embassy still stands, while next door is a copy of the first Japanese embassy. Between Klingel-höferstrasse and Rauchstrasse stands an imposing complex of five embassies. Completed in 1999, these represent Norway, Sweden, Denmark, Finland and Iceland.

Tiergarten ⑯

Map 4 E4, 5 A3, 6 D3. **S** *Tiergarten or Bellevue.* 🚌 *100, 187, 341.*

T HIS IS THE largest park in Berlin. Situated at the geographical centre of the city it occupies a surface area of more than 200 ha (495 acres). Once a forest used as

One of many tranquil areas within the Tiergarten

the Elector's hunting reserve, it was transformed into a landscaped park by Peter Joseph Lenné in the 1830s. A half-kilometre Triumphal Avenue was built in the eastern section of the park at the end of the 19th century, lined with statues of the country's rulers and statesmen.

World War II inflicted huge damage on the Tiergarten, including the destruction of the Triumphal Avenue, many of whose surviving monuments can now be seen in the Lapidarium *(see p138).* Replanting, however, has now restored the Tiergarten which is a favourite meeting place for Berliners. Its avenues are now lined with statues of figures such as Johann Wolfgang von Goethe and Richard Wagner.

By the lake known as Neuer See and the Landwehrkanal are memorials to the murdered leaders of the Spartakus move-ment, Karl Liebknecht and Rosa Luxemburg *(see p26).* Also worth finding is a collection of gas lamps, displayed near the Tiergarten S-Bahn station.

Grosser Stern ⑰

GREAT STAR

Map 5 A4. **S** *Bellevue.* 🚌 *100, 187, 341.*

T HIS VAST ROUNDABOUT at the centre of the Tiergarten has five large roads leading off it in the shape of a star. At its centre is the enormous Siegessäule (Triumphal Column). Surrounding it are various monuments brought over from the nearby Reichstag

building *(see pp130–31)* during the late 1930s. At the same period the Strasse des 17 Juni was widened to twice its size, the square surrround-ing the roundabout was enlarged and much of the existing statuary removed.

In the northern section of the square stands a vast bronze monument to the first German Chancellor, Otto von Bismarck (1815–98). Around it stand allegorical figures, the work of late-19th century sculptor Reinhold Begas. Other statues represent various national heroes including Field Marshal Helmuth von Moltke (1800–91), chief of the Prussian general staff between the years 1858 and 1888, who won the Franco-German war.

Monument to Otto von Bismarck at the Grosser Stern

Siegessäule ⑱

TRIUMPHAL COLUMN

Grosser Stern. **Map** 5 A4.
S *Bellevue.* 🚌 *100, 187, 341.*
◯ *1–6pm Mon, 9am–6pm Tue–Sun.*

T HE TRIUMPHAL column is based on a design by Johann Heinrich Strack, and was built to commemorate victory in the Prusso-Danish war of 1864. After further Prussian victories in wars against Austria (1866) and France (1871), a gilded figure by Friedrich Drake representing Victory, known as the "Goldelse", was added to the top of the column. The monument originally stood in front of the Reichstag building, but was moved to its present location by the Nazi government in 1938. The granite base is decorated with bas-reliefs commemorating battles, while higher up the column a mosaic frieze by Anton von Werner depicts the founding of the German Empire in 1871. An observation terrace at the top of the monument offers magnificent vistas over Berlin.

Siegessäule (Triumphal Column)

Hansaviertel ⓲

Map 4 E3, E4, F3. Ⓢ Bellevue.
🚌 123, 341. **Akademie der Künste**
Hanseatenweg 10. 📞 39 07 60.
🕐 10am–8pm Tue–Sun. 🅿️

T HIS AREA TO the west of Schloss Bellevue is home to some of the most interesting

---

KÖNIGLICHE PORZELLAN-MANUFAKTUR

Established in 1763, the Königliche Porzellan-Manufaktur (Royal Porcelain Factory) was soon producing items of the highest artistic quality, competing with the products of the older Meissen factory in Saxony. The Berlin factory is particularly renowned for its Neo-Classical urns and plates decorated with views of the city. Large collections of porcelain with the markings KPM can be seen at the Ephraim Palais (see p 91), in the Kunstgewerbemuseum (see pp118–21) and at the Belvedere within the grounds of Schloss Charlottenburg (see pp154–55). It is also worth visiting the factory, located at Wegelystrasse 1, which is still producing porcelain, and includes a sales gallery and exhibition hall.

Neo-Classical vase with a view of the Gendarmenmarkt

---

modern architecture in Berlin, built for the 1957 Internationale Bauausstellung (International Architectural Exhibition). Taking on a World War II bomb site, prominent architects from around the world designed 45 projects, of which 36 were realized, to create a varied residential development set in an environment of lush greenery. The list of distinguished architects involved in the project included Walter Gropius (Händelallee Nos. 3–9), Alvar Aalto (Klopstockstrasse Nos. 30–32) and Oskar Niemeyer (Altonaer Strasse Nos. 4–14). The development also includes a school, a commercial services building and two churches.

In 1960, a new headquarters for the **Akademie der Künste** (Academy of Arts) was built at Hanseatenweg No. 10. Designed by Werner Düttmann, the academy has a concert hall, an exhibition area, archives and a library. In front of the main entrance is a magnificent piece, Reclining Figure, by eminent British sculptor Henry Moore.

Schloss Bellevue ⓴

BELLEVUE PALACE

Spreeweg 1. **Map** 5 A3. Ⓢ Bellevue.
🚌 100, 187. ⬤ to the public.

T HIS CAPTIVATING palace with its dazzlingly white Neo-Classical façade is now the official Berlin residence of the German President. Built in 1786 to a design by Philipp Daniel Boumann for the Prussian Prince August Ferdinand, the palace served as a royal residence until 1861. In 1935 it was refurbished to house a Museum of German Ethnology. Refurbished again in 1938, it became a hotel for guests of the Nazi government.

Following bomb damage during World War II, the palace was carefully restored to its former glory, with the oval ballroom rebuilt to a design by Carl Gotthard Langhans. The palace is set within an attractive park laid out to the original late-18th-century design, though unfortunately the picturesque garden pavilions did not survive World War II.

Imposing façade of Schloss Bellevue, now the official Berlin residence of the German President

Haus der Kulturen der Welt or "pregnant oyster" as it is also known

Haus der Kulturen der Welt ㉑

HOUSE OF WORLD CULTURE

John-Foster-Dulles-Allee 10. **Map** 5 C3. 39 78 70 Ⓢ *Unter den Linden.* 100, 248.

THIS FORMER congress hall's squat structure and parabolic roof has given rise to its affectionate nickname "the pregnant oyster". Built between 1956 and 1957 to a design by the American architect Hugh Stubbins, it was intended as the American entry in the international architecture competition "Interbau 1957", (from which the Hansaviertel apartment blocks originated). Partly financed by American institutions, it soon became a symbol of freedom and modernity in West Berlin during the Cold War, particularly when compared to the GDR-era monumental buildings of Karl-Marx-Allee in East Berlin *(see pp164–5).* However, its concept outran current technologies and the roof failed to withstand the test of time, as the building partially collapsed in 1980.

After reconstruction it was re-opened in 1989, with a change of purpose. It is now used to bring world cultures to a wider German audience, and stages various events and performances to this effect. It is known for its jazz festivals in particular *(see pp48–51).*

Standing nearby is the black tower of the Carillon built in 1987 to commemorate the 750th anniversary of Berlin. Suspended in the tower is the largest carillon in Europe, comprising 67 bells. Daily at noon and 6pm, the bells give a brief computer-controlled concert.

Regierungsviertel ㉒

GOVERNMENT DISTRICT

Map 6 D2, E2. Ⓢ *Unter den Linden.* 100, 248.

THIS BOLD CONCEPT for a new government district in keeping with a 21st-century capital was the winning design in a competition held in 1992. Construction of the complex began in 1997 and will be completed in 2003. Axel Schultes and Charlotte Frank's grand design proposed a rectangular site cutting across the meander of the Spree river just north of the Reichstag.

While individual buildings have been designed by other architects, their plans have been adapted to fit within the overall concept. Schultes and Frank have also designed a special building which is to serve as the headquarters of the German Chancellor.

The offices – Alsenblock and Luisenblock – are the work of Stephan Braunfels, as is the office Dorotheenblöcke, built by a consortium of five architects. The whole project will be complemented by an ultra-modern, integrated transport system which will include a road tunnel under the Tiergarten and a vast subterranean railway station – Lehrter Bahnhof. The architects involved in the railway station project are Mainhard von Gerkan, Oswald Mathias Unger and Max Dudler.

Reichstag ㉓

Platz der Republik. **Map** 6 D3, E3. Ⓢ *Unter den Linden.* 100, 248, 257. 227 32 152. **Dome** ◯ 8am-midnight daily. **Assembly Hall** ◯ 9am-4pm Mon-Fri, 10am-4pm Sat, Sun & holidays ◻ noon Tue (in English). ● *1 Jan, 24, 26 & 31 Dec.*

BUILT TO HOUSE the German Parliament, the Reichstag was intended as a symbol of national unity and to show-case the aspirations of the new German Empire, declared in 1871. The Neo-Renaissance design by Paul Wallot captured the prevailing spirit of German optimism. Constructed between the years 1884 and 1894 it was funded by money paid by the French as wartime reparations.

On 23 December 1916, the inscription "*Dem Deutschen Volke*" ("To the German People") was added to the façade. The Reichstag became a potent symbol to the German populace; this power would be exploited in the years to come.

In 1918 Philipp Scheidemann declared the formation of the

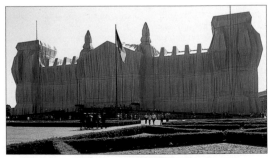

The Reichstag spectacularly wrapped up in 1995 by artist Christo

The Reichstag crowned by a dome designed by Sir Norman Foster

The vast column was made from marble taken from the headquarters of the Chancellor of the Third Reich, when it was being dismantled. The column was designed by Nicolai Sergiejev, while the imposing figure on top, a soldier cast in bronze, is the work of Lew Kerbel. This monument is also a cemetery for around 2,500 Soviet casualties. The site ended up in the British sector, but formed a kind of non-territorial enclave to which Soviet soldiers posted to East Berlin had access.

Weimar Republic from the building. The next time the world heard about the Reichstag was on the night of 28 February 1933, when a fire destroyed the main hall. The Communists were blamed, accelerating a political witch-hunt driven by the Nazis, who subsequently came to power.

With the onset of World War II, the building was not rebuilt. Yet its significance resonated beyond Germany, as shown by the photograph of the Soviet flag flying from the Reichstag in May 1945, which became a symbol of the German defeat. Rebuilding work undertaken between 1957 and 1972 removed the dome and most of the ornamentation on the façades. As well as providing a meeting-place for the lower house of the German Bundestag (Parliament), the Reichstag also made a spectacular backdrop for huge festivals and rock concerts, much to the annoyance of the East German authorities.

On 2 December 1990, the Reichstag was the first meeting place of a newly-elected Bundestag following German reunification. On 23 June 1995 the artist Christo and his wife Jeanne-Claude wrapped the Reichstag in glistening fabric – an artistic statement that lasted for two weeks.

The latest rebuilding project was undertaken between 1995 and 1999 to a design by Sir Norman Foster that transforms the Reichstag into a modern meeting hall crowned with an elliptical dome with a viewing gallery. The first parliamentary meeting in the new building took place on 19 April 1999.

Sowjetisches Ehrenmal ㉔
MONUMENT TO SOVIET SOLDIERS

Strasse des 17 Juni. **Map** 6 D3.
Ⓢ *Unter den Linden.*
🚌 *100, 142, 248, 348.*

THIS HUGE monument near the Brandenburg Gate was unveiled on 7 November 1945, on the anniversary of the start of the October Revolution in Russia. Flanked by the first two tanks into the city, the monument commemorates over 300,000 Soviet soldiers who perished in the battle for Berlin in World War II.

The sculpture of a Soviet soldier atop the Sowjetisches Ehrenmal

BERLIN'S BRIDGES

Despite wartime damage, Berlin's bridges are still well worth seeing. The Spree river and the city's canals have some exemplary architecture on their banks, while many of the bridges were designed and decorated by famous architects and sculptors. Probably the most renowned bridge is the Schlossbrücke designed by Karl Friedrich Schinkel *(see p74)*. Further south along the Kupfergrabenkanal, the Schleusenbrücke dates from c.1914, and is decorated with reliefs of the early history of the city's bridges and sluices. The next bridge, heading south, is the Jungfernbrücke dating from 1798, which is the last drawbridge in Berlin. The next bridge along is the Gertraudenbrücke *(see p85)*. Where Friedrichstrasse crosses the Spree river is the Weidendammer Brücke, designed by Otto Stahn and built in 1897, with an eagle motif decorating its balustrade. On the Spree near the Regierungsviertel is the magnificent Moltkebrücke (1886–91). The bridge is guarded by a huge griffin wielding a shield adorned with the Prussian eagle, while cherubs dressed in a military fashion hold up lamps. On the arches of the bridges are portraits of leaders designed by Karl Begas.

Ornamental feature of a bear on the Liebknechtbrücke

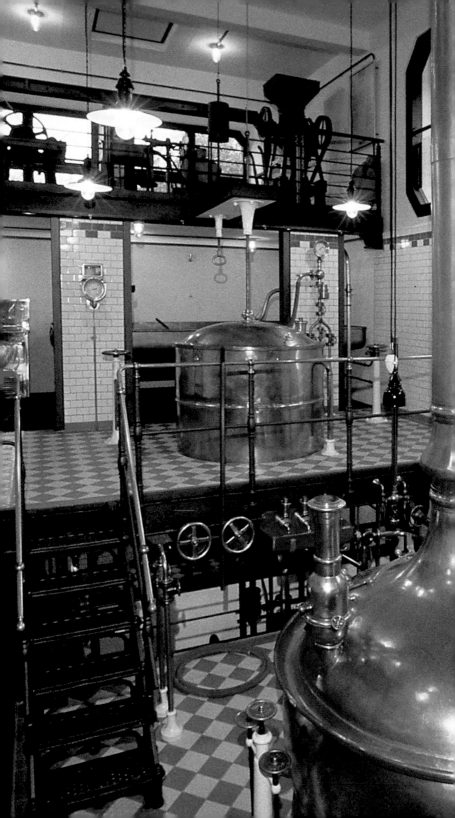

KREUZBERG

THE AREA COVERED in this chapter is only a part of the suburb of the same name. The evolution of Kreuzberg began in the late 19th century when it was a working-class area. After World War II unrepaired buildings were abandoned by those who could afford to move, leaving a population of artists, foreigners, the unemployed and members of a variety of sub-cultures.

Detail from the Martin-Gropius-Bau façade

Kreuzberg is now an area of contrasts, with luxury apartments next to dilapidated buildings. Some parts of Kreuzberg are mainly Turkish, while others are inhabited by affluent young professionals. The district's attractions are its wealth of restaurants and Turkish bazaars, as well as an interesting selection of nightclubs, cinemas, theatres and galleries.

SIGHTS AT A GLANCE

Museums
Berlin-Museum ❺
Checkpoint Charlie ❹
Deutsches Technikmuseum
    Berlin ❾
Jüdisches Museum ❻
Lapidarium ❽
Martin-Gropius-Bau ❷
Topographie des Terrors ❸

Historic Buildings
Anhalter Bahnhof ❶
Flughafen
    Tempelhof ⓭
Riehmers
    Hofgarten ⓫

Squares, Parks and Cemeteries
Friedhöfe vor dem
    Halleschen Tor ❿
Mehringplatz ❼
Viktoriapark ⓬

0 metres   800
0 yards   800

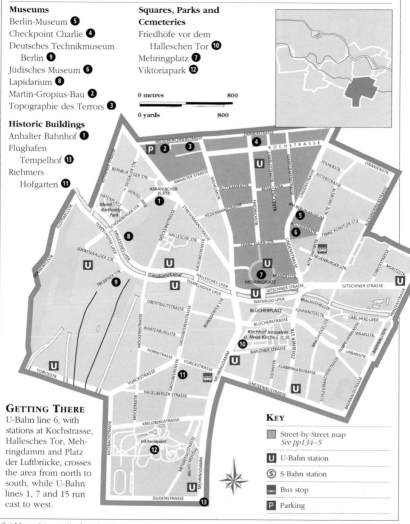

GETTING THERE
U-Bahn line 6, with stations at Kochstrasse, Hallesches Tor, Mehringdamm and Platz der Luftbrücke, crosses the area from north to south, while U-Bahn lines 1, 7 and 15 run east to west.

KEY

	Street-by-Street map *See pp134–5*
U	U-Bahn station
S	S-Bahn station
	Bus stop
P	Parking

◁ **Old machinery displayed at the Deutsches Technikmuseum**

Street-by-Street: Mehringplatz and Friedrichstrasse

T HE AREAS NORTH OF Mehringplatz are the
oldest sections of Kreuzberg. Mehringplatz,
initially called Rondell, together with the
Oktogon (Leipziger Platz) and the Quarré
(Pariser Platz), were laid out in 1734 as part of
the enlargement of Friedrichstadt. World War
II totally changed the character of this area. It
is now full of modern developments such as
the Friedrichstadt Passagen – a huge complex
of shops, apartments, offices, galleries and
restaurants. Only a few buildings recall the
earlier splendour of this district.

★ **Checkpoint Charlie**
*This sign marks the place of the
notorious border crossing between
East and West Berlin* ❹

**Topographie
des Terrors**
*A shocking exhibition
detailing Nazi crimes
is housed within the
former Gestapo and
SS headquarters* ❸

KOCHSTRASSE

FRIEDRICHSTRASSE

WILHELMSTRASSE

PUTTKAMERSTRASSE

Martin-Gropius-Bau
*This interesting, multi-coloured
Neo-Renaissance building was
once home to the Kunstgewerbemuseum (see pp118–21)* ❷

HEDEMANNSTRAS

0 metres	150
0 yards	150

**Deutsches
Technikmuseum** ◄

**Haus am
Checkpoint
Charlie**
*Butterflies on a
piece of the Berlin
Wall mark the
entrance to this
museum.*

STAR SIGHTS

★ **Checkpoint Charlie**

★ **Jüdisches Museum**

Berlin-Museum
The monogram of King Friedrich Wilhelm I decorates the balcony of this former courtroom, now home to a museum that tells the story of the city through prints, crafts and paintings 5

LOCATOR MAP
See Street Finder maps 12 & 13

Märkisches Museum

★ **Jüdisches Museum**
Windows made to resemble cracks create a striking effect in the metallic facing of this new building by architect Daniel Libeskind 6

Mehringplatz
The former Rondell was known for many years as Belle-Alliance-Platz. Completely destroyed during World War II, it was rebuilt by Hans Scharoun, who followed the original design 7

KEY

– – – Suggested route

Anhalter Bahnhof ❶

Askanischer Platz 6–7. **Map** 12 E1.
Ⓢ *Anhalter Bahnhof.* 🚌 *129, 248, 341.*

O NLY A TINY FRAGMENT now remains of what was once Berlin's largest railway station. The hugely ambitious structure was designed by Franz Schwechten and constructed in 1880. The station was intended to be the largest and most elegant in Europe in order to impress official visitors to the capital of the German Empire. The station was taken out of public use in 1943 after its roof was destroyed by Allied bombing.

Despite attempts to preserve the building, it was pulled down in 1960. Only the front portico remains, crowned with still-damaged sculptures, as well as fragments of its once glorious façade.

Martin-Gropius-Bau ❷

Stresemannstrasse 110. **Map** 12 E1.
📞 *25 48 60.* 🕐 *10am–8pm Tue–Sun.* Ⓢ *&* Ⓤ *Potsdamer Platz.* 🚌 *129, 248, 341.*

T HE INNOVATIVE Martin-Gropius-Bau was originally built to fulfil the requirements of an arts and crafts museum. It was designed by Martin Gropius with the participation of Heino Schmieden and constructed in 1881. The building is in a style reminiscent of an Italian Renaissance palace, with a magnificent glazed interior courtyard and unusual, richly decorated elevations. Located between the windows are the crests of German cities, and within the friezes are reliefs illustrating the different arts and crafts. In the plaques between the windows of the top storey are beautiful mosaics containing figures representing the cultures of different eras and countries.

From 1922 the building accommodated the Museum of Ethnology, but after World War II it was abandoned and left in ruins. It was rebuilt in 1981 to house large-scale

Allegorical mosaic on display in the Martin-Gropius-Bau

exhibitions. In 1999 further refurbishment was undertaken and it now houses changing exhibitions of art, photography and architecture. The Berlin Wall stood behind the building, along Niederkirchner Strasse, though the final fragments have now been removed.

Topographie des Terrors ❸

Stresemannstr. 110 (enter on Niederkirchner Strasse). **Map** 6 F5, 12 F1.
📞 *25 48 67 03.* Ⓢ *&* Ⓤ *Potsdamer Platz.* Ⓤ *Kochstrasse.* 🚌 *129, 248, 341.* 🕐 *10am–6pm daily.* 🅰

D URING the Third Reich Prinz-Albrecht-Strasse was probably the most frightening address in Berlin. In 1934, in a block between Stresemann-, Wilhelm-, Anhalter-, and Prinz-Albrecht-Strasse (now Niederkirchner Strasse), three of the most terrifying Nazi political departments had their headquarters. The Neo-Classical Prinz-Albrecht palace which

stands at Wilhelmstrasse No. 102 became the headquarters of Richard Heydrich and the Third Reich's security service (SD). The school of arts and crafts at Prinz-Albrecht-Strasse No. 8 was occupied by the head of the Gestapo, Heinrich Müller, while the neighbouring Hotel Prinz Albrecht at No. 9 became the headquarters of the Schutzstaffel or SS, with Heinrich Himmler in command.

After World War II, the buildings were pulled down. In 1987, however, in cellars that were once torture cells, an exhibition was mounted that documented Nazi crimes. A new museum building, designed by Peter Zumthor, has been under construction on the site since 1998.

Checkpoint Charlie ❹

Friedrichstr. 43–44. **Map** 7 A5.
📞 *253 72 50.* Ⓤ *Kochstrasse.* 🚌 *129.* 🕐 *9am–10pm daily.* 🅰

A LPHA, B Bravo, C Charlie. Not many people remember that the name of this notorious border crossing between the American and Soviet sectors stemmed from the word that signifies the letter C in the international phonetic alphabet. Little remains of the former crossing point, which was witness to a number of dramatic events during the Cold War, including a standoff between Russian and American tanks in 1961.

Exhibition documenting Nazi crimes at the Topographie des Terrors

Today, there are no longer any gates, barriers or barbed wire, but one of the original watch towers is worth visiting at the museum nearby – Haus am Checkpoint Charlie. The museum's rich collection details Cold War border conflicts, and the construction of the Berlin Wall. Of particular interest is a variety of exhibits connected with the escape attempts of East Germans to the West. The ingenuity and bravery of these escapees is astonishing, using devices such as tiny secret compartments built into cars, and specially-constructed suitcases.

A separate exhibition, called "From Gandhi to Wałęsa", illustrates the history of peaceful campaigns in the fight for democracy in a number of totalitarian countries.

Watchtower at Checkpoint Charlie, a famous border crossing

Berlin-Museum ❺

Lindenstrasse 14. **Map** 13 A2.
🅤 *Hallesches Tor or Kochstrasse.*
🚌 *240.*

THE BERLIN-MUSEUM building, by Philipp Gerlach, was one of the first buildings in the new section of the enlarged Friedrichstadt. The Baroque façade dates from the time of King Friedrich Wilhelm I. The main features are the front balconied portal and the triangular pediment with the Prussian crest and the allegorical figures of Justice and Prudence. Inside the building, within the hallway that leads to the left wing, is an integral Baroque portal that came originally from the Palais Danckelmann, which was built in 1690 and designed by Johann Arnold Nering. The building initially served as a

Plaque adorning a window of the Berlin-Museum

college and then, from the beginning of the 19th century, it was the headquarters of the high court. After undergoing post-World War II restoration the structure has accommodated the Berlin-Museum, which illustrates the history of the city, focusing particularly on developments over the last two hundred years.

In 1989 a competition was held to design an annexe to house the collection reflecting the history and culture of Berlin's Jews. Initially it was decided that the annexe should be about 1,000 sq m (10,700 sq ft), but the winning design, by Daniel Libeskind, was ten times the size and, in the end, a separate museum was set up, the Jüdisches Museum.

Jüdisches Museum ❻

Lindenstrasse 14. **Map** 13 A2.
🅤 *Hallesches Tor or Kochstrasse.*
🚌 *240.* 📞 *25 99 33.* ⏰ *Fri 3pm, Sat 1 & 1:30pm, Sun 11 & 11:30am.*
📷 *compulsory.*

THE BUILDING housing the recently-opened Jewish Museum is an exciting and imaginative example of 20th century architecture. Designed

by a team of Berlin-based architects led by Daniel Libeskind, an American of Jewish descent, the plan, shape, style, and interior and exterior arrangement of the building are part of a complicated philosophical programme. The architecture itself conveys something of the tragic history of the millions of Jews who lost their lives in the Holocaust. The zig-zag lay-out recalls a torn Star of David. The interior arrangement is dominated by a gigantic empty crack, which cuts a swathe through the building. Several corridors lead to a windowless Holocaust tower. Another leads the visitor outside, to a garden named after the writer ETA Hoffmann. Wooden posts fill a sloping square, evoking the emptiness and isolation faced by many thousands of German Jews condemned to a life in exile.

The collection focuses on Jewish history and art. Also on display are numerous artifacts which were once part of everyday Jewish life in Berlin. A suite of empty rooms symbolizes lost Jewish culture. Opening in autumn 2000, a new exhibition will include items currently on display in the Berlin-Museum.

The austere, steel-clad walls of the Jüdisches Museum

A representation of Peace, by Albert Wolff, in Mehringplatz

Mehringplatz ❼

Map 13 A2. 🆄 *Mehringplatz.*
🚌 *240, 241.*

MEHRINGPLATZ WAS planned in the 1830s, when the boundaries of the city were extended. Its original name was Rondell, meaning roundabout. This was an appropriate name as Wilhelmstrasse, Friedrichstrasse and Lindenstrasse all converged here.

Mehringplatz was the work of Philipp Gerlach then, in the 1840s, Peter Joseph Lenné designed the decoration of the square. At the centre is the Column of Peace, designed by Christian Gottlieb Cantian, commemorating the Wars of Liberation in 1815. The column is crowned by the figure of Victory by Christian Daniel Rauch. Two sculptures were added in the 1870s: *Peace* by Albert Wolff; and *Clio* (the Muse of History) by Ferdinand Hartzer. In the 19th and early 20th centuries the area was fashionable and populated with politicians, diplomats and aristocrats. The current buildings date from the 1970s.

Lapidarium ❽

Hallesches Ufer 78. **Map** 12 E2.
📞 *25 48 63 41.* ⏱ *10am–8pm Sat–Thu.* 🆄 *Mendelssohn-Bartholdy-Park.*

THIS INTERESTING building, decorated with an enchanting Oriental-style chimney, was once Berlin's pumping station. It was built from 1873 to 1876 and designed by Hermann Blankenstein. The original steam pumps have

survived to this day and can be seen during a visit. The Lapidarium contains numerous sculptures, some of which have been replaced by copies for conservation purposes. Virtually all the sculptures that once decorated the Avenue of Victory in the Tiergarten, known as "Puppenallee", are housed here. These majestic statues of celebrated warriors and rulers stand side by side in their robes and weapons, only slightly diminished by the loss of many heads, arms and other body parts.

Deutsches Technikmuseum Berlin ❾

Trebbiner Strasse 9. **Map** 12 E2.
📞 *25 48 40.* 🆄 *Gleisdreieck.*
🚌 *129.* ⏱ *9am–5:30pm Tue–Fri, 10am–6pm Sat–Sun.* ♿ ⬜

THE TECHNICAL MUSEUM was first established in 1982 with the intention of grouping more than 100 smaller, specialized collections under one roof. The current collection is arranged on the site of the former trade hall, the size of which allows many of the museum's exhibits, such as locomotives, water towers and storerooms, to be displayed full-size and in their original condition.

Of particular interest in the collection are the dozens of locomotives and railway carriages from different eras as well as the vintage cars. There are also exhibitions dedicated to flying, the history of paper manufacture, printing, weaving,

electro-technology and computer technology. There are also two windmills, a brewery and an old forge. The section called Spectrum is especially popular with children as it allows them to conduct "hands-on" experiments.

Friedhöfe vor dem Halleschen Tor ❿

Mehringdamm, Blücher-, Baruther & Zossener Strasse. **Map** 13 A3.
🆄 *Mehringdamm.* 🚌 *219, 341.*

BEYOND THE CITY WALLS, next to the Hallesches Tor, four neighbouring cemeteries were established in 1735. A number of famous people are buried here; among the beautiful gravestones are the greatest of Berlin's artists. Here lie, among others, the composer Felix Mendelssohn-Bartholdy, architects Georg Wenzeslaus von Knobelsdorff, David Gilly and Carl Ferdinand Langhans, portraitist Antoine Pesne and the writer, artist and composer ETA Hoffmann.

Riehmers Hofgarten ⓫

Yorckstr. 83–86, Grossbeerenstr. 56–57 & Hagelberger Strasse 9–12. **Map** 12 F4.
🆄 *Mehringdamm.* 🚌 *119, 140, 219.*

RIEHMERS HOFGARTEN is the name given to the 20 or so exquisite houses arranged around a picturesque garden in the area bordered by the

Headstone in the picturesque Friedhöfe vor dem Halleschen Tor

Renaissance-style façade in Riehmers Hofgarten

streets Yorck-, Hagelberger and Grossbeerenstrasse. These houses were built between 1881 and 1892 to the detailed designs of Wilhelm Riehmer and Otto Mrosk. These respected architects created this unique group of houses, not only designing intricate, Renaissance-style façades but also giving equal splendour to the elevations overlooking the courtyard garden. The streets of Riehmers Hofgarten have been carefully restored and Yorckstrasse also has quite a few cafés. Next to Riehmers Hofgarten is the church of St Bonifaz, which was designed by Max Hasak. Adjacent to the church is a similar complex of houses built in an impressive Neo-Gothic style.

To experience the authentic atmosphere of old Kreuzberg, you need to go no further than Bergmannstrasse. Here, entire districts of 19th-century houses have been restored to their original state. The atmosphere is further enhanced by antique streetlamps, a pedestrianized street, and bars and galleries. This is also true for Marheinekeplatz, where there is a lively covered market.

Viktoriapark ⓬

Map 12 E4, E5, F5. Ⓤ *Platz der Luftbrücke.* 🚌 *119, 140.*

THIS RAMBLING PARK, with several artificial waterfalls, short trails and a small hill, was designed by Hermann Machtig and built between 1884 and 1894. The Neo-Gothic Memorial to the Wars of Liberation at the summit of the hill is the work of Karl Friedrich Schinkel, created

between 1817 and 1821. The monument commemorates the Prussian victory against Napoleon's army in the Wars of Liberation. The cast-iron tower is well ornamented. In the niches of the lower section are 12 allegorical figures by Christian Daniel Rauch, Friedrich Tieck and Ludwig Wichmann. Each figure symbolizes a battle and is linked to a historic figure – either a military leader or a member of the royal family.

Flughafen Tempelhof ⓭

Platz der Luftbrücke. **Plan** 12 F5. Ⓤ *Platz der Luftbrücke.* 🚌 *104, 119, 184, 341.*

SITUATED BEYOND Kreuzberg, the Tempelhof airport was once Germany's largest. Built in 1923, the structure was enlarged during the Third Reich. The building is typical of Third Reich architecture, even though the eagles that decorate the buildings predate the Nazis. The additions to the original structure were designed by Ernst Sagebiel and completed in 1939.

In 1951, a monument was added in front of the airport. Designed by Edward Ludwig, it commemorates the airlifts of the Berlin Blockade. The three spikes on the top symbolize the air corridors used by Allied planes. The names of those who lost their lives during the Blockade appear on the plinth.

THE BERLIN BLOCKADE (1948–9)

On 12 June 1948, as a result of rising tensions between East Germany and West Berlin, Soviet authorities blockaded all the roads leading to West Berlin. In order to ensure food and fuel for the residents, US General Lucius Clay ordered that provisions be flown into the city. British and American planes made a total of 212,612 flights, transporting almost 1.8 million tons of goods, among which were parts of a power station. In April 1949, at the height of the airlifts, planes were landing every 63 seconds. The blockade ended in May, 1949. Although the airlifts were successful, there were casualties: 70 airmen and 8 ground crew lost their lives.

Allied plane bringing supplies during the Berlin Blockade

AROUND KURFÜRSTENDAMM

THE EASTERN AREA of the Charlottenburg region, around the boulevard known as Kurfürstendamm, was developed in the 19th century. Luxurious buildings were constructed along Kurfürstendamm (the Ku'damm), while the areas of Breitscheidplatz and Wittenbergplatz became replete with hotels and department stores. After World War II, with the old centre (Mitte) situated in East Berlin,

Sculpture from the Jüdisches Gemeindehaus

Charlottenburg became the centre of West Berlin. Traces of wartime destruction were removed very quickly and this area was transformed into the heart of West Berlin, and dozens of new company headquarters and trade centres were built. The situation changed after the reunification of Berlin, and although many tourists concentrate on Mitte, the heart of the city continues to beat around Kurfürstendamm.

SIGHTS AT A GLANCE

Museums
Käthe-Kollwitz-Museum ❾

Streets and Squares
Fasanenstrasse ❽
Kurfürstendamm ❹
Savignyplatz ❿
Tauentzien-
strasse ⓭

Parks
Zoologischer
Garten ❶

Historic Buildings
Europa-Center ❷
Hochschule der Künste ⓫
Jüdisches Gemeindehaus ❼
KaDeWe ⓮
Kaiser-Wilhelm-Gedächtnis-
kirche pp146–7 ❸
Ludwig-Erhard-Haus ❺
Technische Universität ⓬
Theater des Westens ❻

KEY

▨	Street-by-Street map *pp142–3*
🚆	Railway station
Ⓢ	S-Bahn station
Ⓤ	U-Bahn station
🚌	Bus station
🅿	Parking

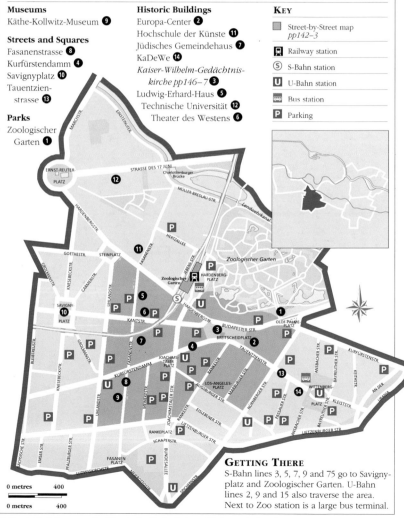

GETTING THERE
S-Bahn lines 3, 5, 7, 9 and 75 go to Savigny-platz and Zoologischer Garten. U-Bahn lines 2, 9 and 15 also traverse the area. Next to Zoo station is a large bus terminal.

0 metres   400

0 metres   400

◁ **Mosaic depicting a standard-bearer inside the Kaiser-Wilhelm-Gedächtniskirche**

Street-by-Street: Breitscheidplatz and Ku'damm

THE AREA SURROUNDING the eastern end of the Ku'damm, especially Tauentzienstrasse and Breitscheidplatz, is the centre of the former West Berlin. Thirty years ago this ultramodern district, full of department stores and office blocks, attracted visitors from all over the world. Today, although the area still retains its unique atmosphere, it is becoming overshadowed by Potsdamer Platz and the arcades of Friedrichstrasse. However, nowhere else in Berlin is there a place so full of life as Breitscheidplatz, a department store with such style as KaDeWe, or streets as refined as Fasanenstrasse.

Kantdreieck
This building, containing only right angles, was designed by Josef Paul Kleihues. The "sail" on the roof makes it instantly recognizable.

Jüdisches Gemeindehaus
Some of the remaining fragments of the old synagogue have been incorporated into the façade of this building ❼

Literaturhaus
contains a charming café and a good bookshop.

Käthe-Kollwitz-Museum
The museum is housed in one of the charming villas on Fasanenstrasse ❾

Fasanenstrasse
This tranquil street features some of the most expensive shops in Berlin ❽

Ku'damm
A stroll along the Ku'damm is a stroll into the heart of Berlin, and an essential part of any visit to the city ❹

STAR SIGHTS

★ Kaiser-Wilhelm-
  Gedächtniskirche

★ Zoologischer
  Garten

KEY

▬ ▬ ▬ Suggested route

Ludwig-Erhard-Haus
The structure of the new Berlin Stock Exchange is based on parabolic arches **5**

LOCATOR MAP
See Street Finder maps 4, 9, 10 & 11.

Theater des Westens
The façade of this musical theatre is fittingly decorated with dancing women **6**

Bahnhof Zoo

Europa-Center
One of the attractions of the Europa-Centre is a glazed courtyard containing a fountain with moving parts **2**

★ **Zoologischer Garten**
The Oriental-style Elephant Gate is one of two entrances to the Zoological Gardens **1**

★ **Kaiser-Wilhelm-Gedächtniskirche**
The mosaics on the wall of the sacristy, by Hermann Schaper, survived World War II undamaged **3**

| 0 metres | | 400 |
| 0 yards | | 400 |

Bao-Bao, one of the star attractions at the Zoologischer Garten

Zoologischer Garten ❶

ZOOLOGICAL GARDEN

Hardenbergplatz 8 or Budapester Strasse 34. **Map** 4 E5, 10 E1. Ⓒ 25 40 10. Ⓢ & Ⓤ *Zoologischer Garten.* ▦ *100, 109, 145, 146, 149, 245, 249.* ◷ *Apr–Sep: 9am–6:30pm daily; Oct–Mar: 9am–5pm daily.* ▨

T HE ZOOLOGICAL garden is undoubtedly one of the greatest attractions in Berlin. It is actually part of the Tiergarten and dates from 1844, which makes this zoo one of the oldest in Germany. You can enter from Hardenbergplatz through the Lion's Gate, and from Budapester Strasse through the decorative Oriental-style Elephant Gate.

The zoo offers a number of attractions, including the monkey house, which contains a family of gorillas, and a specially darkened pavilion for observing nocturnal animals. The hippopotamus pool has a glazed wall that enables visitors to observe these enormous animals moving through the water.

The aquarium, one of the largest in Europe, contains sharks, piranhas and unusual animals from coral reefs. There is also a huge terrarium with an overgrown jungle that is home to a group of crocodiles. One of the best loved animals at the zoo is the giant panda named Bao-Bao.

Europa-Center ❷

Breitscheidplatz. **Map** 10 E1. Ⓢ & Ⓤ *Zoologischer Garten.* ▦ *100, 109, 119, 146, X-9.*

T HE EUROPA-CENTER stands on the site of the legendary Romanisches Café, a famous meeting place for Dada artists in the 1920s. The current building was established in 1965, and since that time it has been one of the largest complexes of its type in Germany. Designed by Helmut Hentrich and Hubert Petschnigg, the Europa-Center is a group of low-rise buildings housing a trade centre, numerous restaurants and pubs, a vast multiplex cinema and a casino. The edifice of the deluxe Palast Hotel (see p222) has been incorporated into the centre, as well as a 22-storey office block.

There are more than 100 shops to browse in as well as some amusing fountains. One of these is the "Flow of Time Clock", designed by Bernard Gitton. Seconds, minutes and hours are measured in vials and spheres of green liquid. The Europa-Center also houses the political cabaret *Die Stachelschweine* and Berlin's largest tourist information centre (see pp278–9).

Kaiser-Wilhelm-Gedächtniskirche ❸

See pp146–7.

One of many outdoor cafés on the Ku'damm

Kurfürstendamm ❹

Map 9 A2, B2, C3, 10 D1. Ⓤ *Kurfürstendamm.* ▦ *109, 119, 129, 219.*

T HIS IS UNDOUBTEDLY one of the most elegant streets in Berlin. The wide avenue was established in the 1880s on the site of a former track that led to the Grunewald forest. It was quickly populated with imposing buildings and grand hotels. In the 20 years between World Wars I and II, the Ku'damm (as it is popularly called) was renowned for its great cafés, visited by famous writers, directors and painters.

After World War II, the damaged houses were replaced with modern buildings, but this did not change the character of the finest street in West Berlin. Elegant shops and cafés with pretty summer gardens attract a chic crowd. A cup of coffee in the corner café in the Kempinski Hotel Bristol or a cake in the Café Kranzler should not be missed.

Ludwig-Erhard-Haus ❺

Fasanenstrasse 83–84. **Map** 4 D5. Ⓢ & Ⓤ *Zoologischer Garten.* ▦ *145, 149, 245, X-9.*

T HIS INNOVATIVE new building houses the headquarters of the Berlin stock exchange as well as a trade and industry

A fountain representing Earth, outside the Europa-Center

centre. Completed in 1998, Ludwig-Erhard-Haus is the creation of British architect Nicholas Grimshaw and has been compared to the skin of an armadillo, a giant skeleton and the ribbing of a shell.

The main structure of the building is composed of 15 elliptical arches, which extend above the roof and through the glass walls of the building. For this reason the entire interior space is completely free of any supports or columns. This allows for freedom and flexibility in the subdivision of the interior.

A system of temperature-sensitive glass Venetian blinds, or louvres, ensures the climate inside the building remains constant. On a windy day, when the sun clouds over, the entire edifice begins to flicker and glisten like a fluttering fish with the movement of the louvres.

Theater des Westens 6

Kantstrasse 9–12. **Map** 10 D1.
⟨⟩ 882 28 88. **Ⓢ** & **U** Zoologischer Garten. **⟨⟩** 149.

THE THEATER DES WESTENS, one of the most picturesque of all Berlin's theatres, was built in 1896 to a design by Bernhard Sehring. The composition of its façade links Neo-Classical elements with Palladian and Art Nouveau details. The interior of the theatre has been designed in a splendid Neo-Baroque style, while the back and the sections that houses the stage have been rebuilt

The façade of the Theater des Westens on Kantstrasse

within a Neo-Gothic structure, incorporating the decorative elements of a chess set.

From its very beginning the theatre catered for lighter forms of musical entertainment. Operettas and vaudeville were staged here, followed by reviews, musicals, and cabaret. Some of the world's greatest stars have appeared on the stage here, including Josephine Baker, who performed her famous banana dance in 1926. Near the theatre is the renowned Delphi cinema and popular jazz club Quasimodo.

Jüdisches Gemeindehaus 7

JEWISH COMMUNITY HOUSE

Fasanenstrasse 79/80. **Map** 10 D1.
U Uhlandstrasse or Kurfürstendamm.
⟨⟩ 109, 119, 129, 219.

THE JEWISH COMMUNITY has its headquarters in this building, constructed on the site of a synagogue that was burned down during *Kristallnacht* on 9 November 1938 *(see p27)*. The original synagogue was designed by Ehenfried Hessel in a Romanesque-Byzantine style and built in 1912. The ruins of the synagogue were removed only in the mid-1950s. The new building, designed by Dieter Knoblauch

The entrance of the Jüdisches Gemeindehaus

and Heinz Heise, was constructed in 1959. The only reminders of the splendour of the former synagogue are the portal at the entrance to the building and some decorative fragments on the façade.

Inside there are offices, a school, a kosher restaurant called Arche Noah and a prayer room covered by three glazed domes. At the rear of the building is a courtyard with a place of remembrance. There is also an emotive statue at the front of the building, depicting a broken scroll of the Torah (the holy book of Jewish Law).

GERMAN CINEMA

The 1920s were a boom time for the arts, and German cinema gained prominence throughout the world with the rise of Expressionism. The opening of the UFA film studios in 1919 in Babelsberg *(see p197)* was a milestone in the development of German cinema. The studios became the heart of the film industry and rivalled Hollywood as a centre for innovation. Many famous films were produced

Marlene Dietrich in the well-known film *The Blue Angel*

there, including the Expressionist masterpiece *The Cabinet of Dr Caligari* (1920) by Robert Wiene, Ernst Lubitsch's *Madame Dubarry* (1919) with Pola Negri and *Nosferatu* (1922) by Friedrich Murnau. Other films released by the studios were Fritz Lang's *Doctor Mabuse* (1922) and his futuristic film *Metropolis* (1927). In April 1930, the studios premiered Joseph von Sternberg's *The Blue Angel* featuring the young Marlene Dietrich in the lead role. After Hitler came to power many directors and actors left Germany.

Kaiser-Wilhelm-Gedächtniskirche ❸

THIS CHURCH MONUMENT is one of Berlin's most famous landmarks, surrounded by a lively crowd of street traders, buskers and beggars. The vast Neo-Romanesque church was designed by Franz Schwechten. It was consecrated in 1895 but was destroyed by bombs in 1943. After World War II the ruins were removed, leaving only the massive front tower at the base of which the Gedenkhalle (Memorial Hall) is situated. This hall documents the history of the church and contains some of the original ceiling mosaics, marble reliefs and liturgical objects from the church. In 1963, Egon Eiermann designed a new octagonal church in blue glass and a new freestanding bell tower.

Kaiser's Mosaic
Kaiser Heinrich I is depicted here in this elaborate mosaic, sitting on his throne.

Bell Tower
The new hexagonal bell tower stands on the site of the former main nave of the destroyed church.

Rose window

Mosaic Decoration
Original mosaics remain on the arches and the walls near the staircase. These feature the Dukes of Prussia among the other decorative elements.

Main Altar
The vast figure of Christ on the Cross is the work of Karl Hemmeter.

Walls of reinforced concrete and blue-coloured glass form a dense grid.

Tower Ruins
The damaged roof of the former church has become one of the best-known symbols of Berlin.

Tower Clock
The tower is decorated with a clock based on a Classical design.

★ Mosaic of the Hohenzollerns
The mosaic of the Hohenzollerns is in the vestibule. The family is led by Queen Luise and the centre is dominated by Kaiser Wilhelm I.

Orthodox Cross
This cross was a gift from the Russian Orthodox bishops from Volokolomsk and Yuruyev, given in memory of the victims of Nazism.

Figure of Christ
This vast sculpture by Hermann Schaper once decorated the church altar. It survived World War II damage.

Main entrance

★ Coventry Crucifix
This modest cross was fashioned from nails found in the ashes of Coventry Cathedral, England. The Cathedral was destroyed during German bombing raids in 1940.

STAR SIGHTS

★ **Mosaic of the Hohenzollerns**

★ **Coventry Crucifix**

Fasanenstrasse – one of the most elegant streets in Berlin

Fasanenstrasse ❽

Map 9 C2, 10 D1, 10 D3.
Ⓤ *Uhlandstrasse.* 🚌 *109, 119, 129, 149, 219, 249.*

THE DISCREET CHARM of Fasanenstrasse, particularly between Lietzenburger Strasse and Kurfürstendamm, has attracted the most exclusive designer shops in the world. Well maintained buildings, *fin-de-siècle* villas set in tranquil gardens and elegant shop windows of jewellers, art galleries and fashion shops will all entice you to take an afternoon stroll along this street.

It is worth seeing the villas at No. 23–5, which are called the Wintergarten-Ensemble. The first one, No. 23, dates from 1889. Tucked away in a garden, the villa is home to the Literaturhaus, which organizes interesting exhibitions and readings. It has an excellent café that extends into a conservatory. At No. 24 is the Käthe-Kollwitz museum, and No. 25, built in 1892 by Hans Grisebach, accommodates an auction house and art gallery.

Käthe-Kollwitz-Museum ❾

Fasanenstrasse 24. **Map** 9 C2.
📞 *882 52 10.* Ⓤ *Uhlandstrasse or Kurfürstendamm.* 🚌 *109, 119, 129, 219, 249.* ⏰ *11am–6pm Wed–Mon* 🖼️🎧

THIS SMALL private museum provides a unique opportunity to become acquainted with the work of Käthe Kollwitz (1867–1945). Born in

Königsberg, the artist settled in Berlin where she married a doctor who worked in Prenzlauer Berg, a working-class district. Her drawings and sculptures portrayed the social problems of the poor, as well as human tragedy and suffering. She frequently took up the theme of motherhood and war after losing a son and grandson in World Wars I and II.

The museum exhibits her work, including posters, drawings and sculptures, as well as her documents, such as letters and photographs.

***Mother and Child,* from the Käthe-Kollwitz-Museum**

Savignyplatz ❿

Map 9 C1. Ⓢ *Savignyplatz.* 🚌 *149.*

SAVIGNYPLATZ IS ENCLOSED on the south side by the arcade of a railway viaduct, which appears in the film *Cabaret* by Bob Fosse. During the day the square does not look interesting – there are no remarkable historic buildings,

only carefully tended greenery and flower beds. However, the area around the square truly comes alive at night. The dozens of cafés and restaurants fill up, while in summer the entire edge of the square and neighbouring streets turn into one big garden filled with tables and umbrellas. People come from outlying districts to visit popular restaurants and cafés such as Zwiebelfisch, Dicke Wirtin, or XII Apostel *(see p240)*. The arcades in the viaduct contain many cafés and bars. One section of the arcades has been taken up by the Bücherbogen bookshop *(see p254)*.

Hochschule der Künste ⓫
COLLEGE OF THE ARTS

Hardenbergstrasse 32–33 and Fasanenstrasse 1b. **Map** 4 D5.
Ⓢ *Zoologischer Garten or* Ⓤ *Ernst-Reuter-Platz.* 🚌 *145, 245, X-9.*

THE HOCHSCHULE der Künste was originally called Preussische Akademie der Künste, which was established in 1696. It continued a long tradition of teaching artists in Berlin and has been headed by well-known figures including Gottfried Schadow and Anton von Werner. As a result of a number of reforms between 1875 and 1882, the Academy was divided into two separate colleges. A complex of buildings was erected for them on Hardenbergstrasse and Fasanenstrasse. The Neo-Baroque buildings were constructed between 1897 and 1902 to a design by Heinrich Keyser and Karl von Grossheim.

After World War II, only two large buildings, both with decorative façades, survived. On the Hardenbergstrasse side was the Hochschule für Bildende Künste (College for Fine Art), while on the Fasanenstrasse side was the Hochschule für Musik und Darstellende Kunst (College for Music and Performing Arts). Unfortunately, the concert hall did not survive. A new one was built in 1955, designed by Paul Baumgarten.

Bas-relief sculpture on the façade of the Hochschule der Künste

A small *fin-de-siècle* building that looks like a castle, at Hardenbergstrasse No. 36, is a college for religious music which belongs to this group of college buildings.

Technische Universität @
TECHNICAL UNIVERSITY

Strasse des 17 Juni 135. **Map** 3 C4.
U *Ernst-Reuter-Platz.* 145, 245, X-9.

THE VAST AREA that lies to the east of Ernst-Reuter-Platz along the Strasse des 17 Juni is occupied by the buildings of the Technische Universität. Officially called Technische Hochschule Berlin (TUB), it was established in 1879 after the unification of the School of Crafts and the renowned Bauakademie. From its inception the Technische Universität had five different departments, which were all housed, from 1884, in a Neo-Renaissance building designed by Richard Lucae, Friedrich Hitzig and Julius Raschdorff. After World War II, the ruined front wing was rebuilt as a flat block without any divisions, while the rear wings and three internal courtyards retained their original appearance.

It is worth continuing along Strasse des 17 Juni towards the colonnade of the Charlottenburger Tor (or gate), dating from 1908. The colonnade is ornamented with the figures of Friedrich and Sophie Charlotte holding a model of Schloss Charlottenburg *(see pp154–5)* in their hands. Beyond the gate and to the right, on the island, is an unusual green building with a gigantic pink pipe. This is the centre that monitors water currents and caters to the needs of seagoing vessels.

Tauentzienstrasse ®

Map 10 E1. **U** *Wittenbergplatz.* 119, 129, 146, 185.

THIS IS ONE OF THE most important streets for trade and commerce in this part of Berlin. The shops are not as expensive or as elegant as on Kurfürstendamm – but they attract more visitors for this reason. One of the highlights of the street is the unusual façade of the department store Peek & Clopenburg. Designed by Gottfried Böhm, the walls of the building are covered with transparent, gently slanting and undulating "aprons".

Other highlights include the central bed of colourful flowers as well as an interesting sculpture entitled *Berlin.* Created by Brigitte and Martin Matschinsky-Denninghoff, the sculpture was erected near Marburger Strasse in 1987 on the occasion of the 750th anniversary of Berlin.

KaDeWe @

Tauentzienstrasse 21–24. **Map** 10 E2.
U *Wittenbergplatz.* 119, 129, 146, 185.

KAUFHAUS DES Westens, or KaDeWe as it is popularly known, is the second largest department store in Europe, ranking just behind Harrods in London. It was built in 1907 to a design by Emil Schaudt, but it has been extended several times from the original building. From the very beginning KaDeWe was Berlin's most exclusive department store with a comprehensive collection of goods for sale and with a slogan that ran "In our shop a customer is a king, and the King is a customer".

After World War II, KaDeWe effectively became the symbol of the economic success of West Berlin. You can buy everything here, however, the main attraction must be the gourmet's paradise, with the largest collection of foodstuffs in the whole of Europe. Here there are exotic fruits and vegetables, live fish and seafood, 100 varieties of tea, more than 2,400 wines and a host of other gastronomic delights. KaDeWe also has a restaurant, the Wintergarten, for busy shoppers who need a rest.

The sculpture *Berlin*, symbolizing the former divided Berlin

AROUND SCHLOSS CHARLOTTENBURG

THE AREA SURROUNDING Schloss Charlottenburg is one of the most enchanting regions of the city, full of greenery and attractive buildings dating from the end of the 19th century. Originally a small settlement called Lützow, it was only when Elector Friedrich III (later King Friedrich I) built his wife's summer retreat here at the end of the 17th century *(see p19)* that this town attained significance. Initially called Schloss

**Urn at Schloss
Charlottenburg**

Lietzenburg, the palace was renamed Schloss Charlottenburg after the death of Queen Sophie Charlotte. By the 18th century Charlottenburg had become a town, and was for many years an independent administration, inhabited by wealthy people living in elegant villas. It became officially part of Berlin in 1920, and despite World War II and the ensuing division of the city, the central section of this area has kept its historic character.

SIGHTS AT A GLANCE

Museums

Ägyptisches Museum
   und Papyrussammlung **9**
Bröhan-Museum **11**
Galerie der Romantik **3**
Museum für Vor-
   und Frühgeschichte **5**
Sammlung Berggruen **10**

Historic Buildings

Belvedere **8**
Luisenkirche **13**
Mausoleum **7**

Neuer Pavillon
   (Schinkel-Pavillon) **4**
*Schloss Charlottenburg
   pp154–5* **1**
Schlossstrasse Villas **12**

Parks and Gardens

Schlosspark **6**

GETTING THERE

The best routes to the palace are bus 109, 110, 145, X-21 and X-26; U-Bahn 7 to Richard-Wagner-Platz, U-Bahn 2 or 12 to Sophie-Charlotte-Platz or S-Bahn 45 or 46 to Westend station.

Monuments

Reiterdenkmal des Grossen
   Kurfürsten **2**

KEY

▦	Street-by-Street map *pp152–3*
U	U-Bahn station
🚌	Bus terminus
P	Parking

0 metres	600
0 yards	600

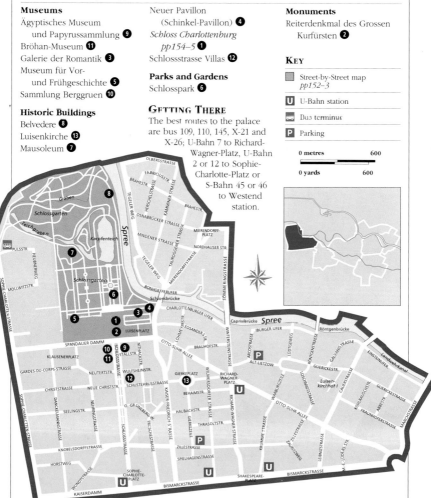

◁ **The façade of Schloss Charlottenburg, originally the summer residence of Elector Friedrich III**

Street-by Street: Around the Schloss

Detail from the main gate

The PARK SURROUNDING the former royal summer residence in Charlottenburg is one of the most picturesque places in Berlin. Visitors are drawn here by the meticulous post-war rebuilding of this luxury Baroque complex and outlying structures, whose marvellous interiors were once home to Prussian nobles. The wings of the palace and its pavilions house interesting exhibitions. After a stroll in the beautiful park, you can take refreshment in the Kleine Orangerie.

★ Schloss Charlottenburg
The central section of the palace is called Nering-Eosanderbau, in honour of the architects who designed the building ❶

Museum für Vor- und Frühgeschichte
The museum is housed in a pavilion which served formerly as the court theatre, designed by Carl Gotthard Langhans ❺

Monument to the Great Elector
The momument to the Great Elector was funded by his son King Friedrich I and designed by Andreas Schlüter ❷

Kleine Orangerie

★ Galerie der Romantik
This gallery of Romantic painting, in the new wing of the palace, houses part of the Nationalgalerie collection (see p78) ❸

KEY

– – – Suggested route

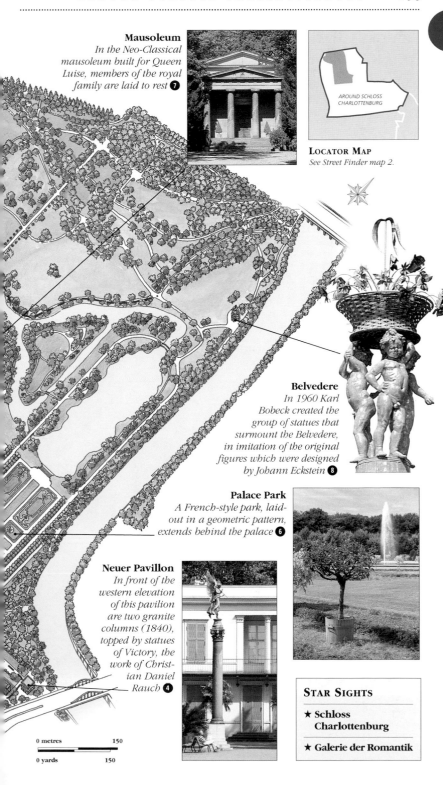

Mausoleum
In the Neo-Classical mausoleum built for Queen Luise, members of the royal family are laid to rest **7**

LOCATOR MAP
See Street Finder map 2.

AROUND SCHLOSS CHARLOTTENBURG

Belvedere
In 1960 Karl Bobeck created the group of statues that surmount the Belvedere, in imitation of the original figures which were designed by Johann Eckstein **8**

Palace Park
A French-style park, laid-out in a geometric pattern, extends behind the palace **6**

Neuer Pavillon
In front of the western elevation of this pavilion are two granite columns (1840), topped by statues of Victory, the work of Christian Daniel Rauch **4**

0 metres   150
0 yards   150

STAR SIGHTS

★ **Schloss Charlottenburg**

★ **Galerie der Romantik**

Schloss Charlottenburg ❶

THE PALACE IN CHARLOTTENBURG was intended as a summer home for Sophie Charlotte, Elector Friedrich III's wife. Construction began in 1695 to a design by Johann Arnold Nering. Between 1701 and 1713 Johann Eosander von Göthe enlarged the palace, crowning it with a cupola and adding the orangery wing. Subsequent extensions were undertaken by Frederick the Great (Friedrich II), who added the east wing, designed by Georg Wenzeslaus von Knobelsdorff, between 1740 and 1746. Restored to its former elegance following World War II, its collection of richly decorated interiors is unequalled in Berlin.

GALLERY GUIDE

The ground floor of the main building must be visited by guided tour. The upper floor and the Neuer Flügel, containing Oriental porcelain and Rococo paintings, can be visited independently.

First floor

Ground floor

★ Porzellankabinett
This exquisite mirrored gallery has walls lined from top to bottom with a fine display of Japanese and Chinese porcelain.

Schlosskapelle
Only the pulpit in the court chapel is original to the palace. All the remaining furniture and fittings, including the splendid royal box, are reconstructions.

Main entrance

Façade
The central section of the palace is the oldest part of the building, and is the work of Johann Arnold Nering.

Cupola
The palace's tall, Baroque cupola completes the perspective from Schlossstrasse.

Fortuna
A new sculpture by Richard Scheibe crowns the palace, replacing the original statue destroyed during World War II.

Eichengalerie
This long gallery, lined with huge oil paintings and decorated with oak-panelling, was completed in 1713.

Weisser Saal

Goldene
Galerie

Neuer Flügel
The new wing holds the elegant apartments and exquisite furniture of Frederick the Great.

Entrance to
Neuer Flügel

★ **Gersaint's Shop Sign** (1720)
An avid collector of French painting, Frederick the Great bought this and seven other fine canvases by Antoine Watteau for his collection.

VISITORS' CHECKLIST

Spandauer Damm. **Map** 2 E2.
Altes Schloss (Nering-Eosander-bau) 32 09 12 75.
Richard-Wagner-Platz & Sophie-Charlotte-Platz, Ⓢ *Westend.*
109, 110, 145, X-26. 9am–5pm Tue–Thu, 9am–7pm Fri, 10am–6pm Sat & Sun.
compulsory on ground floor only.
Neuer Flügel (Knobels-dorff-Flügel) 32 09 12 02.
10am–6pm Mon–Fri, 11am–6pm Sat & Sun.

KEY

☐	Official reception rooms
☐	Apartments of Sophie-Charlotte
☐	Neuer Flügel or Knobelsdorff-Flügel exhibition space
☐	Friedrich Wilhelm II's summer apartments
☐	Mecklenburg apartments
☐	Apartments of Friedrich Wilhelm IV
☐	Friedrich Wilhelm II's winter apartments
☐	Frederick the Great's apartments

STAR SIGHTS

★ **Porzellankabinett**

★ **Gersaint's Shop Sign**

CD Friedrich's *Moonrise over the Sea,* Galerie der Romantik

Reiterdenkmal des Grossen Kurfürsten ❷

MONUMENT TO THE GREAT ELECTOR

Spandauer Damm. **Map** 2 E2.
Ⓤ *Richard-Wagner-Platz &
Sophie-Charlotte-Platz.* Ⓢ *Westend.*
🚌 *109, 110, 145, X-26.*

THE STATUE OF THE Great Elector (Friedrich Wilhelm) is the finest in Berlin and was paid for by his son, Elector Friedrich III (later King Friedrich I). Designed by Andreas Schlüter to be cast in one piece, the statue was started in 1696 but not finished until 1703. It was initially erected near the former Berlin palace, by Lange Brücke (now called Rathausbrücke). The statue was moved to safety during World War II but ironically, on the return journey, the barge transporting the monument sank in the port of Tegel.

In 1949 the statue was retrieved intact from the water and erected in the courtyard of Schloss Charlottenburg. However, it lacked the original base which was left behind in East Berlin, so a copy was commissioned. The original base finally ended up in the Bodemuseum topped with a replica of the statue.

The statue portrays the Great Elector as a warrior in ancient armour (albeit wearing a 17th century wig) mounted on horseback, triumphant over the figures of prisoners of war around the base. The base itself is decorated with patriotic reliefs of allegorical scenes. One scene depicts the kingdom surrounded by figures representing History, Peace and the Spree river; another shows the kingdom protected by embodiments of Faith, Bravery (in the form of Mucius Scaevola) and Strength (represented by Hercules).

Galerie der Romantik ❸

GALLERY OF ROMANTICISM

Spandauer Damm (Schloss Charlottenburg–Neuer Flügel). **Map** 2 E2.
📞 *20 90 55 55.* Ⓤ *Richard-Wagner-Platz & Sophie-Charlotte-Platz.*
Ⓢ *Westend.* 🚌 *109, 110, 145, X-26.* ⭘ *10am–6pm Tue–Fri, 11am–6pm Sat & Sun.* 📷

BUILT BETWEEN 1740 and 1746, the new wing of Schloss Charlottenburg houses a gallery of Romantic paintings that form part of the Nationalgalerie's collection. The gallery on the ground floor has several of Caspar David Friedrich's landscapes, such as *Chalk Cliffs of Rügen.* You can also admire the paintings of Karl Friedrich Schinkel, who was not only a great architect but also a fine painter of fabulous architectural fantasies. There are paintings by Philip Otto Runge and Friedrich Overbeck, as well as some fairy-tale tableaux by Moritz von Schwind. A large collection of views of Berlin, dating from the start of the 19th century, shows how public perceptions of the city have changed over the years.

This superb collection will probably be relocated to the Alte Nationalgalerie once refurbishment is completed in 2001.

Neuer Pavillon (Schinkel-Pavillon) ❹

Spandauer Damm (Schlosspark Charlottenburg). **Map** 2 F2.
📞 *32 09 12 12.* Ⓤ *Richard-Wagner-Platz & Sophie-Charlotte-Platz.*
Ⓢ *Westend.* 🚌 *109, 110, 145, X-21, X-26.* ⭘ *Apr–Oct: 10am–5pm Tue–Fri; Nov–Mar: 9am–5pm Tue–Fri, 10am–5pm Sat & Sun.* 📷

THIS CHARMING Neo-Classical pavilion was built for Friedrich Wilhelm III and his second wife, Princess Auguste von Liegnitz. During a visit to Naples, the king stayed in the Villa Reale del Chiamonte and was so impressed that he commissioned Karl Friedrich Schinkel to build him something similar. The pavilion was completed for the king's birthday on 3 August 1825.

The Neuer Pavillon which was modelled on a Neapolitan villa

Schinkel designed a two-storey structure with a central staircase and ranged the rooms around it in perfect symmetry. Pillared galleries, on the first floor, added variety to the eastern and western elevations. A cast iron balcony runs around the entire structure.

The display inside the pavilion reveals the original splendour and atmosphere of the aristocratic interiors, enhanced with pictures and sculptures of the period. The prize picture is a renowned panorama of Berlin dated 1834, painted by Eduard Gärtner from the roof of the Friedrichswerdersche Kirche *(see p63).*

Urn (c.800 BC) from the Museum für Vor- und Frühgeschichte

Museum für Vor- und Frühgeschichte ❺

MUSEUM OF PRE- AND EARLY HISTORY

Spandauer Damm (Schloss Charlottenburg–Theater). **Map** 2 E2. **C** *32 09 11.* **U** *Richard-Wagner-Platz & Sophie-Charlotte-Platz.* **S** *Westend.* 🚌 *109, 110, 145, X 21.* ◻ *10am–6pm Tue–Fri, 11am–6pm Sat & Sun.* 🖼 🔓

O RIGINALLY USED as the court theatre, this Neo-Classical pavilion was designed by Carl Gotthard Langhans and added to the orangery wing of Schloss Charlottenburg between 1787 and 1791. It now holds a museum that documents the development of early cultures and civilizations. The evolution of mankind from prehistoric times, through the Stone Age, Bronze Age, and Iron Age up to medieval times is portrayed by means of dioramas, skulls (real and imitation) and a large display of pottery, tools, weapons and artifacts. A similar wealth of archaeological finds charts the growth of Celtic, Germanic, Slavic, Baltic and even Sumerian civilizations.

The museum's best display is a magnificent collection from the ancient city of Troy, donated in 1881 by Heinrich Schliemann. The collection contains an array of tools and pottery on the second floor, and a spectacular collection of gold jewellery known as "The Treasure of Priam". Some of the exhibits are replicas, the originals having disappeared after World War II. Many originals, however, are now in the Pushkin Museum, Moscow.

Schlosspark ❻

PALACE PARK

Spandauer Damm (Schloss Charlottenburg). **Map** 2 D1. **U** *Richard-Wagner-Platz & Sophie-Charlotte-Platz.* **S** *Westend.* 🚌 *109, 110, 145, X-21, X-26.*

T HIS EXTENSIVE royal park surrounding Schloss Charlottenburg *(see pp154–5),* criss-crossed with tidy gravel paths, is a favourite place for Berliners to stroll. The park is largely the result of reconstruction work carried out after World War II, when 18th-century prints were used to help reconstruct the varied layout of the original grounds. Immediately behind Schloss Charlottenburg is a French-style Baroque garden, made to a strict geometrical design with a vibrant patchwork of flower beds, carefully trimmed shrubs and ornate fountains adorned with replicas of antique sculptures. Further away from the palace, beyond the curved carp lake, is a less formal English-style landscaped park, the original layout of which was created between 1819 and 1828 under the direction of the renowned royal gardener, Peter Joseph Lenné.

Mausoleum ❼

Spandauer Damm (Schlosspark Charlottenburg) **Map** 2 D2. **C** *32 09 12 80.* **U** *Richard-Wagner-Platz & Sophie-Charlotte-Platz.* **S** *Westend.* 🚌 *109, 110, 145, X-26.* ◻ *Apr–Oct: 10am–5pm Tue–Fri.* 🖼

Q UEEN LUISE, the beloved wife of Friedrich Wilhelm III, was laid to rest in this dignified, modest building, set among the trees in Schlosspark. The mausoleum was designed by Karl Friedrich Schinkel, in the style of a Doric portico-fronted temple.

In the original design, the queen's sarcophagus was housed in the crypt while the tombstone (actually a cenotaph sculpted by Christian Daniel Rauch) stood in the centre of the mausoleum. After the death of Friedrich Wilhelm in 1840, the mausoleum was refurbished; an apse added and the queen's tomb moved to one side, leaving room for her husband's tomb, also designed by Rauch. The second wife of the king, Princess Auguste von Liegnitz, was also buried in the crypt of the mausoleum, but without a tombstone.

Between the years 1890 and 1894, the tombs of Kaiser Wilhelm I and his wife, Auguste von Sachsen-Weimar, were added to the crypt. Both monuments are the work of Erdmann Encke.

French-style garden in the Schloss Charlottenburg park

The Belvedere's Baroque flourishes and clean Neo-Classical lines

Belvedere ❽

Spandauer Damm (Schlosspark
Charlottenburg). **Map** 2 E1.
C 32 09 12 85. **U** Richard-Wagner-
Platz & Sophie-Charlotte-Platz.
S Westend. 109, 110, 145, X-26.
☐ Apr–Oct: 10am–5pm Tue–Sun;
Nov–Mar: noon–4pm Tue–Fri, noon–
5pm Sat & Sun.

THE BELVEDERE IS a summer-
house in the Schlosspark
which served as a tea pavilion
for Friedrich Wilhelm II and,
in times of war, as a watchtower. It dates from 1788 and
was designed by Carl Gotthard
Langhans. The architect mixed
Baroque and Neo-Classical
elements, giving the building
an oval central structure with
four straight-sided annexes.
The building is crowned by
a low dome topped with a
sculpture of three cherubs
dragging a basket of flowers.
Ruined during World War II,
the summer-house was reconstructed between 1956 and
1960 and adapted to serve as
exhibition space. The exhibition is a large collection of
porcelain from the Berlin Königliche Porzellan-Manufaktur
(Royal Porcelain Workshop),
which has pieces from the
Rococo period up to late
Biedermeier, including some
outstanding individual items.

Ägyptisches Museum ❾

EGYPTIAN MUSEUM

Schlossstrasse 70. **Map** 2 E3.
C 32 09 12 61. **U** Richard-Wagner-
Platz & Sophie-Charlotte-Platz.
S Westend. 109, 110, 145, X-
26. **☐** 10am–6pm Tue–Fri,
11am–6pm Sat & Sun.

THE TWO PAVILIONS on either
side of Schlossstrasse were
intended as officers' barracks
for the Kings's Garde du Corps.
Built between the years 1851
and 1859 by Friedrich August
Stüler, they were inspired by
a design by King Friedrich
Wilhelm IV. The eastern
pavilion joins the stable
block and now houses
the collection of the
Egyptian Museum.
Numerous sculptures,
sarcophagi, murals and
architectural fragments
of various eras are on
display, including the
Berlin Green Head, a
4th century BC head
carved from green
stone. The greatest
attraction, however,
is the fascinating
collection from
the 19th century
archaeological
digs by Richard

Lepsius and Ludwig Borchardt
in Tell el-Amarna. This was
the capital of Egypt during
the era of the reign of Amen-
hotep IV, a Pharaoh in the
14th century BC, also called
Akhenaten. He revolutionized
Egyptian religion, introducing
the cult of the god Aton, and
also brought about a radical
change in the basic principles
of representative arts. In a
break from previous traditions
he and his wife, Nefertiti, are
depicted with broad hips and
swollen stomachs. While the
Pharaoh is plainly depicted,
the queen's face is beautiful,
as can be seen from the other
representations in the museum.
The most renowned is the
delicate, long-necked *Nefertiti
Bust*, carved from limestone
and carefully painted. This
delightful exhibit was
discovered in 1912 in the
workshop of the ancient
Egyptian sculptor Thutmosis.

Sammlung Berggruen ❿

Schlossstrasse 1. **Map** 2 E3.
C 32 69 58 11. **U** Richard-Wagner-
Platz & Sophie-Charlotte-Platz.
S Westend. 109, 110, 145,
X-21, X-26. **☐** 10am–6pm Tue–Fri,
11am–6pm Sat & Sun. (free first
Sun of the month).

HEINZ BERGGRUEN assembled
this tasteful collection of
art dating from the late 19th
and first half of the 20th century. Born and educated in
Berlin, he emigrated to the US
in 1936, spent most of his
life in Paris, but finally
entrusted his collection
to the city of his birth.
The museum opened
in 1996, in what was
once the west pavilion
of the barracks using
space freed up by
moving the Antiken-
sammlung to Museum
Island (see p75). The
exhibition halls were
modified according to
the designs of Hilmer
and Sattler, who also
designed the layout of
the Gemäldegalerie.

**Figure from Ägyptisches
Museum (c. 660 BC)**

Pablo Picasso's *Woman in a Hat* (1939), Sammlung Berggruen

The Sammlung Berggruen is particularly well-known for its large collection of quality paintings, drawings and gouaches by Pablo Picasso. In addition to these, the museum displays more than 20 works by Paul Klee and paintings by other major artists Van Gogh, Braque and Cézanne. The exhibition is supplemented by some excellent sculptures, particularly those of Henri Laurens and Alberto Giacometti.

THE GREAT ELECTOR (1620–88)

The Elector Friedrich Wilhelm was one of the most famous rulers of the Hohenzollern dynasty. He inherited the position of Elector of Brandenburg in 1640. Brandenburg-Prussia, founded in 1618, was subject to the Polish crown. One of his first duties was to rebuild the region after the devastation of the 30 Years' War (see p19) and in 1660 he wrested the territory from Poland. During the course of his reign, Berlin became a powerful city. Rich families from all over Europe, fleeing persecution in their own land, chose to settle in Berlin – wealthy Dutch merchants, Huguenots from France and Jews from Vienna following the Edict of Potsdam (1685).

Each of the main halls features an individual artist, but often using an array of artistic media. There is also a display of furniture by Hector Guimard, Eugène Gaillard, Henry van de Velde and Joseph Hoffmann, glasswork by Emile Gallé, and porcelain from the best European manufacturers.

If you continue the walk down the nearby Schustehrusstrasse, there is an interesting school building at No. 39–43 linked to the Villa Oppenheim since the end of the 19th century. In the same area another school building on Nithackstrasse has survived. Built between 1913 and 1914, its sides are covered in pretty terracotta decorations.

Bröhan-Museum ⓫

Schlossstrasse 1a. **Map** 2 E3.
⬛ 321 40 29. Ⓤ Richard-Wagner-Platz & Sophie-Charlotte-Platz.
Ⓢ Westend. 🚌 109, 110, 145, X-26. 🕙 10am–6pm Tue–Sun.
⬛ 24 & 31 Dec. 🖾

LOCATED IN a late-Neo-Classical building which, like the Sammlung Berggruen, was formerly used as army barracks, is a small but interesting museum. The collection of decorative arts was amassed by Karl H Bröhan, who from 1966 collected works of art from the Art Nouveau (Jugendstil or Secessionist) and Art Deco styles. The paintings of the artists particularly connected with the Berlin Secessionist movement, such as Karl Hagermeister and Hans Baluschek, are especially well represented. Alongside the paintings there are fine examples of other media and crafts: furniture, ceramics, glassware, silverwork and textiles.

Art Deco vase, Brohan-Museum

Schlossstrasse Villas ⓬

Schlossstrasse 65–67. **Map** 2 E3.
Ⓤ Sophie-Charlotte-Platz. 🚌 109.

MOST OF THE historic villas and buildings that once graced Schlossstrasse no longer exist. However, careful restoration of a few villas enables the visitor to get a feel for what the atmosphere must have been like at the end of the 19th century. It is worth taking a stroll down Schlossstrasse to look at three of the renovated villas — No. 65, No. 66 and especially No. 67. The latter villa was built in 1873, in a Neo-Classical style to a design by G Töbelmann. After World War II, the building was refurbished to return it to its former splendour. The front garden, however, a characteristic of the area, was only returned to its original state in 1986, when several villas had their gardens restored.

Luisenkirche ⓭

LUISE CHURCH

Gierkeplatz. **Map** 2 F3. Ⓤ Richard-Wagner-Platz & Sophie-Charlotte-Platz. 🚌 109, 110, 145, X-26.

THIS SMALL, MODEST church has undergone a series of re-designs and refurbishments in its lifetime. The original plans by Philipp Gerlach were first adapted by Martin Böhme, before the church was built between the years 1713 and 1716. Its Baroque styling was removed in the next course of rebuilding, undertaken by Karl Friedrich Schinkel from 1823 to 1826, when the church was renamed in memory of Queen Luise, who died in 1810. The church underwent its most recent major refurbishment after suffering major damage during World War II.

The shape of the church is based on a traditional Greek cross, with a tower at the front. The interior fixtures and fittings are not the originals, and the elegant stained-glass windows were only made in 1956.

FURTHER AFIELD

Coat of Arms on the Oberbaumbrücke

BERLIN IS AN EXTENSIVE city with a totally unique character, shaped by its history. Up until 1920 the actual city of Berlin consisted only of the districts which now comprise mainly Mitte, Tiergarten, Wedding, Prenzlauer Berg, Friedrichshain and Kreuzberg. It was surrounded by satellite towns and villages, which for many years had been evolving independently. Each of these had its own administrative centre, parish church, and individual architecture.

In 1920, as part of great administrative reforms, seven towns were incorporated into Berlin, along with 59 communes, and 27 country estates. This reform effected the creation of an entirely new city occupying around 900 sq km (348 sq miles), with a population that had expanded to 3.8 million.

In this way the range of the metropolis extended to small towns with medieval origins, such as Spandau.

Private estates and palaces, such as Britz and Neuschönhausen, were absorbed into Berlin. So were many old villages, such as Marienfelde with its 13th century parish church. Suburban housing developments full of luxury villas were also incorporated.

Over the last hundred years the faces of many of these places have changed. Modern housing developments have arisen together with industrial centres, although the character of individual areas has remained intact. Thanks to this diversity, a stay in Berlin is like visiting many cities simultaneously. A short journey by S-Bahn enables you to travel from a metropolitan city centre of the 21st century to the vast forests of the Grunewald or the beach at Wannsee. You can explore everything from Dahlem's tranquil streets lined with villas to Spandau with its Renaissance citadel and vast Gothic church of St Nicholas.

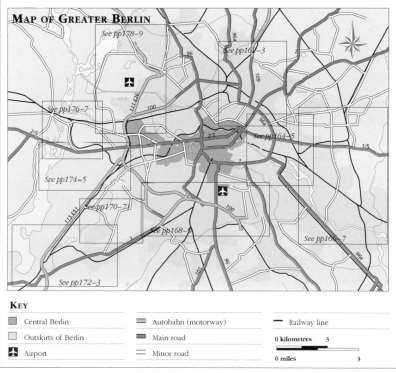

MAP OF GREATER BERLIN

See pp178–9

See pp162–3

See pp176–7

See pp164–5

See pp174–5

See pp170–71

See pp168–9

See pp166–7

See pp172–3

KEY

▨ Central Berlin	═ Autobahn (motorway)	▬ Railway line
☐ Outskirts of Berlin	═ Main road	0 kilometres 3
✈ Airport	═ Minor road	0 miles 3

◁ **The Funkturm or radio tower in Berlin's western outskirts, illuminated at night** (*see p175*)

Northeast Berlin

IN THE NORTHEAST of Berlin, but still within the Mitte district, a fragment of the Berlin Wall has survived; this has been earmarked as a place of remembrance. Further east extends Prenzlauer Berg, which is currently the most fashionable area for alternative youth culture. In the southern part of Pankow is the Baroque palace of Niederschönhausen. From here it is also worth setting off to see the Weissensee district, which has one of the largest Jewish cemeteries in Europe.

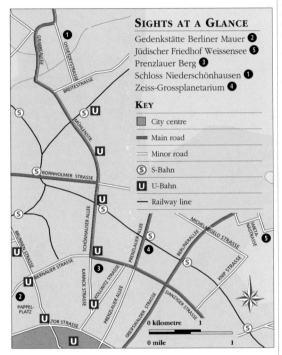

SIGHTS AT A GLANCE

Gedenkstätte Berliner Mauer ❷
Jüdischer Friedhof Weissensee ❺
Prenzlauer Berg ❸
Schloss Niederschönhausen ❶
Zeiss-Grossplanetarium ❹

KEY

▨	City centre
▬	Main road
—	Minor road
Ⓢ	S-Bahn
Ⓤ	U-Bahn
—	Railway line

0 kilometre   1
0 mile   1

Schloss Nieder-schönhausen ❶

Ossietzkystrasse 〖 47 47 38 55.
Ⓢ Pankow. 🚇 52. 🚌 107, 150, 250. **Schloss** ⏰ noon–5pm Sat, Sun & holidays. 🎟 noon, 2pm, & 4pm. **Park** ⏰ 8am–7pm daily. 🅿

THIS PALACE, located in an extensive and picturesque park, belonged to the von Dohna family during the 17th century. Ownership of the estate passed to the Elector Friedrich III in 1691, for whom Johann Arnold Nering designed the palace. In 1704 it was extended to a design by Johann Friedrich Eosander von Göthe, who added side wings. The palace was home

to Queen Christine, estranged wife of Frederick the Great, between 1740 and 1797. In 1763 further extensive refurbishment was undertaken by architect Johann Boumann.

A section of the garden elevation of Schloss Niederschönhausen

The property remained in the hands of the Prussian royal family for the next hundred years. Among those who resided here were Princess Augusta of Liegnitz, following the death of her husband, King Friedrich Wilhelm III.

After World War II the rebuilt palace was occupied by the president of the German Democratic Republic, Wilhelm Pieck. In 1990 Round Table discussions were held here and the treaty to reunify Germany was signed here.

It is worth strolling through the vast park, which has kept its character bestowed by Peter Joseph Lenné in the 1820s.

Gedenkstätte Berliner Mauer ❷

Bernauer Strasse 111. 〖 46 41 03.
Ⓢ Nordbahnhof. Ⓤ Bernauer Strasse. 🚌 120, 328.

ON THE NIGHT OF 12 and 13 August 1961 the East German authorities decided to close the border around the western sectors of Berlin (die Mauer) consisted of rolls of barbed wire, which were soon replaced by a 4-m (13-ft) wall safeguarded by a second wall made from reinforced concrete. This was topped with a thick pipe to prevent people from reaching the top of the Wall with their fingers.

Along the Wall ran a "death zone", controlled by guards with dogs. Where the border passed close to houses, the inhabitants were relocated while windows onto the "western" street were bricked up. Along the border with West Berlin there were 293 watch towers and 57 bunkers. Later, there were alarms, too.

On 9 November 1989, with the help of Soviet leader Gorbachev, the Wall was finally breached. Dismantling it took much longer, however, with more than a million tons of rubble to be removed.

Only small fragments of the Wall have survived. One of these, along Bernauer Strasse between Acker- and Berg-strasse, is now an official place of remembrance.

Prenzlauer Berg ❸

Map 8 D1, E1. **Sammlung Industrielle Gestaltung** Knaackstrasse 97.
◖ *443 93 82.* **Ⓢ** *Senefelderplatz or
Eberswalderstrasse.* **◯** *2–9pm
Tue–Sun.* **Museum Berliner Arbeiterleben** Husemannstrasse 12. **◖** *442
25 14.* **◯** *10am–3pm Mon–Thu.*

TOWARD THE END of the 19th
century this was one of the
most impoverished, densely
populated districts of Berlin.
Although it was not damaged
during World War II, it was
very badly neglected by the
East German authorites, and
became a centre for anti-
Communist opposition.

After 1989 it took over the
role once played by Kreuzberg.
Artists, journalists and students
began to gather here from all
parts of Berlin, creating a
colourful, vibrant community.
This is clear to see at night
when various bars, restaurants
and cafés begin to fill up.

On Senefelderplatz is a monument to Alois Sencfelder,
who invented the process
of producing lithographs.
Schönhauser Allee, which
cuts through this square, is
the main thoroughfare of
Prenzlauer Berg. The vast Neo-
Gothic brick building at the
junction with Sredzkistrasse is
the former Schultheiss brewery,
built by Franz Schwechten
between 1889 and 1892. Now
known as KulturBrauerei, it
houses a cultural centre. In one
of the buildings is the headquarters of a department of the
city museum – **Sammlung
Industrielle Gestaltung** –
with a collection of industrial
designs from East Germany.

Heading along Sredzkistrasse
you reach Husemannstrasse,
the only street to be restored
prior to reunification. It now
features popular restaurants.
At No. 12 is the **Museum
Berliner Arbeiterleben** – a
museum with interiors that
typify a worker's *fin-de-siècle*
house. Husemannstrasse leads
to Kollwitzplatz. The monument to the artist in the middle
of the square is by Gustav
Seitz. Nearby at Rykestrasse
No. 53 is one of the few
synagogues to have survived.
Dating from 1903–4, it was
designed by Johann Hoeniger.

Buildings on Hagenauer Strasse, Prenzlauer Berg

Amid the greenery around
Belforter Strasse is a water
tower built during the mid-
19th century. Nearby, on
Schönhauser Allee, an old
Jewish cemetery dating from
1827 has survived, with many
gravestones. Among those
buried here is the renowned
painter Max Liebermann.

Zeiss-Gross-
planetarium ❹

Prenzlauer Allee 80 (Ernst-Thalmann-
Park) **◖** *42 18 45 12.* **Ⓢ** *Prenzlauer
Allee, then* **▦** *1.* **◯** *10am–noon
Mon–Fri, 1:30–9pm Wed & Sat,
6–10pm Thu & Fri, 1:30–6pm Sun.* **◪**

THE SILVERY DOME visible from
afar is the huge planetarium, built in the grounds of a
park dedicated to the inter-war
communist leader Ernst Thäl-
mann, who died at Buchen-
wald concentration camp.
The foyer of the planetarium
houses an exhibition of optical
equipment and accessories
produced by the renowned
factory of Carl-Zeiss-Jena.

Jüdischer Friedhof
Weissensee ❺

Herbert-Baum-Strasse 45. **Ⓢ** *Greifswalder Strasse, then* **▦** *2, 3, 4, 13,
23, 24.*

THIS EXTENSIVE Jewish cemetery is the final resting
place for more than 115,000
Berliners, many of whom were
victims of Nazi persecution.
The cemetery was established
in 1880 according to a design
created by Hugo Licht.

By the main entrance is a
place of remembrance for the
victims of the Holocaust, with
plaques bearing the names
of the concentration camps.
Buried here are renowned
figures from Berlin's Jewish
cultural and commercial past.
Among others here rest the
publisher Samuel Fischer and
the restaurateur Berthold
Kempinski. Some tombstones
are outstanding works of art,
such as that of the Panowsky
family designed by Ludwig
Hoffman, or the Cubist
tombstone of Albert Mendel,
designed by Walter Gropius.

Silvery dome of the Zeiss-Grossplanetarium

Friedrichshain and Treptow

BOTH THESE DISTRICTS are situated to the southeast of Mitte and provide excellent opportunities for walks amid some spectacular remnants of Berlin's most recent history. Visitors can see the official face of the German Democratic Republic, as shown in the Socialist Realist architecture of Karl-Marx-Allee, and the Soviet ideals of nationalism in the huge monument to the Red Army in Treptower Park. A sharp contrast is provided by stark reminders of a less glorious past – the Berlin Wall, East Side Gallery and the grim watchtower on the border.

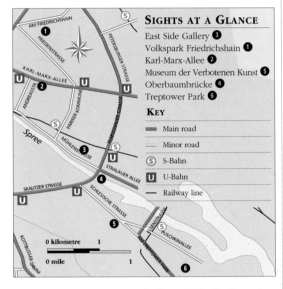

SIGHTS AT A GLANCE

East Side Gallery **❸**
Volkspark Friedrichshain **❶**
Karl-Marx-Allee **❷**
Museum der Verbotenen Kunst **❺**
Oberbaumbrücke **❹**
Treptower Park **❻**

KEY

▬▬	Main road
▬	Minor road
Ⓢ	S-Bahn
Ⓤ	U-Bahn
▬	Railway line

0 kilometre 1
0 mile 1

The park has undergone frequent re-designs in its history including, during World War II, the construction of two large bunkers. After the war, the site was covered with a mound of earth.

Between the years 1969 and 1973 a sports and games area was established in the park, although there is still plenty of room for leisurely strolls.

Fragment of Socialist Realist decoration from Karl-Marx-Allee

Karl-Marx-Allee **❷**

Map 8 F3. **Ⓤ** *Strausberger Platz or Weberwiese.*

THE SECTION OF Karl-Marx-Allee between Strausberger Platz and Frankfurter Tor is effectively a huge open-air museum of Socialist Realist architecture. The route to the the east, leading on to Poland and Moscow, was named Stalinallee in 1949 and chosen as the site for the construction showpiece of the new German Democratic Republic. The avenue was widened to 90 m (300 ft) and in the course of the next ten years, huge residential tower blocks and a row of shops were built on it. The designers, led by Hermann Henselmann, succeeded in combining three sets of architectural guidelines. They used the style known in the Soviet Union as "pastry chef" according to the precept: "nationalistic in form but socialist in content", and linked the whole work to Berlin's own traditions. Hence there are motifs taken from famous Berlin architects Schinkel and Gontard, as well as from the renowned Meissen porcelain.

The buildings on this street, renamed Karl-Marx-Allee in 1961, are now considered historic monuments. The buildings have been cleaned up and the crumbling details are gradually being restored.

Volkspark Friedrichshain **❶**

Am Friedrichshain/Friedenstrasse.
Map 8 F1. 🚌 *100, 142, 257.*

THIS EXTENSIVE PARK complex of Friedrichshain, with its picturesque nooks and crannies, was one of Berlin's first public parks. It was laid out in the 1840s on the basis of a design by Peter Joseph Lenné, with the idea of creating an alternative Tiergarten for the inhabitants of the eastern districts of the city.

The greatest attraction of the park is the Fountain of Fairy Tales – Märchenbrunnen by Ludwig Hoffmann, built from 1902 until 1913. It is a spectacular feature, in a Neo-Baroque style with fountain pools made from Tivoli stone, decorated with small statues of turtles and

other animals. The fountain is surrounded by well-known characters from the fairy tales by the Brothers Grimm.

Neo-Baroque Märchenbrunnen in Volkspark Friedrichshain

East Side Gallery ❸

Mühlenstrasse. Ⓢ & Ⓤ *Warschauer Strasse.* Ⓢ *Hauptbahnhof.* 🚌 *147.*

SINCE 1990, this 1300-m (one mile) section of the Berlin Wall, running along Mühlenstrasse between Hauptbahnhof and Oberbaumbrücke, has been known as the East Side Gallery. A huge collection of graffiti is on display here, comprising the work of 118 different artists from 21 countries. This expansive display was organized by the Scottish artist Chris MacLean.

Oberbaumbrücke ❹

Ⓢ & Ⓤ *Warschauer Strasse* Ⓤ *Schlesisches Tor.* 🚌 *147.*

THIS PRETTY BRIDGE crossing the Spree river was built from 1894 to 1896 to a design by Otto Stahn. It is actually made from reinforced concrete, but the arches are covered with red brick. The most decorative element of the bridge is a Neo-Gothic arcade which supports a line of the U-Bahn. The central arch of the bridge is marked by a pair of crenellated Neo-Gothic towers.

The bridge was not open to traffic for 12 or so years prior to reunification, as it linked districts from opposing sides of the Berlin Wall. Only pedestrians with the relevant documents were able to use this bridge. After reunification and renovation, it was returned to full working order.

The picturesque Neo-Gothic archway of Oberbaumbrücke

Museum der Verbotenen Kunst ❺

MUSEUM OF FORBIDDEN ARTS

Im Schlesischen Busch (Puschkinallee/ Schlesische Strasse) ☎ 204 20 49. Ⓤ *Schlesisches Tor.* Ⓢ *Treptower Park.* 🚌 *265.* 🕐 *noon–6pm Sat, Sun & holidays.*

IN A NEGLECTED PARK near the former Berlin Wall stands the last remaining watchtower in the border control system that divided East and West Berlin. The ground floor has been converted into a small museum featuring artists whose work was outlawed by the German Democratic Republic.

The upper floor has been preserved as it was when the building was used by border guards to monitor the various control points along the Wall.

Museum der Verbotenen Kunst in the last remaining watchtower

Treptower Park ❻

Archenhold-Sternwarte. Ⓢ *Treptower Park.* 🚌 *166, 167, 177, 265.* **Archenhold Sternwarte** 🕐 *2–6:30pm Wed–Sun.* 🎦 *8pm Thu, 3pm Sat & Sun.*

THE VAST PARK in Treptower was laid out in the 1860s on the initiative and design of Johann Gustav Meyer. In 1919 it was where revolutionaries Karl Liebknecht, Wilhelm Pieck and Rosa Luxemburg assembled 150,000 striking workers.

The park, however, is best known for the colossal monument to the Red Army. Built between 1946 and 1949, it stands on the grave of 5,000

Gigantic wreath commemorating the Red Army in Treptower Park

Soviet soldiers killed in the battle for Berlin in 1945. The gateway is marked by a vast granite sculpture of a grieving Russian Motherland surrounded by statues of Red Army soldiers. This leads to the mausoleum, topped by an 11-m (35-ft) high figure of a soldier rescuing a child and resting his mighty sword on a smashed swastika. The whole scheme was the work of architect Jakow Biełopolski and sculptor Jewgien Wuczeticz.

In the farthest section of the park it is worth going to see the astronomical observatory, **Archenhold Sternwarte**, built for a decorative arts exhibition held here in 1896. Given a permanent site here in 1909, the observatory was used by Albert Einstein for a lecture on the Theory of Relativity in 1915. It is also home to the longest reflecting telescope in the world (21-m or 70-ft), and a small planetarium.

Beyond Treptower Park lies another park, Plänterwald, while the Spree river provides an ideal place for a riverside stroll or maybe a trip on one of the rowing or pedal boats.

At the beginning of the 19th century, Berliners flocked to the banks of the Spree to enjoy themselves at the weekend. However, from the many dance halls and restaurants, only one historic building has remained – Eierschale-Zenner. This can trace its history back as far as the 17th century.

The small Insel der Jugend can be reached via the Abteibrücke, an ornamental bridge built by French prisoners of war in 1916. The island was once home to an abbey, but it now houses a fashionable arts complex and nightclub.

Southeast Berlin

AN EXPEDITION to Berlin's furthest corners, Lichtenberg and Hohenschönhausen, provides an occasion to visit shocking museums documenting the work of the German Democratic Republic's security services (Stasi). However, you can just as easily stroll through the zoological garden in the park at the Baroque Schloss Friedrichsfelde or enjoy a leisurely break in Köpenick, which has retained the atmosphere of a small town.

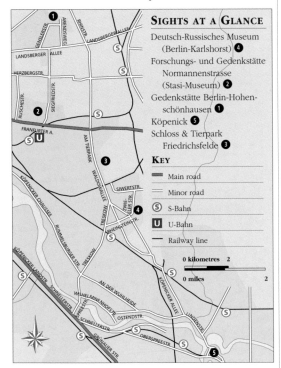

SIGHTS AT A GLANCE

Deutsch-Russisches Museum
  (Berlin-Karlshorst) ❹
Forschungs- und Gedenkstätte
  Normannenstrasse
  (Stasi-Museum) ❷
Gedenkstätte Berlin-Hohen-
  schönhausen ❶
Köpenick ❺
Schloss & Tierpark
  Friedrichsfelde ❸

KEY

▬▬ Main road

══ Minor road

Ⓢ S-Bahn

Ⓤ U-Bahn

▬ Railway line

0 kilometres   2

0 miles   2

Gedenkstätte Berlin-Hohen-schönhausen ❶

Genslerstrasse 66. [982 42 19.
Ⓢ Landsberger Allee, then [5, 6, 7, 15, 17. [256. [1pm Mon–Thu, 11am & 1pm Fri–Sat. [

THIS MUSEUM was established in 1995 within the former custody building of the Stasi – the dreaded security service of the GDR. The custody building was part of a huge complex built in 1938. In May 1945 the occupying Russian authorities created a special transit camp here, in which they interned war criminals who were subsequently

transported to Siberia. Shortly thereafter they started to bring anyone under political suspicion to the camp. During this time more than 20,000 people passed through here.

From 1946 this group of buildings was refashioned into the custody area for the KGB (Soviet Secret Service), and in 1951 it was given over for the use of the Stasi.

During a visit to the complex you can see prisoners' cells and interrogation rooms, two of which have no windows and are lined with rubber. Housed in the cellars was the "submarine" – a series of cells without daylight to which the most "dangerous" suspects were brought.

Forschungs- und Gedenkstätte Normannenstrasse (Stasi-Museum) ❷

Ruschestrasse 103 (Haus 1).
[553 68 54. Ⓤ Magdalenenstrasse.
[11am–6pm Tue–Fri, 2–6pm Sat–Sun. [

UNDER THE GERMAN Democratic Republic, this huge complex of buildings at Ruschestrasse housed the Ministry of the Interior. It was here that the infamous Stasi (GDR secret service) had its headquarters. The Stasi's "achievements" in infiltrating its own community were without equal in the Eastern block.

Since 1990 one of the buildings has housed a museum that displays photographs and documents depicting the activities of the Stasi. You can see a model of the headquarters, and equipment used for bugging and spying on citizens suspected of holding an unfavourable view of the political regime. You can also walk around the office of infamous Stasi chief Erich Mielke. A "big-brother"-like figure, Mielke's legacy of suffering still lives on in the memory of millions of German citizens.

Stasi chief Erich Mielke's office at the Stasi Museum

Schloss & Tierpark Friedrichsfelde ❸

Am Tierpark 125. Ⓤ Tierpark. [194, 296. **Schloss** [513 81 41. [10am–6pm (9am–4pm in winter) Tue–Fri, 10am–4pm Sat–Sun. **Tierpark** [51 53 10. [9am–7pm (until dusk in winter) daily. [

THIS CHARMING Baroque palace was built for the Dutchman Benjamin von Raule around 1695, to a

The façade of Schloss Friedrichsfelde

design by Johann Arnold Nering. Under successive owners, it underwent extensive renovations. In 1719 it was redesigned by Martin Heinrich Böhme. The second renovation, designed by Peter Biron in 1786, gave this residence its current appearance.

The well-balanced structure, typical of the style during the transition from Baroque to Neo-Classical, was extensively restored in the 1970s. It now houses a museum of interiors, and is chiefly furnished with 18th and 19th century pieces. The palace's park was redesigned into the zoological garden of East Berlin in 1957.

Deutsch-Russisches Museum (Berlin-Karlshorst) ❹

Zwieseler Strasse 4/Rheinsteinstrasse
📞 50 15 08 10. Ⓢ Karlshorst.
🚊 26, 27, 28. 🚌 396. 🕐 10am–6pm Tue–Sun.

THIS BUILDING was erected in the 1930s as the casino of the Wehrmacht (armed services of the Third Reich). It was here on the night of 8 May 1945 that Hitler's successor Grossadmiral Karl Dönitz, Field-Marshall Wilhelm Keitel, Admiral Hans Georg von Friedeburg and General Hans-Jürgen Stumpff signed the unconditional surrender of Germany's armed forces. You can visit the renowned hall in which the surrender was signed, the office of Marshal Žukov, and see an exhibition documenting the history of World War II.

Köpenick ❺

Kunstgewerbemuseum Ⓢ *Spindlersfeld, then* 🚌 *167 or* Ⓢ *Köpenick, then* 🚌 *269, 360.* 🚊 *26, 60, 61, 63, 67, 68.* 🚫 *closed for renovation until 2002.*

KÖPENICK IS MUCH older than Berlin. Already in the 9th century AD this island contained a fortified settlement called Kopanica. It was inhabited by Slavs from the Łaba river region, which in the 12th century was ruled by Duke Jaksa, who was waging a war against the Ascanian Albrecht the Bear over Brandenburg *(see p17)*. From the later part of the 12th century Köpenick belonged to the Margrave of Brandenburg, also an Ascanian. In about 1240 a castle was built, around which a town began to evolve, though over the years it lost out in importance to Berlin. Craftsmen settled here, and after 1685 a large colony of Huguenots also settled here.

A reconstructed drawing room dating from 1548 in Köpenick's Kunstgewerbemuseum

In the 19th century Köpenick recreated itself as an industrial town. Despite wartime devastation it has retained its historic character. There are no longer any 13th century churches, which in the years 1838 to 1841 were replaced by buildings in the style of Schinkel, nevertheless it is worth strolling around the old town. By the old market square and the neighbouring streets, such as Alt Köpenick and Grünstrasse, modest houses have survived which recall the 18th century, next to buildings from the end of the 19th century.

At Alt Köpenick No. 21 is a vast brick town hall built in the style of the Brandenburg Neo-Renaissance between the years 1901 and 1904 by Hans Schütte and Hugo Kinzer. It was here on 16 October 1906 that a famous swindle took place. Wilhelm Voigt dressed himself in a Prussian officer's uniform and proceeded to arrest the mayor and then fraudulently empty everything from the city treasury. This incident became the inspiration for a comedy *The Captain from Köpenick* by Carl Zuckmayer, which is still popular.

Part of the Neo-Gothic façade the town hall

Köpenick's greatest attraction is a magnificent palace built on the island in the southern part of town. It was built between 1677 and 1681 for the heir to the throne Friedrich (later King Friedrich I), according to a design by the Dutch architect Rutger van Langfeld. The three-storey Baroque building that resulted was extended to a design by Johann Arnold Nering, but until 1693 only part of the extension was completed: the chapel, entrance gate and a small gallery wing.

Since 1963 the palace has housed the craft museum, a part of the **Kunstgewerbemuseum** *(see pp118–21)*, but until 2002 restoration work will prevent public access to the collection.

Southwest Berlin

A N EXCURSION TO BRITZ provides a chance to visit one of the few surviving manor houses in the suburbs of Berlin, Schloss Britz. In Schöneberg you can see the town hall from which President Kennedy gaves his famous speech, or visit the grave of Berlin-born actress and singer, Marlene Dietrich. The Botanical Gardens are great for those who enjoy a stroll through cultivated and wild gardens, but you should allow at least half a day.

Neo-Classical Königskolonnaden, gateway to the Kleistpark

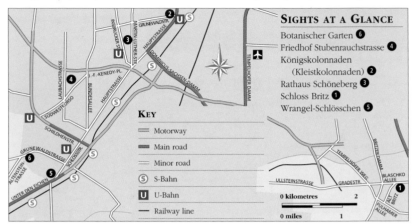

SIGHTS AT A GLANCE

Botanischer Garten **6**
Friedhof Stubenrauchstrasse **4**
Königskolonnaden
    (Kleistkolonnaden) **2**
Rathaus Schöneberg **3**
Schloss Britz **1**
Wrangel-Schlösschen **5**

KEY

▬▬	Motorway
▬▬	Main road
—	Minor road
Ⓢ	S-Bahn
Ⓤ	U-Bahn
—	Railway line

0 kilometres   2

0 miles   1

Schloss Britz **1**

Alt-Britz 73. **C** 606 60 51.
U Parchimer Allee. **▬** 144, 174,
181. **○** 2–6pm Wed. **✦** compulsory.

O RIGINALLY A small manor house built in 1706 for Sigismund von Erlach, Schloss Britz was extended to its current size between 1880 and 1883 to a design by Carl Busse. It is a one-storey palace with a modest Neo-Classical aspect adorned with Baroque statues at the front and a tower on the garden side. As well as housing a permanent museum, the building is often used as a venue for concerts and temporary exhibitions.

The palace displays furnishings from the *Gründerzeit* – the years after the founding of the German Empire in 1871. The 19th century interiors are excellent but it is also worth strolling through the park, where there is a bust of one of the former owners, Rüdiger von Ilgen. This statue once stood on the Avenue of Triumph in the Tiergarten.

Next to the palace is a housing estate called Hufeisensiedlung (Horseshoe Colony), built in the late 1920s to a design by Bruno Taut and Bruno Schneidereit. The architects' aim was to create spacious and affordable housing for Berliners.

Königskolonnaden (Kleistkolonnaden) **2**

Potsdamer Strasse **Map** 11 B4.
U Kleistpark. **▬** 148, 187, 348.

A SHORT WALK north of U-Bahn Kleistpark, the unremarkable architecture of Potsdamer Strasse suddenly transforms dramatically. Leading to the park, the elegant sandstone Königskolonnaden captivates the passer-by with its Baroque ornamental sculptures. The royal colonnade, designed by Carl von Gontard and built between 1777 and 1780, once graced the route from Königsstrasse to Alexanderplatz. In 1910, to protect it from traffic, it was moved to this new site.

The huge Kammergericht at the far boundary of the park was built between 1909 and 1913 to a design by Carl Vohl, Rudolf Mönnich and Paul Thoemer. The site of the notorious Nazi Volksgericht or "People's Court", it was also used to try members of the failed 1944 July Bomb Plot against Hitler (see p127).

Schloss Britz's Neo-Classical façade

Rathaus Schöneberg ❸

SCHÖNEBERG TOWN HALL

John-F-Kennedy-Platz.
Ⓤ *Rathaus Schöneberg.*

THE GIGANTIC BUILDING with a tower is the Schöneberg town hall, built between 1911 and 1914. From 1948 to 1990 it was used as the main town hall of West Berlin. Here, on 26 June 1963, the US President John F Kennedy gave his famous speech. More than 400,000 Berliners assembled to hear the young president say *"Ich bin ein Berliner"* – "I am a Berliner", intended as an expression of solidarity from the democratic world to a city defending its right to freedom.

While Kennedy's meaning was undoubtedly clear, pedants were quick to point out that, strictly speaking, he said "I am a small doughnut".

Rathaus Schöneberg – the site of President Kennedy's speech

Friedhof Stuben-rauchstrasse ❹

STUBENRAUCHSTRASSE CEMETERY

Stubenrauchstrasse/Südwestkorso.
Ⓢ & Ⓤ *Bundesplatz.* 348.

THIS SMALL CEMETERY in the shadow of a motorway, achieved renown in 1993 as the burial place of Marlene Dietrich, who died on 6 May. Born Maria Magdalena von Losch in 1901, she grew up at Leberstrasse No. 65 in Schöneberg. For a few years she struggled to make a career as an actress, playing small parts.

The pleasantly cultivated spaces of the Botanischer Garten

In 1929 she was discovered in Berlin by Hollywood director Josef von Sternberg who was filming *The Blue Angel*, based on Heinrich Mann's novel *Professor Unrat*. The ensuing role of Lola took Marlene to the height of fame. She sang only once more in Berlin, giving a concert at the Titania-Palast in 1960. Although she died in Paris, she was laid to rest in the city of her birth.

Wrangel-Schlösschen ❺

Schlossstrasse 48. 79 04 39 21.
Ⓤ *Rathaus Steglitz.* 148, 185, 186, 280, 285.

THIS COMPACT Neo-Classical palace derives its name from Field Marshal Wrangel, the building's mid-19th century owner. However, the house was built much earlier, in 1804, following a design by Heinrich Gentz. The simplicity and clarity of its details make it a prime example of early Neo-Classical architecture. It currently houses the cultural centre for the district of Steglitz.

Botanischer Garten ❻

BOTANICAL GARDEN

Unter den Eichen 5–10 & Königin-Luise-Strasse 6–8. 83 00 60.
Ⓤ *Dahlem-Dorf.* Ⓢ *Botanischer Garten.* 101, 148, 183. ☐ Mar & Oct: 9am–5pm daily; Apr & Sep: 9am–8pm daily; May–Aug: 9am–9pm daily; Nov–Feb: 9am–4pm daily.
Museum ☐ 10am–5pm Tue–Sun, (Nov–Feb: until 4pm).

THE BOTANICAL GARDEN is one of the most beautiful places in Berlin. The expansive park was created towards the end of the 19th century and has a romantic character with gentle hills and picturesque lakes. Of particular interest is the 19th-century palm house, designed by Alfred Koerner. The new greenhouses were built from 1984 to 1987 to a design by Engelbert Kremser. The most popular plants are the exotic species such as the orchids and cacti. By the entrance on the Königin-Luise-Platz side is the Botanisches Museum, home to an excellent collection of plant specimens.

COUNTRY CHURCHES

The establishment of Greater Berlin in 1920 swallowed up nearly 60 villages, some of which were older than the city itself. Now they have evolved into large residential estates, and many of the parish churches (more than 50) have survived. The most treasured, dating from the 13th century, can be seen in the south of Berlin, for instance in Britz by Backbergstrasse, Buckow (Alt-Buckow) or in Mariendorf (Alt Mariendorf). The oldest church, dating from the 13th century, has survived in Marienfelde (Alt Marienfelde).

St Anna's in Dahlem   **Wittenau**   **Marienfelde**

Dahlem

D AHLEM IS FIRST MENTIONED in 1275 and it remained a small village surrounded by private estates until the 19th century. Retaining its Gothic parish church and its manor house, Dahlem was transformed into an affluent, tranquil city suburb with grand villas and a clutch of museums, designed by Bruno Paul, at the beginning of the 20th century. The district was confirmed as a major cultural and educational centre after World War II with the establishment of the Freie Universität and the completion of the museum complex. The Botanischer Garten also sits on the borders of Dahlem *(see p169).*

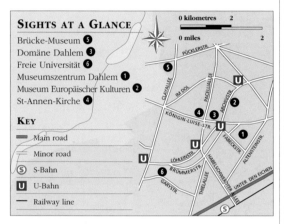

SIGHTS AT A GLANCE

Brücke-Museum ❺
Domäne Dahlem ❸
Freie Universität ❻
Museumszentrum Dahlem ❶
Museum Europäischer Kulturen ❷
St-Annen-Kirche ❹

KEY

▬ Main road
⌐ Minor road
Ⓢ S-Bahn
Ⓤ U-Bahn
▬ Railway line

0 kilometres   2
0 miles   2

Museumszentrum Dahlem ❶

Lansstrasse. ☎ 830 14 38.
Ⓤ *Dahlem Dorf.* 🚌 110, 183, X-11.
Museum für Indische Kunst
◑ *until 2002.* **Museum für Ostasia-**
tische Kunst, Museum für
Völkerkunde, Museum für Kunst
Afrikas & Nordamerika Ausstellung
◯ *10am–6pm Tue–Fri, 11am–6pm*
Sat & Sun. 🎫

D AHLEM'S FIRST museums were built between 1914 and 1923. After World War II, with many of Berlin's collections fragmented, a large miscellany of art and artifacts was put on display here. In the 1960s the museums were extended considerably: the new Museumszentrum was created to rival East Berlin's Museum Island. Reunification in 1990 meant the collections could be reunited and reorganized. Paintings were moved to the Kulturforum *(see pp122–5),* and sculptures to the Bodemuseum *(see p79).* Five

museums are now housed at Dahlem: the Museum für Völkerkunde (Museum of Mankind); the Museum für Indische Kunst (Museum of Indian Art); the Museum für Ostasiatische Kunst (Museum of Far Eastern Art); the Museum für Kunst Afrikas (Museum for African Art) and

Japanese woodcut from the
Museum für Ostasiatische Kunst

the newly-opened Nord-amerika Ausstellung (Exhibition of Native North American Cultures).
Highlights from the collections include bronzes from Benin at the Museum of African Art, gold Inca jewellery at the Museum of Mankind, and Japanese woodcuts and Buddhist cave paintings from Chinese Turkestan at the Museum of Far Eastern Art. Opened in 1999, the Exhibition of Native North American Cultures includes a collection of 600 ceremonial objects.

An East Prussian carpet from the
Museum Europäischer Kulturen

Museum Europäischer Kulturen ❷

MUSEUM OF EUROPEAN CULTURE

Im Winkel 6. ☎ 839 01 01.
Ⓤ *Dahlem Dorf.* 🚌 110, 183, X-11,
X-83. ◯ *10am–6pm Tue–Fri,*
11am–6pm Sat & Sun. 🎫

T HIS ETHNOGRAPHIC museum specializes in European folk art and culture, documenting the daily life of its inhabitants. It hosts long-running but temporary exhibitions, often in conjunction with museums from other European countries. Among the exhibits you can expect to see are earthenware items, costumes, jewellery, toys and tools.

Domäne Dahlem ❸

DAHLEM CITY FARM

Königin-Luise-Str. 49. ☎ 832 50 00.
Ⓤ *Dahlem Dorf.* 🚌 110, 183, X-11,
X-83. ◯ *10am–6pm Wed–Mon.* 🎫
(museum only).

D OMÄNE DAHLEM, a manor house and farming estate, is a rare oasis of country life in the Berlin suburbs. The Baroque house was built for Cuno Johann von Wilmersdorff

The combined museum and working farm of Domäne Dahlem

around 1680 and still retains its original character. Part of the Stadtmuseum Berlin (Museum of the City of Berlin), the manor house boasts period interiors, while the 19th-century farm buildings hold a collection of agricultural tools. Also on show is a large and varied collection of beehives.

Domäne Dahlem is a farm and a museum with a garden, workshops and farm animals. Festivals and markets are held here with demonstrations of rural crafts and skills – you can learn how to shoe a horse or milk a cow, or, if you prefer, you can just relax with a glass of cold beer.

Gothic St-Annen-Kirche dating back to the 14th century

St-Annen-Kirche ❹

Königin-Luise-Strasse/Pacelliallee.
U *Dahlem Dorf.* 🚌 *110, 183, X-11.*

AT THE CENTRE of a small leafy cemetery stands the Gothic 14th-century St-Annen-Kirche. The church was built

initially with a plain roof. The chancel was completed in the 15th century, the vaulting in the 17th century and the tower was added in the 18th century.

Inside the church, 14th-century wall paintings depict scenes from the life of St Anna, alongside several interesting items of ecclesiastical furnishings. These include a 15th-century painting called *The Crucifixion*, 11 late-Gothic figures of saints and a 17th-century Baroque pulpit.

Brücke-Museum ❺

Bussardsteig 9. 📞 *831 20 29.*
🚌 *115.* 🕐 *11am–5pm Wed–Mon.*

ONE OF THE MORE interesting museums dedicated to 20th-century art is hidden away on a leafy, tranquil street lined with picturesque villas. The elegant Functionalist building was built by Werner Düttmann in 1966 to 1967. The museum houses a collection of German Expressionist painting linked to the artistic group known as Die Brücke, which originated in Dresden in 1905 and was based in Berlin from 1910. The members of this group included Karl Schmidt-Rottluff, Emil Nolde, Max Pechstein, Ernst Ludwig Kirchner and Erich Heckel. The collection is based on almost 80 works by Schmidt-Rottluff bequeathed to the town in 1964. The collection quickly grew, thanks to donations and acquisitions. In addition to displaying other works of art contemporary to Die Brücke (which was disbanded in 1913), there are also some paintings from the later creative periods of these artists, as well as works of other closely associated artists.

Nearby, at Käuzchensteig No. 8, lie the foundation's headquarters, established in the former studio of the sculptor Bernhard Heliger. The garden, which borders the Brücke-Museum, has a display of his metal sculptures.

A Bernhard Heliger sculpture outside the Brücke-Museum

Freie Universität ❻

Henry-Ford-Bau Garystrasse 35–39.
U *Thielplatz.* 🚌 *111.*

THE FREE UNIVERSITY was established on 4 December 1948 on the initiative of a group of academics and activists, led by Ernst Reuter. This was a reaction to the restrictions introduced at the Humboldt-Universität in the Soviet sector and further evidence of the competition between the two halves of the city. The new university was initially located in rented buildings. It was only thanks to the American Ford Foundation that the university's Henry-Ford-Bau, housing the rector's office, the auditorium and the library, was built. Designed by Franz Heinrich Sobotka and Gustav Müller, and built from 1951 to 1954, the building is distinguished by its fine proportions.

Henry-Ford-Bau, the rector's office and library at the Freie Universität

Zehlendorf

WITH NEARLY HALF of Zehlendorf covered by forests, lakes and rivers, the region has a quiet, rustic atmosphere that belies the fact that it is a mere 20 minutes away from the hustle and bustle of a huge metropolis. The area is dotted with picture-postcard villas and small settlements where life carries on at an unchanging, slow pace. It is worth taking a walk *(see pp200–203)* to see the stunning lakeside summer residences and royal parks, Pfaueninsel and Klein Glienicke, which are located in the furthest corner of this district.

Reconstructed medieval settlement at the Museumdorf Düppel

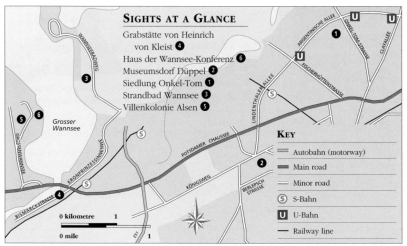

SIGHTS AT A GLANCE

Grabstätte von Heinrich von Kleist ❹
Haus der Wannsee-Konferenz ❻
Museumsdorf Düppel ❷
Siedlung Onkel-Tom ❶
Strandbad Wannsee ❸
Villenkolonie Alsen ❺

KEY

═══	Autobahn (motorway)
▬▬	Main road
───	Minor road
Ⓢ	S-Bahn
Ⓤ	U-Bahn
───	Railway line

0 kilometre   1

0 mile   1

Siedlung Onkel-Tom ❶

Argentinische Allee. Ⓤ *Onkel-Toms-Hütte.*

THIS HOUSING ESTATE, known as "Uncle Tom's Estate" represents one of the most interesting urban architectural achievements of the Weimar Republic. It was built from 1926 to 1932, to a design by

The Siedlung (estate) Onkel-Tom, built between 1926 and 1932

Bruno Taut, Hugo Häring and Otto Rudolf Salvisberg. Their primary intention was to solve the city's housing shortage by building large developments that were both pleasant to live in and fairly inexpensive. This project in Zehlendorf was the realization of the English concept of garden cities. The result is an enormous housing estate comprising single- and multiple-family houses. It is set in lush greenery on the borders of Grunewald and accommodates nearly 15,000 people.

Museumsdorf Düppel ❷

Clauerstrasse 11. ☎ 802 66 71. Ⓢ *Mexikoplatz* or Ⓤ *Krumme Lanke,* then 115, 211, 629. ☐ Apr–Oct: 3–6pm Tue–Thu, 10am–5pm Sun.

A VISIT TO THE Museumsdorf Düppel takes the visitor on a trip back in time. A reconstruction of a medieval village has been made on the site of a 13th-century settlement, discovered in the 1940s. It is a living village surrounded by still cultivated gardens and fields, where traditional breeds of pigs and sheep are raised in the sheds and pigsties.

On Sundays the village puts on displays of traditional crafts. Here you can see how primitive saucepans and tools were fashioned; how wool was spun, dyed and woven; and how baskets were made.

Strandbad Wannsee ❸

Wannseebadweg. Ⓢ *Nikolassee.* 513.

THE VAST PICTURESQUE lake of Wannsee, situated on the edge of Grunewald, is a principal destination for Berliners who are looking for some kind of recreation. Here you can take part in water sports, enjoy a lake cruise, bathe, or simply enjoy relaxing on the

Boarding point for lake cruises on the Wannsee

shore. The most developed part is the southeastern corner of the lake. Here, near S-Bahn Wannsee, there are yachting marinas and harbours, while further north is one of the largest inland beaches in Europe – Strandbad Wannsee. It has been in use since the beginning of the 20th century, and was developed between 1929 and 1930 by the construction of a complex of changing rooms, shops and cafés on top of man-made terraces.

On sunny summer days, sun-worshippers completely cover the sandy shore, while the lake is filled with yachts and windsurfers. It is also quite pleasant to take a walk around Schwanenwerder island. It has many elegant villas, one of which, Inselstrasse No. 24/26, was built for Axel Springer, the German newspaper publisher.

Grabstätte von Heinrich von Kleist ❹

GRAVE OF HEINRICH VON KLEIST

Bismarckstrasse (near No. 3).
Ⓢ *Wannsee.* 🚌 *114, 116, 118, 211, 216, 316, 318.*

A NARROW STREET running from Königstrasse at the viaduct of the S-Bahn Wannsee leads to the spot where the playwright Heinrich von Kleist committed suicide. On 21 November 1811 he shot his companion Henriette Vogel and then turned the pistol on himself. They are both buried

here, with a stone marking the location of their grave, on which flowers and lit candles are left by well-wishers.

Villenkolonie Alsen ❺

Am Grossen Wannsee. Ⓢ *Wannsee, then* 🚌 *114.*

T HIS CLUTCH OF VILLAS forms a delightful holiday resort – the oldest of its kind in Berlin. The villas are thought to be the most beautiful, not just because of their picturesque lakeside location, but also because of the quality of their architecture. Development in the area started in the 1860s on the initiative of the banker Wilhelm Conrad. One by one, the richest industrialists settled here, giving commissions to the most illustrious architects of that time. These days most of these elegant villas are occupied by yacht clubs.

Strolling along Am Grossen Wannsee, it is worth looking at the villa at No. 39/41, known as Haus Springer. It was designed by Alfred Messl in 1901 and is covered with shingles which reflect contemporary American designs. At No. 42 stands a villa that was designed by Paul Baumgarten in 1909 for the painter Max Liebermann, who spent many summers here painting. The luxurious residence at No. 52 was designed in 1891 by Wilhelm Mertens and is particularly striking because it looks like a medieval castle.

Haus der Wannsee-Konferenz ❻

Am Grossen Wannsee 56/58.
📞 *805 00 10.* Ⓢ *Wannsee, then* 🚌 *114.* ◯ *10am–6pm Mon–Fri, 2–6pm Sat & Sun.*

T HIS IS ONE OF THE most beautiful of the luxury Alsen holiday villas, and yet the most abhorrent. Designed by Paul Baumgarten between 1914 and 1915 for the businessman Ernst Marlier, it is in the style of a small Neo-Baroque palace with an elegant portico leading to an oval hall. In 1940 its next owner, Friedrich Minou, sold the villa to the Nazi SS. On 20 January 1942, a meeting took place between Richard Heydrich and 14 other officers from the secret service and the SS, among them Adolf Eichmann. It was then that the decision was taken about "the final solution on the question of Jews". Their plans for the outright extermination of 11 million Jews embraced the whole of Europe, including Great Britain and neutral countries.

Since 1992 there has been a museum and place of remembrance here. In the rooms there is an exhibition depicting the history of the Holocaust from 1933 to 1945 which has some shocking documents and photographs from the ghettos and extermination camps. For security reasons, the gate to the villa is always locked, and to enter the park you have to announce yourself through the intercom.

Haunting sculptures in front of Haus der Wannsee-Konferenz

Western Berlin

WEST OF CHARLOTTENBURG, beyond the city ring road, stretches an area notable for its striking Funkturm (Radio Tower) and Internationales Congress Centrum, as well as a number of large exhibition centres. After World War II, a residential estate of villas was built here, one of which belonged to the sculptor, Georg Kolbe and now houses a museum of his works. A radio station has its recording studios in a very large building nearby; its plain, almost boring looking façade hides one of Berlin's most beautiful art deco interiors.

The futuristic exterior of the Internationales Congress Centrum

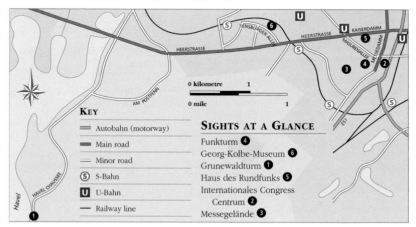

KEY

▬▬▬	Autobahn (motorway)
▬▬▬	Main road
───	Minor road
Ⓢ	S-Bahn
Ⓤ	U-Bahn
───	Railway line

SIGHTS AT A GLANCE

Funkturm ❹
Georg-Kolbe-Museum ❻
Grunewaldturm ❶
Haus des Rundfunks ❺
Internationales Congress
   Centrum ❷
Messegelände ❸

Grunewaldturm ❶

Havelchaussee. 🚌 *218.*

THE NEO-GOTHIC tower built on a hill at the edge of the Havel river is one of the most prominent features of the area. This type of tower became popular in Germany during the 19th century as a way of commemorating important events or people. The Grunewaldturm was built in 1899 on the centenary of the birth of Wilhelm I. After 1871, he was the first Emperor of the Second Reich, and the tower was initially named "Kaiser-Wilhelm-Turm". The 56-m (185-ft) tower was designed by Franz Schwechten and is made of red brick with plaster details. The tower is made all the more striking by the green background provided by the surrounding leafy trees.

Currently used as an observation tower, the view from the top is magnificent and worth climbing the 204 steps. There is a popular restaurant in the base of the tower and

above, in the domed hall, is a marble statue monument to the Emperor, which was designed by Ludwig Mansel.

The impressive red-brick Neo-Gothic Grunewaldturm

Internationales Congress Centrum ❷

Messedamm 19. Ⓢ *Witzleben.* Ⓤ *Kaiserdamm.* 🚌 *104, 149, 204.*

THIS SILVER FUTURISTIC structure stands on a peninsula of land, surrounded on two sides by a continuous stream

of fast moving cars. The Internationales Congress Centrum (ICC) marked yet another stage in the rivalry between East and West Berlin – it was built in reply to the East's Palast der Republik.

Constructed between 1973 and 1979, to a design by Ralf Schüler and Ursulina Schüler-Witte, the building is a mass of angular aluminium shapes, that disguise its well thought-out construction. The conference area has been sited independently of the concert halls, for good sound-proofing. One of the most modern buildings of its type in the world, it has a state-of-the-art electronic security system and an advanced means of co-ordinating and directing the several thousand people who come here to attend various meetings and conferences. More than 80 rooms and halls enable the venue to host a variety of events, from rock concerts for up to 5,000 spectators to a small artistic workshop or seminar. The building also has a roof garden, where you can rest during intervals. In front of the main entrance stands *Alexander the Great in front of Ekbatana*, by French sculptor Jean Ipoustéguy (born 1920).

Monumental façade of the Ehren-hall part of the Messegelände

Messegelände ❸

Hammarskjöldplatz. Ⓢ *Witzleben.* Ⓤ *Kaiserdamm.* 🚌 *104, 149, 204, 219.*

T HE PAVILIONS of the vast exhibition and trade halls which lie south of Hammarsk-jöldplatz cover more than 160,000 sq m (1,700,000 sq ft). Many of the international events organized here, inclu-ding the food and agricultural fair Grüne Woche, are among the largest events of their kind in Europe. Even so, the exhi-bition areas are constantly enlarged and updated.

The original exhibition halls on this site were built before World War I, but nothing of these buildings remains. The oldest part is the **Funkturm** and the group of pavilions which surround it. The huge building at the front – Ehren-halle – was built in 1936 to a design by Richard Ermisch, and is one of the few surviving buildings in Berlin designed in a Fascist architectural style.

The straight motorway which lies at the rear of the halls, in the direction of Nikolassee, is the famous Avus, the first Ger-man autobahn, built in 1921. It was adapted for motor racing, and became Germany's first car-racing track. It was here that the world speed record was broken before World War II. Now it forms part of the autobahn system.

Funkturm ❹

Hammarskjöldplatz. Ⓢ *Witzleben.* Ⓤ *Kaiserdamm.* 🚌 *104, 149, 204.* **Observation Terrace** ⬛ *10am–11pm daily.*

T HE RADIO TOWER, resem-bling Paris' Eiffel tower, has become one of Berlin's most recognizable landmarks. Built in 1924 to a design by Heinrich Straumer, it was conceived as a 150-m (500-ft) radio mast. It now operates as both an air-traffic control tower and a radio mast. Visitors can enjoy splendid views on the observation terrace at 125-m (400-ft), or dine at the Funkturm's lofty restaurant at 55 m (180 ft).

Haus des Rundfunks ❺

Masurenallee 8–14. Ⓢ *Witzleben.* Ⓤ *Theodor-Heuss-Platz.* 🚌 *104, 149, 204.*

T HIS BUILDING'S depressing, flat, brick-covered façade hides an interior of startling beauty. The huge edifice was constructed as a radio station between 1929 and 1931 to a design by Hans Poelzig. The building has a triangular shape, with three studio wings radia-ting from the central five-storey hall. The impressive Art Deco interiors, which are spectacu-larly lit from above, are enhanced by geometrically-patterned rows of balconies and large, pendulous,

Clean, geometric shapes in the Art Deco lobby, Haus des Rundfunks

octagonal lamps. They represent one of the finest architectural achievements of this era in Berlin.

From the studio concert hall, concerts are often broadcast on radio SFB.

Fountain in the garden of the sculptor Georg Kolbe's villa

Georg-Kolbe-Museum ❻

Sensburger Allee 25. 📞 *304 21 44.* Ⓢ *Heerstrasse.* 🚌 *149, X-34, X-49.* ⬛ *10am–5pm Tue–Sun.*

O NE OF THE MOST renowned German sculptors, Georg Kolbe (1877–1947) bequeathed the house in which he lived and worked almost his entire life to the city of Berlin. The villa was built by the Swiss architect, Ernst Reutsch, between 1928 and 1929 in a Functionalist style. Extended a few years later by the archi-tect Paul Lindner, it was given an old-fashioned styling with rooms that open onto a large hall. Kolbe also left the city 180 of his sculptures, as well as his own art collection, which includes works by the Expres-sionist painter Ernst Ludwig Kirchner and the sculptor Wilhelm Lehmbruck. Visiting here is not only a rare chance to get to know Kolbe's works but also an opportunity to see his house and workshop, which display the tools and various devices for lifting a heavy or large sculpture.

Northwest Berlin

A VISIT TO THIS PART of the city provides a chance to see the grandeur of the Olympia-Stadion, which was inspired by the monumental architecture of ancient Rome. Nearby stands the monolithic Le Corbusier Haus, once regarded as the model for future housing. The historic town of Spandau has some pretty medieval streets and a well-preserved Renaissance citadel. A number of original timber-framed houses remain and are well worth seeing, along with the Gothic St-Nikolai-Kirche.

500 two-storey apartments with integral services, such as a post office, shops, a sports hall and nursery school. The structure fell short of Le Corbusier's aspirations as financial pressure meant the estate lacked some service elements; in addition, structural alterations changed the building's proportions from the original plans.

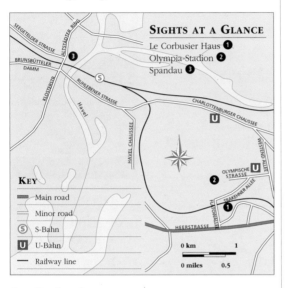

SIGHTS AT A GLANCE
Le Corbusier Haus **1**
Olympia-Stadion **2**
Spandau **3**

KEY
- Main road
- Minor road
- Ⓢ S-Bahn
- Ⓤ U-Bahn
- Railway line

0 km — 1
0 miles — 0.5

Two sculptures of athletes decorating the Olympia-Stadion

Olympia-Stadion **2**

Olympischer Platz. Ⓢ & Ⓤ Olympia-Stadion. 🚌 218.

Le Corbusier Haus **1**

Reichssportfeldstrasse 16.
Ⓢ Olympia-Stadion. 🚌 218.

THIS APARTMENT building by Le Corbusier, on a hill near the site of the Olympia-Stadion, was this architect's entry to the 1957 Interbau Exhibition (see p129). Following World War II,

there was a housing shortage all over Europe, especially in the bomb-damaged cities. Le Corbusier's innovative design for what he called a *Unité d'Habitation* was his attempt to create fully self-sufficient housing estates in answer to this problem. He built three of these complexes, the most famous being in Marseilles. For his Berlin design, Le Corbusier wanted to build over

THE OLYMPIA-STADION, or Reichssportfeld as it was originally known, was built specifically for the 1936 Olympic Games in Berlin. It was designed by Werner March in the Nazi architectural style and was inspired by the architecture of ancient Rome. The Olympia-Stadion was immortalized in the dramatic final scenes of István Szabó's classic film *Mefisto*. To the west of the stadium lie the Maifeld and what is now called the Waldbühne. The former is an enormous assembly-ground surrounded by grandstands and fronted by the Glockenturm, a 77-m (250-ft) tower, while the latter is an open-air amphitheatre. Stretching north is a group of sports grounds and swimming pools. The entire complex provided the infrastructure for Berlin to hold the Olympics. However, it also provided Hitler plenty of opportunities to use it for his own propagandist purposes.

Le Corbusier Haus, by the renowned French architect

Interior of the Gothic St-Nikolai-Kirche in Spandau

Spandau ❸

Zitadelle Spandau Am Juliusturm.
☎ 354 94 42 00. Ⓤ *Zitadelle.*
◯ 9am–5pm Tue–Fri, 10am–5pm Sat
& Sun. 🅰

SPANDAU IS ONE of the oldest
towns within the area of
greater Berlin, and it has
managed to retain a distinct
character for itself. Evidence
of the earliest settlement dates
back to the 8th century,
although the town of Spandau
was only granted a charter in
1232. The area was spared
the worst of the World War II
bombing, so there are still
some interesting sights to visit.

The heart of the town is a
network of medieval streets
with a picturesque market
square and a number of
original timber-framed
houses; in the north of
Spandau sections of
town wall still stand,
dating from the
15th century. In
the centre of
town is the
magnificent
Gothic St-Nikolai-
Kirche dating from
the 15th century. The
church holds many
valuable ecclesiastical
furnishings, such as a
splendid Renaissance
stone altar from the end of
the 16th century, a Baroque
pulpit from around 1700 which
came from a royal palace in
Potsdam, a Gothic baptismal
font and many epitaphs.

**Crowned black
Prussian eagle**

A castle was first built on the
site of the **Zitadelle Spandau**
(citadel) in the 12th century,
but today only the 36-m (120-
ft) Juliusturm (tower) remains.
In 1560 the building of a fort
was begun here, to a
design by Francesco
Chiaramella da
Gandino. It took
30 years to bring to
completion how-
ever, and most of
the work was
supervised by archi-
tect Rochus Graf von
Lynar. Although the
citadel had a jail, the
town's most infamous
resident, Rudolf Hess,
was incarcerated a short distance away in a military prison
after the 1946 Nuremberg trials.
In 1986 the former deputy
leader of the Nazi party died,
and the prison was torn down.

The Hohenzollern coat of arms above the main gate of the citadel

ZITADELLE SPANDAU

This magnificent and perfectly proportioned
16th-century citadel stands at the confluence of
the Spree and Havel rivers. Both the main
citadel and its various 19th-century additions
are still in excellent condition. The "Iron
Chancellor", Otto von Bismarck *(see p22),*
moved the gold treasure of the Reichskriegs-
schatz (Imperial War Fund) here in 1874, where
it remained until 1919. The citadel now holds
museums of local history, and an observation
terrace on the crenellated Juliusturm (tower).

KEY

Bastion Kronprinz ①
Bastion Branden-
burg ②
Palace ③
Main gate ④

Bastion König ⑤
Bastion Königin ⑥
Juliusturm ⑦
Ravelin Schweine-
kopf ⑧

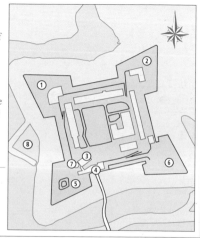

Northern Berlin

BEYOND THE TIERGARTEN lie the AEG-Turbinenhalle, designed by Peter Behrens, and the Gedenkstätte Plötzensee, a sombre memorial to those executed for their supposed crimes against the Third Reich. Further north past the airport, the Tegel area contains the picturesque Schloss Tegel and the IBA-Viertel, an unusually colourful, modern housing estate designed by a team of architects. It is worth taking a cruise boat to Tegel and linking together sight-seeing in this area and a visit to Spandau with a relaxing voyage along the Havel river.

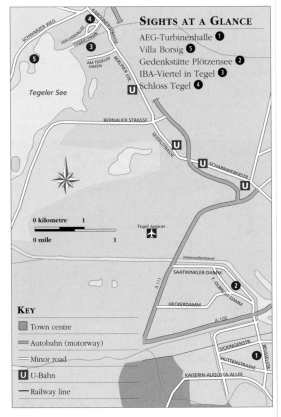

SIGHTS AT A GLANCE

AEG-Turbinenhalle ❶
Villa Borsig ❺
Gedenkstätte Plötzensee ❷
IBA-Viertel in Tegel ❸
Schloss Tegel ❹

Tegeler See

KEY

▮ Town centre

▬ Autobahn (motorway)

— Minor road

Ⓤ U-Bahn

— Railway line

AEG-Turbinen-halle ❶

Huttenstrasse 12–16. Ⓤ *Turmstrasse, then* 🚌 *227.*

THIS BUILDING IS one of the most important textbook examples of modern architecture dating from the beginning of the 20th century. It was commissioned by the electronics company, AEG, in 1909 and designed by Peter Behrens in conjunction with Karl Bernhardt. It was among the earliest structures not to incorporate any element, decorative or otherwise, that reflected previous architectural styles. A huge hangar of a building, it has enormous windows and stretches 123 m (400 ft) down Berlichingenstrasse. The principal design imperative for this structure was to maintain a streamlined profile, while making no effort to disguise the materials used in its construction.

Gedenkstätte Plötzensee ❷

PLÖTZENSEE MEMORIAL

Hüttigpfad. 📞 *344 32 26.*
Ⓤ *Jakob-Kaiser-Platz, then* 🚌 *123.*
🕐 *Jan & Nov: 9am–4:30pm; Feb & Oct: 9am–5:30pm; Mar–Sep & Dec: 9am–6pm.*

A NARROW street leads from Saatwinkler Damm to the site where nearly 2,500 people convicted of crimes against the Third Reich were hanged. The Gedenkstätte Plötzensee is a simple memorial in a brick hut, which still has the iron hooks from which the victims were suspended. The main figures in the unsuccessful assassination attempt against Hitler, on July 20 1944, were executed in Bendlerblock *(see p127)*, although the remainder of the conspirators were killed here. Count Helmut James von Moltke, one of the leaders of the German resistance movement, was also killed here. He organized the Kreisauer Kreis – a political movement which gathered and united German opposition to Hitler.

Memorial to concentration camp victims at Gedenkstätte Plötzensee

IBA-Viertel in Tegel ❸

Karolinenstrasse & Am Tegeler Hafen.
Ⓤ *Alt Tegel.*

THE DEVELOPMENT around the southern edge of the port of Tegel is an essential stop for lovers of modern, and

The elegant Neo-Classical façade of Schloss Tegel

particularly post-modern, architecture. This complex developed out of the IBA (Internationale Baustellung) building exhibition in 1987. Over 30 architects were involved in this project, although the main designers were Charles Moore, John Ruble and Buzz Yudell. Within this complex stands the Humboldt-Bibliothek, which draws on Neo-Classical themes. In 1997 a monument was established to the eminent scientists Wilhelm and Alexander von Humboldt in front of this library.

Running the length of Am Tegeler Hafen street is a large housing estate where each unit has been designed by a different architect. As a result, each one has its own colour scheme, and reflects a distinct style. For instance, at No. 8, the house by Stanley Tigerman recalls a style popular in Hanseatic architecture, while the red house at No. 10, designed by Paolo Portoghesi, looks as though it has been cracked lengthwise in two.

To the north, the IBA-Viertel estate borders another modern building, the Hotel Sorat, carefully built around the remaining section of an old windmill that was once part of the Humboldt estate.

Schloss Tegel ❹

Adelheidallee 19–21. **📞** 434 31 56.
U Alt Tegel. **🚌** 124, 133, 222.
🕐 May–Sep: 10am–noon & 3–5pm
Mon. **📷** compulsory.

S CHLOSS TEGEL is one of the most interesting palace complexes in Berlin. In the

16th century there was already a manor house on this site, which in the second half of the 17th century was rebuilt into a hunting lodge for the Elector Friedrich Wilhelm. In 1766 the ownership of the property passed to the Humboldt family, and between the years 1820 and 1824, Karl Friedrich Schinkel thoroughly rebuilt the palace, giving it its current style.

There are tiled bas-reliefs decorating the elevations on the top floor of the towers. These were designed by Christian Daniel Rauch and depict the ancient wind gods. Some of Schinkel's marvellous interiors have survived, along with several items from what was once a large collection of antique sculptures. The palace is still private property, owned by descendants of the Humboldt family, but guided tours are offered on Mondays.

It is also worth visiting the park. On its western limits lies the Humboldt family tomb designed by Schinkel and decorated with a copy of a splendid sculpture by Bertel Thorwaldsen; the original piece stands inside the palace.

Villa Borsig ❺

Reiherwerder. **U** Alt Tegel.
🚌 124, 133, 222, 824, then a 15-minute walk.

T HIS VILLA SITS on a peninsula which cuts into the Tegeler See and is reminiscent of Schloss Sanssouci in Potsdam. It was built much later, however, between 1911 and 1913. It was designed by Alfred Salinger and Eugen Schmohl, for the Borsig family, one of the wealthiest industrialist families in Berlin. This villa is particularly picturesque when observed from the lake, so it is worth looking out for it while cruising in a boat.

The Villa Borsig façade viewed from the garden

KARL FRIEDRICH SCHINKEL (1781–1841)

Schinkel was one of the most renowned German architects; even today his work forms an essential element of the architectural landscape of Berlin. He graduated from the Berlin Bauakademie, and for many years held a high-profile position in the Prussian Building Ministry. He was equally skilled in producing both Neo-Classical and Neo-Gothic designs. In Berlin and Potsdam he designed a few dozen buildings – palaces, civic buildings and churches, many of which still stand today. He also excelled at painting and even designed scenery for the opera house on Unter den Linden, among others. You can admire his paintings in the Galerie der Romantik in Schloss Charlottenburg. Schinkel's creativity had a truly enormous influence on the next generation of architects working in Prussia.

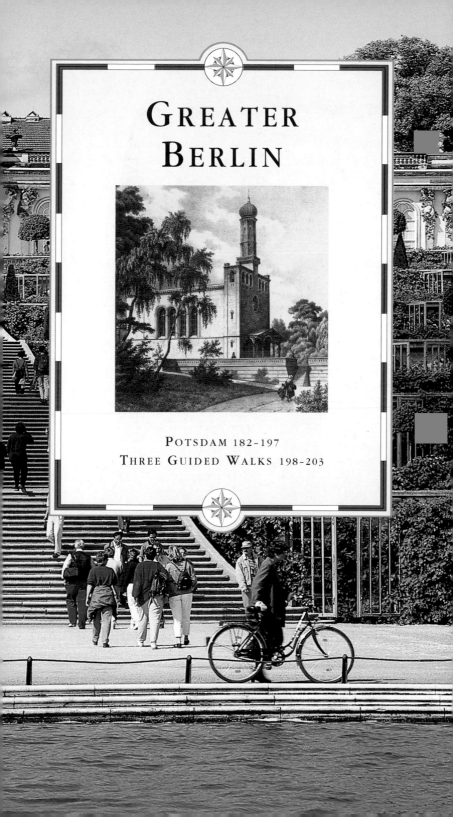

GREATER BERLIN

POTSDAM

POTSDAM IS AN independent city bordering Berlin. It is also the capital of Brandenburg, with almost 140,000 inhabitants. The first historical reference to Potsdam dates from AD 993. The town blossomed in the 1600s, during the era of the Great Elector *(see p18)*, and then again during the 18th century. Potsdam suffered very badly during World War II, particularly on the nights of 14 and 15 April 1945, when the Allies bombed the town's centre. Today, despite its

Sculpture from Park Sanssouci

wartime losses, Potsdam is one of the most interesting cities in Germany. Tourists flock to see the royal Park Sanssouci and palaces such as the Marmorpalais and Schloss Cecilienhof. It is also worth strolling around Neuer Garten and the historic area around the Rathaus. The Russian colony of Alexandrowka, the Holländisches Viertel, the film studios of Babelsberg and Babelsberg park *(see pp202–203)* also rate among the attractions of Potsdam.

SIGHTS AT A GLANCE

Historic Buildings
Altes Rathaus ㉑
Bildergalerie ⑪
Chinesisches Teehaus ⑥
Communs ③
Historische Mühle ⑫
Marmorpalais ⑯
Marstall (Filmmuseum) ㉒
Neue Kammern ⑨
Neues Palais pp186–7 ①
Orangerie ⑦
Römische Bäder ⑤
Schloss Cecilienhof ⑮
Schloss Charlottenhof ④

Schloss Sanssouci pp192–3 ⑩
Wasserwerk Sanssouci ㉔

Historic Areas
Alexandrowka ⑬
Holländisches Viertel ⑰

Churches
Französische Kirche ⑲
Friedenskirche ⑧
Nikolaikirche ⑳
Peter und Paul Kirche ⑱

Parks
Neuer Garten ⑭
Park Sanssouci ②
Telegrafenberg ㉕

Museums
Potsdam-Museum ㉓

KEY

Street-by-Street map pp184–5

P Parking

Railway station

0 metres   750
0 yards   750

GETTING THERE

S-Bahn 7 goes to Potsdam from Berlin. From Potsdam station, bus 606 goes to Neues Palais and trams 91, 92 and 96 go to the centre of town. Bus 695 travels between Park Sanssouci and Neuer Garten.

◁ **Colonnaded cloister at the Friedenskirche**

Street-by-Street: Park Sanssouci

THE ENORMOUS Park Sanssouci, occupying an area of 287 hectares, is among the most beautiful palace complexes in Europe. The first building to be constructed was Schloss Sanssouci, the summer palace of Frederick the Great. It was built on the site of an orchard in 1747. Over the years, Park Sanssouci was expanded considerably and enriched by the addition of other palaces and pavilions. Allow yourself at least a whole day to enjoy the park fully.

Flower-filled urn, Park Sanssouci

Communs
This house for the palace staff has an unusually elegant character, and is situated next to a pretty courtyard ❸

★ **Neues Palais**
This monumental building of the New Palace, constructed between 1763 and 1769, is crowned by a massive dome ❶

Römische Bäder
The Roman baths include a mock-Renaissance villa and a suite of Roman-style rooms ❺

| 0 metres | 200 |
| 0 yards | 200 |

STAR SIGHTS

★ **Schloss Sanssouci**

★ **Neues Palais**

Schloss Charlottenhof
This Neo-Classical palace gained its name from Charlotte von Gentzkow, the former owner of the land on which the palace was built ❹

Park Sanssouci
The extensive parkland is made up of several gardens. The one near the Orangerie is called the Lustgarten (pleasure garden) ❷

Orangerie
This Neo-Renaissance palace, the largest in the park, was built in the mid-19th century to house foreign royalty and guests ❼

Neue Kammern
This Rococo pavilion was once the orangerie of the Sanssouci Palace, but was rebuilt as a guest house ❾

★ Schloss Sanssouci
A beautifully terraced vineyard creates a grand approach to Schloss Sanssouci, the oldest building in the complex ❿

Bildergalerie
Built between 1755 and 1764, this pavilion houses an art gallery. It is Germany's oldest purpose-built museum building ⓫

Chinesisches Teehaus
The small Rococo-style Chinese Tea House features an exhibition of exquisite Oriental porcelain ❻

Friedenskirche
The Neo-Romanesque Church of Peace is modelled on the Basilica of San Clemente in Rome ❽

Neues Palais **❶**

THIS IMPOSING BAROQUE PALACE, on the main avenue in Park Sanssouci, was built at the request of Frederick the Great. The initial plans were prepared in 1750 by Georg Wenzeslaus von Knobelsdorff. However, construction only began in 1763, after the Seven Years' War *(see p19)*, to a design by Johann Gottfried Büring, Jean Laurent Le Geay and Carl von Gontard. The result was a vast two-storey building, decorated with hundreds of sculptures and more than 200 richly adorned rooms, which together make up one of Germany's most beautiful palaces.

Cabinet from the study

Façade
The entrance to the Neues Palais is through the gate on the western façade. The imposing gate is flanked by stone sentry boxes.

The Schlosstheater
was completed in 1768, and designed by JC Hoppenhaupt.

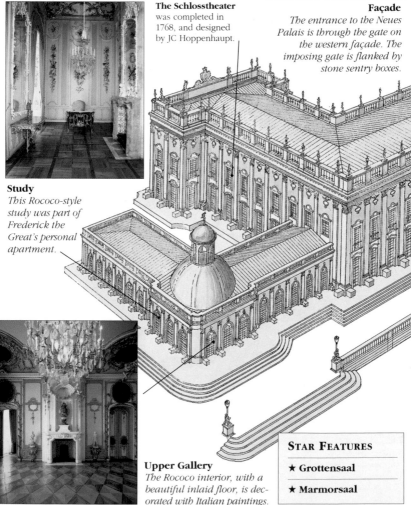

Study
This Rococo-style study was part of Frederick the Great's personal apartment.

Upper Gallery
The Rococo interior, with a beautiful inlaid floor, is decorated with Italian paintings.

STAR FEATURES
★ **Grottensaal**
★ **Marmorsaal**

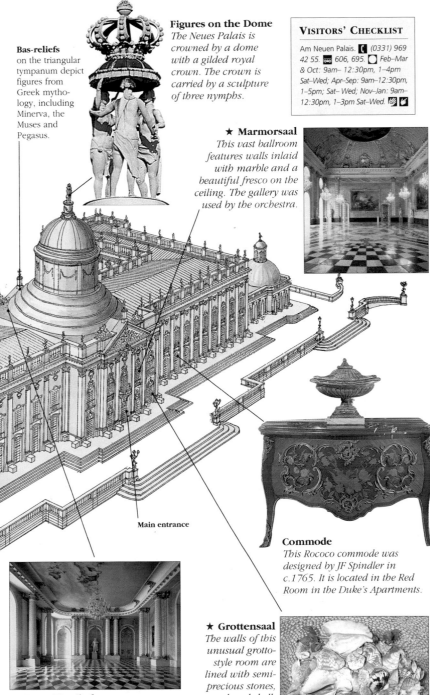

Bas-reliefs
on the triangular tympanum depict figures from Greek mythology, including Minerva, the Muses and Pegasus.

Figures on the Dome
The Neues Palais is crowned by a dome with a gilded royal crown. The crown is carried by a sculpture of three nymphs.

VISITORS' CHECKLIST

Am Neuen Palais. ☎ (0331) 969
42 55. 🚌 606, 695. ◯ Feb–Mar
& Oct: 9am– 12:30pm, 1–4pm
Sat–Wed; Apr–Sep: 9am–12:30pm,
1–5pm; Sat– Wed; Nov–Jan: 9am–
12:30pm, 1–3pm Sat–Wed. ♿ ⬛

★ Marmorsaal
This vast ballroom features walls inlaid with marble and a beautiful fresco on the ceiling. The gallery was used by the orchestra.

Main entrance

Commode
This Rococo commode was designed by JF Spindler in c.1765. It is located in the Red Room in the Duke's Apartments.

Upper Vestibule
This elegant room was designed by Carl von Gontard. The walls are covered with Silesian marble and the ceiling depicts Venus and the Graces.

★ Grottensaal
The walls of this unusual grotto-style room are lined with semi-precious stones, coral and shells as well as man-made stalactites.

Park Sanssouci ❷

Schopenhauerstrasse/ Zur Historischen Mühle. 🚌 612, 614, 695.

THIS VAST PARK, covering some 287 ha (700 acres), was established in 1725 on the site of an orchard. However, it was only transformed into an enormous landscaped park when construction work began on Schloss Sanssouci *(see pp192–3)*. Today, the park is made up of smaller gardens dating from different eras, each of which has been maintained in the original style. At the foot of Schloss Sanssouci is the oldest section of the park, containing the Dutch garden, a number of fountains and the French-style Lustgarten (pleasure garden), with a symmetrical layout and lovely rose beds. Surrounding Friedenskirche is the Marlygarten, created in the mid-19th century by Ludwig Persius.

The eastern part of the park is called the Rehgarten, a beautifully landscaped park in the English style, designed by Peter Joseph Lenné, and established on the site of former hunting grounds. This park extends right up to the Neues Palais. To the south, surrounding the small palace,

extends the Charlottenhof Park, also designed by Lenné. In the northern section of the park, next to the Orangerie, is the Nordischer Garten and the Paradiesgarten.

The range of different garden styles makes a simple stroll through this park particularly pleasant. There are also a large number of sculptures, columns, obelisks and grottoes for the visitor to explore. The perspectives that suddenly open up across the park, and the picturesque groupings of trees, are also beautiful.

Communs ❸

Am Neuen Palais. 🚌 606, 695.

THIS AREA OF the park consists of a pair of two-storey pavilions linked by a semi-circular colonnade. They are unusually elegant buildings considering they were used for servants' quarters and the palace kitchens. However, they also served to screen from view the cultivated fields that extended past the park from the palace.

The Communs were built between 1766 and 1769 by Carl von Gontard, to a design by Jean Laurent Le Geay. The

Elegant façade of the Communs, the servants' quarters

buildings are enclosed by an elegant courtyard reflected in the style of the buildings. The kitchen was in the south pavilion, linked to the palace by an underground passage-way, and the north pavilion accommodated the servants of the king's guests. Today, the rectors' offices of the University of Potsdam are located here in the Communs.

Schloss Charlottenhof ❹
CHARLOTTENHOF PALACE

Geschwister-Scholl-Strasse (Park Charlottenhof). 📞 (0331) 969 42 02. 🚌 606. 🚊 91, 94, 96, 98. ◯ 15 May–15 Oct: 10am–12:30pm & 1–5pm Tue–Sun.

THIS SMALL Neo-Classical palace is located in the southern extension of Park Sanssouci, Park Charlottenhof. It was designed by Friedrich Schinkel and Ludwig Persius in 1829 for the heir to the throne, later King Friedrich Wilhelm IV. This small one-storey building was built in the style of a Roman villa. The rear of the palace has a portico that opens out onto the garden terrace.

Some of the wall paintings in the so-called Pompeiian style, designed by Schinkel, are still in place. There is also a collection of Italian engravings. The most interesting part of the interior is the Humboldt Room, also called the Tent Room due to its resemblance to a tent. The palace is surrounded by a picturesque landscaped park designed by Peter Joseph Lenné.

One of the many sculptures on display in Park Sanssouci

Römische Bäder ❺
ROMAN BATHS

Lenné-Strasse (Park Charlottenhof).
📞 (0331) 969 42 02. 🚌 606. 🚃 91,
94, 96, 98. ⭘ 15 May–15 Oct:
10am–5pm Tue–Sun.

THIS PICTURESQUE group of
pavilions, situated by the
edge of a lake, forms the
Roman Baths, which actually
served as accommodation for
the king's guests. It was
designed by Karl Friedrich
Schinkel, with the involve-
ment of Ludwig Persius,
between 1829 and 1840. At
the front is the gardener's
house, which is adjacent to
an asymmetrical low tower in
the style of an Italian
Renaissance villa. In the background, to the left, extends
the former bathing pavilion,
which is currently used for
temporary exhibitions. All of
the pavilions are arranged
around an internal garden
planted with a multi-coloured
carpet of shrubs. A closer
look will reveal that many of
these colourful plants are
actually vegetables.

Spring of water, Römische Bäder

Chinesisches Teehaus ❻
CHINESE TEAHOUSE

Ökonomieweg (Rehgarten). 📞 (0331)
969 42 02. 🚌 606. 🚃 91, 94, 96, 98.
⭘ 15 May–15 Oct: 10am–12:30pm
& 1–5pm Tue–Sun.

THE LUSTROUS, GILDED pavilion
that can be seen glistening
from a distance is the Chinese
Teahouse. Chinese art was

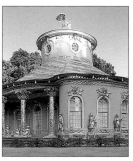

**The Chinesisches Teehaus, now
housing a collection of porcelain**

popular during the Rococo
period – people wore Chinese
silk, rooms were wallpapered
with Chinese designs, furniture
was lacquered, drinks were
served in Chinese porcelain,
and Chinese pavilions were
built in gardens.
   The Chinesisches Teehaus
was built in Park Sanssouci
between 1754 and 1756 to a
design by Johann Gottfried
Bühring. It is circular in shape
with a centrally located main
hall surrounded by three
studies. Between each of
these are pretty *trompe l'oeil*
porticos. Ornaments, together
with gilded figures of Chinese
gentlemen and ladies, surround
the pavilion. Originally the
Chinesisches Teehaus served
as a tea room and a summer
dining room. Today, it houses
a collection of porcelain.

Orangerie ❼

Maulbeerallee (Nordischer Garten).
📞 (0331) 29 61 89. 🚌 695. ⭘
15 May–15 Oct: 10am–12:30pm &
1–5pm Tue–Sun. **Observation terrace**
1 Apr–14 May: 10am–12:30pm &
1–5pm Sat–Sun; 15 May–15 Oct:
10am–12:30pm & 1–5pm Tue–Sun.

TOWERING ABOVE the park is
the Orangerie, designed in
the Italian Renaissance style
and crowned by a colonnade.
The Orangerie was built to
house guests, not plants. It
was constructed between
1851 and 1860 by Friedrich
August Stüler, on the initiative
and direction of Friedrich
Wilhelm IV. The final design
was partly based on the plans
of Ludwig Persius. It served
as a guest residence for the

king's sister and her husband
Tsar Nicholas I. The rooms
were grouped around the
Raphael Hall, which was
based on the Regia Hall in the
Vatican and decorated with
copies of the works of Italian
artist Raphael. It is also worth
climbing up to the observation
terrace, from where the view
extends over Potsdam.

Friedenskirche ❽

Allee nach Sanssouci (Marlygarten).
🚌 692, 695. 🚃 94, 98. ⭘
15 May–15 Oct: 10am–6pm Tue–Sun.

CLOSE TO SCHLOSS Sanssouci
is Friedenskirche, or the
Church of Peace. The foundation stone was laid by King
Friedrich Wilhelm IV in 1845
and the church was com-
pleted in 1848. Designed by
Ludwig Persius, Friedrich
August Stüler and Ludwig
Hesse, the church is based
on San Clemente in Rome.
   Inside, the vaulted ceiling
of the apse is almost completely covered by an
enchanting 12th-century
mosaic depicting the figure of
Christ as a judge. This
Byzantine mosaic was
originally located in the
church of San Capriano on
the island of Murano in
Venice, Italy. Next to the
church is a colonnaded
atrium and a mausoleum containing the tombs of Freidrich
Wilhelm I, Freidrich Wilhelm
IV and Kaiser Friedrich III.

**Long flight of stairs leading to the
Renaissance-style Orangerie**

Neue Kammern ❾
NEW CHAMBERS

Zur Historischen Mühle (Lustgarten).
📞 *(0331) 969 42 02.* 🚌 *612, 614, 695.* 🕐 *mid-May–mid-Oct: 10am–12:30pm & 1–5pm Tue–Sun; Apr–mid-May: 10am–12:30pm & 1–5pm Sat–Sun.* 🎫 ♿

T HE NEUE KAMMERN contains residential apartments. It is the mirror image of the Bildergalerie and was originally built as an orangery in 1747 to a design by Georg Wenzeslaus von Knobelsdorff. In 1777 Frederick the Great (Friedrich II) ordered the building to be remodelled as guest accommodation. The architect, Georg Christian Unger, left the elegant Baroque exterior of the orangery largely untouched and concentrated on converting the interior. As well as the sumptuous guest suites, the architect built four elegant halls. The best of these is the Ovidsaal, with its rich reliefs and marble floors. The interior décor has been maintained in Frederick's Rococo style. The building also has a collection of Meissen figurines.

Schloss Sanssouci ❿

See pp192–193.

Detail of Caravaggio's *Doubting Thomas*, in the Bildergalerie

Bildergalerie ⓫

Zur Historischen Mühle. 📞 *(0331) 969 42 02.* 🚌 *612, 614, 695.* 🕐 *mid-May–mid-Oct: 10am–12:30pm & 1–5pm Tue–Sun.* ♿

T HE PICTURE GALLERY housed in the building adjacent to Schloss Sanssouci is the first purpose-built gallery in Germany. It was constructed between 1755 and 1764 to a design by JG Büring. The garden elevation reveals an allegorical tableau representing Art, Education and Crafts, while busts of renowned artists have been placed in the windows.
   The gallery contains an exhibition of Baroque paintings once owned by Frederick the Great, although part of the collection can be found in the Gemäldegalerie *(see pp122–5).* Highlights include Caravaggio's *Doubting Thomas* and Guido Reni's *Cleopatra's Death,* as well as a number of canvases by Rubens and van Dyck.

Historische Mühle ⓬
HISTORIC WINDMILL

Zur Historischen Mühle. 📞 *(0331) 969 42 02.* 🚌 *612, 614, 695.* 🕐 *Apr–Oct: 10am–12:30pm & 1–6pm Sat–Thu.* ♿

A MILL HAS BEEN located here since the early 18th century, although this is actually a reconstruction, dating from 1993. According to local legend, the old windmill was so noisy that Frederick the Great ordered it to be dismantled. However, a court upheld the miller's cause and the mill was not demolished. In 1790 a new windmill was built in its place, which lasted until 1945. The building currently houses a small museum of mechanical windmills.

Alexandrowka ⓭

Russische Kolonie Allee/ Puschkinallee.
🚊 *92, 95.* 🚌 *138, 604, 609, 650, 692, 697.*

A TRIP TO Alexandrowka takes the visitor into the world of Pushkin's stories. Wooden houses made from logs,

A Russian-style wooden house in the settlement of Alexandrowka

decorated with carved motifs and set in their own gardens, create a very pretty residential estate. Although they appear to be picturebook, traditional Russian houses, they were constructed in 1826 under the direction of a German military architect called Captain Snethlage. What is interesting is that the estate was created for the singers of a Russian choir. The choir was set up in 1812 to entertain the troops and was recruited from over 500 Russian prisoners of war, who had fought with Napoleon. In 1815, when the Prussians and the Russians joined forces, the choir was retained by Friedrich Wilhelm III.

Peter Joseph Lenné was responsible for the overall appearance of the estate, and it was named Alexandrowka after the Tsarina, the Prussian Princess Charlotte. It is based on the shape of the cross of St Andrew inscribed within an oval. In all, 12 houses were built here, as well as an outhouse which now contains a small museum. Some of the dwellings are still owned by the ancestors of the choir. To the north of this estate stands the Russian Orthodox church of Alexander Nevski (1829).

Schloss Cecilienhof, summer residence of the Hohenzollern family

the current layout was created by Peter Joseph Lenné in 1816. It is a Romantic park ornamented with numerous pavilions and sculptures. The charming Marmorpalais stands beside the lake, while the northern section contains the early 20th-century Schloss Cecilienhof. Elsewhere you can see the red and green gardeners' houses, the pyramid-shaped ice house and a Neo-Gothic library pavilion completed in 1794.

Schloss Cecilienhof 🕔

Am Neuen Garten. 📞 *(0331) 969 42 44.* 🚌 *695.* ⏱ *Apr–Oct: 9am–5pm; Nov–Mar: 9am–4pm Tue–Sun.*

THE CECILIENHOF residence played a brief but important part in history because it was here that the 1945 Potsdam

Conference took place. Built between 1914 and 1917, the palace is the most recent of the Hohenzollern dynasty buildings and was designed by Paul Schultze-Naumburg in the style of an English country manor. It is a sprawling, asymmetrical building with wooden beams making a pretty herringbone pattern on its walls. The gatehouse passageways leading to the courtyards are decorated with Baroque reliefs.

The palace was the Hohenzollern family residence after they lost the crown; the family remained in Potsdam until February 1945. It now functions as a first-class hotel and restaurant, where history lovers can relax amid carefully tended shrubbery. Most of the historic furnishings used during the famous Potsdam conference are on display.

Orange growing in the Neuer Garten's Marmorpalais

Neuer Garten 🕓

NEW GARDEN

Am Neuen Garten. 🚌 *695.*

RUNNING ALONG the edge of Heiliger See, on what was once the site of palace vineyards, is a park laid out between 1787 and 1791. It was landscaped originally by Johann August Eyserbeck the Younger on the instructions of Friedrich Wilhelm II, while

THE POTSDAM CONFERENCE OF 1945

On 17 July 1945 the heads of government for Great Britain (Winston Churchill, later represented by Clement Attlee), the United States (Harry Truman) and the Soviet Union (Joseph Stalin) met in Schloss Cecilienhof to confirm the decisions made earlier that year at Yalta. The aim of both conferences was to resolve the problems arising at the end of World War II. They decided to abolish the Nazi Party, to limit the size of the German militia and monitor it indefinitely, and also to punish war criminals and establish reparations. They also revised the German borders and

arranged the resettlement of Germans from Poland. The conference played a major part in establishing the political balance of power in Europe, which continued for the next 45 years.

Attlee, Truman and Stalin at Cecilienhof

Schloss Sanssouci ❿

THE NAME SANSSOUCI is French for "without a care" and gives a good indication of the flamboyant character of this enchanting Rococo palace, built in 1745. The original sketches, made by Friedrich II (Frederick the Great) himself, were finalized by Georg Wenzeslaus von Knobelsdorff. The glorious interiors were designed by Knobelsdorff and Johann August Nahl. The king clearly loved this palace, as his final wishes were that he should be buried here, near the tomb of his Italian greyhounds. He was actually interred in the Garnisonkirche, Potsdam, but his final wishes were carried out in 1991.

Bacchanalian Figures
The curved male and female bacchanalian figures on the pilasters are the work of Friedrich Christian Glume.

The colonnade frames the view of the artificial ruins on the hill.

The wings were added to the building between 1841 and 1842.

Voltaire Room
This room, located in the Damenflügel (Ladies' wing), is decorated with naturalistic carvings of birds, flowers and fruit.

Domed Roof
The oxidized green dome covers the Marmorsaal. It is decorated with Baroque sculptures.

Marmorsaal
The imposing marble hall is decorated with pairs of columns made from Carrara marble. Frederick the Great wanted this room to be loosely based on the Pantheon in Rome.

STAR SIGHTS

★ **Konzertzimmer**

★ **Fêtes Galantes by Antoine Watteau**

Arbour
The palace design is completed by picturesque arbours and pergolas decorated with sun motifs.

VISITORS' CHECKLIST

Zur Historischen Mühle.
☎ (0331) 969 42 02.
🚌 695. 🚃 91, 94, 96, 98.
🕐 1 Apr–31 Oct: 8:30am–5pm daily; 1 Nov–31 Mar: 9am–4pm daily. **Damenflügel** 15 May–15 Oct: 10am–12:30pm & 1–5pm Sat–Sun.

★ Fêtes Galantes (c. 1715)
The real jewels in the palace are the enchanting paintings by Antoine Watteau. He was one of Frederick the Great's favourite artists.

Weimar Urn (1785)
This Neo-Classical urn from the Berlin company KPM (see p129) is a copy of the original urn, which was presented to the Duchess of Weimar.

★ Konzertzimmer
The walls of the salon are decorated with paintings by Antoine Pesne, based on Greek mythology.

Bibliothek
The library of Frederick the Great contains about 2,100 books. The walls are lined with cedar panelling to create a contemplative atmosphere.

Marmorpalais ⑯
MARBLE PALACE

Am Ufer der Heiligen Soor (Neuer Garten). **[C]** (0331) 969 42 46.
[bus] 695. **[O]** 15 May–31 Oct:
10am–5pm Tue–Sun; 1 Nov–14 May:
10am–4pm Sat–Sun.

T HE MARMORPALAIS is situated on the edge of the lake in Neuer Garten (see p191), a park northeast of the centre of Potsdam. This small palace is a beautiful example of early Neo-Classical architecture. The palace owes its name to its façade, which is lined with Silesian marble.

The square main body of the palace was the initiative of King Friedrich Wilhelm II. The original building was completed in 1791 to a design by Carl von Gontard, under the direction of Carl Gotthard Langhans. The single-storey building had small rooms around a central staircase, but this turned out to be too small, and in 1797 it was extended. An extra floor and two projecting wings were added. This gave the Marmorpalais the character of a Palladian villa.

The main part of the palace contains Neo-Classical furnishings from the late 1700s, including furniture from the workshops of Roentgen and porcelain from Wedgwood, the English firm. The interiors of the wings date from slightly later, from the 1840s. The concert hall in the right hand wing is particularly beautiful. King Friedrich Wilhelm II died in this palace in 1797.

Neo-Classical Marmorpalais, with its inlaid marble façade

The historic Dutch district known as the Holländische Viertel

Holländisches Viertel ⑰
DUTCH QUARTER

Friedrich-Ebert-/Kurfürsten-/Hebbel-/Gutenbergstr. **[bus]** 138, 601, 602, 603, 604, 606, 607, 608, 609, 610, 611, 612, 614, 631, 632, 650. **[tram]** 92, 95.

J UST AS AMAZING as the Russian district of Alexandrowka (see p190) is this Dutch district. The area is popular with tourists, with numerous shops, galleries, cafés and beer cellars, especially along Mittelstrasse.

Dutch workers, invited by Friedrich Wilhelm I, arrived in Potsdam at the beginning of the 18th century. Between 1733 and 1742 a settlement was built for them, comprising 134 gabled houses arranged in four groups, according to plans by Johann Boumann the Elder. They were built from small red bricks, and finished with stone and plaster details. These houses are typically three-storey, with picturesque roofs and gables. The gardens were lost as a result of widening the streets.

Peter und Paul Kirche ⑱

Bassinplatz. **[bus]** 138, 601, 602, 603, 604, 606, 607, 608, 609, 610, 611, 612, 614, 631, 632, 650. **[tram]** 92, 95.

T HIS 19TH-CENTURY church was the first large Catholic church built in Potsdam, at the initiative of Friedrich Wilhelm IV. The first designs came from Friedrich August Stüler, though the final version is the work of Wilhelm Salzenberg. It was built in 1870, in the

shape of a Neo-Romanesque cross. Its slender tower is a copy of the campanile of San Zeno Maggiore in Verona, Italy. Inside are three beautiful paintings by Antoine Pesne.

The colonnaded portico of the Französische Kirche

Französische Kirche ⑲
FRENCH CHURCH

Bassinplatz. **[bus]** 138, 601, 602, 603, 604, 606, 607, 608, 609, 610, 611, 612, 614, 631, 632, 650. **[tram]** 92, 95.

T HIS CHURCH, reminiscent of the Pantheon in Rome, was built especially for the Hugenots in 1752. Following their expulsion from France, they were given the option of settling in Prussia in 1685 (see p19). Those who settled in Potsdam initially benefited from the hospitality of other churches, then eventually the Französische Kirche was built for them. It was designed by Johann Boumann the Elder in the shape of an ellipse. The front elevation is supported by a grand columned portico. The side niches, which are the entrances of the church, are decorated with the allegorical figures of Faith and Knowledge. The interior of the church dates from the 1830s and is based on designs by Karl Friedrich Schinkel.

Nikolaikirche ⑳

Am Alten Markt. 🚌 601, 603, 692, 694, 🚃 91, 92, 93, 95, 96, 98. ⏰ 2–5pm Mon, 10am–5pm Tue–Sat, 11:30am–5pm Sun.

THIS IMPOSING church, built in a late Neo-Classical style, is undoubtedly the most beautiful church in Potsdam. It was designed in 1830 by Karl Friedrich Schinkel and the building work was overseen by Ludwig Persius. The main body of the church is based on a square cross, with a semi-circular presbytery.

It was decided only in the 1840s to crown the church with a vast dome, supported on a colonnaded tambour (wall supporting a dome). Schinkel had envisaged this from the beginning of the project, but it was not included in the orders of the king. Initially it was thought that the dome would be supported by a wooden structure, though ultimately it was built using iron between 1843 and 1848, according to a design by Persius and Friedrich August Stüler. The interior decoration and the furnishings of the church date back to the 1850s, and in the main area of the church they were based on the earlier designs by Schinkel.

In front of the church stands an obelisk built between 1753 and 1755, according to a

design by Georg Wenzeslaus von Knobelsdorff. Initially it was decorated by medallions depicting the portraits of Prussian rulers, but during the post-World War II restorations, they were replaced with portraits of renowned Prussian architects.

Altes Rathaus ㉑
OLD TOWN HALL

Am Alten Markt. 🚌 601, 603, 692, 694. 🚃 91, 92, 93, 95, 96, 98.

THIS ELEGANT, colonnaded building, located on the eastern side of Alter Markt, is the old town hall. Designed by Johann Boumann the Elder, it was built in 1753 on the site of an earlier building that served a similar purpose. The uppermost storey, which features an ornamental attic roof, is decorated with the crest of Potsdam and allegorical sculptures. At the summit of the small tower are two gilded figures

Atlas at Altes Rathaus

of Atlas, each carrying a globe of the earth. The Altes Rathaus is currently used as a cultural centre. The interior of the neighbouring mid-18th century building was also refurbished, and a glassed-in passageway was built, linking the two buildings.

The Potsdam Royal Palace was located at one time on the west side of Alter Markt. It was a massive two-storey building with three wings. There was also an elegant courtyard and a superb gateway crowned by a tower. The palace was built in 1662 on the site of a former castle, on the initiative of the Great Elector. Over the following years the palace was greatly enlarged and modernized for members of the royal family, including Frederick the Great (Friedrich II). After a bombing raid in 1945 the palace remained in ruins for many years, but the East German Government decided finally to pull down the remains in 1960. A temporary theatre now occupies the site.

POTSDAM TOWN GATES

The city of Potsdam was enclosed by a wall in 1722. This wall did not serve a defensive purpose – it was supposed to contain criminals and stop soldiers deserting. When the borders of the town were extended in 1733, new districts were also enclosed by the wall. There was a total of five city gates, of which three have survived. Jägertor has survived in its original condition and dates from 1733. Featuring solid, wide pillars, the gate is crowned with a group of sculptures depicting hunting dogs attacking a deer. Nauener Tor was redesigned in 1755 by Johann Gottfried Büring and, interestingly, it is one of the earliest examples of Neo-Gothic design occurring outside Great Britain. The most imposing of the gates is the Brandenburger Tor. It was rebuilt in 1770 in a Neo-Classical style to commemorate victory in the Seven Years' War (see p19). The designers, Gontard and Unger, gave it the appearance of an ancient triumphal arch. At the very top is a number of different groups of sculptures. These include figures from Greek mythology, such as Hercules and Mars.

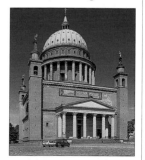
Nikolaikirche's imposing exterior, with its green, weathered dome

Nauener Tor   **Jägertor**   **Brandenburger Tor**

Stately building of the Marstall (Filmmuseum)

Marstall (Filmmuseum) ㉒

Alter Markt. 27 18 10. 10am–6pm Tue–Sun. 601, 603, 692, 694. 91, 92, 93, 95, 96, 98.

THIS BAROQUE PAVILION, once used as a royal stables, hence the name Marstall, is the only remaining building of a former royal residence. It was first established in 1714 by refashioning the orangery built by Johann Nering in 1685. In 1746 it was extended and refashioned once more, according to a design by the architect GW von Knobelsdorff. It suffered extensive damage in World War II and in 1977, after major restoration, it was converted to a film museum. As well as temporary exhibitions, this museum documents the history and work of the Babelsberg studios, Germany's earliest film studios. Exhibits include old projectors, cameras and other equipment as well as props used in some of the most famous German films.

Potsdam-Museum ㉓

Breite Strasse 8–12. 289 66 00. 9am–5pm Tue–Sun.

THE POTSDAM-MUSEUM'S collection embraces natural science and historical exhibits equally, including a display illustrating the geography and nature of the basin of the Havel river. In the main building, the history of Potsdam is documented up until 1900 and the exhibition continues in two smaller buildings, called the Hiller-Brandt's Häuser (houses). These twin structures were built in 1769 by Georg Christian Unger and were a deliberate copy of Inigo Jones's Banqueting House on Whitehall, London.

Cherubs decorating the façade of the Potsdam-Museum

Wasserwerk Sanssouci ㉔

Breite Strasse. (0331) 969 42 48. 15 May–15 October: 10am–5pm Sat–Sun. 606. 91, 94, 96, 98.

ALTHOUGH POTSDAM once boasted a Russian and Dutch community, the remarkable mosque was not built to serve the needs of an Islamic community. Rather, it was built to disguise the special steam pump that serviced the fountains in Park Sanssouci. This Moorish-style building, with its slender minaret and Oriental dome, was designed by Ludwig Persius in 1842. The dome does not serve any useful purpose, although within the minaret there is a huge chimney. While visiting the mosque you can see the preserved steam-powered machinery manufactured by the Borsig company.

Telegrafenberg ㉕

Albert-Einstein-Strasse. 694. **Einsteinturm** (0331) 288 233 33 8f 29 17 41. Jul. compulsory.

THE BUILDINGS on the Telegrafenberg are considered to be some of the most beautiful 20th-century structures in the world and attract many admirers of modern architecture. The hill received its current name in 1832, when an optical telegraph station linking Berlin and Koblenz was built there. In the late 19th century, various educational institutes were located here. These included the Institute of Astrophysics, for which the complex of buildings in yellow brick was constructed.

The meandering avenues lead to a picturesque clearing where the small Einsteinturm (Einstein's Tower) breaks through the surrounding trees. Specially designed to observe the solar system, the tower was intended to provide information that would support Einstein's Theory of Relativity. It was built in 1920 by Erich Mendelsohn and is regarded as one of the finest architectural examples of German Expressionism. Its fantastical appearance was intended to show what could be achieved with reinforced concrete. However, the costs of the complicated form limited the use of concrete, and above the first storey the building is made from brickwork covered in plaster.

Moorish Wasserwerk Sanssouci, complete with minaret

Filmpark Babelsberg

THIS AMAZING FILM PARK was laid out on the site of the film studios where Germany's first films were produced in 1912. From 1917 the studio belonged to Universum-Film-AG (UFA), which produced some of the most renowned films of the silent era, such as *Metropolis (see p145).* Subsequently, Nazi propaganda films were also made here. The studio is still operational today, although part of the complex is open to visitors. Expect to see the sets from old films, special effects at work and stuntmen in action.

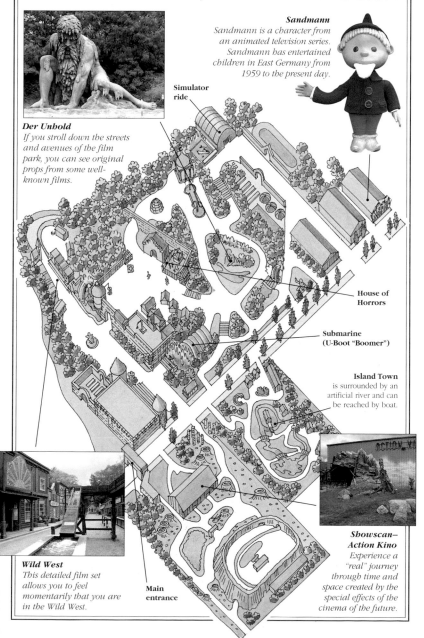

Sandmann
Sandmann is a character from an animated television series. Sandmann has entertained children in East Germany from 1959 to the present day.

Simulator ride

Der Unhold
If you stroll down the streets and avenues of the film park, you can see original props from some well-known films.

House of Horrors

Submarine (U-Boot "Boomer")

Island Town
is surrounded by an artificial river and can be reached by boat.

Wild West
This detailed film set allows you to feel momentarily that you are in the Wild West.

Main entrance

Showscan– Action Kino
Experience a "real" journey through time and space created by the special effects of the cinema of the future.

THREE GUIDED WALKS

BERLIN IS FULL of enchanting parks, gardens, lakes and interesting monuments, and one of the best ways to enjoy them is by going on a guided walk. The three walks suggested in this chapter provide for relaxation far from the hustle and bustle of the city centre. The first takes you onto the picturesque Pfaueninsel (Peacock Island), which at the end of the 18th century was refashioned into a romantic English-style park with garden pavilions and an enchanting little palace. After visiting the island you can pay a short visit to Nikolskoe – a Russian-style *dacha* (country house) built for the future Tsar Nicholas I and his wife, the daughter of King Friedrich Wilhelm III. The second walk begins in Berlin and takes you first through the grounds of the Klein

Statue at Klein Glienicke

Glienicke Park, which was laid out in the 1820s for Prince Karl of Prussia. This route continues across the former border between East and West Germany, in an area which is now part of Potsdam. There you can visit the Romantic-era park of Babelsberg, and the Neo-Gothic palace designed for Prince Wilhelm by Karl Friedrich Schinkel. The third walk, around the forest called Grunewald, takes you initially through a deluxe villa resort of the late 19th century, and then along forest paths to the Grunewaldsee. On the shores of this lake stands an enchanting hunting lodge. From there you can continue walking to the Brücke-Museum. Because each of these three walks leads you across unpaved paths, remember to wear comfortable shoes.

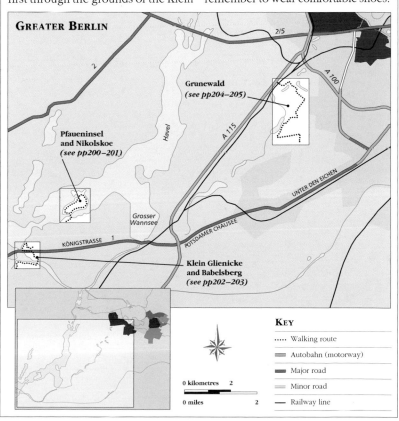

GREATER BERLIN

Grunewald
(see pp204–205)

Pfaueninsel
and Nikolskoe
(see pp200–201)

Havel

A 115

UNTER DEN EICHEN

Grosser
Wannsee

KÖNIGSTRASSE

POTSDAMER CHAUSSEE

Klein Glienicke
and Babelsberg
(see pp202–203)

KEY

····· Walking route

═══ Autobahn (motorway)

▬▬ Major road

══ Minor road

── Railway line

0 kilometres 2

0 miles 2

◁ **A picturesque corner of the Neo-Gothic Babelsberg palace**

Pfaueninsel and Nikolskoe

THIS WALK takes you around Pfaueninsel (Peacock Island). This picturesque park, now a nature reserve, was laid out in 1795 according to a design by Johann August Eyserbeck. Its final form, which you see today, is the work of the renowned landscape architect Peter Joseph Lenné. This pleasant, relaxing walk allows you to explore several interesting sights, and to encounter the peacocks for which the island is named. Afterwards you can have refreshments at the lakeside, or head straight to Nikolskoe, the location of one of Berlin's finest restaurants.

Statue at the small palace

James's Well, deliberately built to resemble a picturesque ruin

One of the colourful peacocks on Pfaueninsel (Peacock Island)

Around Pfaueninsel

At the jetty ① you board a small passenger ferry which takes you to the island in a few minutes. After disembarking, follow the path which leads to the left. It continues along the edge of the island, gently uphill past the Castellan's House ② and further on to the Swiss House, dating from 1830, in which the gardener lived. Continue along the path to the extensive clearing with a picturesque flower garden, beyond which is the small romantic palace of Schloss Pfaueninsel ③. Dating from 1794, it was designed by

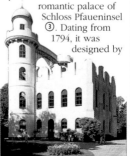

The Neo-Gothic Schloss Pfaueninsel designed by Johann Brendel

Johann Gottlieb Brendel for Friedrich Wilhelm II and his mistress Wilhelmine Encke (the future Countess Lichtenau). The palace was built of wood, with a façade (hidden away) fashioned in the form of a ruined medieval castle. The façade was visible from Neuer Garten in Potsdam. The cast-iron bridge which links the towers was built in 1807. During the summer months you can go inside the palace to see its furnishings from the 18th and 19th centuries.

After leaving the palace follow the path that leads along the edge, passing by the kitchen pavilion ④ on the left, which is set amid greenery. At the next junction turn gently right into the depths of the island. You will pass by the James's Well ⑤ which was built to resemble an ancient ruin, and cross a meadow heading towards a small wood which contains the Kavalierhaus ⑥. This building was used to provide the

royal household with accommodation. At the front of the house, Karl Friedrich Schinkel installed an authentic façade from a late Gothic house brought over from Danzig (now Gdansk in Poland). From here you proceed further in the same

PFAUENINSELCHAUSSEE

NIKOLSKOER WEG

| 0 metres | 200 |
| 0 yards | 200 |

KEY

•••• Suggested route

– – Ferry route

⚓ Ferry boarding point

direction, and emerge again in a large clearing. To the left you can marvel at the Parschenkessel bay ⑦ in the distance, surrounded by dead trees on which cormorants nest. Take the path on the left to the Neo-Gothic Dairy ⑧

Guests on the terrace of the Blockhaus Nikolskoe in summer

mausoleum in Schlosspark Charlottenburg *(see p157)* in 1829. The path leads further along the edge of the lake, while on the right side among the trees you pass the stone commemorating Johannes Kunckel, an alchemist who lived on Pfaueninsel in the 17th century. In his quest to uncover how to make gold he, in fact, discovered a method of producing ruby-coloured glass. Carry on further through the forest, passing the Gothic Bridge ⑪, and then take the path to the right up towards the hill of the Aviary ⑫, home to multi-coloured parrots and pheasants. From here you continue towards the tall column of a Fountain ⑬ designed by Martin Friedrich Raabe in 1824 . Next, walk onward to the jetty, passing the market gardens with their hothouses on the way.

From the Jetty to Nikolskoe
Once you've taken the little ferry back to the mainland, head off to the right, going

Havel

and the Dutch House ⑨. This was a cow shed and dates from 1802, while the Dairy is an artificial ruin of a medieval abbey dating from 1795. From here take the path along the edge of the lake heading south; you can marvel at the wonderful views. To the right by the edge of the forest you can see Luisentempel ⑩ in the form of a Greek temple. Its sandstone portico at the front was moved to the island from the

> **TIPS FOR WALKERS**
>
> **Beginning of the walk:** the jetty for the ferry to Pfaueninsel.
> **Length:** 4.4 km (2.7 miles).
> **Duration:** 2.5–3 hours.
> **Getting there:** bus A16 or 316 from S-Bahn Wannsee; or ferry from Wannsee or Potsdam.
> **Stops:** There are no cafés or restaurants on Pfaueninsel itself. By the jetty on the mainland is "Wirtshaus zur Pfaueninsel," a little place to eat with a summer beer garden. In Nikolskoe is a restaurant with a terrace called "Blockhaus Nikolskoe."

south. When you come to the fork take the left hand path leading gently uphill. This leads to the church of Saint Peter and Paul ⑭, which rises above a large terrace from where there are pretty views of Pfaueninsel. The church was built between the years 1834 and 1837, according to a design by Friedrich August Stüler. The small, orderly, body of the church is fronted by a tower crowned by an onion-shaped dome, which reflects Russian Orthodox sacral architecture. This links to the adjacent Blockhaus "Nikolskoe" ⑮, a Russian-style wooden *dacha* (country house), built in 1819 by the architect Snethlage, who created the Alexandrowka estate in Potsdam. The *dacha* was a present from King Friedrich Wilhelm III to his daughter and son-in-law, the future Tsar Nicholas I. Following a fire in 1985 the *dacha* was reconstructed, and it currently houses a restaurant. Nearby you will find a bus-stop where you can catch buses back to the S-Bahn Wannsee.

The little ferry on the Havel river which takes passengers to Pfaueninsel

Klein Glienicke and Babelsberg

THIS GUIDED WALK takes you through an area covered by two interesting palace-park complexes – Klein Glienicke and Babelsberg. They were built originally for members of the royal family during the mid-19th century. The buildings of Klein Glienicke were designed by Schinkel, Persius and von Arnim in a Neo-Classical style. Peter Joseph Lenné created the charming park in which they are located. Babelsberg has a more romantic park that was completed by Hermann von Pückler-Muskau. It is maintained in a completely different style, with regal Neo-Gothic pavilions.

A griffin in Klein Glienicke

Mosaic from the Klosterhof in the gardens of Klein Glienicke

Around Klein Glienicke

The walk begins by the main gate leading into the park. The southern section of the park has the feel of an Italianate Arcadian garden. Soon on the left you will see the Stibadium ①, a roofed pavilion designed by Ludwig Persius. Nearby you can marvel at the imposing Fountain of Lions ②, decorated with gilded figures of these royal beasts. The fountain stands on the axis of the palace ③ which was built in 1825, according to a design

The reconstructed Gothic Gerichts-laube (arcaded courthouse)

by Karl Friedrich Schinkel for Prince Karl of Prussia. During summer weekends you can visit the palace between 10am and 5pm. Beyond the symmetrical, Neo-Classical building extends an irregular cluster of buildings, grouped around a courtyard with a veranda, which include a pergola and staff cottages. You pass by the palace and approach the Coach House ④, designed by Schinkel but refurbished several times. This now houses the Coach House restaurant (see p243).

Beyond the Coach House you can see the orangery and greenhouses built by Persius. A path leads in the direction of the lake, but on the way it is worth diverting to the right to the Klosterhof ⑤, a mock monastery with pavilions, also by Persius. In the walls of these buildings are numerous Byzantine and Romanesque architectural elements from Italy. Further to the north extends a second "wild" section of the park created to resemble an alpine and Carpathian landscape, with man-made waterfalls, planks

for crossing the water, and hunting lodges. You can return in the direction of the lake and go up to the Casino ⑦, which once contained guest apartments. From here a path extending along the lake takes you to the Grosse Neugierde ⑧, a circular pavilion with a roof supported by Doric columns, based on the Athenian monument to Lysikrates from the 4th century BC. From here there are beautiful views across the Havel river and Glienicker Brücke ⑨, known paradoxically as the bridge of unity under the East German

contain original Roman and Byzantine fragments.

From Klein Glienicke to Babelsberg

On leaving the park you cross to the other side of Potsdamer Chaussee and proceed along Mövenstrasse, passing the massive building of the Jagdschloss Glienicke ⑪ on the right. Located on the site of an earlier hunting lodge, its Neo-Mannerist appearance is the result of a massive rebuilding process undertaken in 1889 by Albert Geyer, on behalf of Prince Friedrich Leopold. It now houses an international meeting centre as well as an academy of folk art. Passing the Jagdschloss you turn right into Waldmüllerstrasse, then right again into Lankestrasse, which leads you to the bridge linking Glienicke with Babelsberg.

Around Schloss Babelsberg

From the bridge you head right towards the engine house ⑫, designed by Persius to look like a medieval castle with a tall tower covering the chimney. From here you head towards Schloss Babelsberg ⑬, designed by Karl Friedrich Schinkel for the future Kaiser Wilhelm I of Germany. The palace was built between 1833 and 1835 in a Neo-Gothic style and shows the influence of English architecture on Schinkel. This beautiful, irregular building with many

Babelsberg's Neo-Gothic Flatowturm dating from 1853 to 1856

towers and bay windows is one of Schinkel's greatest works. Visitors can go inside.

From here, take the path leading along the edge of the Havel to the so-called Kleines Schloss ⑭. Another Neo-Gothic palace, although much smaller in scale, this was where ladies of the court once resided. It now houses a café.

From here you proceed further to the edge of the lake, taking the left branch to the Neo-Gothic stable ⑮, and further to the Gerichtslaube (Gothic arcaded courthouse) ⑯ which was moved here from Berlin. The final sight on this walk is the Flatowturm ⑰, a Neo-Gothic tower dating from 1853 to 1856, from which there are marvellous views of the surrounding area. From here follow the path to the park exit at Grenzstrasse. Turning left, you reach the bus stop for the No. 690 and No. 691 which go to S-Bahn Babelsberg station.

regime. The border with West Berlin ran across this bridge, where the exchange of spies was conducted during the Cold War. You return via a path along the wall of the main gate, passing the Kleine Neugierde ⑩, a pavilion serving as a tea room. This was built in the form of an ancient temple, and its walls

| 0 metres | 300 |
| 0 yards | 300 |

KEY

•••• Suggested route

⛴ Ferry boarding point

The Neo-Gothic Schloss Babelsberg, designed by KF Schinkel

TIPS FOR WALKERS

Beginning of the walk: bus stop at Klein Glienicke. **Length:** 4.2 km (2.6 miles). **Duration:** 3 hours. **Getting there:** bus 116 from S-Bahn station Wannsee or ferry from Wannsee or Potsdam. **Stops:** Café at Park Babelsberg; Coach House at Klein Glienicke. **Schloss Babelsberg** ☐ Apr–Oct: 10am–12:30pm & 1–5pm Tue–Sun; Nov–Mar: 10am–12:30pm & 1–4pm Sat–Sun.

Grunewald

THIS WALK leads initially through one of Berlin's most elegant residential areas established in 1889. Once the haunt of politicians, wealthy industrialists, renowned artists and academics, some villas now serve as the headquarters of academic institutes. This walk continues through the forest to a small hunting lodge with an interesting art collection, and ends at the edge of the Grunewald in a residential estate of elegant villas, home of the Brücke-Museum.

The elegant villa at Winklerstrasse No. 11

From Bahnhof Grunewald to Hagenstrasse

From the S-Bahn Grunewald station follow the signs to "Grunewald (Ort)". Be sure to take a close look at the station itself ① – this picturesque wooden framed building was built in 1899. From the square in front of the station go along Winklerstrasse, which turns left. Along the way you will pass stunningly beautiful villas. The Neo-Classical house at No. 15, dating from 1899, was home to architect Ewald Becher ②. Not much further on the same side of the road, at No. 11, is an interesting villa dating from 1906 ③. It was designed by Hermann Muthesius, who transplanted onto German soil the style of English rustic building. On the right at No. 12 is Villa Maren, dating from 1897, an interesting example of a Neo-Renaissance building in the style of an Italian palazzo with *sgraffito* decorations ④. The villa at No. 8–10, dating from 1902, boasts costly stone elevations, which fan out richly with decorations in the German

Renaissance style ⑤. By this villa turn right into Hasensprung, which leads across the bridge decorated with running hares, dividing Diana-see from Königssee. You reach Königsallee and turn left before immediately turning right into Lassen-strasse, and then right again into Bismarck-strasse, which leads to a small square where you can marvel at the picturesque Neo-Gothic Grunewald-Kirche ⑥, from 1902 to 1904. This asymmetrical building has two naves and a tower by the presbytery. From here go left into Furt-wänglerstrasse, where it is worth looking at the villa at No. 15, a beautiful example of a southern German country house ⑦. Next turn right into Hubertusbader Strasse, where at No. 25 an interesting villa has survived with Neo-Classical motifs ⑧, which is the work of Arnold Hartmann dating from 1896. He is also responsible for the villa at No. 23

Rose window, Grunewald-Kirche

Seebergsteig, featuring fantastic elevations decorated with Secessionist motifs ⑨. From here continue along Hubertus-bader Strasse to Hagenstrasse.

From Hagenstrasse to the Brücke-Museum

You cut through Hagenstrasse and continue further, straight into Wildpfad, where you turn left in Waldmeisterstrasse, which leads along the fence of the grounds of private clubs. Turn right into Eichhörn-chensteig, which gradually becomes surrounded by forest and changes from being a

road into a forest path. Once past the grounds of the private clubs, follow a road which goes gently to the right, and down to the edge of the picturesque Grunewaldsee. Turn left and continue along its edge to Jagdschloss Grunewald ⑩. This is one of the oldest civic buildings to survive in Berlin. It was built for the Elector Joachim II in 1542, and around 1700 it was rebuilt in a Baroque style. Through the gate you enter a courtyard enclosed on three sides with household buildings. In the small palace is Berlin's only surviving Renaissance hall. Currently this houses a collection of paintings, with canvases by Rubens and van Dyck among others. In the east wing is the small Waldmuseum, with illustrations that depict forest life and the history of forestry. Opposite the Jagdschloss, a hunting museum (Jagdmuseum) features historic weapons and equipment.

From the palace you proceed further along the edge to Forsthaus Paulsborn ⑪. This picturesque building was constructed in 1905, according to a design by Friedrich Wilhelm Göhre (see p242). The entire building is maintained in the style of a hunting lodge with decorations that reflect hunting themes. During the summer the garden is filled

The household buildings in the hunting lodge in Grunewald

with tables, where you can enjoy a tasty meal and have a rest, following the walk.

From Paulsborn you return to Jagdschloss Grunewald; at the crossroads you should take the central avenue sign-posted "Wilmersdorf". This leads through the forest and emerges on Pücklerstrasse. Passing modern deluxe villas you continue straight on, and then turn right into Fohlenweg, then turn right again into Bussardsteig, at the end of which is the Brücke-Museum (see p171) ⑫. It is also worth looking at the exhibition of sculptures by Bernhard Heliger arranged in the garden surrounding the villa at Käuzchensteig No. 8. From here you continue to Clayallee where buses on the No. 115 route operate.

Decorative detail from Seebersteig No. 23

Restaurant in the Forsthaus Paulsborn near Jagdschloss Grunewald

KEY

····· Suggested route

Ⓢ S-Bahn

0 metres 400

0 yards 400

TIPS FOR WALKERS

Beginning of the walk: Grunewald S-Bahn station.
Distance: 3 km (1.8 miles).
Duration: 2.5–3 hours.
Getting there: S-Bahn line 3 or 7; U-Bahn Oskar-Helene-Heim; Bus 115. **Museum:** Jagdschloss Grunewald. 🕿 813 35 97.
⭘ May–Oct: 10am–1pm & 1:30–5pm Tue–Sun; Nov–Apr: 10am–1pm & 1:30–4pm Sat & Sun.
Stops: There are numerous cafés and restaurants in the Grunewald residential area. Near Jagdschloss Grunewald there is a very good restaurant, Forsthaus Paulsborn.

Travellers' Needs

WHERE TO STAY

ERLIN HAS A good selection of hotels to suit any budget. Many of the expensive hotels belong to well-known international chains, but you can also find reasonably priced rooms in and around the centre. There are good-quality mid-range hotels in eastern Berlin, where many new hotels have been built recently. There is no lack of luxurious hotels in eastern Berlin, either, particularly around Unter den Linden. Many of the more affordable hotels in the western part of Berlin require urgent repairs. The area around Grunewald is an oasis of peace that will guarantee a good rest. From the numerous hotels in Berlin, this section highlights some of the best; these have been categorized according to location and price on pages 214–16. Details about each one can be found on pages 217–25. Information about alternative ways of spending a night can be found on pages 210–11.

Reception area in the Sorat Art'otel *(see p222)*

WHERE TO LOOK

THERE ARE A FEW areas in Berlin with large concentrations of hotels. In each area there is usually at least one luxury hotel as well as several more affordable places. In Charlottenburg, around Kurfürstendamm and Tauentzienstrasse, are well-known hotels, such as the Kempinski, Savoy, Palace Berlin and the Steigenberger. Bear in mind that this part of Berlin was severely damaged during World War II and the majority of these hotels occupy modern buildings; hotels in old buildings, like the Brandenburger Hof, are a rarity. Inexpensive hotels and pensions can be found in the side streets off the main road, but ask to see the rooms before you decide. Good hotels are also situated in the east part of Charlottenburg, around Lützowufer.

There have been changes in recent years to hotels in the former East Berlin. These hotels have been privatized and the majority of them have been refurbished extensively. In addition, many new hotels have been built. The Adlon, Hilton and Grand, situated in the western part of Mitte around Unter den Linden, are the most luxurious. In the eastern part of this area, around Marx-Engels-Forum and Alexanderplatz, the hotels are more reasonably priced and offer good-quality rooms.

Grunewald is an oasis of peace far from the bustle of Berlin. There is the luxurious Ritz hotel, as well as cosy pensions and little hotels, some of them operating from 19th-century villas and palaces.

If you want to be certain of finding a room and you don't mind staying outside the centre of Berlin, you should head for Neukölln. Here, close to Treptower Park, is the recently opened Estrel – the largest hotel in Germany.

HOTEL PRICES

THE PRICE OF a hotel room in Berlin does not alter much with the season. Major events, such as trade fairs, do push up prices however. Many more luxurious hotels offer weekend discounts and often, if you just turn up without a reservation, you can find yourself a good deal. If you intend to stay for an extended period of time, it is worth trying to negotiate a better rate.

HIDDEN EXTRAS

IN GERMANY, taxes are included in hotel room rates, but like anywhere else, you are expected to tip for any additional services, such as bringing luggage to the room or booking a theatre ticket. Hotels from the Dorint chain are an exception: they provide a range of services (such as free bicycle hire) at no additional cost.

Swimming pool at the Grand Hotel Esplanade *(see p219)*

Café at the Hilton hotel *(see p217)*

There is no hard and fast rule about breakfast: it is best to ask if it is included in the price when making a reservation.

The majority of Berlin hotels have their own parking spaces, but sometimes their rates are exorbitant. Ask about telephone charges before using the phone in your room and check the exchange rates and the commission for cashing travellers' cheques before using this service. Items from the minibar and paid-television channels can also turn out to be surprisingly costly.

FACILITIES

THERE IS NO standardized system of categorizing hotels by stars in Germany, although the price of a room usually reflects the quality. Small hotels usually include breakfast in the price of the room – they will probably not have a restaurant and their services are limited. If you choose to stay for a longer period, an Aparthotel might be an option to consider. This type of accommodation is an apartment, complete with a fully equipped kitchen.

HOW TO BOOK

YOU CAN BOOK A ROOM in Berlin by mail, telephone or fax, and some rooms can also be booked through the internet. If you prefer, you can also make use of the company **Berlin Tourismus Marketing** *(see p211)*, which can be contacted via the internet or by telephone or fax. This company can make

your booking in hotels throughout Berlin. When making a reservation, however, be prepared to give your credit card details.

If you are already in Berlin and would like to find a comfortable room, your best option is to go to one of the large tourist information bureaux. Some of the best of these are situated in the **Europa-Center**, at the **Brandenburg Gate**, and at **Tegel Airport** *(see p211)*.

PRIVATE ROOMS

BED & BREAKFAST-style accommodation is not particularly popular in Berlin, although this kind of service can be found in some of the residential districts far from the city centre. You can obtain information about them from tourist information bureaux and the other organizations whose numbers are listed in the Directory *(see p211)*.

Conference room in the Villa Kastania *(see p224)*

The luxurious lounge at the Kempinski Hotel *(see p222)*

TRAVELLING WITH CHILDREN

TRAVELLING WITH CHILDREN in Berlin should not present a problem. A cot can be requested in most hotels, and there is usually no extra charge for having a small child in the room, although an extra bed for an older child may sometimes incur a cost. In better hotels, a reliable babysitter can be obtained at a few hours' notice. In hotel restaurants, high chairs for children are standard.

Elegant hallway in the Four Seasons Hotel *(see p217)*

DISABLED TRAVELLERS

NEARLY ALL TOP-QUALITY and luxury hotels are able to accommodate disabled travellers – at least one entrance will have wheelchair access and some rooms will have specially-adapted bathrooms. Unfortunately, the situation in mid-range and lower standard hotels is not as promising; special equipment is a rarity

and in many cases these hotels are not situated on the ground floor. In very old buildings, there may not be an elevator. The **Hotel Mondial** *(see p221),* located near Kurfürstendamm, is recommended for disabled travellers. It has many facilities for wheelchair users in all its public rooms and has as many as 22 bedrooms equipped for people with special needs.

DEPOSITS

IN MANY BERLIN HOTELS, a deposit may be requested either when reserving the room or upon checking in at the hotel. A credit card number is the most common way to secure a room over the telephone. If you do not have one, however, be prepared to use a cheque or cash to pay about 20 to 40 per cent of the price for one night's stay. The amount you pay as a deposit should always be credited to the final bill. In some smaller hotels or

pensions, don't be surprised if you are asked to pay for your first night's accommodation when you arrive.

YOUTH HOSTELS

IT IS EASY to find inexpensive accommodation in Berlin at a youth hostel. The **DJH (Deutsches Jugendherbergswerk)**, an organization that belongs to the International Youth Hostels Association, gives discounts to all its members. Membership is usually inexpensive and if you are not a member, you will have to join to stay at the hostel. The DJH has hostels in different locations throughout Berlin. There are also several independent youth hostels as well as hotels for students in Berlin that do not belong to any organization.

The type of accommodation offered usually consists of dormitory-style rooms containing bunk beds. There is often a communal bathroom on each floor and a kitchen is usually also available for cooking your own meals. Most youth hostels have a dining room where breakfast and a hot evening meal are served. Some youth hostels are closed during the day, allowing no access to the rooms; confirm this in advance.

CAMPING

CAMPING IS a popular pastime throughout Germany, and the **Deutscher Camping Club** has a lot of information about campsites in and around Berlin. This organization also

Illuminated façade of the Westin Grand *(see p217)*

provides information about other independently run campsites in Berlin.

Campsites are open usually from the beginning of April until the end of October. There are two exceptions: the Berlin-Kladow in Spandau and the Am Krossinsee in Köpenick, which are open year round. The majority of people that choose to stay at campsites are young, particularly during the Oktoberfest *(see p50)* and the weekend in July when the famous Love Parade takes place *(see p49)*. During these times campsites can be very busy and noisy.

Spacious suite at the Palace Hotel *(see p222)*

ORGANIZED YOUTH GROUPS

Berlin has a large base of accommodation for organized youth groups. Most of these consist of hostel-style accommodation, situated on the outskirts of the city, often in green belt areas. They were established not only for the purpose of school trips to Berlin but also for children from West Berlin; until the unification of Germany in 1990, it was difficult for youth groups to organize trips to the countryside so they had to opt for trips to the Grunewald instead. Information about availability and reservations is offered by **Berlin Tourismus Marketing** and by larger tourist information centres, such as the one in the Europa-Center.

DIRECTORY			

INFORMATION AND BOOKING

Berlin Tourismus Marketing
Am Karlsbad 11
10785 Berlin.
Map 12 D1.
☎ 25 00 25.
FAX 25 00 24 24.
w www.berlin.de

Tourist Information
Europa-Center
Budapester Strasse.
Map 10 E1.
⏰ 8:30am–8:30pm Mon–Sat, 10am–6pm Sun.

Brandenburg Gate
Pariser Platz.
Map 6 E3, 15 A3.
⏰ 9:30am–6pm daily.

Tegel Airport
⏰ 5am–10:30pm daily.

Potsdam Information
Friedrich-Ebert-Strasse 5.
☎ (0331) 275 58 0.
FAX (0331) 275 58 99.

CAMPING

Deutscher Camping Club
Geisbergstrasse 11
10777 Berlin.
Map 10 E3, 10 F3.
☎ 218 60 71.
⏰ 10:30am–6pm Mon, 8am–4pm Wed, 8am–1pm Fri.

DCC-Campingplatz Berlin-Kladow (Spandau)
Krampnitzer Weg 111–117
14089 Berlin.
☎ 365 27 97.
FAX 365 12 45.

DCC-Campingplatz Am Krossinsee
Wernsdorfer Strasse 45
12527 Berlin.
☎ 675 86 87.
FAX 675 91 50.

YOUTH HOSTELS

DJH (Deutsches Jugendherbergs-werk)
Tempelhofer Ufer 32
10963 Berlin.
Map 12 E2.
☎ 264 95 20.
FAX 262 04 37.

Jugendgästehaus
Kluckstrasse 3
10785 Berlin.
Map 11 C1.
☎ 25 79 98 08.
FAX 265 03 83.

Jugendherberge Ernst Reuter
Hermsdorfer Damm 48–50
13467 Berlin.
☎ 404 16 10.
FAX 404 59 72.

Jugendgästehaus Am Wannsee
Badeweg 1, 14129 Berlin.
☎ 803 20 34.
FAX 803 59 08.

DISABLED TRAVELLERS

Berliner Behinderten-verband
Jägerstrasse 63d
10117 Berlin-Mitte.
☎ 204 38 47.

Informations und Beratungsgruppe für Behinderte
Sächsische Strasse 28–30
10707 Berlin.
☎ 867 61 14
or 867 63 71.

Hotel Mondial
Kurfürstendamm 47.
Map 10 D1.
☎ 88 41 10.
FAX 884 11 150.

BED & BREAKFAST

Bed & Breakfast in Berlin
☎ 746 14 46.
FAX 441 31 15.

Erste Mitwohn-zentrale in Charlottenburg
Sybelstrasse 53.
10629 Berlin-Charlottenburg.
Map 9 A2.
☎ 324 30 31.
FAX 324 99 77.

Last Minute
☎ 3082 0885.
FAX 3082 0887.

Wohnwitz
Holsteinische Strasse 55.
10717 Berlin-Wilmersdorf.
Map 9 C4, 9 C5.
☎ 861 82 22.
FAX 861 82 72.

Berlin's Best: Hotels

BERLIN BOASTS MANY splendid and luxurious hotels. While some of them belong to international chains, others are private establishments with an intimate, family atmosphere. The hotels chosen here have been selected because they offer unique interiors, excellent service and a price that is a true representation of the accommodation and service provided.

Savoy Hotel
The beautiful and stylish Savoy hotel offers its guests Berlin's first cigar bar. One can relax here in a comfortable armchair while enjoying a newspaper and a Havana (see p222).

Hotel Palace Berlin
The rooms – individually decorated in subtle tones – are only part of the attraction of this hotel, which is often visited by international movie celebrities (see p222).

Around Schloss Charlottenburg

Tiergarten

Around Kurfürstendamm

Villa Kastania
This cosy hotel is situated on a side street, offering a high level of service, peace and quiet as well as proximity to the heart of the metropolis (see p224).

Kempinski Hotel Bristol Berlin
The understated elegance of this hotel has attracted a regular clientele for many years. Its rooms are luxurious and its service unintrusive (see p222).

Brandenburger Hof
This hotel is located in a beautifully restored building and offers sophisticated interiors and a unique family atmosphere (see p221).

Hotel Adlon
This super-luxurious hotel has a stunning interior. Walls and windows in the rooms have excellent sound-proofing (see p217).

Hackescher Markt
This charming hotel, opened in 1998, has bright, elegant rooms and a beautiful façade that matches the surrounding historic architecture (see p218).

Four Seasons Hotel
This hotel, one of the top three in Berlin, offers opulent interiors with magnificent flower arrangements and impeccable service (see p217).

North of the Centre

East of the Centre

Museum Island

Around Unter den Linden

Kreuzberg

Berlin Hilton
Its proximity to the Gendarmenmarkt and the amazing choice of restaurants distinguish this hotel. Some of the rooms offer spectacular views (see p217).

DeragHotel Grosser Kurfürst
Guests of this modern hotel are offered numerous additional services, such as free bicycle hire, that set it apart from other hotels in the same category (see p218).

| 0 metres | 750 |
| 0 yards | 750 |

Choosing a Hotel

THE CHOICE OF HOTELS selected in this guide is based on quality of accommodation and service as well as location. The list of hotels covers all the areas and price categories with additional information to help you choose a hotel that best meets your needs. Hotels within the same price category are listed alphabetically. More details can be found on pages 217–25.

	Number of Rooms	Business Facilities	Children's Facilities	Recommended Restaurant	Close to Shops	Quiet Location	24-Hour Room Service
AROUND UNTER DEN LINDEN *(see p217)*							
Hotel Unter den Linden	320		■		■		
Madison City Suites	84	●			■		
Berlin Hilton	493	●	■	●	■		■
Maritim proArte Hotel Berlin	401	●	■		■		■
Dorint Select Hotel am Gendarmenmarkt	92	●	■	●	■		■
Westin Grand	358	●	■		■		■
Four Seasons Hotel	204	●	■	●	■		■
Hotel Adlon	337	●	■	●	■		■
MUSEUM ISLAND *(see pp217–8)*							
art'otel Ermelerhaus Berlin	109	●	■	●		●	■
DeragHotel Grosser Kurfürst	144	●	■			●	■
EAST OF THE CENTRE *(see p218)*							
Forum Hotel	1006	●			■		■
Mercure Alexander Plaza Berlin	92	●					
Radisson SAS Hotel Berlin	540	●		●	■		■
NORTH OF THE CENTRE *(see p218)*							
EKOS Boardinghouse	21				■		
Artist Apartment Hotel Die Loge	35	●	■		■		
Hackescher Markt	31	●	■	●	■	●	
Hotel Albrechtshof	107	●					■
Märkischer Hof	20				■	●	
Taunus Hotel	18				■		
TIERGARTEN *(see p219)*							
Blue Band Hotel Berlin	701	●	■	●			■
Hotel Hamburg	200	●	■		■		■
Dorint Hotel Schweizerhof	384	●	■				■
Grand Hotel Esplanade Berlin	400	●	■	●		●	■
Inter-Continental Berlin	511	●	■	●		●	■
Grand Hyatt Berlin	340	●		●	■		■
KREUZBERG *(see pp219–20)*							
Hotel am Anhalter Bahnhof	33						
Hotel Transit	49						
Jugendgästehaus der DSJ	124		■				
Hotel Antares	85	●	■				■
Hotel Riehmers Hofgarten	25			●	■	●	
Best Western Hotel Stuttgarter Hof	110	●	■	●			■

Price categories for a double room per night, including all taxes (in Deutsch Marks):
- (DM) under DM150
- (DM)(DM) DM150–250
- (DM)(DM)(DM) DM250–350
- (DM)(DM)(DM)(DM) DM350–450
- (DM)(DM)(DM)(DM)(DM) more than DM450

BUSINESS FACILITIES
There are telephones and fax machines in bedrooms, a conference or meeting room within the hotel and computers with Internet access for guests.

CHILDREN'S FACILITIES
Family rooms and/or extra bed in a double room. Cots and babysitting service available. There are creche areas in some hotels, or a games room with toys and other suitable equipment.

QUIET LOCATION
Hotel is located on a quiet street.

CLOSE TO SHOPS
Within a five-minute walk to a good choice of shops and restaurants.

Hotel	Price	Number of Rooms	Business Facilities	Children's Facilities	Recommended Restaurant	Close to Shops	Quiet Location	24-Hour Room Service
AROUND KURFÜRSTENDAMM (see pp220–22)								
Hotel Pension Augusta	(DM)	26				■		
Hotel Pension Funk	(DM)	14				■	●	
Alpenland	(DM)(DM)	35				■		
Best Western Hotel Boulevard	(DM)(DM)	57	●	■		■		
Blue Band Berlin Mark Hotel	(DM)(DM)	233	●	■		■		
Blue Band Berlin Plaza Hotel	(DM)(DM)	131	●		●			
Comfort Hotel Frühling am Zoo	(DM)(DM)	66				■		■
Consul	(DM)(DM)	75				■		■
Hotel Ambassador Berlin	(DM)(DM)	200	●	■	●	■		■
Hotel Askanischer Hof	(DM)(DM)	16		■				
Hotel Astoria	(DM)(DM)	32				■		
Hotel Berliner Hof	(DM)(DM)	80				■		
Hotel California	(DM)(DM)	45	●	■				
Propeller Island City Lodge	(DM)(DM)	31				■	●	
Remter	(DM)(DM)	31				■		
Alsterhof	(DM)(DM)(DM)	200	●	■				
Best Western Hotel President	(DM)(DM)(DM)	187	●			■		■
Bleibtreu Hotel	(DM)(DM)(DM)	60	●	■		■		■
Blue Band Berlin Excelsior Hotel	(DM)(DM)(DM)	320	●	■				■
Concept Hotel	(DM)(DM)(DM)	106		■			●	
Hecker's Hotel	(DM)(DM)(DM)	72	●	■				■
Holiday Inn Crowne Plaza Berlin	(DM)(DM)(DM)	425	●	■				■
Hotel Avantgarde	(DM)(DM)(DM)	27		■				
Hotel Brandenburger Hof	(DM)(DM)(DM)	87	●	■	●		●	■
Hotel Mondial	(DM)(DM)(DM)	75	●	■	●			
Hotel Residenz Berlin	(DM)(DM)(DM)	80		■				
Sorat Art'otel Berlin	(DM)(DM)(DM)	133	●					
Hotel Palace Berlin	(DM)(DM)(DM)(DM)	282	●	■	●	■		■
Savoy Hotel	(DM)(DM)(DM)(DM)	125	●			■		■
Steigenberger Berlin	(DM)(DM)(DM)(DM)	397	●	■	●	■		■
Kempinski Hotel Bristol Berlin	(DM)(DM)(DM)(DM)(DM)	301	●	■	●	■		■
AROUND SCHLOSS CHARLOTTENBURG (see p222)								
Hotel an der Oper	(DM)(DM)	46				■		
Schlossparkhotel	(DM)(DM)(DM)	39	●	■			●	
FURTHER AFIELD (see pp222–5)								
Die Fabrik	(DM)	41				■		
Hotel Ahorn	(DM)	28				■		
Hotel Belvedere	(DM)	18					●	
Hotelpension Alpina	(DM)	17					●	
Alfa Hotel	(DM)(DM)	33	●				●	■
Artemisia	(DM)(DM)	8	●					
Best Western Kanthotel Berlin	(DM)(DM)	70				■		■
East-Side Hotel	(DM)(DM)	36	●				●	
Estrel Residence & Congress Hotel	(DM)(DM)	1125	●	■				■

Price categories for a double room per night, including all taxes (in Deutsch Marks):
ⓦ under DM150
ⓒⓜ DM150–250
ⓒⓜⓒⓜ DM250–350
ⓒⓜⓒⓜⓒⓜ DM350–450
ⓒⓜⓒⓜⓒⓜⓒⓜ more than DM450

BUSINESS FACILITIES
There are telephones and fax machines in bedrooms, a conference or meeting room within the hotel and computers with Internet access for guests.

CHILDREN'S FACILITIES
Family rooms and/or extra bed in a double room. Cots and babysitting service available. There are play areas in some hotels, or a games room with toys and other suitable equipment.

QUIET LOCATION
Hotel is located on a quiet street.

CLOSE TO SHOPS
Within a five-minute walk to a good choice of shops and restaurants.

	NUMBER OF ROOMS	BUSINESS FACILITIES	CHILDREN'S FACILITIES	RECOMMENDED RESTAURANT	CLOSE TO SHOPS	QUIET LOCATION	24-HOUR ROOM SERVICE
FURTHER AFIELD CONT. *(see pp222–5)*							
Forsthaus Hubertusbrücke	22					●	
Forsthaus Paulsborn	10			●		●	
Holiday Inn Gustavo Berlin	122	●	■				
Hotel Igel	70	●		●		●	
Hotel Pension Wittelsbach	31		■				
Hotel Rheinsberg am See	81	●	■			●	
Ibis Hotel	198	●			■		
Ibis Hotel Berlin-Messe	168	●			■		
Imperator	11				■		
Jurine	50		■			●	
Modena	19				■		
Queens Hotel Berlin	109	●	■		■	●	■
Villa Kastania	43	●	■			●	
Villa Toscana	16					●	
Hotel Luisenhof	27	●	■			●	
Hotel Seehof Berlin	77	●	■	●		●	■
SORAT Hotel Humboldt-Mühle Berlin	120	●	■			●	■
SORAT Hotel Spree-Bogen Berlin	220	●	■			●	■
Ritz-Carlton Schlosshotel	54	●		●		●	■
GREATER BERLIN *(see p225)*							
art'otel potsdam	123	●		●			
Hotel Voltaire	143				■		
Schloss Cecilienhof	42	●				●	■

AROUND UNTER DEN LINDEN

Hotel Unter den Linden

Unter den Linden 14, 10117 Berlin.
Map 7 A3, 16 C3. **☎** 238 110.
FAX 238 11 100. **Rooms:** 320. 🛏
🔲 ⚏ 📺 ⚡ ♨ 🐾 🅿 🍴
🍽 🍷 AE, DC, MC, V, JCB, EC.
ⓂⓂ

This is the cheapest hotel in this part of Berlin. It was one of the best hotels during the GDR era but now, in order to withstand competition, it has reduced its prices. Do not expect luxury – the furniture in bedrooms and bathrooms is slightly worn, but it is not a bad address for those who are looking to stay in the town centre on a budget.

Madison City Suites

Friedrichstrasse 185–190, 10117 Berlin. **Map** 6 F4, 15 C4. **☎** 20 29 20. **FAX** 20 29 20. **Rooms:** 84. 🛏 📺 ⚡ ♨ 🐾 🅿 🍷 AE, DC, MC, V, JCB, EC. ⓂⓂ

This hotel offers only suites, the price of which depend upon the size of the suite and on the duration of the stay. The hotel offers many services, including car and bicycle rental, shopping and even clothes repair. There are also CD players in all rooms. It pays to stay here for at least for a week but, even on a per-night basis, the prices are much lower than in many of the neighbouring hotels.

Berlin Hilton

Mohrenstrasse 30, 10117 Berlin.
Map 7 A4, 16 D4. **☎** 20 23 0.
FAX 20 23 42 69. **Rooms:** 400.
🛏 🔲 ⚏ ⚏ 📺 🍷 ⚡ ♨ 🍴
🍽 ♨ 🐾 ♿ ⚡ 🐾 🅿
🍷 🍴 🍽 AE, DC, MC, V, JCB.
ⓂⓂⓂⓂ

The Berlin Hilton is in a good location, near the Gendarmenmarkt. There is a spectacular view from the bedrooms at the front of the building. These take in Konzerthaus and the twin churches of Deutscher Dom and Französischer Dom. The rooms are wonderfully furnished and spacious, and there is a wide selection of places to eat and drink in the hotel. These include bars, cafés, a pub and a bistro in addition to two splendid restaurants – visitors can choose between the Brandenburg and Fellini (an Italian restaurant), both of which attract guests from the whole of Berlin.

Maritim proArte Hotel Berlin

Friedrichstrasse 151, 10117 Berlin.
Map 6 F3, 15 C2. **☎** 203 35.
FAX 20 33 42 09. **Rooms:** 401. 🛏
🔲 ⚏ ⚏ 📺 🍷 ⚡ ♨ 🍴 🍽 🍴 ♨
🐾 AE, DC, MC, V, JCB, EC.
ⓂⓂⓂ
🔲 www.maritim.de

Although this hotel aims to attract mainly conference business, its central location and excellent facilities make it one of the most attractive hotels in Berlin. It is an ultra-modern building, with furnishings and art displays to match – each floor features the work of a different artist. Its luxurious rooms are divided into three categories and have marble and granite bathrooms. There is also a swimming pool and recreation centre.

Dorint Select Hotel am Gendarmenmarkt

Charlottenstrasse 50–52, 10117 Berlin.
Map 7 A4, 16 D4. **☎** 26 55 35 91.
FAX 26 55 35 94. **Rooms:** 92. 🛏 🔲
⚏ ⚏ 📺 🍷 ⚡ ♨ 🍴 🍽 🍴 ♨
🐾 🅿 🍷 🍴 AE, DC, MC, V, JCB, EC. ⓂⓂⓂ

Very nice, cosy hotel located near Gendarmenmarkt, not far from Unter den Linden and Friedrichstrasse. The hotel belongs to the Dorint chain, so guests can expect well-furnished rooms and excellent service.

Westin Grand

Friedrichstrasse 158–164, 10117 Berlin. **Map** 6 F3, 15 C3. **☎** 20 27 0.
FAX 20 27 33 62. **Rooms:** 358. 🛏 🔲
⚏ ⚏ 📺 🍷 ⚡ ♨ 🍴 🍽 🍴 ♨
♿ 🐾 🅿 🍷 🍴 🍽 AE, DC, MC, V, JCB, EC. ⓂⓂⓂⓂ
🔲 www.westin-grand.com

A lavish hotel built at the end of the 19th century in Empire and Secessionist styles. The main hall is particularly impressive, with an atrium that extends the length of the building and a breathtaking staircase. Its excellent location means you are within minutes of all the most important historic sites.

Four Seasons Hotel

Charlottenstrasse 49, 10117 Berlin.
Map 7 A4, 16 D3. **☎** 20 33 8.
FAX 20 33 61 66. **Rooms:** 204. 🛏
🔲 ⚏ ⚏ 📺 🍷 ⚡ ♨ 🍴 🍽 🍴 ♨
🐾 ♿ 🐾 🍷 E, DC, MC, V, JCB, EC. ⓂⓂⓂⓂ
🔲 www.fourseasons.com

This hotel is ranked as one of the three best hotels in Berlin. Situated just around the corner from Gendarmenmarkt, the hotel

is a modern building with an impressive façade laid with travertine and green marble. The interiors will astonish with the opulence of their Neo-Baroque objects and magnificent flower arrangements. The hotel offers luxurious rooms in three categories, a comfortable business centre and impeccable service. Excellent light cuisine is served in the Seasons restaurant.

Hotel Adlon

Unter den Linden 77, 10117 Berlin.
Map 6 E3, 15 A3. **☎** 226 10.
FAX 22 61 22 22. **Rooms:** 337. 🛏
🔲 ⚏ ⚏ 📺 🍷 ⚡ 🍴 🍽 🍴
🐾 ♿ 🐾 🅿 🍷 🍴 🍽 AE, DC, MC, V, JCB. ⓂⓂⓂⓂ
🔲 www.hotel-adlon.com

This deluxe hotel is located near the Brandenburg Gate. It opened in 1997 and continues the traditions of its predecessor of 1907, which was destroyed in 1945 *(see p68)*. The most expensive materials were used for interiors: marble, leather, exotic woods, all put together by the best designers. The hotel prides itself on its excellent service and has a host of special services: special rooms for people with allergies; electronic security systems for doors; cordless telephone handsets that can be taken to the restaurant and excellently sound-proofed walls and windows in all rooms. The extremely comfortable bedrooms are decorated in tones of green, brown and beige and the bathrooms are panelled in wood.

MUSEUM ISLAND

art'otel Ermelerhaus Berlin

Wallstrasse 70–73, 10179 Berlin.
Map 7 C4. **☎** 240 62 0. **FAX** 240 62 222. **Rooms:** 109. 🛏 🔲 ⚏ ⚏ 📺 🍷 ⚡ ♨ 🐾 ♿
🅿 🍷 🍴 AE, DC, MC, V, EC.
ⓂⓂⓂ 🔲 www.artotel.de

This well-situated hotel overlooks the Spree river. It has the U-Bahn Märkisches Museum station just opposite its entrance and the museum is just nearby. Reasonably priced for its location, it is one of the most popular hotels in Mitte. The hotel itself is modern with simple and elegant furniture. The ... rooms on the Märkisches Ufer side are situated in Ermeler Haus *(see pp84–5)*. The Ermeler Haus restaurant *(see p237)* is decorated with a Rococo ceiling, or you can try traditional Berlin food at Raabe Diele *(see p237)*. In the summer there is a café on a riverboat tied to the bank of the river.

For key to symbols see back flap

DeragHotel Grosser Kurfürst

Neue Roß-Strasse 11–12, 10179 Berlin.
Map 7 C4. 24 60 00. **FAX** 24 60 03 00. **Rooms:** 144. 1 24
TV ☎ ⚐ ▥ ♨ 🐕 ♿ ⚲ 🍽 ☎ 🍴
AE, DC, MC, V, EC. DM DM DM
www.deraghotels.de.

This is a good middle-range hotel, with modern facilities and a convenient location close to the U-Bahn station Märkisches Museum. The hotel opened in 1997 and it belongs to the DeragHotel chain, which specializes in additional services for tourists and business travellers alike. For example, the price of a room also includes free public transport or bicycle hire.

EAST OF THE CENTRE

Forum Hotel

Alexanderplatz, 10178 Berlin. **Map** 8 D2.
23 89 0. **FAX** 23 89 43 05.
Rooms: 1006. 1 24 TV ☎
⚐ ▥ 🐕 ♿ ⚲ 🐕 📶 P 🍽 🍴
AE, DC, MC, V, JCB, EC. DM DM

It is impossible to miss the Forum Hotel. This 37-storey tower building was constructed under the GDR government and, despite radical modernization in the 1990s, it has an ugly exterior. However, inside it does have an elegant hall, a very good restaurant, a casino on the top floor and a huge conference area. Unfortunately, the rooms tend to be small and without air-conditioning so any rooms that catch the sun can get a bit hot in summer. If you don't mind the sun in the morning and have a head for heights, the upper rooms on the east side of the hotel have wonderful views over the city.

Mercure Alexander Plaza Berlin

Rosenstrasse 1, 10187 Berlin. **Map** 7 B2, 16 F1. 24 00 10. **FAX** 240 01 777. **Rooms:** 92. 1 24
🍽 ☎ 🐕 ♿ ⚲ 🐕 📶 P 🍽 🍴
AE, DC, MC, V, EC. DM DM DM

This top-quality hotel, opened in 1997, is located near the S-Bahn Hackescher Markt station. It is also not very far from Marienkirche and from the restaurants on Oranienburger Strasse. The large and comfortable rooms are full of light and, with soundproof windows, guarantee a good rest. Modern facilities have been incorporated together with older elements of architecture which date from around 1900.

Radisson SAS Hotel Berlin

Karl-Liebknecht-Strasse 5, 10178 Berlin. **Map** 7 C3, 16 F2. 23 828.
FAX 23 82 75 91. **Rooms:** 540. 1
⚐ 24 TV ☎ ⚐ ▥ 🍽 ♨ ▥ 🐕 ♿
📶 P 🍽 🍴 AE, DC, MC, V.
DM DM DM

The Radisson SAS hotel, situated in close proximity to Museum Island, is worth recommending after its modernization in 1994. The rooms are fairly large, and the executive rate includes additional services to facilitate a business trip. Older guests are offered a discount, 1 per cent off for every year above 65. The hotel's dining rooms are very popular, particularly its restaurant called Orangerie.

NORTH OF THE CENTRE

EKOS Boardinghouse

Mulackstrasse 1, 10119 Berlin.
Map 7 C1. 283 88 488. **FAX** 283 88 489. **Rooms:** 21. 1 TV ⚐
⚐ 🐕 P 🐕 🍴 AE, DC, MC, V. DM

The EKOS Boardinghouse consists of single and double apartments. These must be rented for a minimum of three nights. Breakfast is included in the price, but you might wish to prepare it yourself in your own kitchen. Alternatively, take it in one of the many cafés in the neighbourhood. This is an ideal place for people planning a longer stay in Berlin.

Artist Apartment Hotel Die Loge

Oranienburger Strasse 44, 10117 Berlin.
Map 6 F1. 280 75 13. **FAX** 280 75 13. **Rooms:** 35. 1 TV 🍽
⚐ 🍽 ☎ 🐕 ♿ ⚲ 🐕 📶 P 🍽 🍴
AE, DC, MC, V, EC. DM DM

The Artist Apartment Hotel Die Loge is situated on a busy street but it is close to restaurants and shops. It is a warm and cosy hotel and has plenty of modern facilities, which make this establishment worth its price.

Hackescher Markt

Grosse Präsidentenstrasse 8, 10178 Berlin. **Map** 7 B2, 16 F1. 28 00 30. **FAX** 280 03 111. **Rooms:** 31. 🍽
1 TV 🍽 ☎ 🐕 ⚲ 🐕 📶 P 🍽
🍴 AE, DC, MC, V, JCB, EC. DM DM

Built in 1998, this charming hotel has an excellent location, situated opposite Hackesche Höfe. Its façade was designed to blend in with the historic architecture of this district. The Hackescher Markt has a cosy atmosphere and its service is discreet. The rooms are bright and elegantly furnished and the hotel offers excellent cuisine in its restaurant, Maps. There is also a small patio where guests can have coffee outside during summer days. This is altogether an attractive place to stay.

Hotel Albrechtshof

Albrechtstrasse 8, 10117 Berlin.
Map 6 F2, 15 B1. 30 88 60.
FAX 308 86 100. **Rooms:** 107.
🍽 1 🍽 24 TV ☎ 🐕 ♿ ⚲
🐕 🍽 P 🍽 🍴 🍽 AE, DC, MC,
V, JCB, EC. DM DM

Situated near the Spree river, this hotel is well placed, close to Friedrichstrasse. This makes it ideally located for tourists who plan to visit sites near Unter den Linden and Museum Island. The Hotel Albrechtshof belongs to the oldest association of hoteliers in Germany – Verband Christlicher Hotels. It is sited in a modernized early 19th-century building, and caters not only for the corporeal with a bar, restaurant and banqueting hall, but also for the spiritual with a chapel. The hotel offers large discounts for weekend stays.

Märkischer Hof

Linienstrasse 133, 10115 Berlin. **Map** 6 F1. 282 71 55. **FAX** 282 43 31.
Rooms: 20. 1 🍽 TV 🍽 🍽
🍽 P 🍽 🍴 MC, V. DM DM DM

This is a small, cosy hotel with a pleasant family atmosphere. The hotel is well located near the busy Oranienburger Strasse. The building itself dates from the 19th century and its recently redecorated rooms are of a surprisingly high standard considering their prices. There is also a hotel café, where a traditional Berlin-style breakfast is served.

Taunus Hotel

Monbijouplatz 1, 10178 Berlin.
Map 7 B2, 16 E1. 283 52 54.
FAX 283 52 55. **Rooms:** 18. 🍽 1
TV P 🍽 🍴 AE, DC, MC, V. DM DM

This is a pleasant hotel, situated in a building that has been completely redecorated inside. Outside, it has an eye-catching façade of yellow and red brick with decorative details picked out in sapphire-blue. The rooms are quite modest, simply furnished and, most importantly, very clean. The hotel has a bar that is open in the evenings, however, if you are looking for something a little more adventurous, you can head for nearby Hackesche Höfe, an area that stays busy till the early hours of the morning.

TIERGARTEN

Blue Band Hotel Berlin

Lützowplatz 17, 10785 Berlin.
Map 11 A1. 26 05 27 00.
FAX 260 52 716. **Rooms:** 701.
🏨 🔟 🏥 24 TV 🏋 🍽 📶 🛗
⚙️ 📶 📶 🏪 📶 📶 🏥 AE, DC,
MC, V, JCB, EC. 📶 📶 📶

Despite the fact that it this is one of the largest hotels in Berlin, its welcoming service and good organization mean that you will not feel overwhelmed by its size. There is a good chance of finding a vacant room here, even without a reservation. The hotel offers bright and spacious rooms with classically decorated interiors.

Hotel Hamburg

Landgrafenstrasse 4, 10787 Berlin.
Map 11 A1. 26 47 70. **FAX** 262 93 94. **Rooms:** 200. 🏨 🔟
TV 🏥 🏋 📶 🏪 📶 📶 P 🏥 🍽
⚙️ AE, DC, MC, V, JCB, EC. 📶 📶 📶

Located in the southern part of the Tiergarten district, the Hotel Hamburg is quite close to Tauentzienstrasse. It was completely redecorated in 1994, but the elegant rooms, in all shades of warm red, are a bit on the small side. Because of its location, the hotel is popular with both tourists and business travellers.

Dorint Hotel Schweizerhof

Budapester Strasse 21, 10787 Berlin.
Map 10 F1. 269 60.
FAX 269 61 000. **Rooms:** 384. 🏨 🔟
🏥 🏥 TV 🏋 📶 🏪 📶 🍽 🏥 🛗
⚙️ 📶 🏪 P 🏥 🍽 🏥 AE, DC,
MC, V, EC. 📶 📶 📶

This luxurious hotel, opened in 1999, is one of the most modern hotels in the entire city. Work only began on the site in 1997, soon after the demolition of a hotel with the same name. It sports an elegant, sand-finished façade, and offers beautifully furnished rooms, two restaurants, a large conference centre and a ballroom.

Grand Hotel Esplanade Berlin

Lützowufer 15, 10785 Berlin.
Map 11 A1. 25 47 80. **FAX** 265 11 71. **Rooms:** 400. 🏨 🔟 🏥 24
TV 🏥 🏋 📶 🏪 📶 🍽 🏥 🏥 📶
🍽 🏥 AE, DC, MC, V, JCB, EC.
📶 📶 📶 📶

A modern, lavish establishment overlooking the Landwehrkanal, the Grand Hotel Esplanade is situated not far from Bauhaus-Archiv (see p127) and the

Kulturforum (see pp114–15). The cosy, well-furnished rooms attract prominent guests from artistic and political circles. Harry's New York Bar is famous across Berlin and the Harlekin restaurant is one of the city's best. As an additional attraction, the hotel's own boat offers trips along the Spree river and the Landwehrkanal.

Inter-Continental Berlin

Budapester Strasse 2, 10787 Berlin.
Map 10 F1. 260 20. **FAX** 26 02 26 00. **Rooms:** 511. 🏨 🔟 🏥 24
TV 🏥 🏋 📶 🏪 📶 🍽 🏥 🏥 🛗
🏪 P 🏥 🍽 ⚙️ AE, DC, MC, V,
JCB, EC. 📶 📶 📶 📶

This hotel belongs to an international chain of hotels, which ensures its guests receive five-star service. It is situated on the outskirts of the Zoologischer Garten (see p144). The massive building is hard to miss, with a glass dome covering its main lobby. The hotel offers large rooms in several categories. A swimming pool and a rejuvenating salon provide the chance for tired guests to relax, while the restaurant Zum Hugenotten (see p240) attracts gourmets from all over the city.

Grand Hyatt Berlin

Marlene-Dietrich Platz 2, 10785 Berlin. **Map** 6. 25 53 12 34.
FAX 25 53 12 35. (0180) 523 12 34.
Rooms: 340. 🏨 🔟 🏥 24 TV 🏥
🏋 📶 🏪 📶 🍽 🏥 P 🏥 🍽 🏥
AE, DC, MC, V, JCB, EC. 📶 📶 📶 📶
🔲 www.hyatt.com

The Grand Hyatt is one of the most modern hotels in Berlin and is situated near the Potsdamer Platz complex. It is conveniently located near a shopping centre, music theatre and a multiplex cinema (where the Berlin Film Festival takes place). There is also a casino, restaurants and the Kulturforum (see pp114–15) nearby. This is one of the more splendid hotels in Berlin with a sushi bar, bistro, good restaurant called Vox, and a quiet café called Tizian.

KREUZBERG

Hotel am Anhalter Bahnhof

Stresemannstrasse 36, 10963 Berlin.
Map 12 E1. 251 03 42.
FAX 251 48 97. **Rooms:** 33. 🔟 TV
🏋 ⚙️ MC, V, EC. 📶

This small and friendly hotel is situated in an old apartment block. Its low prices only apply to rooms without bathrooms, so expect to

pay more for rooms with a bath. The more expensive rooms face onto a courtyard and are so quieter, while the cheaper rooms overlook a busy street.

Hotel Transit

Hagelberger Strasse 53–54, 10965 Berlin. **Map** 12 F4. 789 04 70.
FAX 789 04 777. **Rooms:** 49. 🏨 🏋
🏥 P 🏥 🍽 AE, MC, V. 📶

This is a small, inexpensive hotel in the west part of Viktoriapark. If you don't expect luxury, you will be pleased with the easy access to the town centre. The area around the hotel is also quite lively.

Jugendgästehaus der DSJ

Franz-Künstler-Strasse 4–10, 10969 Berlin. **Map** 13 B2. 615 10 07.
FAX 61 40 11 50. **Rooms:** 124. 🏥
🏥 🏪 P 📶

This pleasant, though very large, youth hostel is excellently located in the central part of Kreuzberg, near the Jüdisches Museum (see p137). The rooms do not have bathrooms, but there are shower rooms on the corridors. For those on a tight budget who do not mind sharing, the hostel's cheapest rate is for a bed in a dormitory room.

Hotel Antares

Stresemannstrasse 97, 10963 Berlin.
Map 12 E1. 254 16 0. **FAX** 261 50 27. **Rooms:** 85. 🏨 🔟 🏥 24
TV 🏥 🏋 📶 🏪 📶 🍽 🏥 🍽
🍽 🏥 AE, DC, JCB, MC, V, EC. 📶 📶

The Hotel Antares is a modern establishment located close to Martin-Gropius-Bau (see p136) and Potsdamer Platz. An economy room is pleasant enough for a short tourist visit, but there are business-class rooms available, too. The extra level of comfort is worth the higher cost if you are planning to work during your stay. It is also well worth enquiring about special weekend rates.

Hotel Riehmers Hofgarten

Yorckstrasse 83, 10 965 Berlin.
Map 12 F4. 78 09 88 00.
FAX 78 09 88 08. **Rooms:** 25. 🏨 🔟
🏥 TV 🏥 🏋 P 🏥 🍽 ⚙️ AE,
DC, MC, V. 📶 📶

This beautiful building is part of a Gothic red-brick complex in Kreuzberg (see p139) and dates from the end of the 19th century. The hotel itself is situated in a converted apartment block. The rooms are comfortable with high ceilings and very elegant bathrooms. The best rooms overlook the inner courtyard.

Best Western Hotel Stuttgarter Hof

Anhalter Strasse 9, 10693 Berlin.
Map 12 F1. 264 830. **FAX** 264 83 900. **Rooms:** 110. AE, DC, MC, V, EC.

This is a pleasant, top-quality hotel dating back to 1907. The hotel, which has an interesting façade, is situated near the city centre, behind Potsdamer Platz. It has good-sized rooms, a restaurant called Gershwin and a charming, green courtyard – one of the main features of this hotel.

AROUND KURFÜRSTENDAMM

Hotel Pension Augusta

Fasanenstrasse 22, 10719 Berlin.
Map 10 D1. 883 50 28. **FAX** 882 47 79. **Rooms:** 26. MC, V.

This relatively inexpensive guest-house is located in the very heart of Berlin. As it is based in a 19th-century building, the rooms are spacious and quiet. Some rooms lack *en suite* bathrooms and so are much cheaper. There is no hotel restaurant but that hardly matters with so many good places in the neighbourhood.

Hotel Pension Funk

Fasanenstrasse 69, 10719 Berlin.
Map 10 D2. 882 71 93. **FAX** 883 33 29. **Rooms:** 14. (most). AE, MC, V.

This small, charming hotel is located on Fasanenstrasse, one of Berlin's finest streets, and is within easy reach of many famous theatres, cabarets and restaurants. The building dates from the turn of the 20th century, and it was once the home of Asta Nielsen, star of the silent screen. Many of the original features are still in place, including decorative coved ceilings and Art Nouveau stained-glass windows.

Alpenland

Carmerstrasse 8, 10623 Berlin. **Map** 3 C5. 312 39 70. **FAX** 313 84 44. **Rooms:** 35. AE, DC, MC, V.

Centrally located in a narrow street joining Savignyplatz with Steinplatz, the Alpenland is a modest hotel. Occupying an old apartment building, not all the rooms have bathrooms. Those without, on the fourth floor, are much cheaper than the others. The hotel's restaurant has traditional Berlin food on the menu.

Best Western Hotel Boulevard

Kurfürstendamm 12, 10719 Berlin.
Map 10 D1. 001 060. **FAX** 884 25 451. **Rooms:** 57. AE, DC, MC, V, EC.

Well located on Kurfürstendamm, this hotel belongs to a good-quality hotel chain. The lack of a restaurant is compensated by the number of places to eat in the area. During summer, there is a very charming garden café on the roof of the building, with a beautiful view of the whole area.

Blue Band Berlin Mark Hotel

Meinekestrasse 18–19, 10719 Berlin.
Map 10 D2. 88 00 20. **FAX** 880 02 804. **Rooms:** 233. AE, DC, MC, V, EC.
W www.markhotel.de

This is a comfortable three-star hotel located close to Kurfürstendamm. The pleasant rooms are lightly furnished. Sixteen of the rooms have a slightly higher standard to cater for the needs of business travellers. The rates also vary depending on the time of year and if there are trade fairs, conventions or other events taking place in Berlin.

Blue Band Berlin Plaza Hotel

Knesebeckstrasse 63, 10719 Berlin.
Map 9 C2. 884 130. **FAX** 884 13 754. **Rooms:** 131. AE, DC, MC, V, JCB, EC.

Its proximity to Kurfürstendamm and functional, bright rooms are not the only good things about this hotel. It is worth trying the food at the hotel restaurant, called Knese, which is famous for its Berlin dishes. Enquire about their special weekend rates.

Comfort Hotel Frühling am Zoo

Kurfürstendamm 17, 10719 Berlin.
Map 10 D1. 881 80 83. **FAX** 881 64 83. **Rooms:** 66. AE, DC, MC, V, JCB, EC.

This is a mid-range hotel, situated in an old 19th-century building on the corner of Kurfürstendamm and Joachimstaler Strasse. It doesn't have a restaurant, and the hotel is located above a row of shops. The windows in the bedrooms overlook a busy street. Although the windows have been soundproofed,

there is no air-conditioning, so in summer the noise may affect light sleepers. The hotel also offers apartments with small kitchens.

Consul

Knesebeckstrasse 8–9, 10623 Berlin.
Map 3 C5. 311 060. **FAX** 312 20 60. **Rooms:** 75. AE, DC, MC, V, JCB.

Located not far from Kurfürstendamm, this hotel has rooms of varying standards and prices. Some of the rooms have been recently equipped with a private bathroom, minibar and television.

Hotel Ambassador Berlin

Bayreuther Strasse 42–3, 10787 Berlin.
Map 10 F1. 219 020. **FAX** 219 02 380. **Rooms:** 200. AE, DC, MC, V, EC.

This high-standard hotel is in a quiet street near Wittenbergplatz and KaDeWe (*see p149*). Its rooms are comfortable, traditionally furnished and have soundproofed windows. The restaurant, with its rustic interior, offers an à la carte menu or a Swedish-style buffet.

Hotel Askanischer Hof

Kurfürstendamm 53, 10707 Berlin.
Map 9 B2. 881 80 33. **FAX** 881 72 06. **Rooms:** 16. AE, DC, MC, V, JCB, EC.

Small and full of charm, this guesthouse-type hotel near Schlüterstrasse is one of the few hotels that survived World War II. The rooms are not big but are very comfortable. The interior is decorated in the style of the 1920s and contains some authentic furniture. Famous authors Franz Kafka and Arthur Miller used to stay here, and even now it attracts important guests who appreciate the cosy atmosphere.

Hotel Astoria

Fasanenstrasse 2, 10623 Berlin.
Map 4 D5. 312 40 67. **FAX** 312 50 27. **Rooms:** 32. AE, DC, MC, V, JCB.

An intimate hotel, managed by the same family for three generations, the Hotel Astoria occupies a 19th-century building. The rooms are comfortable and the lack of a restaurant is compensated for by the hotel's proximity to Savigny-platz. Special rates are offered over weekends but during popular trade fairs, the prices go up.

Hotel Berliner Hof

Tauentzienstrasse 8, 10789 Berlin.
Map 10 E1. 254 95 0. **FAX** 262 30 65. **Rooms:** 80. ⬚ ▯ ⬚ TV ⬚ ⬚ ⬚ ⬚ P ⬚ AE, DC, MC, V. ⬚

Situated near the famous Europa-Center (see p144), this is a small guesthouse-type hotel – hence no restaurant. With plenty of places to eat in the area this is not really a drawback. The rooms on the Tauentzienstrasse side have sound-proofed windows, but if you like to sleep with the windows open, you should ask for a room at the back of the building. All the rooms were redecorated in 1998. They are large and light, complete with all modern facilities.

Hotel California

Kurfürstendamm 35, 10719 Berlin.
Map 9 C1. 880 120. **FAX** 880 12 111. **Rooms:** 45. ⬚ ▯ ⬚ TV ⬚ ⬚ ⬚ ⬚ ⬚ ⬚ P ⬚ ⬚ AE, DC, MC, V, JCB, EC. ⬚⬚

Not too large and overwhelming, this is a very pleasant hotel in an excellent location. Hotel California occupies a 19th-century building and, as is often the case in Berlin, the reception desk is on the first floor. The fact that there is no restaurant should not be a problem in this part of Berlin.

Propeller Island City Lodge

Albrech-Achilles Strasse 58, 10709 Berlin-Wilmersdorf. 891 90 16.
FAX 891 87 21. **Rooms:** 31.
⬚ ▯ TV ⬚ ⬚ ⬚ www. propeller-island.com

Situated in a 19th-century apartment block, in one of the quiet streets off Kurfürstendamm, this hotel is known as an art hotel. Each room is differently and often outrageously themed – they are real works of art – full of fantasy and flair. This is an ideal place for those looking for a more aesthetic and truly memorable stay.

Remter

Marburger Strasse 17, 10789 Berlin.
Map 10 E1. 23 50 88 0. **FAX** 213 86 12. **Rooms:** 31. ⬚ ▯ ⬚ TV ⬚ P ⬚ ⬚ AE, DC, MC, V. ⬚⬚

This is a pleasant, quiet hotel, and is well located for tourists – it is only about 200 m (650 ft) from the historic landmark Kaiser-Wilhelm-Gedächtniskirche. Although the prices for its rooms are not the cheapest in Berlin, the Remter is one of the best-value hotels in this central location.

Alsterhof

Augsburger Strasse 5, 10789 Berlin.
Map 10 E2. 212 42 719.
FAX 212 42 731. **Rooms:** 200.
⬚ ▯ ⬚ 24 TV ⬚ ⬚ ⬚ ⬚ ⬚ ⬚ ⬚ ⬚ P ⬚ ⬚ AE, DC, V, EC. ⬚⬚⬚

This establishment is ideal for those who value its location near the KaDeWe department store (see p149). The Alsterhof is especially recommended for non-smokers, who can have a special non-smoking bedroom and can also dine in their non-smoking breakfast room. The inner courtyard is an additional feature where, during summer, coffee is served under a pretty chestnut tree.

Best Western Hotel President

An der Urania 16–18, 10787 Berlin-Schöneberg. **Map** 10 F2. 21 90 30. **FAX** 21 41 200. **Rooms:** 187. ⬚ ▯ ⬚ 24 TV ⬚ ⬚ ⬚ ⬚ ⬚ ⬚ P ⬚ ⬚ AE, DC, MC, V. ⬚⬚⬚ W www. bestwestern.com

This large hotel, centrally located, is near to Nollendorfplatz. With comfortable, functional bedrooms in several categories, this is suitable for tourists and for business travellers alike. Special rates are offered during holidays and weekends.

Bleibtreu Hotel

Bleibtreustrasse 31, 10707 Berlin.
Map 9 B2. 88 47 40. **FAX** 884 74 444. **Rooms:** 60. ⬚ ▯ ⬚ 24 TV ⬚ ⬚ ⬚ ⬚ ⬚ ⬚ ⬚ P ⬚ ⬚ AE, DC, MC, V, EC. ⬚⬚⬚

This hotel occupies a restored 19th-century building, which is located on a quiet street quite close to Kurfürstendamm. The sophisticated interiors will appeal to guests who appreciate natural materials. The restaurant serves mainly organic food from farms outside Berlin. The pretty garden inside the inner courtyard comes into its own in summer, when it serves as a particularly relaxing place for tourists and business travellers alike.

Blue Band Berlin Excelsior Hotel

Hardenbergstrasse 14, 10623 Berlin.
Map 4 D5. 31 55 0.
FAX 31 55 10 02. **Rooms:** 320.
⬚ ▯ ⬚ 24 TV ⬚ ⬚ ⬚ ⬚ ⬚ ⬚ P ⬚ ⬚ ⬚ AE, DC, MC, V, JCB, EC. ⬚⬚⬚

This is a good-quality hotel next to the famous Ludwig-Erhard-Haus (see p144). It offers helpful service and good food. It is worth

considering this hotel if you have children under 16 because they can stay for free.

Concept Hotel

Grolmanstrasse 41–43, 10623 Berlin.
Map 9 C1. 884 260. **FAX** 884 26 500. **Rooms:** 106. ⬚ ▯ ⬚ 24 TV ⬚ ⬚ ⬚ ⬚ ⬚ ⬚ ⬚ AE, DC, MC, V, JCB, EC. ⬚⬚⬚

This welcoming hotel is situated in a quiet street. The building itself is modern and some of its rooms have extra long beds for taller guests. The terrace on the roof overlooks the area and during summer, dinner is served in the inner courtyard.

Hecker's Hotel

Grolmanstrasse 35, 10623 Berlin.
Map 9 C1. 88 900. **FAX** 88 90 260. **Rooms:** 72. ⬚ ▯ ⬚ 24 TV ⬚ ⬚ ⬚ ⬚ ⬚ ⬚ P ⬚ ⬚ AE, DC, MC, V, JCB. ⬚⬚⬚

Situated in the very heart of town, very close to Kurfürstendamm, this low-key, private hotel caters not only for its guests' needs but tries for a more individual approach. The plain façade hides a more sophisticated interior. If you like simple furniture in the style of Frank Lloyd Wright and Hans Martin Unger as well as contemporary art, this place will suit your needs.

Holiday Inn Crowne Plaza Berlin

Nürnberger Strasse 65, 10787 Berlin.
Map 10 E2. 21 00 70.
FAX 213 20 09. **Rooms:** 425. ⬚ ▯ ⬚ 24 TV ⬚ ⬚ ⬚ ⬚ ⬚ ⬚ ⬚ ⬚ P ⬚ ⬚ AE, DC, MC, V, EC. ⬚⬚⬚

This luxurious hotel is located near Kaiser-Wilhelm-Gedächtnis-kirche and Tauentzienstrasse. It has a swimming pool, a good restaurant, large rooms and a pleasant atmosphere. It offers special weekend rates combined with sightseeing tours.

Hotel Avantgarde

Kurfürstendamm 15, 10719 Berlin.
Map 10 D1. 882 64 66. **FAX** 882 40 11. **Rooms:** 27. ⬚ ▯ ⬚ TV ⬚ ⬚ ⬚ ⬚ AE, DC, MC, V, JCB. ⬚⬚⬚

Occupying the upper floors of a Neo-Baroque building since the end of the 19th century, this hotel offers large rooms with sound-proof windows and decorative stucco ceilings. Although the hotel does not have its own dining room, there is a Mövenpick restaurant on the ground floor.

Hotel Brandenburger Hof

Eislebener Strasse 14, 10785 Berlin. **Map** 10 E2. 214 050.
FAX 214 95 100. **Rooms:** 87.
AE, DC, MC, V, JCB.
www.brandenburger-hof.com

Elegance, an intimate family atmosphere, impeccable service and the quiet and luxurious rooms of the Hotel Brandenburger Hof make this one of the most desirable addresses in Berlin. This enchanting building has been carefully restored and furnished with items from the Bauhaus period. The staff have a reputation for an attitude of caring and understanding towards all guests. Its restaurant, Die Quadriga (see p241), is one of the best in Berlin.

Hotel Mondial

Kurfürstendamm 47, 10707 Berlin. **Map** 9 B2. 88 41 10.
FAX 8841 11 50. **Rooms:** 75.
AE, DC, MC, V, JCB, EC.

Wonderfully located near George-Grosz-Platz, this hotel is very pleasant, offering a high standard of service. It is recommended for the disabled as it is wheelchair accessible and more than one-quarter of the rooms have special facilities for disabled guests.

Hotel Residenz Berlin

Meinekestrasse 9, 10719 Berlin. **Map** 10 D2. 88 44 30.
FAX 882 47 26. **Rooms:** 80.
AE, DC, MC, V.
www.hotel-residenz.com

The Hotel Residenz is based in a recently restored 19th-century building. It is quite a pleasant mid-range hotel, situated in a side street close to Kurfürstendamm. The interior features stucco ornamentation and decorative banisters. The restaurant, Grand Cru, has many Art Deco objects including a decorated ceiling. First-class suites are available as well as comfortable rooms and cosy apartments with a studio kitchen. The price of the room also includes a buffet breakfast. If you intend to stay for a while, be sure to ask about special prices for long-stay guests. There is also a small room available for business meetings or functions.

Sorat Art'otel Berlin

Joachimstaler Strasse 29, 10719 Berlin. **Map** 10 D2. 88 44 70.
FAX 00 147 700. **Rooms:** 133.
AE, DC, MC, V, JCB, EC.
www.sorat-hotels.com

The Sorat Art'otel, located close to Kurfürstendamm, can be easily recognized from a distance by the figure of a discus-thrower on the façade. Belonging to a young hotel chain, its interiors are boldly designed in an ultra-modern style, and colourful elements are used to give the rooms a unique character. Contemporary art works decorate the walls. In fact, due to the work of Johann and Gernotow Nalbach and the attention to detail, the whole hotel is like a carefully considered work of art. If one fails to appreciate the extravagant interior concept, the high quality of service will undoubtedly impress on its own.

Hotel Palace Berlin

Europa-Center, 10789 Berlin. **Map** 10 E1. 250 20.
FAX 262 65 77. **Rooms:** 282.
AE, DC, MC, V, JCB, EC.
www.palace.de

This is a luxurious hotel, located at the Europa-Center opposite Kaiser-Wilhelm-Gedächtnis-kirche. The simple, uninspiring shape of the building hides its charming interior, which is full of discreet elegance. The hotel is distinguished by the extraordinary lengths taken to create an intimate atmosphere and its personal approach towards the individual needs of guests. That is why this establishment is popular with politicians and celebrity film stars: former guests include Julia Roberts, Kevin Costner, Isabella Rosellini. The type of room available ranges from double rooms and junior suites to country suites and presidential suites. It also has a number of bars and restaurants, including a bar called Sam's Bar and the excellent restaurant called First Floor (see p 241).

Savoy Hotel

Fasanenstrasse 9–10, 10623 Berlin. **Map** 10 D1. 31 10 30.
FAX 311 03 333. **Rooms:** 125.
AE, DC, MC, V, CB.
www.hotel-savoy.com

Established since 1930, the Savoy Hotel is one of the most beautiful

hotels in Berlin. It has an excellent location on the elegant Fasanen-strasse, with a range of fine boutiques, shops and entertainment nearby. Comfortable rooms and a friendly atmosphere attract an exclusive clientele – former guests include Greta Garbo and Thomas Mann. The suites on the 6th floor offer good views over the rooftops of Berlin. (You can choose from the Greta Garbo, Henry Miller or the Miró suites). The hotel's facilities include a babysitting service, theatre ticket service, secretarial services and free newspapers. Apart from an exquisite restaurant and several bars, it also boasts Berlin's first cigar bar, Casa Del Habano, which has its own unique atmosphere. There is also a car rental service and hotel car park.

Steigenberger Berlin

Los-Angeles-Platz 1, 10789 Berlin. **Map** 10 E2. 212 70.
FAX 212 71 17. **Rooms:** 397.
AE, DC, MC, V, EC.

With a very good location (on quiet Los-Angeles-Platz near the Europa-Center) the Steigenberger offers cosy rooms and several categories of apartments. In addition, one can find here everything to cater for the needs of business traveller and tourist alike. These include a swimming pool, sauna, massage, a pleasant bar and good Berlin cuisine served in the hotel restaurant, Berliner Stube. For lighter meals the hotel offers its excellent restaurant called Aromaküche.

Kempinski Hotel Bristol Berlin

Kurfürstendamm 27, 10719 Berlin. **Map** 10 D1. 884 340.
FAX 883 60 75. **Rooms:** 301.
AE, DC, MC, V, JCB.

One of the most famous hotels in Berlin, the Kempinski Hotel is known to locals as the Kempi. It occupies a distinctive semi-circular building that is quite hard to miss on Kurfürstendamm. The hotel first opened its doors in 1953 but was extensively redecorated in the 1990s. It has a classic interior – well balanced with modern elements. Its luxurious rooms are also very comfortable, decorated in navy or brown and with marble en suite bathrooms. There are 56 non-smoking rooms available and 18 rooms with wheelchair access. Equally famous is its restaurant, Kempinski-Grill, which serves international food and its bistro-café, Kempinski-Eck and Terrace, serving traditional Berlin cuisine.

AROUND SCHLOSS CHARLOTTENBURG

Hotel an der Oper

Bismarckstrasse 100, 10625 Berlin.
Map 3 A4. 315 830. FAX 315 83
109. **Rooms:** 46. AE, DC, MC, V,
JCB.

As its name suggests, the Hotel an
der Oper is located near the opera
house in Charlottenburg. Although
the rooms overlook the busy and
noisy Bismarckstrasse, the windows have been soundproofed.
However, if you like sleeping with
your windows open, request a
room on the courtyard side of the
building. The hotel has a non-smoking breakfast room, but smoking is permitted in guest rooms.

Schlossparkhotel

Heubnerweg 2a, 14059 Berlin.
Map 2 D2. 326 90 30. FAX 325
88 61. **Rooms:** 39.
AE, DC, MC, V, JCB, EC.

Schlossparkhotel is a very pleasant,
small hotel, near the beautiful
gardens of Schlosspark Charlottenburg. There is no convenient U-Bahn station nearby, but S-Bahn
Westend is within walking distance.
When making a reservation, it is
worth asking for a room with a
balcony that overlooks the garden.

FURTHER AFIELD

Die Fabrik

Schlesische Strasse 18, 10997
Berlin-Kreuzberg. 611 71 16.
FAX 618 29 74. **Rooms:** 41.
AE, DC, MC, V, JCB, EC.

Die Fabrik is a type of youth hostel,
set in an old factory building. Its
simple furnishings are made from
pale wood, and there are shared
bathrooms along the corridors.
However, its easy-going atmosphere appeals not only to young
people. Apart from single and
double rooms, it also offers rooms
for three and four people and
even larger group rooms, where
the price of a bed is very cheap.

Hotel Ahorn

Schlüterstrasse 40, 10707 Berlin-
Charlottenburg. **Map** 9 B2. 881 43
44. FAX 881 65 00. **Rooms:** 28.
AE, DC,
MC, V, JCB, EC.

Hotel Ahorn is a pleasant guest-house-style hotel. It has a prime
location only a few steps away
from Kurfürstendamm. As well as
double and triple rooms, apartments with kitchens are available
for longer stays.

Hotel Belvedere

Seebergsteig 4, 14193 Berlin-
Wilmersdorf. 82 60 010. FAX 82 60
0163. **Rooms:** 18.

This little hotel is located in a
quiet street, in the district of
Grunewald. It is a quaint, charming villa, surrounded by a
romantic garden. The atmosphere
is very homely and rooms are
furnished with some stylish pieces.
Those who like colourful carpets,
crystal chandeliers and old-fashioned wallpaper will feel at
home in the Belvedere.

Hotelpension Alpina

Trabener Strasse 3, 14193 Berlin-
Wilmersdorf. 891 35 17. FAX 893
53 42. **Rooms:** 17.

The Hotelpension Alpina is similar
to the Hotel Belvedere, which is
owned by the same people. It is
located in a nice, quiet street of
Grunewald, surrounded by pretty
greenery. The building itself is a
Neo-Baroque villa that dates from
the beginning of the 20th century.
The hotel does have a family
atmosphere. The rooms are
decorated in an old-fashioned
style and only some of the rooms
have en suite bathrooms.

Alfa Hotel

Ufnaustrasse 1, 10553 Berlin-
Tiergarten, Berlin. 344 00 31.
FAX 345 21 11. **Rooms:** 33.
AE, DC, MC, V, JCB, EC.

This is a well-equipped modern
establishment that nevertheless
maintains an intimate atmosphere,
due to its location in a quiet street
not far from the centre of Berlin.
The rooms at the Alfa Hotel are
comfortable and of a high standard. Although the hotel does not
have a restaurant, there is a small
informal café that offers excellent
food. The service at the café is
extremely polite.

Artemisia

Brandenburgische Strasse 18, 10707
Berlin-Wilmersdorf. 873 89 05.
FAX 861 86 53. **Rooms:** 8.

The Artemisia is the only hotel in
Berlin that caters exclusively for
women. This hotel is often visited
by women travelling on business.
Men are only allowed into the
conference room. Its comfortable
rooms are decorated in pastel
colours and are located on the
fourth and fifth floors of this old
building. Some rooms do not have
en suite bathrooms and have only
basins, with a bathroom located in
the corridor. The hotel also has a
small breakfast room with a
terrace that overlooks Berlin.

Best Western Kanthotel Berlin

Kantstrasse 111, 10627 Berlin-
Charlottenburg. **Map** 9 A1.
323 020. FAX 324 09 52.
Rooms: 70. AE, DC, EC, V.
www.kanthotel.com.

This good-quality mid-range hotel
is located in the vicinity of
Charlottenburg railway station,
very close to the heart of the
shopping centre in Wilmersdorfer
Strasse. Some of the rooms have
special facilities for business
travellers, and non-smoking
rooms are also available. The
hotel offers extra services, such as
babysitting and clothes laundering.
There is no hotel restaurant but
there are many places to eat
in the neighbourhood.

East-Side Hotel

Mühlenstrasse 6, 10243 Berlin-
Friedrichshain. **Map** 8 F5. 29 38
33. FAX 29 38 35 55. **Rooms:** 36.
AE, DC, MC, V, EC.

The East-Side Hotel is located in
a modernized hotel opposite the
East-Side-Gallery (see p165), in a
building that was formerly used to
house workers. It opened in 1996,
and has big, bright rooms with
modern facilities and spacious
bathrooms. The hotel has a
comfortable family atmosphere.

Estrel Residence & Congress Hotel

Sonnenallee 225, 12057 Berlin-
Neukölln. **Map** 14 F5. 68 31 0.
FAX 68 31 23 45. **Rooms:** 1125.
AE, DC, MC, V,
EC.

Opened in 1994, the Estrel Residence & Congress Hotel belongs
to one of the biggest hotel chains
in Germany. It was designed to
house major conferences, but it is
also popular among tourists as
well as various visitors of fairs and
conventions. Conveniently linked
by S-Bahn to the town centre, it
offers so many rooms that one is
always sure to find something
vacant. You can leave children in
a crèche at the hotel, or dine in
one of five restaurants. During
summer, you can also have a beer
in the garden along the canal.

For key to symbols see p209

Forsthaus Hubertusbrücke

Stolpchenweg 45, 14109 Berlin-Wannsee. **(** *805 30 00.* **FAX** *805 35 24.*
Rooms: 22.

This is the ideal place for those looking for rest after a full day of sightseeing. The hotel is situated in green surroundings and is very intimate. Staying here allows you to forget that you are only 20 minutes away from one of the busiest cities in the world.

Forsthaus Paulsborn

Am Grunewaldsee/Hüttenweg 90, 14193 Berlin-Grunewald. **(** *818 19 10.* **FAX** *81 81 91 50.* **Rooms:** 10.
AC, DC, V.

Only a few miles away from the centre of Berlin, a stay here should banish any thought of inner city stress, as it is located next to a lake, deep in the Grunewald. There are only ten rooms in this stylish former hunting lodge, built at the beginning of the 20th century. It is full of character – its walls bristle with deer antlers, its windows have stained glass, there is a fireplace in the lobby and the restaurant offers a full range of venison dishes. The Forsthaus Paulsborn is best suited to visitors with a car, due to its secluded location.

Holiday Inn Gustavo Berlin

Prenzlauer Allee 169, 10409 Berlin-Prenzlauer Berg. **(** *44 66 10.* **FAX** *44 66 16 61.* **Rooms:** 122.
AE, DC, MC, V, EC.

The hotel is named after the Spanish artist Gustavo, whose works decorate its interiors. This includes walls, carpets and even keyrings. The amusing, colourful paintings and sculptures perfectly match the character of the whole district. The rooms are modern and clean and there is a hand-signed Gustavo print in every room. There is good public transport on the hotel's doorstep and special rates offered for weekend stays.

Hotel Igel

Friederikestrasse 33–34, 13505 Berlin-Tegelort. **(** *436 00 10,* **FAX** *436 24 70.* **Rooms:** 70.
EC, AE, V, DC

This is a perfect establishment for those travellers who not only want to see the attractions of the city, but who want to relax as well. Situated near Tegeler See, the

Hotel Igel offers quiet, comfortable rooms. The hotel's restaurant is very good and specializes in venison and fish dishes.

Hotel Pension Wittelsbach

Wittelsbacher Strasse 22, 10707 Berlin-Wilmersdorf. **(** *864 98 40.* **FAX** *862 15 32.* **Rooms:** 31.
AE, MC, V, JCB.

This is a pleasant pension located in a 19th-century building. The bedrooms are huge, and some are decorated with stucco. This hotel is recommended for families that are travelling with small children; one floor is dedicated to them. There are plenty of toys and the nursery rooms are decorated in the style of a palace and the "Wild West". Guests can also rent almost everything required to cater for children, including bottle heaters for babies.

Hotel Rheinsberg am See

Finsterwalder Strasse 64, 13435 Berlin-Reinickendorf. **(** *402 10 02.* **FAX** *403 50 57.* **Rooms:** 81.
MC, V, EC.

If you place more value on peace, picturesque surroundings overlooking a lake and comfortable, reasonably-priced rooms than on proximity to the town centre, then this hotel will meet your needs. The amusing shape of the building and its rustic interiors make it a rather unusual place to stay.

Ibis Hotel

Prenzlauer Allee 4, 10405 Berlin-Mitte. **Map** 8 D1. **(** *44 33 30.* **FAX** *44 33 31 11.* **Rooms:** 198.
AE, DC, MC, V, JCB, EC.

One of the three Berlin hotels belonging to this chain, the Ibis hotel is situated in Mitte, only a few hundred metres from Alexanderplatz. Modern rooms (on the small side), pleasant service and relatively low prices make it a popular place. The 24-hour shop in the nearby petrol station is handy.

Ibis Hotel Berlin-Messe

Messedamm 10, 14057 Berlin-Charlottenburg. **Map** 1 C5. **(** *30 39 30.* **FAX** *301 95 36.* **Rooms:** 168.
AE, DC, EC, V.

Visitors to the frequent trade fairs held in this area only have to cross the street to reach this hotel.

It has been newly refurbished and the hotel chain is known for its reliable standard of accommodation and good service. It is located next door to the Funkturm, which has the best view of the city, and it is also well placed for the Kurfürstendamm and Mitte areas.

Imperator

Meinekestrasse 5, 10719 Berlin-Charlottenburg. **Map** 10 D2. **(** *881 41 81.* **FAX** *885 19 19.*
Rooms: 11.

Just a stone's throw away from the Ku'damm, this comfortable hotel provides a very attentive service. It is a favourite hotel of artists and others who appreciate its individual atmosphere. The late 19th-century building, set in an exclusive street, recalls a more prosperous time for the Ku'damm.

Jurine

Schwedter Strasse 15, 10119 Berlin-Mitte. **(** *443 29 90.* **FAX** *44 32 99 99.* **Rooms:** 50.
AE, DC, EC, MC, V.

This small hotel is located in a side street near Senefelderplatz, in the centre of Prenzlauer Berg. It is an excellent base for visiting the area and a good opportunity to experience Berlin nightlife. At the same time, the nearby U-Bahn station gives easy access to the town centre. The recently redecorated rooms are of a high standard and there is a hotel garden.

Modena

Wielandstrasse 26, 10707 Berlin. **Map** 9 B2. **(** *885 70 10.* **FAX** *881 52 94.* **Rooms:** 19.

This typical, intimate Berlin pension occupies an apartment block dating from the end of the 19th century. Although the price includes breakfast, there are also many restaurants and cafés in the neighbourhood. Situated around Kurfürstendamm and Olivaer Platz, it is an excellent base for tourists. Not all rooms have bathrooms; those with only a washbasin are less expensive.

Queens Hotel Berlin

Güntzelstrasse 14. 10717 Berlin-Wilmersdorf. **Map** 10 D4. **(** *873 02 41.* **FAX** *861 93 26.*
Rooms: 109.
AE, DC, MC, V, EC.

This is a comfortable hotel located near a U-Bahn station in a quiet street. The hotel is not far from the centre and the nice bars in Schöneberg. It has cosy rooms with good facilities and its service is helpful. It also serves a good breakfast and the peace and quiet guarantee a pleasant stay.

Villa Kastania

Kastanienallee 20, 14052 Map 1 A5. Berlin-Charlottenburg. **C** *30 00 02 0.* FAX *30 00 02 10.* **Rooms:** *43.*
AE, DC, MC, V, JCB, EC.

This is a pleasant, intimate hotel with high standard of service. It is located in a quiet street, a few minutes by foot from Messegelände (a complex of trade fair halls) and with excellent links to the town centre. All the rooms have balconies and the standard rooms have small kitchenettes as well. This is worth recommending not only to those attending fairs and conferences, but also to tourists looking for reasonable, convenient accommodation.

Villa Toscana

Bahnhofstrasse 19, 12207 Berlin-Steglitz. **C** *76 89 270.* FAX *773 44 88.* **Rooms:** *16.*
AE, DC, MC, V.

This hotel is situated in an Italian-style villa, dating from the end of the 19th century. It is more convenient for tourists with cars as it is far from the centre and from any S- and U-Bahn stations. Instead, it offers a quiet and romantic atmosphere. The rooms are furnished with some antiques and the marble bathrooms are elegant.

Hotel Luisenhof

Köpenicker Strasse 92, 10179 Berlin-Mitte. **Map** 8 D5. **C** *241 59 06.* FAX *279 29 83.* **Rooms:** *27.*
AE, DC, MC, V, JCB, EC.

Situated near the Märkisches Museum, this hotel occupies the oldest building (1882) in this part of Berlin. Extensive restoration in 1993 changed the neglected building into a charming, small hotel with nice rooms and a pleasant restaurant in the cellar. During weekends, attractive room rates are available.

Hotel Seehof Berlin

Lietzenseeufer 11, 14057 Berlin-Charlottenburg. **Map** 2 D5. **C** *32 00 20.* FAX *32 00 22 51.* **Rooms:** *77.*
AE, DC, MC, V, JCB, EC.

...is is an amazing hotel situated ...he town centre. It is only 10 ...tes by foot from Messegelände

(the complex of trade fair halls) but at the same time it overlooks a picturesque lake and an apartment block dating from time of Kaiser Wilhelm. The modern structure of this hotel does not reveal the stylish interiors. If you like large rooms with mahogany furniture and a lakeside view, you will love this place. Its restaurant, Restaurant Au Lac, is one of the best in Berlin.

SORAT Hotel Humboldt-Mühle Berlin

An der Mühle 5–9, 13507 Berlin-Reinickendorf **C** *43 90 40.* FAX *43 90 44 44.* **Rooms:** *120.*
AE, DC, MC, V, JCB, EC.

Located near Tegel airport, this hotel occupies a former grain mill. It is furnished in a modern style using light-coloured woods and old architectural elements. Because of its history, dishes offered in the breakfast bar and in the restaurant contain wholemeal grains.

SORAT Hotel Spree-Bogen Berlin

Alt-Moabit 99, 10559 Berlin-Tiergarten. **Map** 4 F1. **C** *399 200.* FAX *399 20 999.* **Rooms:** *220.*
AE, DC, MC, V, JCB, EC.
W *www.sorat-hotels.com.*

Beautifully located on the bank of the Spree river, the hotel is surrounded by modern tower blocks not far from the Tiergarten and the government residential district. The building used to be an old dairy but has been completely modernized inside. The most attractive rooms have a view of the river and the hotel also has its own yacht, which can be used for short trips to Museum Island or the Reichstag.

Ritz-Carlton Schlosshotel

Brahmsstrasse 10, 14193 Berlin-Wilmersdorf. **C** *895 840.* FAX *895 84 800.* **Rooms:** *54.*
AE, DC, MC, V, JCB, EC.

This is one of the most exclusive, comfortable and undoubtedly one of Berlin's most expensive hotels, situated in a quiet part of Grunewald. The hotel was formerly a palace, built in 1912 for Walter von Pannwitz, the personal lawyer of the Kaiser. The contemporary interiors were created by Karl Lagerfeld. There is a breathtaking

lobby with a magnifice... ceiling, decorative woodc... and a restaurant hall in Reg... style. The restaurant, Vivaldi *p243*), has a very good reputa...

GREATER
BERLIN

art'otel potsdam

Zeppelinstrasse 136, 14471 Potsdam. **C** *(0331) 98 15 0.* FAX *(0331) 98 15 555.* **Rooms:** *123.*
AE, DC, MC, V.

This beautiful, luxurious hotel on the bank of Havel river has carefully designed interiors. Part of the hotel occupies an old granary dating from the 19th century. This older part is joined with a modern structure that houses the second wing. Rooms in the granary have beautiful ceilings with restored beams and simple furniture designed by Jasper Morrison. The best feature of the rooms in the modern wing is their balconies overlooking the Havel. The hotel restaurant specializes in fish dishes.

Hotel Voltaire

Friedrich-Ebert-Strasse 88, 14467 Potsdam. **C** *(0331) 23 170.* FAX *(0331) 23 17 100.* **Rooms:** *143.*

This is a top-quality hotel in the centre of town, near Holländische Viertel. Comfortably furnished rooms each have a different atmosphere due to their individual colour schemes and carefully chosen details. The modern part of the building is joined to a Baroque palace that was adapted to meet the needs of the hotel.

Schloss Cecilienhof

Am Neuen Garten, Potsdam. **C** *(0331) 37 050.* FAX *(0331) 29 24 98.* **Rooms:** *42.*
AE, DC, MC, V, JCB, EC.

This is undoubtedly a treat for history lovers who want to relax in pleasant and green surroundings. The hotel occupies most of the Cecilienhof palace (see p191), which is a large and picturesque complex. The meeting room, where the Potsdam Conference (see p191) took place in 1945, is now a museum, but the rest of the wing is reserved for guests. In the evening, when the daytrippers have left, hotel guests are able to take a stroll in the pleasant gardens or even a boat trip on the lake.

For key to symbols see p209

STAURANTS, CAFÉS AND BARS

Shield of the Forst-
haus Paulsborn restaurant

IVEN THAT BERLIN is so cosmopolitan, you will find a wider range of restaurants here than in any other city in Germany. This includes Indian, Greek, Chinese, Thai and Turkish as well as Alsatian and Cambodian. Recently, new places have been opened by famous chefs, which maintain high European standards of international-style cuisine. There are also plenty of restaurants specializing in local dishes: the food can be a little heavy but it is usually very tasty and served in large portions. Wherever you are in Berlin, you won't have to travel far to find somewhere to eat – every area has its own cluster of restaurants, cafés and bars, covering a range of styles and prices. Some of the best places are listed on pages 234–6. These have been chosen for their delicious food or good value. More detailed information about these places is given on pages 237–43. The listings on pages 244–9 should help those who would like a bite to eat but want the more relaxed setting of a café or bar.

**The intimate interior of
Bamberger Reiter (see p243)**

WHERE TO GO

ALTHOUGH GOOD restaurants and cafés can be found all over Berlin, some of the best gourmet restaurants tend to be located in exclusive hotels, including **Die Quadriga** in the Brandenburger Hof *(see p241)* or **First Floor** in the Hotel Palace Berlin *(see p241)*. Alternatively, good restaurants can also be found on quiet streets far away from the centre of the city, such as **Rockendorfs** *(see p243)*, **Grand Slam** *(see p243)*, or **Bamberger Reiter** *(see p243)*.

The largest concentrations of restaurants are in a number of well-known districts. In the former West Berlin, for example, the most famous restaurants are clustered around Savignyplatz. Good places to eat in the centre can be found in and around Oranienburger Strasse. One of the recent top spots in Berlin that is popular with young people is in Prenzlauer Berg, near Kollwitzplatz. Despite all the changes that have taken place in the eastern part of Berlin over the past few years, restaurants in Kreuzberg (particularly along Oranien-strasse) are among the busiest in the city. The places in these areas are all consistently good and offer a wide choice in style and price.

WHAT TO EAT

IN THE MORNING, nearly all eateries, including those in most hotels, will offer a substantial breakfast. This usually consists of eggs, ham or cold cuts and different kinds of cheese. On Sundays some places also serve a German buffet-style brunch (breakfast combined with lunch) until 2pm. At lunchtime, one can easily find an elaborate salad or a bowl of steaming soup almost anywhere. In addition many restaurants may also offer their standard menus with slightly reduced prices.

The options for an evening meal are practically unlimited. In a restaurant serving local food one can have, for example, a tasty pork knuckle or potato soup *(see pp230–31)*. Lovers of Italian cuisine can easily find a good pizzeria or an Italian restaurant that serves sophisticated regional Italian dishes. Fans of Oriental food can choose between many Asian national cuisines, a great variety of which are situated along Prenzlauer Berg and around Savignyplatz. In addition,

The open-air summer terrace in front of the Operncafé

Russian restaurant, Pasternak (see p242), in Prenzlauer Berg

Berlin also has very good Mexican restaurants, particularly around Oranienburger Strasse and in Kreuzberg, and the food served at Greek restaurants is usually quite good and very inexpensive. Vegetarians can easily find something suitable at almost every restaurant, however, places that offer a significant choice of meat-free dishes are specially marked in the restaurant listings (see pp234–6).

PRICES AND TIPPING

MENUS, SHOWING meals and their prices, are usually on display outside restaurants and cafés. The prices of meals can vary a great deal. It is possible to eat a three course meal, without alcohol, for DM20–25, but in the centre of Berlin the price rises up to DM35–45. In a top-notch establishment the cost of a meal can be over DM150. The price of alcohol varies as well, but the most popular and cheapest drink is beer. Although prices include service and tax, many Germans will round up the bill. In more expensive restaurants a 10 per cent tip is customary.

EATING HOURS

IN GENERAL, cafés open at 9am and restaurants at noon; the latter sometimes also close between 3 and 6pm. However, there are a lot of places that stay open very late, sometimes until 2 or 3am. Some of the most expensive and best restaurants are only open in the evening and are sometimes closed on one day during the week as well.

BOOKING

IN THE MOST up-market restaurants, reservations are almost certainly required – in popular places it is advisable to book well in advance. For the majority of good restaurants it is necessary to book only for Friday or Saturday evenings, when all restaurants are at their busiest. If you do not have a reservation, look for a street or square with a large concentration of restaurants – there is bound to be an empty table among these.

DISABLED DINERS

IN ORDER TO avoid any problems in advance, you should discuss wheelchair access when booking. Bear in mind, however, that even if a dining room may be accessible on the ground floor, the toilets may be up or down stairs or through a narrow corridor.

CHILDREN

CASUAL RESTAURANTS usually welcome children, though this may not be the case in more upmarket establishments. Those that do cater for children may provide high chairs as well as light dishes, particularly during lunchtime. Some places will offer a separate children's menu with small portions. Children are also allowed in pubs and bars.

READING THE MENU

MENUS ARE WRITTEN OUT, in many places, in German and English, although some restaurants will provide menus in French as well. If you find yourself in a casual restaurant or bar, where the menu is perhaps hand-written, you can ask a waiter for help. Apart from the standard menu many restaurants will sometimes also offer a menu of the day containing seasonal dishes or the chef's specials, which are always worth considering.

The interior of Olive (see p242)

SMOKING

SMOKING IS ALLOWED everywhere in Berlin – except in some fast-food places. There are special non-smoking rooms in some restaurants, but this is a rarity. To avoid a smoky meal, sit near a door or window, or look for a restaurant with high ceilings.

Restaurant in film studio, Babelsberg

Berlin's Best: Restaurants

A S BEFITS A MAJOR cosmopolitan city, Berlin
boasts a huge range of marvellous places to
eat. The variety is enormous, from cheap and
cheerful restaurants serving anything from traditional German food to Thai, Italian and Greek,
through to more expensive places, often em-
ploying famous chefs. Below are some of the
best restaurants, many with a long history in the
city, and all with excellent reputations.

Ana e Bruno
*Stylish Italian cuisine with a
speciality of carpaccio (raw
beef) that attracts fans from
across the city (see p242).*

Around Schloss
Charlottenburg

Around
Kurfürstendamm

Alt Luxemburg
*Karl Wannemacher's
cuisine will impress even
the choosiest guests, and
the cosy, old-fashioned
interior makes an
evening here a relaxing
experience (see p243).*

Die Quadriga
*Plenty of refined
German and French
dishes are listed on the
menu at this charming
and very popular
restaurant (see p240).*

Bamberger Reiter
*French cuisine is the
speciality of Franz
Raneburger's chic,
cosy restaurant (see
p243), as well known
for its welcoming
atmosphere as for the
top-notch food.*

0 metres   750

0 yards   750

Rockendorf's Restaurant

Situated some way from the centre of the city, Rockendorf's does require a special trip, but the journey is always worthwhile (see p243).

First Floor

This restaurant is famous for its sophisticated German dishes with the additional attraction of an excellent wine list (see p241).

North of the centre

West of the centre

Museum Island

Tiergarten

Around Unter den Linden

Kreuzberg

Ermeler-Haus

Good old-fashioned Berlin cuisine is served in the Rococo dining room of the historic Ermeler-Haus (see p237).

Harlequin

The funky interior of this modern restaurant is dominated by a large Harlequin figure overlooking the widely-spaced tables (see p239).

L'Etoile

Part of the Hotel Adlon (see p237), this restaurant maintains the same standards of unpretentious luxury.

What to Eat in Berlin

Loaf of Berlin bread

B ERLIN CUISINE is richly varied but its many wonderful and tasty dishes are often overshadowed by German food's reputation as rich and stodgy. Concentrating on fresh ingredients from local forests and lakes, Berlin chefs create excellent seasonal cuisine, including particularly delicious wild mushrooms *(Pfifferlingen)*, crayfish, and river fish such as eel, which is often cooked with a green sauce *(Aal grün)*. You can always rely on finding excellent potato soup *(Kartoffelsuppe)*, while veal or pork knuckle with cabbage is also popular.

Käsestange

Brezel

Mohn-
brötchen

Berlin Breads
A wide range of excellent breads, rolls and pretzels is consumed in Berlin every day.

Zander mit Radieschenpfann-kuchen *is sautéed fillets of zander served with delicate pancakes stuffed with radishes.*

Zander

Radish-stuffed pancakes

Forelle mit Spargel, *or fresh trout from the Wannsee, is often filleted and served with delicate green asparagus.*

Kalb mit Petersilienmousse, *slices of stewed veal with a light parsley mousse, is accompanied by* Spätzle *(German noodles) and herb dumplings.*

Wilde Pilze in Aspik *is carefully chosen wild mushrooms covered in aromatic aspic, which makes an elegant seasonal starter.*

Geräucherte Barbell mit Kartoffelpuffern *is slices of smoked barbel (a carp-like fish) served with crispy grated-potato pancakes.*

Rote Bete mit Schlagsahne, *a beetroot soup, is blended with cream and served with highly-flavoured meatballs.*

Kartoffelsuppe, *or creamy potato soup, is flavoured with marjoram, and served with slices of pork sausage.*

Brotsuppe, *made of brown bread and enriched with cream, is served with crisp bacon pieces and croûtons.*

Entenbraten mit Kraut, *a traditional dish, is roast duck served in an aromatic sauce with new potatoes and slowly braised spring cabbage.*

Ochsenschwanz mit Lendenfilet, *or stuffed oxtail, is simmered slowly in wine and served with rare sirloin steak and spring vegetables.*

Eisbein mit Kraut und Erbsenpüree *is a braised pork knuckle on a bed of cabbage cooked in champagne with puréed peas.*

Hühnerfrikassee mit Languste
This tasty fricassée of chicken is served with crayfish and squares of flaky pastry.

Crayfish

Fried chicken

Flaky pastry

Gefüllte Forelle, *wild trout from the river Havel, is stuffed and served with a salad of mixed leaves and mushrooms.*

BERLIN DESSERTS

The classic Berlin dessert is *Rote Grütze,* a compôte of mixed berries served with vanilla sauce. A simpler dessert is the famous *Berliner* or doughnut.

Savarin mit Blaubeeren und Minzsorbet *is sponge-cake soaked in syrup and served with blueberries and refreshing mint sorbet.*

Berliner mit Holunder-sorbet, *are mini* Berliner *doughnuts filled with plum mousse and served with elderflower sorbet, sliced pears and a fruit coulis.*

CURRYWURST

One of the most popular of Berlin snacks is the *Curry-wurst.* Invented in the city and sold on every street corner, a *Currywurst* is a spicy sausage served in a bread roll with a curried tomato sauce.

What to Drink in Berlin

IN BERLIN, AS THROUGHOUT the rest of Germany, beer is the most widely drunk alcoholic beverage. There are no productive vineyards around Berlin, but wines from the Rhine and Mosel regions are always popular. As an *aperitif*, or with pork dishes, Berliners often enjoy a shot of rye vodka *(Korn)*, sometimes flavoured with herbs. With dessert, a glass of herbal liqueur often fits the bill.

Engelhardt brewery logo

Pilsner beers from Berlin breweries

LAGER *(PILSNER)*

BERLINERS DRINK BEER on every occasion, and Germany's many beers are some of the best and purest in the world. Some of the best-known Berlin breweries are Schultheiss, Berliner Kindl, Berliner Pils and Engelhardt, but beers brewed in other parts of Germany are just as popular. Although beer is available in all sorts of venues and *"Ein Bier bitte"* can be heard in pubs, cafés and restaurants, it is worth experiencing the atmosphere of an old-fashioned beerhouse, or *Kneipe*. The most highly esteemed beer is draught beer, drawn from the cask *(vom Fass)* and poured slowly into tall glasses. Pouring in a thin trickle is essential to achieve a thick head of foam, and a good barman will take a few minutes to fill your glass. Berliners drink mostly lager *(Pils)*, but other beers are also popular.

Strong, dark Bock beer

OTHER BEERS

IN ADDITION TO THE USUAL light, Pilsner-type beers, Berlin's breweries, many of them small and independent, also make a number of more adventurous brews. Dark, sweetish beer, known as *Schwarzbier* or black beer, is becoming more and more popular and has rather more than the standard four per cent alcohol. *Weizenbier* is made from wheat rather than barley, and is usually served in half-litre (one pint) glasses wth a slice of lemon. Another unusual drink is *Bock*, an especially strong beer made with barley. *Maibock* is a special version, available only in May.

A *Brezel* makes a good snack with beer

Berliner Weisse, a light malted-wheat beer

Berliner Weisse with raspberry and woodruff cordials

BERLINER WEISSE MIT SCHUSS

A BERLIN SPECIALITY, called *Berliner Weisse mit Schuss*, is a light, newly-fermented wheat beer that continues fermenting in the bottle. On its own, it is not very palatable as it is rather watery and sour, but when mixed with raspberry cordial it becomes fruity and delicious. Mixing with sweet woodruff syrup gives it a vivid green colour and a slightly medicinal flavour. *Berliner Weisse mit Schuss* is served in large wine glasses with a straw, and makes a very refreshing drink, particularly popular during the hot summer months.

WINE

N O WINE IS PRODUCED around Berlin as the climate here is too cold for vines, but a variety of wines from Germany's southern and western regions are available in Berlin. The most famous are the white wines, particularly those made from Riesling grapes. Most expensive are those from the Rheingau region. The northern climate dictates that most German wines are white, but lovers of red wine can try the Rhine Assmanshausen Spät-burgunder, made from Pinot Noir grapes. Although there is no regional system of classification like the French *Appellation d'Origine Contrôlée*, a national quality control system divides German wines into three categories: *Tafelwein* or table wine is the most basic; next comes *Qualitätswein*, and the highest is *Qualitätswein mit Prädikat*, which includes wines made from specially selected grapes. *Trocken* means dry, *halbtrocken* means medium dry and *süss* means sweet. You can also find some very good sparkling wines known as *Sekts*.

A prize-winning bottle of German red wine

Riesling from Schloss Vollrads

OTHER ALCOHOLIC BEVERAGES

V ODKA IS OFTEN DRUNK with more substantial meals, particularly those based on pork. Especially recommended is one of the rye vodkas, such as *Weizendoppelkorn*, that are popular in Berlin. Many establishments also serve brandies, known generically as *Weinbrand*. In addition, various digestive liqueurs and vodkas flavoured with plant extracts are quite popular, particularly *Kümmerling*, *Jägermeister* and a Berlin favourite, *Kanlzzdorferkräuter Likör*. In many restaurants you will come across a speciality honey liqueur from east Prussia known as *Bärenfang*. More of an acquired taste is *Goldwasser* from Danzig, a traditional herbal liqueur containing flakes of gold leaf. It is made according to a secret 16th-century German recipe.

Weizendoppel-korn rye vodka

Herbal digestive liqueur

Bitter-sweet Jägermeister liqueur

NON-ALCOHOLIC COLD DRINKS

A LTHOUGH BERLIN TAP WATER is safe to drink, it is not usually served with restaurant meals. If you want water you should order a bottle of mineral water *(Mineralwasser)* adding *"ohne Gas"* if you prefer still water. A wide variety of canned sparkling soft drinks, ubiquitous across Europe and the US, are popular in Berlin. Fruit juices are also widely drunk and a wide selection is available in every restaurant and café. Another popular soft drink is *Apfel-Schorle*, apple juice mixed in equal proportions with sparkling mineral water.

Apfel-Schorle

COFFEE AND TEA

C OFFEE IS VERY POPULAR IN BERLIN and is served in a variety of ways. The most usual is filter coffee, served by the cup or the pot, generally with condensed milk and sugar. If you prefer something stronger and more aromatic you should go for an espresso. It is also easy to enjoy a good cup of tea in Berlin, herbal or otherwise. Germans drink a lot of herbal teas, two of the most common being peppermint *(Pfefferminz-tee)* and camomile *(Kamillentee)*. If you want a cup of non-herbal tea, you can make a point of ordering *Schwarzen Tee*. If you want milk with your tea, then ask for *Tee mit Milch*.

Peppermint and camomile, two widely available herbal teas

Choosing a Restaurant

THE RESTAURANTS in this section were chosen because of their good value, good food and attractive interiors. This list includes some criteria that should help make your choice easier. Places in each area are listed alphabetically within a given price range. More details can be found on pages 237–243.

	Price	REGIONAL CUISINE	LATE OPENING	FIXED-PRICE MENU	VEGETARIAN MEALS	OUTSIDE TABLES	RECOMMENDED WINE LIST	ATTRACTIVE LOCATION
AROUND UNTER DEN LINDEN *(see p237)*								
XII Apostel *(Italian)*	DM		■		■			●
Borchardt *(International)*	DM DM DM		■	●	■			
Möve *(German)*	DM DM DM	●		●	■		■	●
Königin Luise im Opernpalais *(German)*	DM DM DM DM	●		●	■	●		●
Seasons *(International)*	DM DM DM			●	■			●
L'Etoile *(International)*	DM DM DM DM DM			●	■		■	●
Vau *(Austrian and International)*	DM DM DM DM DM				■		■	
MUSEUM ISLAND *(see p237)*								
Raabe Diele *(Berlin)*	DM DM	●	■	●				●
Ermeler-Haus *(International)*	DM DM DM	●	■	●			■	●
EAST OF THE CENTRE *(see pp237–8)*								
Historische Weinstuben *(Berlin)*	DM DM	●		●				●
Mutter Hoppe *(German)*	DM DM	●			■			●
Podewil *(Italian)*	DM DM				■	●		●
Reinhard's *(International)*	DM DM	●	■	●	■		■	●
T.G.I. Friday's *(American)*	DM DM		■		■			
Zum Nussbaum *(German)*	DM DM	●	■				●	
Zur Letzten Instanz *(German)*	DM DM	●	■					
La Riva *(Italian)*	DM DM DM				■	●	■	●
NORTH OF THE CENTRE *(see pp238–9)*								
Las Cucarachas *(Mexican)*	DM		■		■	●	■	
Yosoy *(Spanish)*	DM		■		■			
Bar-Celona *(Spanish)*	DM DM		■		■			
Brazil *(Brazilian)*	DM DM		■		■			
Fridas Schwester *(International)*	DM DM		■		■			
Goa *(Asian)*	DM DM		■		■	●		
Kamala *(Thai)*	DM DM		■		■			
Kartoffelkeller *(International)*	DM DM		■	●	■			
Kellerrestaurant im Brecht-Haus *(Austrian)*	DM DM		■		■		●	
Kurvenstar *(International)*	DM DM		■		■			
Orange *(Italian)*	DM DM		■		■			
Oren *(Jewish and Arabic)*	DM DM		■		■		●	●
Ständige Vertretung *(German)*	DM DM	●	■					
Ganymed *(International)*	DM DM DM		■		■			
Hackescher Hof *(International)*	DM DM DM DM		■	●	■	●	■	●
Mare Bê *(Mediterranean)*	DM DM DM		■		■	●		
Modellhut *(International)*	DM DM DM	●			■			
Schwarzenraben *(Italian, Mediterranean)*	DM DM DM		■		■		■	
TIERGARTEN *(see pp239–40)*								
Tony Roma's *(American)*	DM DM					●		●
Am Karlsbad *(Italian)*	DM DM DM			●	■	●	■	
Du Pont *(French)*	DM DM DM			●	■		●	
Il Sorriso *(Italian)*	DM DM DM			●	■	●	■	
Harlekin *(International)*	DM DM DM DM DM			●	■		■	
Zum Hugenotten *(International)*	DM DM DM DM DM			●	■		■	

Price categories for a three-course meal per person, including tax and service but not alcohol (in marks):
(DM) up to DM35
(DM)(DM) DM35–50
(DM)(DM)(DM) DM50–70
(DM)(DM)(DM)(DM) DM70–100
(DM)(DM)(DM)(DM)(DM) over DM100

FIXED-PRICE MENU
A restaurant offering a set menu: usually three courses.
VEGETARIAN DISHES
A restaurant with a particularly good selection of vegetarian dishes.
LATE OPENING
Places open after midnight.
ATTRACTIVE LOCATION
Restaurant with a good view or situated in a historic building, for example, a palace.

Restaurant	Price	Regional Cuisine	Late Opening	Fixed-Price Menu	Vegetarian Meals	Outside Tables	Recommended Wine List	Attractive Location
KREUZBERG (see pp239–40)								
Bar Centrale (Italian)	(DM)(DM)			●	●	●		
Bergmann 103 (German)	(DM)(DM)	●		●	●			
Parlamento (Italian)	(DM)(DM)			●	●	●		
Thürnagel (Vegetarian, Fish)	(DM)(DM)			●	●	●		
Tres Kilos (Mexican)	(DM)(DM)(DM)			●	●	●		
Altes Zollhaus (German)	(DM)(DM)(DM)(DM)	●		●			●	●
AROUND KURFÜRSTENDAMM (see pp240–1)								
Marché (International)	(DM)			●	●	●		
Satyam (Indian)	(DM)				●			
XII Apostel (Italian)	(DM)			●	●	●		
Don Quijote (Spanish)	(DM)(DM)			●	●	●		
El Bodegon (Spanish)	(DM)(DM)			●	●	●		
Hamlet (International)	(DM)(DM)			●	●	●		
Schildkröte (Berlin)	(DM)(DM)	●		●	●	●		
Bacco (Italian)	(DM)(DM)(DM)				●		●	
Bovril (International)	(DM)(DM)(DM)	●		●	●	●		
Fischküche (Fish)	(DM)(DM)(DM)	●			●			●
Florian (International)	(DM)(DM)(DM)			●	●	●	●	
Istanbul (Turkish)	(DM)(DM)(DM)				●	●		
Kashmir Palace (Indian)	(DM)(DM)(DM)				●	●		
Kuchi (Japanese)	(DM)(DM)(DM)			●	●			
Le Canard (French)	(DM)(DM)(DM)				●			
Ottenthal (Austrian)	(DM)(DM)(DM)			●	●		●	●
Paris Bar (French)	(DM)(DM)(DM)			●				
Peppino (Italian)	(DM)(DM)(DM)				●	●	●	
Heising (French)	(DM)(DM)(DM)(DM)				●			
Die Quadriga (French)	(DM)(DM)(DM)(DM)(DM)				●		●	
First Floor (German)	(DM)(DM)(DM)(DM)(DM)	●			●		●	
AROUND SCHLOSS CHARLOTTENBURG (see pp241–2)								
Angkor (Cambodian)	(DM)(DM)				●	●		
Hitit (Turkish)	(DM)(DM)				●	●		
Woolloomooloo (Australian)	(DM)(DM)			●			●	
Ponte Vecchio (Italian)	(DM)(DM)(DM)			●	●		●	
Ana e Bruno (Italian)	(DM)(DM)(DM)(DM)(DM)				●		●	
GREATER BERLIN (see pp242–3)								
Blockhaus Nikolskoe (Berlin)	(DM)(DM)	●		●	●	●		●
Blue Goût (International)	(DM)(DM)			●	●	●		●
Mao Thai (Thai)	(DM)(DM)			●	●			
Merhaba (Turkish)	(DM)(DM)				●	●		
Nola (Californian)	(DM)(DM)			●	●	●		
Olive (Berlin)	(DM)(DM)	●		●	●			
Ostwind (Chinese)	(DM)(DM)			●	●	●		
Pasternak (Russian)	(DM)(DM)			●	●	●		
Restauration 1900 (International)	(DM)(DM)	●		●	●	●		
Trattoria Lappeggi (Italian)	(DM)(DM)			●	●	●		

Price categories for a three-course meal per person, including tax and service but not alcohol (in marks):
- ⓓ up to DM35
- ⓓⓓ DM35–50
- ⓓⓓⓓ DM50–70
- ⓓⓓⓓⓓ DM70–100
- ⓓⓓⓓⓓⓓ over DM100

FIXED-PRICE MENU
A restaurant offering a set menu: usually three courses.

VEGETARIAN DISHES
A restaurant with a particularly good selection of vegetarian dishes.

LATE OPENING
Places open after midnight.

ATTRACTIVE LOCATION
Restaurant with a good view or situated in a historic building, for example, a palace.

Restaurant	Price	REGIONAL CUISINE	LATE OPENING	FIXED-PRICE MENU	VEGETARIAN DISHES	OUTSIDE TABLES	RECOMMENDED WINE LIST	ATTRACTIVE LOCATION
Abendmahl *(Vegetarian)*	DMDMDM		■		■			
Chalet Suisse *(Swiss)*	DMDMDM	●			■	●		●
Forsthaus Paulsborn *(German)*	DMDMDM	●		●	■	●		●
Grunewaldturm *(German)*	DMDMDM	●		●	■	●	■	●
Jelängerjelieber *(International)*	DMDMDM		■	●	■			
Maxwell *(International)*	DMDMDM			●	■	●	■	
Spree-Athen *(Berlin)*	DMDMDM	●	■					
Storch *(Alsatian)*	DMDMDM		■			●		
Paris-Moskau *(French)*	DMDMDMDM		■				■	
Remise im Schloss Klein-Glienicke *(German)*	DMDMDMDM	●		●	■	●	■	●
Restaurant im Logenhaus *(German)*	DMDMDMDM	●	■	●		●	■	
Alt Luxemburg *(French)*	DMDMDMDMDM		■	●			■	
Bamberger Reiter *(French)*	DMDMDMDMDM		■	●		●	■	
Grand Slam *(French)*	DMDMDMDMDM			●		●	■	●
Rockendorf's Restaurant *(German)*	DMDMDMDMDM	●		●			■	●
Vivaldi *(French)*	DMDMDMDMDM		■	●			■	●

AROUND
UNTER DEN LINDEN

XII Apostel (Italian)

Georgenstrasse 2 (S-Bahnbögen 177–180). **Map** 7 A2, 16 D2. 201 02 22. 9am–2am daily.

Picturesquely situated in the old arcade of an S-Bahn railway bridge, this restaurant offers popular Italian cuisine. On Mondays you can have unlimited amounts of pizza for the price of one portion.

Borchardt (International)

Französische Strasse 47. **Map** 6 F4, 15 C3. 20 38 71 10. V. 11:30am–1am.

One of the restaurants in Berlin with its original interior, including marble columns, mosaics and patterned floors in the Wilhelmine style. Prices are reasonable and the food is very good. Favoured by German politicians.

Möve (German)

Am Festungsgraben 1. **Map** 7 A3, 16 E2. 201 20 29. AF, DC, V. 6pm–midnight Mon–Sat.

Situated inside the Palais am Festungsgraben (see p63), Möve serves good-quality German cuisine in its lighter form. The elegant interior is furnished with comfortable, soft sofas.

Königin Luise im Opernpalais (German)

Unter den Linden 5. **Map** 7 A3, 16 E3. 20 26 83. AE, DC, MC, V. 6pm–midnight Tue–Sat.

The interior of this Rococo-style ballroom on the first floor of the Prinzessinnenpalais (see p69) is part of the dining experience. With views of the Neue Wache and Zeughaus, the restaurant offers good, light German food, a decent wine list and a good ambience. Reservations are required.

Seasons (International)

Charlottenstrasse 49. **Map** 7 A4, 16 D3. 20 33 63 63. AE, DC, MC, V. 6:30–11:30am, noon–2:30pm & 6–11:30pm daily.

This restaurant is based in the Four Seasons Hotel (see p217). Wood-panelled rooms are lit by chandeliers, candles and the glow from the fireplace. It is an ideal place for a romantic evening and for sampling light meals of international cuisine. The restaurant is sensitive to the particular needs of its patrons, offering low-cholesterol dishes and a full vegetarian selection, as well as a non-smoking area. Prices are lower for lunch.

L'Etoile (International)

Unter den Linden 77. **Map** 6 E4, 15 A3. 22 610. AE, DC, MC, V, JCB. 9:30–11am, noon–3pm, 6–11:00pm daily.

This establishment is worthy of the hotel in which it is based, the Adlon. From the day it opened, the restaurant was rated among the best in Berlin. L'Etoile, under the guidance of its chef – Karlheinz Hauser – has maintained its position among the ten best restaurants in Berlin.

Vau (Austrian and International)

Jägerstrasse 54–55. **Map** 6 F4, 15 C4. 202 97 30. AE, DC, EC, V. noon–2pm & 7–11.30pm Mon–Sat

This establishment stands out among the first-class restaurants located around Gendarmenmarkt. The interior is elegant though unpretentious. The excellent Austrian- and French-based dishes are created by well-known chefs, and the food is appreciated by regulars, who include politicians and celebrities. The service is welcoming and there is a large selection of good wines, mainly from France and Austria. The small courtyard is used during the lunch service.

MUSEUM ISLAND

Raabe Diele (Berlin)

Märkisches Ufer 10. **Map** 7 C4. 24 06 20. AE, DC, MC, V. noon–2am daily.

A pleasant restaurant that specializes in Berlin cuisine and is based in the cellar of Ermeler-Haus (see pp84–5). The huge portions will satisfy any appetite. Pork knuckle with pureed peas and sauerkraut (Eisbein mit Erbsenpuree und Sauerkraut) seems to be the main item on the menu. There are also other typical Berlin dishes, including wild mushrooms and potato salad, as well as river fish such as Zander (pike-perch) and Aal (eel). Everything served is immersed in heavy but tasty sauces, which is typical of the cuisine of this region.

Ermeler-Haus (International)

Märkisches Ufer 10. **Map** 7 C4. 24 06 20. AE, DC, MC, V. 6pm–1am Tue–Sat.

Good regional cuisine in a modern, light style, with a Mediterranean flair. The restaurant is part of the gastronomic complex of art'otel and is situated in a unique room, featuring a Rococo ceiling, on the first floor of an 18th century palace (see pp84–5).

EAST OF
THE CENTRE

Historische Weinstuben (Berlin)

Poststrasse 23. **Map** 7 C3. 242 41 07. 11am–midnight, 11am–1am in summer.

This popular wine bar is located in Knoblauchhaus (see p91), which dates from the 18th century and is one of the most decorative buildings of the Nikolaiviertel. Guests can dine either on the ground floor, which is furnished with pieces from the Biedermeier period, or in the cellar, where the atmosphere is more relaxed. Mainly traditional dishes from Berlin are offered on the menu, and the wine list offers an amazing selection from some of Germany's most famous vineyards.

Mutter Hoppe (German)

Rathausstrasse 21. **Map** 7 C3. 241 56 25. 11:30am–midnight daily.

Based in the Nikolaiviertel, Mutter Hoppe is situated in an arched cellar, and its interior is decorated in a rustic style. Traditional German cuisine with the full repertoire of regional specialities is served here in huge portions. There is also entertainment, in the form of live guitar music, on Friday and Saturday evenings.

Podewil (Italian)

Klosterstrasse 68–70. **Map** 8 D3. 242 67 45. noon–midnight daily.

This restaurant, with a pleasant and relaxed atmosphere, is part of the Palais Podewils complex (see p97). The restaurant specializes in good Italian cuisine, where pizza and pasta have not completely taken over the rest of the menu. There is also a large choice of salads as well as lighter meat dishes. In summer, diners can sit in the garden.

For key to symbols see back flap

...d's
...tional)

Poststrasse 28. **Map** 7 C3. 238
42 95. ▦ **V** ▦ ▦ AE, DC, V.
◯ 9am–1am.

An enchanting place where the
interior is decorated in the style of
the Roaring Twenties. The food is
excellent and the house speciality
is *Das Geheimnis aus dem
Kaiserhof* (the secret of the
Kaiser's court). This consists of a
succulent steak served with a
special sauce that was apparently
created for Max Liebermann.

T.G.I. Friday's
(American)

Karl-Liebknecht-Strasse 5. **Map** 7 B3.
238 279 60. **V** ▦ AE, DC,
EC, V. ◯ noon–midnight Mon–Thu,
11:30am–1am Fri–Sat.

Huge restaurant with a wide
choice of American food from all
over the United States. Typical
items on the menu include steaks,
burgers, and nachos. Portions are
reassuringly large and filling.

Zum Nussbaum
(German)

Am Nussbaum 3. **Map** 7 C3. 242
30 95. ▦ ◯ noon–2am daily. ▦▦

Situated in one of the alleys off
the Nikolaiviertel, this inn is one
of the best in town. It is a reconstruction of a 16th-century country
inn and serves traditional Berlin
cuisine, with tender pork knuckle
and rollmops (rolled pickled herring) on the menu. During the
summer months guests can sit in
its small but pleasant garden.

Zur Letzten Instanz
(German)

Waisenstrasse 16. **Map** 8 D3. 242
55 28. ▦ AE, DC, V. ◯ noon–
1am Mon–Sat, noon–11pm Sun. ▦▦

One of the oldest restaurants in
Berlin, this establishment used to
be a meeting place for lawyers
after court sessions, and this is
reflected in the names of many
dishes. Situated near the old town
wall, it specializes in traditional,
heavy German food. So, if you
feel like pork knuckle (*Eisbein*),
beef olive (*Rinderroulade*) or a
huge plate of a selection of cold
meats (*Altberliner Schlachtplatte*),
you are in the right place.

La Riva (Italian)

Spreeufer 2. **Map** 7 C4. 242
51 83. **V** ▦ ▦ AE, DC, V.
◯ 11:30am–midnight daily. ▦▦▦

This restaurant, serving good-
quality Italian food, can be found
at the back of the Ephraim-Palais

in the Nikolaiviertel, on the bank
of the Spree river. Many different
types of pasta and good Italian
wines appear on the menu here.
During summer, diners can sit on
the terrace overlooking the boats
and barges that are found all
along the river.

NORTH OF
THE CENTRE

Las Cucarachas
(Mexican)

Oranienburger Strasse 38. **Map** 7 A1.
282 20 44. **V** ▦ ▦ MC, DC, V.
◯ 11:30am–4am Mon–Fri, 10am–
4am Sat & Sun.

This place is completely jam-
packed with people at the
weekends. It has a pleasant
interior where you can eat the
usual Mexican fare, including
burritos, tacos, fajitas and enchiladas, all for a very reasonable
price. The vegetarian equivalents
of these dishes are also available.
Alcohol, including cocktails, is
served here, too, and one of the
best drinks on the menu is the
strawberry Margarita.

Yosoy (Spanish)

Rosenthaler Strasse 37. **Map** 7 B2.
283 912 13. **V** ◯ 5pm–late,
daily. ▦

A pleasant and inexpensive
restaurant with a large selection
of Spanish wines and dishes. The
tapas are excellent and well
worth sampling.

Bar-Celona (Spanish)

Hannoversche Strasse 2. **Map** 6 F1.
282 91 53. **V** ♫ ▦ AE, DC,
MC, V. ◯ noon–2am daily. ▦▦

Catalan cuisine and Spanish wines
are served at Bar-Celona in an
attractively decorated interior.
Paella, in all its variations, is the
speciality, but you can also choose
from grilled meats and fish. On
Thursdays, live flamenco is
performed on the premises.

Brazil (Brazilian)

Gormannstrasse 22. **Map** 7 C1.
28 59 90 26. **V** ▦ ◯ 6pm–2am
daily. ▦

With a combination of good
Brazilian food and a casual,
friendly atmosphere, it is no
surprise that this place is always
busy. Brazil is an ideal place for a
relaxed, low-key supper. If you
don't feel like eating a meal, you
can order snacks called pastel –
delicious fried balls stuffed with
various ingredients.

Fridas Schwester
(International)

Neue Schönhauser Strasse 11.
Map 7 B2. 283 84 710. **V**
◯ 10am–2am Mon–Fri, 10am–3am
Sat & Sun. ▦▦

Pleasant surroundings, an original
buffet and amusing furniture
create an inviting atmosphere for
both a short lunch break and an
evening's relaxation. International
cuisine appears on the menu, with
the majority of dishes coming from
Italy and Austria.

Goa (Asian)

Oranienburger Strasse 50. **Map** 6 F1.
28 59 84 51. **V** ▦ ▦ AE, DC,
EC, V. ◯ 10am–late daily. ▦▦

An extraordinary place, with an
interior that looks as if it were
designed by a hippie just returned
from a trip around Asia. The
general Asian menu features dishes
from all over the region, with a
number of different Indian curries,
Chinese stir-fries and Thai starters.

Kamala (Thai)

Oranienburger Strasse 69. **Map** 7 A1.
283 27 97. **V** ▦ ◯ 11:30am–
midnight daily. ▦▦

A small restaurant with very
simple furnishings, located in the
basement of a building. The service
is pleasant and prompt and the
quality of food is as good as it is
authentic. Among the delectable
items on offer, the menu features
excellent soups flavoured with
delicate Thai herbs, such as ginger
and lemon grass.

Kartoffelkeller
(International)

Albrechtstrasse 14b. **Map** 6 F2.
282 85 48. **V** ▦ ▦ AE, V.
◯ 11am–1am daily. ▦▦

This restaurant features dishes
where the humble potato is the
main ingredient. Baked, stuffed,
fried, boiled and mashed, these
international dishes will fill you up
very quickly. Unfortunately the
interior is not very interesting.

Kellerrestaurant
im Brecht-Haus
(Austrian)

Chausseestrasse 125. **Map** 6 E1.
282 38 43. ▦ ▦ AE, MC. ◯
noon–3pm & 6pm–1am Mon–Fri. ▦▦

This restaurant is located in the
cellar of the house where Bertolt
Brecht used to live (*see p109*).
Apparently, the dishes served here
are prepared according to the
recipes of Helene Weigel, the wife
of this famous writer.

Kurvenstar
(International)

Kleine Präsidentenstrasse 3. **Map** 7 B2,
16 F1. 🕿 28 59 97 10. V 🔲 🔲 DC,
MC, V. ◯ 9pm–late daily. ⓓ ⓓ

An unusual place that links
together a restaurant, a music club
and a bar: you can eat, drink and
dance all under the one roof. The
menu offers mainly exotic cuisine
from all over the world. Highly
recommended is the sushi, the
calaloo (from the Caribbean) or
any of the Chinese specialities.
European dishes are also served.

Orange
(Italian)

Oranienburger Strasse 32. **Map** 7 A1.
🕿 28 38 52 42. V 🔲 ◯ 9am–late
daily. ⓓ ⓓ

Diners sit in a very pleasant and
simple interior in the style of a
café-restaurant, offering basic
Italian dishes. You can have a
leisurely three-course meal or a
quick, light snack.

Oren (Jewish and
Middle Eastern)

Oranienburger Strasse 28. **Map** 7 A1.
🕿 282 82 28. V 🔲 🔲 🔲
◯ 10am–1am daily. ⓓ ⓓ

This establishment specializes in
vegetarian Jewish and Middle
Eastern cuisine and is situated
near the synagogue in the vicinity
of the Centrum Judaicum (see
p102). You can order falafel (fried
spiced chick-pea balls), peppers
stuffed with tofu or an excellent
array of aubergine (eggplant)
dishes. The standard tahina and
hummus are served, too. The
Israeli wines are recommended.

Ständige Vertretung
(German)

Schiffbauerdamm 8. **Map** 6 F2.
🕿 282 39 65. V 🔲 🔲 ◯ 11am–late
Sun–Fri, 4pm–late Sat. ⓓ ⓓ

Regional food and drink from the
Rhine are served in this friendly
establishment. Dishes include
Flammekuchen, a type of quiche
with meat, vegetables and shrimp,
or Zander (a pike-perch) served
on sauerkraut.

Ganymed
(International)

Schiffbauerdamm 5. **Map** 6 F2, 15 C1.
🕿 ▨▨▨▨▨▨. ▨▨▨▨▨
Mon–Fri; 11am–1am Sat & Sun.
V 🔲 🔲 V. ⓓ ⓓ

A good-quality restaurant in
pleasant surroundings. The chef
favours fish dishes, and the menu
includes Berlin fish specialities.

Hackescher Hof
(International)

Rosenthaler Strasse 40/41. **Map** 7 B2.
🕿 283 52 93. 🔲 V 🔲 🔲
🔲 AE, DC, MC, V. ◯ 7am–1am
Mon–Thu, 7am–3am Fri–Sun,
9am–3am Sun. ⓓ

A very popular spot situated in the
newly restored Hackescher Höfe
complex (see p103). This café-
restaurant serves breakfast from
early in the morning, followed by
inexpensive fixed-price lunches
and finally a large selection of
Italian dishes in the evenings. It is
always full, so booking is advisable.

Mare Bê
(Mediterranean)

Rosenthaler Strasse 46–48. **Map** 7 B2.
🕿 283 65 45. 🔲 V 🔲 EC, V.
◯ noon–1am daily. ⓓ ⓓ ⓓ

The perfect place for fans of
southern-French, Italian and
Spanish cuisines, all with a hint of
Middle Eastern influence. Oysters
are served on Tuesdays. During
the summer, some tables are
placed in the garden, which is
within a quiet courtyard.

Modellhut
(International)

Alte Schönhauser Strasse 28. **Map**
7 C1. 🕿 283 55 11. V 🔲 🔲 EC, V.
◯ 7pm–2am daily. ⓓ ⓓ

This place is worthy of recommendation mainly because of its
nouvelle cuisine dishes from France,
Germany and Italy. The food and
interesting interior make it very
popular among Berlin yuppies.

Schwarzenraben
(Italian,
Mediterranean)

Neue Schönhauser Strasse 13. **Map**
7 B2. 🕿 28 39 16 98. V 🔲 🔲 AE,
DC, MC, V. ◯ 10am–midnight daily.
ⓓ ⓓ ⓓ

A fashionable venue consisting of
a bistro in the front and a restaurant at the back which operates
only in the evening. It serves good
Italian food prepared with flair as
well as a decent selection of
cheeses and wines.

TIERGARTEN

Tony Roma's
(American)

Marlene-Dietrich-Platz 3. **Map** 6 D5.
🕿 25 29 58 30. 🔲 ◯ 11:30am–
midnight, daily. ⓓ ⓓ

A new restaurant situated in the
centre of the city near Potsdamer

Platz. A treat for meat eate▨▨
menu features grilled marinated
ribs served with large portions of
chips (fries) as well as favourites
such as corn on the cob.

Am Karlsbad
(Italian)

Am Karlsbad 11. **Map** 12 D1. 🕿 264
53 49. 🔲 V 🔲 🔲 ◯ noon–3pm
& 7pm–midnight Tue–Fri; 7pm–
midnight Sat. ⓓ ⓓ ⓓ

A bistro-style modern restaurant,
hidden in the courtyard of a huge
skyscraper. The interior features
granite, wood, chrome and glass
walls. The excellent, light cuisine
makes the most of seasonal
variations. The lunch menu is
usually less expensive.

Du Pont
(French)

Budapester Strasse 1. **Map** 10 F1.
🕿 261 88 11. 🔲 AE, DC, EC, V.
◯ noon–3pm & 6pm–midnight
Mon–Fri; 6pm–midnight Sat & Sun.
ⓓ ⓓ ⓓ

Good, classical French cuisine,
however, the prices are rather
extravagant. The intimate room,
charming atmosphere and pleasant
service almost make up for it.

Il Sorriso
(Italian)

Kurfürstenstrasse 76. **Map** 11 A1.
🕿 262 13 13. 🔲 V 🔲 🔲
🔲 AE, DC, V. ◯ noon–midnight
Mon–Sat. ⓓ ⓓ

This restaurant is located in a
restored apartment block that once
housed a workers' canteen. It
serves very good Italian cuisine
with a large selection of traditional
dishes. The menu changes
according to the season and
during the summer months diners
can sit outside.

Harlekin
(International)

Lützowufer 15. **Map** 11 A1.
🕿 25 47 88 58. 🔲 V 🔲 🔲 AE,
DC, MC, V, JCB. ◯ 6–11pm Tue–Sat.
ⓓ ⓓ ⓓ

The pride and joy of the Grand
Hotel Esplanade is one of the best
restaurants in the town, run by the
master chef from Austria, Kurt
Jäger. A figure of a Harlequin
▨▨▨▨▨▨▨▨▨▨▨▨▨▨▨ the
large room, which is designed in a
modern style. The open kitchen
allows guests to observe the chefs
at work. All the dishes are
beautifully presented and served
in an impeccable manner.
Booking is necessary at this
popular venue.

For key to symbols see back flap

Zum Hugenotten (International)

Budapesterstrasse 2. **Map** 10 F1.
☎ 26 02 12 63. **¶DM** **V** **♨** **≋** AE,
DC, MC, V. **◻** 6:30–midnight
Mon–Sat. **DM** **DM** **DM** **DM**

The Inter-Continental hotel is the
location of Zum Hugenotten, one
of the best restaurants in Berlin.
Unusual French dishes prepared
with a German influence attract a
steady clientele that comes from
all over Berlin. Any fish or seafood
dish proves the real mastery of the
chef. Reservations are necessary.

KREUZBERG

Bar Centrale (Italian)

Yorckstrasse 82. **Map** 12 F4.
☎ 786 29 89. **¶DM** **V** **≋** EC, V.
◻ noon–2am Mon–Sat. **DM** **DM**

A popular bistro with a modern-
style interior, it is often frequented
by a younger group of diners. The
Italian cuisine is experimental
rather than traditional.

Bergmann 103 (German)

Bergmannstrasse 103. **Map** 12 F4.
☎ 694 83 23. **V** **◻** 9:30am–1am
daily. **DM** **DM**

This restaurant's dining room has
tables set on the bases of old
sewing-machines. The food is
generally German, but is sometimes influenced by other cuisines.

Parlamento (Italian)

Bergmannstrasse 3. **Map** 12 F4.
☎ 694 77 45. **V** **≋** **◻** noon–midnight, 6pm–midnight in winter. **DM** **DM**

Delicious Italian dishes that taste
like they were home-made and a
pleasant atmosphere enable this
place to compete easily with other
restaurants in the Kreuzberg area.

Thürnagel (Vegetarian and Fish)

Gneisenaustrasse 57. **☎** 691 48 00.
V **◻** 8pm–1am daily. **DM** **DM**

This neat vegetarian restaurant
offers a wide range of well-
prepared vegetarian dishes. The
menu is also enriched by excellent
fish dishes. Reservations required.

Tres Kilos (Mexican)

Marheinekeplatz 3. **Map** 13 A4.
☎ 693 60 44. **¶DM** **V** **♫** **◻** 6pm–
late daily. **DM** **DM** **DM**

If you like spicy-hot Mexican food,
a range of tortillas, burritos and
enchiladas, Corona beer served in

bottles with a wedge of lemon,
loud music and a relaxed atmosphere, then you'll feel at home
here. Drawing on the paper
tablecloths with crayons and
throwing peanut shells on the
floor are welcomed.

Altes Zollhaus (German)

Carl-Herz-Ufer 30. **Map** 13 B3.
☎ 692 33 00. **¶DM** **♨** **≋** AE, DC,
MC, V. **◻** 6pm–1am Tue–Sat.

This place is situated on the picturesque bank of the Landwehrkanal, in a old building that used
to be a border control point.
Excellent gourmet-style German
cuisine is served here, but without
the heavy sauces that are so
typical of the traditional versions.
Dishes that are based on wild
mushrooms, when in season,
are highly recommended.

AROUND KURFÜRSTENDAMM

Marché (International)

Kurfürstendamm 14. **Map** 10 D1.
☎ 882 75 78. **V** **≋** **≋** AE, DC, MC,
V, JCB. **◻** 8am–midnight daily. **DM**

A self-service restaurant under the
Mövenpick umbrella, Marché caters
for the many tourists visiting Kaiser-
Wilhelm-Gedächtniskirche. Choose
from meat and fish dishes, salads,
plenty of desserts, beer and wine.

Satyam (Indian)

Goethestrasse 5. **Map** 3 C5. **☎** 312
90 79. **V** **◻** 9am–11pm daily. **DM**

If you don't mind a shabby
interior, you will enjoy feasting
(very inexpensively) on vegetarian
Indian dishes, and many of them
are not too spicy. Dishes made
from panir (Indian fresh cheese)
are the speciality of the house.

XII Apostel (Italian)

Bleibtreustrasse 49. **Map** 9 B1.
☎ 312 14 33. **V** **≋** **◻** 7am–5am
daily. **DM**

The Italian food served here is
available nearly 24 hours, but it is
always busy. The menu includes
all types of pastas and pizzas,
which are available all night.

Don Quijote (Spanish)

Bleibtreustrasse 41. **Map** 9 B1.
☎ 881 32 08. **V** **≋** **≋** AE, DC,
MC, V. **◻** 4:30pm–1am Mon–Fri,
noon–1am Sat–Sun. **DM** **DM**

The food in this restaurant is
wonderfully prepared, the kitchen

smells like a tavern on the Iberian
peninsula and there is even an
excellent affordable Rioja.

El Bodegon (Spanish)

Schlüterstrasse 61. **Map** 9 B1.
☎ 312 44 97. **V** **≋** **≋** AE, DC,
EC. **◻** 7pm–1:30am daily. **DM** **DM**

Spanish specialities like tapas and
paella are served here and an
assortment of Spanish wines features on the wine list. Live music
on Fridays; flamenco on Saturdays.

Hamlet (International)

Uhlandstrasse 47. **Map** 9 C3.
☎ 882 13 61. **V** **≋** **≋** AE, DC,
MC, V. **◻** 8am–2am daily. **DM** **DM**

Do not be misled by the name –
the menu offers mainly French
and a few Oriental dishes, but surprisingly, nothing English or Danish.

Schildkröte (Berlin)

Kurfürstendamm 212. **Map** 9 C1.
☎ 881 67 70. **≋** AE, DC, MC, V.
◻ noon–1am daily. **DM** **DM**

An interesting dining room in the
old, pre-war Berlin style. Good,
traditional German cooking is
on the menu, featuring pork
roasted in a vinegar marinade
(Sauerbraten) and stuffed cabbage
leaves (Kohlrouladen).

Bacco (Italian)

Marburger Strasse 5. **Map** 10 E1.
☎ 211 86 87. **V** **♨** **≋** AE, DC, EC
V. **◻** noon–3pm & 6pm–midnight
Mon–Fri, 6pm–midnight Sat. **DM** **DM** **DM**

An intimate restaurant, with a
modern interior and marvellous
food from Tuscany. Prices are fairly
high and the portions are small
and light, but the excellent quality
of the food and wine list make it
not too painful on the wallet.

Bovril (International)

Kurfürstendamm 184. **Map** 9 B2.
☎ 881 84 61. **¶DM** **V** **≋** **≋** AE,
DC, MC, V. **◻** 10am–2am Mon–Sat.
DM **DM** **DM**

A popular bistro, although a bit
elitist. During lunchtime, it is
usually visited by people working around
the Ku'damm. Good, light food
influenced by German cuisine.

Fischküche (Fish)

Uhlandstrasse 181–183. **Map** 9 C1.
☎ 882 48 62. **♨** **≋** AE, MC, V.
◻ noon–3pm & 6pm–12:30am
Mon–Fri, noon–12:30am Sat.
DM **DM** **DM**

A branch of its namesake in Hamburg, this is an excellent restaurant

serving very fresh fish of excellent quality. Recommended dishes include the fish soup, a Hamburg speciality, or the superbly cooked sole. Booking in advance is advisable: crowds have recently turned their attention to restaurants in this area and this is one of the most popular places.

Florian (International)

Grolmannstrasse 52. **Map** 3 C5.
📞 313 91 84. 🍴 🎵 V 🍷 ⬛ 6pm–3am daily. 🅳🅼 🅳🅼 🅳🅼

This restaurant is particularly popular among journalists and worth visiting because of its good food and wide selection of wines. The daily specials vary constantly with the seasons. Recommended dishes include anything created during the asparagus or wild mushroom season. Reservations required.

Istanbul (Turkish)

Knesebeckstrasse 77. **Map** 9 C1.
📞 883 27 77. V 🎵 🍷 AE, DC, MC, V. ⬛ noon–midnight daily. 🅳🅼 🅳🅼

This is one of the best traditional Turkish restaurants in Berlin and the menu offers food from every region of the country. Belly-dancing shows on Saturdays and Sundays.

Kashmir Palace (Indian)

Marburger Strasse 14. **Map** 10 E1.
📞 214 28 40. V 🎵 🍷 AE, DC, MC, V. ⬛ noon–3pm & 6pm–midnight Tue–Fri, noon–midnight Sat, 5pm–midnight Sun–Mon. 🅳🅼 🅳🅼 🅳🅼

A good Indian restaurant in the best Colonial style. The food is authentic, but not overly spiced.

Kuchi (Japanese)

Kantstrasse 30. **Map** 9 B1.
📞 31 50 78 15. V 🍷 AE, EC, V. ⬛ noon–midnight Mon–Thu, noon–2am Fri–Sun. 🅳🅼 🅳🅼 🅳🅼

Considering the quality of food, this is undoubtedly one of the best-value Japanese restaurants in Berlin. A simple, unpretentious interior and welcoming service make it a perfect venue for a dinner for two. The menu offers sushi as well as regional dishes.

Le Canard (French)

Knesebeckstrasse 88. **Map** 3 C5.
📞 312 26 45. V 🍷 AE, DC, V. ⬛ noon–late Mon–Sat, 7pm–late Sun. 🅳🅼 🅳🅼 🅳🅼

The wonderful, popular French food served in this bistro includes a magnificent dish of duck after which the restaurant is named.

Ottenthal (Austrian)

Kantstrasse 153. **Map** 10 D1.
📞 313 31 62. 🍴 🍷 AE, V. ⬛ 6pm–1am daily. 🅳🅼 🅳🅼 🅳🅼

The simple interior is adorned by a clock from the Ottenthal Church in Austria and the background music is mainly of Mozart. Austrian cuisine is served here in fine style, plus a fantastic wine list including some examples from the owner's vineyards. Reservations are usually required.

Paris Bar (French)

Kantstrasse 152. **Map** 9 C1.
📞 313 80 52. V 🍴 🍷 AE. ⬛ noon–1am daily. 🅳🅼 🅳🅼 🅳🅼

This is an exclusive bistro frequented by artists and politicians. Relatively expensive, but the food is excellent – the blood sausage with potatoes (*Blutwurst mit Kartoffeln*) is recommended. Book to avoid disappointment.

Peppino (Italian)

Fasanenstrasse 65. **Map** 10 D2.
📞 883 67 22. V 🍴 🍷 🍷 AE, DC, V. ⬛ noon–3pm & 6pm–midnight daily. 🅳🅼 🅳🅼

A good-quality Italian restaurant serving mainly dishes from the region of Tuscany in Italy. Fish dishes are among the house specialities, and they are prepared in an exquisite manner. The menu varies according to season.

Heising (French)

Rankerstrasse 32. **Map** 10 E1.
📞 213 39 52. 🍴 🍷 🍷 ⬛ 7pm–midnight Mon–Sat. 🅳🅼 🅳🅼

This is one of the most traditional restaurants in Berlin, with a Neo-Rococo interior and impeccable service. The food is straight classic French with no extravagant experiments. This place is for the mature and demanding guest.

Die Quadriga (French)

Eislebener Strasse 14. **Map** 10 E2.
📞 214 05 0. 🍴 🍴 🍷 🍷 AE, DC, MC, V, JCB. ⬛ 7pm–late Mon–Fri. 🅳🅼 🅳🅼 🅳🅼

The Hotel Brandenburger Hof has many attractions, but one of the most obvious is its gourmet restaurant (definitely among the best in Berlin). The small dining room is filled with furniture designed by Frank Lloyd Wright. The restaurant serves unusual French dishes accompanied by perfect service and a cosy atmosphere. Reservations are required.

First Floor (German)

Budapester Strasse 42. **Map** 10 E1.
📞 25 02 10 20. 🍴 🍷 🍷 AE, DC, MC, V, JCB. ⬛ noon–2pm & 6pm–1am Mon–Fri, 6pm–1am Sat. 🅳🅼 🅳🅼 🅳🅼 🅳🅼

An elegant restaurant of the highest quality that makes you realize that German cuisine, when it is well prepared, is as good as any other European cooking. The menu offers the usual German standards, such as pork knuckle with cabbage, as well as some unrivalled creations with fish, crayfish and aromatic truffles. Prices are lower during lunch. Reservations are necessary.

AROUND SCHLOSS CHARLOTTENBURG

Angkor (Cambodian)

Seelingstrasse 34–36. **Map** 2 E4.
📞 325 59 94. V ⬛ 6–11pm Mon–Fri, 4pm–midnight Sat–Sun. 🅳🅼 🅳🅼

A pleasant restaurant whose interior is slightly more gaudy than the usual Asian restaurant. The menu offers very aromatic dishes that often include an array of delicate spices and coconut milk, typical of Cambodian cuisine.

Hitit (Turkish)

Knobelsdorffstrasse 35. **Map** 2 D4.
📞 322 45 57. V ⬛ noon–midnight Mon–Fri, noon–1am Sat–Sun. 🅳🅼 🅳🅼

The slightly extravagant dining room is adorned with modern sculptures inspired by contemporary Turkish art. For lovers of kofta and kebab this is a true paradise. In addition, there is a good selection of Turkish wines.

Woolloomoolloo (Australian)

Röntgenstrasse 7. **Map** 3 B3.
📞 34 70 27 77. 🍴 🎵 ⬛ 5pm–1am daily. 🅳🅼 🅳🅼

As its Aboriginal name suggests, this restaurant is situated "where rivers cross", in this case the Spree and Landwehrkanal. The menu includes kangaroo, ostrich and crocodile meat. Australian music is performed live here on Sundays.

Ponte Vecchio (Italian)

Spielhagenstrasse 3. **Map** 2 F4.
📞 342 19 99. 🍴 🍷 DC. ⬛ 6:30pm–1am daily. 🅳🅼 🅳🅼 🅳🅼

An unpretentious restaurant that specializes in dishes from the region of Tuscany. It attracts many regular guests, who are quite

For key to symbols *see back flap*

happy to follow the chef's recommendations. Alternatively, food can be prepared to your own specifications. It is advisable to book a table in advance.

Ana e Bruno (Italian)

Sophie-Charlotten-Strasse 101. **Map** 2 D3. █ 325 71 10. 🍴 🎵 🍷 🎵 AE. ◯ 6pm–midnight Tue–Sat. ⑩⑩⑩⑩

This is without doubt one of the best Italian restaurants in Berlin. An elegant interior and quiet Italian music create the perfect atmosphere to sample the magnificent creations prepared by the chef. Everything is delicious, including the onion stuffed with chocolate. Menus given to women do not show any prices, but they do provide the calorie count for each of the dishes.

FURTHER AFIELD

Blockhaus Nikolskoe (Berlin)

Nikolskoer Weg (Wannsee). █ 805 29 14. 🍷 🎵 🍷 V. ◯ 16 Apr–31 Oct: 10am–10pm daily; 1 Nov–15 Apr: 10am–7pm daily. ⑩⑩

This restaurant is in an old *dacha* (Russian-style log cabin) built for King Friedrich Wilhelm III of Prussia's son-in-law, who later became Tsar Nicholas I *(see p201)*. The terrace, which is open in summer, has a wonderful view of the lake. The menu offers classical German dishes (pork shank, fish, game) and wonderful cakes.

Blue Goût (International)

Anklamer Strasse 38 (2nd courtyard) (Mitte). █ 448 58 40. 🍷 🎵 🍷 V. ◯ 7pm–1am. ⑩⑩

A nice place with a pleasant atmosphere. The door to the kitchen is open, so you can watch food being prepared while you wait. Mainly vegetarian dishes are served here, but meat-eaters won't go hungry.

Mao Thai (Thai)

Wörtherstrasse 30. █ 441 92 61. 🍴 🍷 🎵 🍷 V. ◯ noon–midnight daily. ⑩⑩⑩

This is one of the best Thai restaurants in Berlin with an interior filled with beautiful antiques from Burma. The menu offers a full range of aromatic dishes but they have been slightly toned down from the original to better suit European tastes.

Merhaba (Turkish)

Hasenheide 39. **Map** 13 C5, 14 E5. █ 692 17 13. 🎵 🍷 AE, EC, V. ◯ 4pm–midnight Mon–Fri, 4pm–1am Sat, noon–midnight Sun. ⑩⑩

This charming restaurant attracts guests from all over Berlin, joining the local Turks and Germans to enjoy the Turkish food served here. There is outdoor dining in summer and belly dancing.

Nola (Californian)

Dortmunder Strasse 9 (Moabit). **Map** 4 E2. █ 399 69 69. 🍷 🍷 🍷 AE, V. ◯ 5pm–1am daily. ⑩⑩

Sometimes it is difficult to explain why certain places are so popular. There is nothing unusual about the interior and the food is a typical Californian-Mexican mixture. However, the atmosphere here is fantastic and during weekends it is necessary to make a booking.

Olive (Berlin)

Tegeler Weg 97 (Charlottenburg). **Map** 2 F2. █ 344 33 96. 🍷 V. ◯ 5pm–1am Mon–Sat, 10am–1am Sun. ⑩⑩

This is one of the best restaurants serving traditional Berlin cuisine. The cosy interior has a very real "Altberliner" kitchen. If you order a pork knuckle you can be sure that it will probably weigh more than one kilo (two pounds), a roast will be the size of your plate and the *Aal grün* (eel in green sauce) will be simply magnificent. The restaurant was apparently named after the time Kaiser Wilhelm sampled his first ever olive here.

Ostwind (Chinese)

Husemannstrasse 13. █ 441 59 51. 🍴 🍷 🍷 V ◯ 6pm–1am Mon–Sat, 10am–1am Sun. ⑩⑩

This restaurant opens only in the evening, as well as Sunday during the day. The interior is a bit garish but the food is excellent, however, and there are plenty of tasty specialities from the different regions of China.

Pasternak (Russian)

Knaackstrasse 22–24. █ 441 33 99. 🍷 🍷 ◯ noon–2am Mon–Sat, 10am–2am Sun. ⑩⑩

A charming room, comfortable armchairs and food from the St Petersburg area can all be found in this restaurant. The menu offers all kinds of Russian specialities: beetroot soup *(borsht)*, blinis and of course beef strogonov served with buckwheat noodles. Vodka or champagne and caviar are also available for brunch.

Restauration 1900 (International)

Husemannstrasse 1. █ 449 40 52. 🍷 🍷 🍷 AE. ◯ noon–1am Mon–Fri, 10am–1am Sat–Sun. 🍷🍷

This restaurant offers light cuisine with some dishes of German origin and a large selection for vegetarians. It is worth visiting for the excellent views over eastern Berlin from the terrace and for the substantial breakfast they serve every Sunday.

Trattoria Lappeggi (Italian)

Kollwitzstrasse 56. █ 442 63 47. 🍷 🍷 🍷 AE, V. ◯ noon–2am daily. ⑩⑩

A rustic-styled restaurant, complete with a terracotta floor and unseasoned wooden furniture. On the menu here is good, home-made pasta and many other mouth-watering traditional dishes from the Italian peninsula.

Abendmahl (Vegetarian)

Muskauer Strasse 9 (Kreuzberg). **Map** 14 F2. █ 612 51 70. 🍷 ◯ 6pm–1am daily. ⑩⑩⑩

This rather gaudy restaurant is loosely vegetarian, but fish is also included on the menu. Everything comes from organic farms and the large choice of salads guarantees a sufficient dose of vitamins and minerals. The food is healthy and tasty, but not exactly cheap.

Chalet Suisse (Swiss)

Clayallee 99. █ 832 63 62. 🍷 🍷 🍷 AE, DC, EC, MC, V. ◯ 11:30am–midnight daily. ⑩⑩⑩

This restaurant is not hard to miss – it occupies a picturesque wooden building resembling a chalet and is a perfect place for a rest after walking in the Grunewald forest. There is a large selection of Swiss dishes as well as some German, including asparagus and wild mushrooms, when in season, or game.

Forsthaus Paulsborn (German)

Hüttenweg 90 (Grunewald). █ 818 19 10. 🍷 🍷 🍷 AE, DC, MC, V, JCB. ◯ Mar–Oct & Dec: 11am–11pm Tue–Sun; Jan–Feb & Nov: 11am–6pm Tue–Sun. ⑩⑩⑩

This former hunting palace is located deep in the forest. Now used as a lodge, the ground floor is occupied by this excellent restaurant which, in summer, extends into the garden. The food is magnificent and the porcini mushroom (cepes) soup, when mushrooms are in season, is highly recommended.

Grunewaldturm (German)

Havelchaussee 61. **C** 304 12 03. **†OM** **V** **🔥** **🍷** **🍴** AE, V. **○** 10am–11pm daily. **DM DM DM**

Combining a meal in this restaurant with a trip to Grunewald forest or a walk along the river is a very fine way of spending an afternoon. A lunch or supper with a wonderful view of the Havel River and a game or wild mushroom dish on the table can be an ideal end for this kind of outing.

Jelängerjelieber (International)

Göhrener Strasse 1. **C** 201 20 29. **†OM** **V** **○** 6pm–2am daily. **DM DM**

This restaurant is furnished with pieces from the Palast der Republic and serves dishes from all over the world. The menu also includes an original soup made from broccoli and red cabbage with a pinch of nettle. The name translates roughly as "the longer the better", presumably referring to the length of time you should stay there.

Maxwell (International)

Bergstrasse 22 (Mitte). **C** 280 71 21, **†OM** **V** **🔥** **🍷** **🍴** AE, DC, V. **○** 1 May–30 Sep: noon–3pm & 6pm–midnight daily; 1 Oct–30 Apr: 6pm–midnight daily. **DM DM DM**

This highly regarded and very popular restaurant is known for its good food with Mediterranean influences. There is a less expensive menu for lunch but there are not enough affordable wines. It has an elegant interior, with tables in a charming courtyard during summer time.

Spree-Athen (Berlin)

Leibnizstrasse 60 (Charlottenburg). **Map** 9 B1. **C** 324 17 33. **♫** **🍴** AE, DC, EC, V. **○** 6pm–1am Mon–Sat. **DM DM**

This is an excellent place to try typical Berlin dishes. There is a stylish and nostalgic atmosphere inside and old German tunes are played in the background. The menu changes daily, however, pork knuckle with potatoes and cabbage is always available.

Storch (Alsatian)

Wartburgstrasse 54 (Schöneberg). **Map** 11 A5. **C** 784 20 59. **🔥** **🍴** EC, MC. **○** 6pm–1am daily. **DM DM DM**

Highly esteemed restaurant specializing in dishes from the German-French border. Alsatian fare, such as sausages, sauerkraut, and fried mushrooms, is simply but wonderfully prepared. Sweet and savoury tarts are the main specialities. Excellent service is provided by waiters in dress coats. The only drawback is that the large tables usually require sharing with strangers.

Paris-Moskau (French)

Alt Moabit 141. **Map** 5 C2. **C** 394 20 81. **🍷** **○** 6pm–1am daily. **DM DM**

This is an extraordinary place: in the middle of a building site stands a lone building that houses one of the best restaurants in Berlin. The menu features sublime French food and the wine list is exquisite.

Remise im Schloss Klein-Glienicke (German)

Königstrasse 36 (Klein-Glienicke). **C** 805 40 00. **†OM** **V** **🔥** **🍷** **🍴** **○** Apr–Oct: noon–10pm daily; Nov–Mar: noon–10pm Tue–Sun. **DM DM DM**

This is an ideal place for an elegant meal in the outskirts of Berlin. The name of the owner – Rockendorf – is a guarantee of excellent food. The menu offers typical German cuisine, with perch, crayfish and game all prepared with a dose of imagination.

Restaurant im Logenhaus (German)

Emser Strasse 12–13 (Wilmersdorf). **Map** 9 B3. **C** 873 25 60. **†OM** **🍷** **🍴** AE, V. **○** 7pm–1am Mon–Sat. **DM DM DM**

Very good cuisine inspired by the region of Baden in Germany. The kitchen is open: diners can watch the chef at work while they wait – and what a performance.

Alt Luxemburg (French)

Windscheidstrasse 31. **Map** 2 E5. **C** 323 87 30. **†OM** **🍷** **🍴** AE, DC, MC, V. **○** 7pm–1am Mon–Sat. **DM DM DM DM**

Food for a true gourmet is created here by a real master, Karl Wannemacher, and set in a tastefully understated atmosphere. The best of European cooking has been given a personal touch inspired by aromatic flavours of the East. Reservations are required.

Bamberger Reiter (French)

Regensburger Strasse 7. **Map** 10 E3. **C** 218 42 82. **†OM** **🍷** **🍴** AE, DC, MC, V. **○** 6pm–1am Tue–Sat. **DM DM DM DM**

Undoubtedly one of the largest restaurants in Berlin, this is the domain of Austrian chef Franz Raneburger. The cosy dining room, intimate atmosphere and impeccable service guarantee a perfect dining experience. Reservations should be made well in advance. If the prices are too expensive, similar food is offered next door at the informal Bistro Bamberger Reiter.

Grand Slam (French)

Gottfried-von-Cramm-Weg 47–55 (Grunewald). **C** 825 38 10. **†OM** **🔥** **🍷** **🍴** AE, DC, V. **○** 6:30pm–midnight Tue–Sat. **DM DM DM**

This restaurant is rather hard to find, as it is based on the site of a tennis club called Rot-Weiss in one of Grunewald's small streets. The elegant, classic interior with enchanting views of the lake are very appealing. The chef, Johannes King, is certainly rated among the best. His cuisine is light, original, sophisticated and definitely worth its price. Reservations are necessary.

Rockendorf's Restaurant (German)

Düsterhauptstrasse 1/ Waidmannsluster Damm (Reinickendorf). **C** 402 30 99. **🍷** **🍴** AE, DC, MC, V. **○** noon–2pm & 7–11pm Tue–Sat. **DM DM DM DM**

Due to the talents of its chef, Siegfried Rockendorf, this establishment occupies a high position among German restaurants – some consider it the best. The menu features regional cooking, mainly from Brandenburg, but with a modern twist. House specialities include a venison brioche and sea bass and lobster with a fennel confit.

Vivaldi (French)

Brahmsstrasse 10. **C** 89 58 45 21. **†OM** **🍷** **🍴** AE, DC, MC, V, JCB. **○** 6:30pm–late Tue–Sat. **DM DM DM DM**

A luxurious restaurant in the most expensive hotel in Berlin, the Ritz-Carlton. The interior, which was designed by Karl Lagerfeld, features panelled walls, gold leaf and chandeliers. The impeccable food is very French with some German and Mediterranean influences. This restaurant has long been considered one of the best in Berlin. Reservations required.

For key to symbols see back flap

Light Meals and Snacks

There are many popular fast-food bars and restaurants in Berlin that serve the all-pervading burgers, French fries and pizzas, some of them run by well-known international chains. By way of contrast, many of the self-service places specialize in local foods. The city's cafés are ideal stopping places for a quick meal and always offer something on the menu that will fill you up. Even more convenient are the many bars on wheels or small kiosks – *Imbissbude* – that serve the traditional Berlin *Currywurst*.

IMBISSBUDE AND SNACK BARS

The classic *Imbissbude* is a simple little kiosk selling drinks and a few light snacks, such as *Currywurst* or French fries *(Pommes)* served with mayonnaise or ketchup (or both). The former is a genuine Berlin speciality consisting of grilled, sliced sausage *(Bratwurst)*, topped with a spicy sauce, and served on a paper plate with a plastic fork. These kiosks are usually located in convenient sites near the S-Bahn or U-Bahn stations, or on busy streets and junctions. **Ku'damm 195**, **Amtsgerichtsplatz** and **Konnopke** are considered the best places to experience traditional *Currywurst*, which is served with home-made spicy sauce instead of the now standard tomato ketchup sprinkled with curry powder and fiery paprika.

Other popular snacks sold on the streets include various grilled sausages, collectively referred to as *Bratwurst*. The most common types are frankfurters *(Wienerwurst)* and a thicker kind of sausage known as *Bockwurst*. These are heated in hot water. The German variation on the hamburger theme is called *Boulette*.

Unfortunately there are few places similar to the *Imbissbude* that offer visitors the chance to try food from other regions of Germany. One of the exceptions is the aptly named **Spätzle** which can be found in an arcade under the S-Bahn railway bridge, near Bellevue station. Short, thick noodles called *Spätzle* feature in many dishes on its typically southern German menu.

SPECIALITIES FROM AROUND THE WORLD

Traditional berlin specialities are facing stiff competition from further afield. Turkish restaurants serving excellent *Döner Kebab* are on every corner. Typically a kebab is a piece of warmed flat *pitta* bread stuffed with hot sliced meat, lettuce, cucumber, and tomatoes, and covered with a thick, aromatic, yogurt-based sauce. Obviously the best kebabs are made by the Turks living around Kreuzberg, but you can also have an excellent version of this dish in most of the other Berlin districts. The restaurants worth trying are **Kebab** or indeed any of the places around Kottbuser Tor or Oranienstrasse.

Although Turkish cuisine does have a reputation for not catering for vegetarians, **Kulinarische Delikatessen** goes some way to disprove this by offering many delicious kinds of vegetarian kebabs.

Also suitable for vegetarians are *falafel*, a Middle Eastern speciality widely available in Berlin. Balls of chickpeas and coriander or parsley are rolled in breadcrumbs and deep fried, then served stuffed inside flat bread with salad and yogurt sauce. The best places to try this excellent snack are around Winterfeldt-platz, for example, **Habibi**, **Dada Falafel** and **Baharat Falafel**, or **Safran** in the eastern part of the city.

Fragrant Thai dishes are offered by **Fish & Vegetables** in Goltzstrasse, while those with a passion for Chinese food should eat at **Pagode** in Kreuzberg on Bergmann-strasse. If you wish to try

Korean cuisine, then go to **Kwang-Ju-Grill**, where the variety of starters, soups and main courses is quite over-whelming. A visit to **Vietnam Imbiss** is a good opportunity to try out some Vietnamese specialities, and if you fancy genuine Mexican tacos and burritos, visit **Viva Mexico!** which is managed by a Mexican family. There are also many restaurants offering Indian food, mainly along Grolmanstrasse, around Savignyplatz, where the **Ashoka** deserves a special recommendation.

Berlin's Japanese restau-rants tend to be of the more exclusive type but still offer excellent soups and sushi. The best are **Sushi Bar Ishin**, **Cat Food sushi bar**, **Sushi-Bar**, **FUKU Sushi**, **Mäcky Messer** and **Musashi**.

LIGHT SNACKS

Those with an appetite for more traditional snacks are easily catered for in the estab-lishments around S- and U-Bahn stations and along the main streets offering fresh baguettes filled with ham or cheese. For an instant solution to hunger pangs, try one of the bakeries that offer delicious freshly baked croissants or excellent *Brezeln* (pretzels) covered with coarse salt. During lunchtime, the popular **Nordsee** chain restaurants, in addition to their normal dishes, offer sandwiches to take away. Some sandwich bars offer mouth-watering quiches and tarts alongside baguettes and rolls. If this is what you want, it is worth visiting the snackbar **Fressco** in Oranienburger Strasse or one of the two other branches situated in Kreuzberg.

If a traditional American-Jewish bagel bar is required, then **Bagels & Bialys** in Rosenthaler Strasse or **Salomon Bagels** in Joachims-taler Strasse are the places to go, where the variety of fillings is quite staggering.

Some places also specialize in one particular kind of dish or food. For example **Soup-Kultur** serves only soup, but in a multitude of varieties –

hot, cold, exotic, spicy or mild. Garlic lovers should visit **Knofel** in Prenzlauer Berg, while vegetarians can take comfort in the **Little Shop of Foods** in Kreuzberg, an establishment that offers delicious meat-free dishes from all over the world. Also worth mentioning are **Deli** and **Curry 36**.

Another way to ensure a quick fill-up is to visit one of the self-service pizzerias such as **Piccola Italia**.

EATING IN SHOPPING CENTRES

O NE OF THE PROBLEMS for the dedicated shopper is that eating can seriously cut down on shopping time. Fortunately, many snack bars in shopping centres have put the emphasis on fast service. Some, however, such as **KaDeWe** manage this in stylish surroundings. A visit to this enormous shop features on most tourists' list of things to do, and its self-service café is therefore very popular. Lunch at one of the tables with a view of Wittenbergplatz is a very pleasant adjunct to a Berlin shopping trip.

Another equally busy venue is the self-service café situated in the basement of the chic **Galeries Lafayette** in Friedrichstrasse. If you are visiting the boutiques of Quartier 205, it is also worth stopping by **Bio Insel**, which specializes in organic food, or having a quality cup of coffee in **E33**.

For those reluctant shoppers who put more emphasis on the food, a new oasis of bars and cafés has opened near to Potsdamer Platz, in the **Arkaden** shopping centre. As well as a branch of Salomon Bagels, this centre provides a taste of the Orient in Asia Pavillon, while fans of potatoes should pay a visit to Pomme de Terre. Here, the humble potato becomes the star of the meal and is served in a myriad of guises and with just as many different fillings.

For short stops, both the dedicated and the reluctant shopper should visit the classic **Wiener Café** for coffee and cakes and the **Caffè e Gelato** for delicious ice cream.

CAFÉS

B ERLIN IS well served by cafés that provide a wide range of light snacks or cakes to suit everyone's budget and tastes. They are normally open from 9 or 10 in the morning until late at night. In the mornings they serve breakfast, either à la carte or as a buffet. After that the regular café menu comes into force, although breakfast items are often still available. Main meals on the menu might include several salads, several hearty soup-type stews (*Eintöpfe*) and a few simple hot dishes. Prices are quite reasonable, not greater than DM 15-20. Invariably, every café has a great choice of desserts, ice creams and cakes, as well as a range of alcoholic drinks.

Around the Ku'damm, **Café Adlon** and **Café Kranzler**, the latter established since 1932, are worth a visit as is **Café Möhring**. Around the Technical University, **Café Hardenberg** is popular with students, and near Kantstrasse you can visit **Schwarzes Café**, which is open 24 hours a day. If you are on Savignyplatz you might want to try **Café Aedes**, which has two good branches, one by the architecture gallery and the other in the second courtyard of Hackesche Höfe in Mitte. **Café am Neuen See** is situated near the lake in the Tiergarten Park. **Patisserie Buchwald**, in Hansaviertel, offers a wide range of *Baumkuchen* (so-called "tree cakes" that resemble tree stumps).

Other renowned cafés include the charming **Café Wintergarten**, located in the Literaturhaus on Fasanenstrasse, and the Viennese-style **Café Einstein**. Here you can enjoy coffee made with beans fresh from the café's own roasting room. The original café, in Kurfürstenstrasse, has been joined by another branch in Mitte, on Unter den Linden, whose delicious cakes are in welcome competition with those of the nearby **Opernpalais** (see p63).

If you prefer Hungarian cakes and desserts then you should pay a visit to **Café Szolnay**. While taking a walk

around Checkpoint Charlie, you could drop in to **Sale e Tabacchi**, where, along with an excellent Italian restaurant, you will find the equally admirable **Café Adler**.

There are many places that offer light lunches and coffee around Oranienburger Strasse and Alte and Neue Schönhauser Allees. In the evening they attract livelier crowds in search of decent music and good beer. You can stop by **Boon's**, a smoky and atmospheric café, and the **Café Cinema**, which is decorated with film ephemera. If that is not to your taste, **Café Zucca** serves Italian cuisine, while **Café Döblin** is the place to take in an art exhibition or to listen to some jazz.

An interesting evening can be spent investigating the options in Prenzlauer Berg. You can join the in-crowd at **Anita Wronski** then move on to **Tantalus**, which serves excellent pancakes. If you prefer a cosier environment, then **Chagall** is the place to visit, with an open fire and Russian ballads. During hot days a good spot to enjoy the sun is on the terrace in **November** or at **Seeblick**, which is a good place to eat. Other reliable cafés are **Atlantic**, **Café Berio**, **Keyser Soze**, **Rathauscafé**, **Telecafé**, **Voltaire** and **Café Savigny**, where the menu changes daily.

COFFEE BARS AND TEA ROOMS

T HERE ARE NOT many coffee bars in Berlin, but they are easily spotted as they tend to be run by well-known coffee producers such as Eduscho or Tschibo. **Barcomi's** is a real treat, an American-style coffee bar with its own roasting room and a large selection of coffees. If you need more sustenance than coffee and muffins, try **Barcomi's Deli** where you can build your own sandwiches.

If you want a good cup of tea, then you should go to **Tadschikische Teestube**, or **TTT (Tee, Tea, Thé)**, where the choice is quite amazing – but smokers beware, it has a no-smoking policy. **Mittendrin** also has a wide choice of teas.

DIRECTORY

IMBISSBUDEN AND SNACK BARS

Amtsgerichtsplatz
Kantstrasse/Suarezstrasse.
Map 2 E5. ◯ 11:30am–
11pm Mon–Fri, 1pm–
11pm Sat–Sun. ◉ Tue.

Konnopke
Schönhauser Allee 44a
(U-Bahnhof Eberswalder Str).
◖ 442 77 66.
◯ 4:30am–8pm Mon–Fri.

Ku'damm 195
Kurfürstendamm 195.
Map 9 B2. ◯ 6pm–
1am Mon–Fri, 5pm–7am
Sat–Sun.

Spätzle
Lüneburger Strasse
(arcade under S-Bahn
bridge near Bellevue).
Map 5 A3. ◖ 394 20 57.
◯ 6–11pm daily.

SPECIALITIES FROM AROUND THE WORLD

Ashoka
Grolmanstrasse 51.
Map 3 C5. ◖ 313 20 66.
◯ noon–midnight daily.

Baharat Falafel
Winterfeldtstrasse 37.
Map 11 B3. ◖ 216
83 01 ◯ noon–2pm
Mon–Sat, from 1pm Sun.

Cat Food sushi bar
Körterstrasse 8.
Map 13 C4. ◖ 693 02 27.
◯ 6pm–1am daily.

Dada Falafel
Linienstrasse 132.
Map 6 F1. ◖ 282 83 17.
◯ 11am–midnight daily.

Fish & Vegetables
Goltzstrasse 32.
Map 11 A3. ◖ 215 74 55.
◯ 9am–2pm Mon–Fri,
10am–3am Sat–Sun.

FUKU Sushi
Rosenthaler Strasse 61.
Map 7 B1. ◖ 28 38 77 83.
◯ noon–midnight Mon–
Thu, noon–2am Fri–Sat,
4pm–midnight Sun.

Habibi
Goltzstrasse 24.
Map 11 A3. ◖ 215 33
32. ◯ 11am–3pm Thu,
11am– 5pm Fri–Sat,
11am– 3pm Sun.

Kebab
Goltzstrasse 37a.
Map 11 A3, 11 A4.
◯ 10am–11pm daily.

Kulinarische Delikatessen
Oppelner Strasse 4.
◖ 618 67 58.
◯ 9am–1am Mon–Sat,
10am–1am Sun.

Kwang-Ju-Grill
Emser Strasse 24.
Map 9 B3. ◖ 883 97 94.
◯ noon–midnight Mon–
Thu, noon–2am Fri–Sat.

Mäcky Messer
Mulackstrasse 29.
Map 7 C1. ◖ 283 49
42. ◯ 6pm–midnight
Tue–Sun.

Musashi
Kottbusser Damm 102.
Map 14 E3. ◖ 693 20 42.
◯ noon–10:30pm Mon–
Sat, 2–10pm Sun.

Pagode
Bergmannstrasse 88.
Map 13 A4. ◖ 691 26 40.
◯ noon–midnight daily.

Safran
Knaackstrasse 14.
◖ 44 04 33 78.
◯ 11am–2am daily.

Sushi
Pariser Strasse 44.
Map 9 B2. ◖ 881 27 90.
◯ noon–midnight Mon–
Sat, 4pm–midnight Sun.

Sushi-Bar
Friedrichstrasse 115.
Map 6 F1. ◖ 281 51 88.
◯ noon–10pm Mon–Fri,
noon–midnight Sat–Sun.

Sushi Bar Ishin
Schlossstrasse 101.
Map 2 E4. ◖ 797 10 49.
◯ 11am–8pm Mon–Fri,
11am–4pm Sat, noon–
5pm Sun.

Vietnam Imbiss
Damaschkestrasse 30.
◖ 324 93 44. ◯ noon–
9pm Mon–Fri.

Viva Mexico!
Chausseestrasse 36.
Map 6 F1. ◖ 280 78 65.
◯ noon–midnight Mon–
Sat, 5pm–midnight Sun.

LIGHT SNACKS

Bagels & Bialys
Rosenthaler Strasse 46–48.
Map 7 B2. ◖ 283 65 46.
◯ 9am–4pm daily.

Curry 36
Mehringdamm 36.
Map 12 F3, 12 F5.
◯ 10am–late daily.

Deli
Kollwitzstrasse 44.
◖ 442 05 60. ◯ 10am–
7pm Mon–Thu, 10am–
8pm Fri, 10am–2am Sat.

Fressco
Oranienburger Strasse 48.
Map 6 F1. ◖ 261 94 93.
◯ 10am–1am Mon– Sat,
11am–1am Sun.

Stresemannstrasse 34.
Map 12 F2. ◖ 25 29 93 09.
◯ 10am– 11:30pm daily.

Zossener Strasse 24.
Map 13 A4. ◖ 69
40 16 13. ◯ 10am–
midnight daily.

Knofel
Wichertstrasse/Dunckerstrasse. ◖ 447 67 17. ◯
6pm–late Mon–Thu, 2pm–
late Fri, 1pm–late Sat–Sun.

Little Shop of Foods
Kollwitzstrasse 90.
◖ 44 05 64 44.
◯ noon–10pm Mon–Fri.

Nordsee
Karl-Liebknecht-Strasse 6.
Map 7 C3, 16 F2. ◖ 213
98 33. ◯ 10am–9pm
Mon–Sat.

Piccola Italia
Oranienburger Strasse 6.
Map 7 B2. ◖ 283 58 43.
◯ noon–1am daily.

Salomon Bagels
Joachimstaler Strasse 13.
Map 10 D2. ◖ 881 81 96.
◯ 9am–9pm Mon–Fri,
10am–8pm Sat–Sun.

Soup-Kultur
Kurfürstendamm 224.
Map 10 D1. ◖ 74 30 82
95. ◯ 11am–8pm Mon–
Fri, 11am–4pm Sat.

EATING IN SHOPPING CENTRES

Bio Insel
Friedrichstadtpassage,
Friedrichstrasse 67.
Map 6 F4, 15 C4.
◯ 8am–10pm daily.

E33
Friedrichstadtpassage,
Friedrichstrasse 67.
Map 6 F4, 15 C4.
◯ 9am–9pm daily.

Galeries Lafayette
Französische Strasse 23.
Map 6 F4, 15 C3. ◖ 20
94 80. ◯ 9:30am–8pm
Mon–Fri, 9am–4pm Sat.

KaDeWe
Tauentzienstrasse 21.
Map 10 E1. ◯ 9am–8pm
Mon–Fri, 9am–4pm Sat.

Potsdamer Platz Arkaden
Alte Potsdamer Strasse 7.
Map 6 D5. ◯ 9:30am–
8pm Mon–Fri; 9:30am–
4pm Sat.

CAFES

Anita Wronski
Knaackstrasse 26–28.
◖ 442 84 83.
◯ 10am– 2am daily.

Atlantic
Bergmannstrasse 100.
Map 12 F4. ◖ 691 92
92. ◯ 9am–late daily.

Boon's
Monbijouplatz 12.
Map 7 B2, 16 E1. ◖ 28
53 98 90. ◯ 5pm–late
Mon–Fri, 1pm–late Sat–Sun.

Buchwald
Bartningallee 29.
Map 4 F2. ◖ 391 59 31.
◯ 9am–6pm Mon–Sat,
10am–6pm Sun.

Café Adler
Friedrichstrasse 206.
251 89 65.
9:30am–midnight
Mon–Sat, 9:30am–
7pm Sun.

Café Adlon
Kurfürstendamm 69.
Map 9 A2. 883 76 82.
9am–midnight daily.

Café Aedes
Savignyplatz (arcade
under the S-Bahn bridge)
Map 9 C1. 312 55 04.
10am–late daily.

Rosenthaler Strasse 40–41
(Hackesche Höfe,
second courtyard).
Map 7 B2. 282 21 03.
10am–late daily.

Café am Neuen See
Lichtensteinallee 1.
Map 4 F5. 254 49 30.
10am–11pm daily.

Café am Schiffbauerdamm
Schiffbauerdamm 8.
282 39 65. 10am–
midnight daily.

Café Berio
Maassenstrasse 7.
Map 11 A2. 216 19
46. 8am–1am daily.

Café Cinema
Rosenthaler Strasse 39.
Map 7 B2. 280 64 15.
noon–3am daily.

Café Döblin
Alte Schönhauser Str. 46.
Map 7 C1. 241 99 07.
4pm–late Mon–Sat
10am–late Sun.

Café Einstein
Kurfürstenstrasse 58.
Map 11 A2. 261 50
96. 10am–2am daily.

Unter den Linden 42.
Map 6 F3, 15 C3. 204
36 32. 8am–1am daily.

Café Ephraim's
Spreeufer 1.
Map 7 C4. 24 72
59 47. 10am–mid-
night daily.

Café Hardenberg
Hardenbergstrasse 10.
Map 3 C5. 312 33 30
9am–1am daily.

Café Harder
Leipziger Strasse 30.
Map 7 A5, 15 C5.
20 45 20 75. 9am–
midnight daily.

Café Kranzler
Kurfürstendamm 18.
Map 10 D1. 885 77
20 or 882 69 11.
8am–midnight daily.

Café Lebensart
Unter den Linden 69–73.
Map 6 E3, 15 B3. 229
00 18. 7am–7:30pm
Mon–Fri, 8am–7:30pm
Sat, 9am–7:30pm Sun.

Café Möhring
Kurfürstendamm 213.
Map 10 D1. 881 20
75. 7am–midnight daily.

Charlottenstrasse 55.
Map 7 A4. 20 90 22
40. 9am–7pm daily.

Café Savigny
Grolmanstrasse 51.
Map 3 C5, 9 C1. 312
81 95. 9am–1am daily.

Café Silberstein
Oranienburger Strasse 27.
Map 7 A2. 281 28 01.
noon–midnight daily.

Café Szolnay
Karl-Liebknecht-Strasse 9.
Map 7 C2. 241 57 15.
2–10pm Mon – Tue,
noon–10pm Wed–Thu,
10am–10pm Fri–Sun.

Café Wellenstein
Kurfürstendamm 190.
Map 9 B2. 882 15 55.
9am–3am daily.

Café Wintergarten im Literaturhaus
Fasanenstrasse 23.
Map 10 D1. 882 54
14. 9:30am–1am daily.

Café Zucca
Am Zwirngraben 11–12
(in the S-Bahn arcade).
24 72 12 12.
10am–3am daily.

Chagall
Kollwitzstrasse 2.
441 58 81. 9am–
late daily, (10am–late daily
in winter).

Eckstein
Pappelallee 73.
441 99 60.
9am– 2am daily.

Filmbühne am Steinplatz
Hardenbergstrasse 12.
Map 4 D5. 312 65
89. 9am–2am Sun–
Thu, 9am–3am Fri–Sat.

Kaffeestube am Nikolaiplatz
Poststrasse 19.
Map 7 C3. 242 71 20.
10am–8pm Sun–Thu,
10am–10pm Fri–Sat.

Keyser Soze
Tucholskystrasse 33.
Map 7 A1.
28 59 94 89.
10am–late daily.

Kleine Orangerie
Spandauer Damm 20.
Map 2 E3. 322 20 21.
10am–10pm daily
(10am–8pm in winter).

November
Husemannstrasse 15.
442 84 25.
10am–2am daily.

Opernpalais
Unter den Linden 5.
Map 7 A3, 16 E3.
20 26 83. 9am–
midnight daily.

Pasticceria Italiana
Leibnizstrasse 45.
Map 9 B1. 10am–
9pm daily.

Rathaus-café
Rathausstrasse 17.
Map 7 C3. 242 36 46.
9am–10pm daily

Sale e Tabacchi
Kochstrasse 18.
252 11 55.
9am–2am Mon– Fri,
10am–2am Sat–Sun.

Schwarzes Café
Kantstrasse 148.
Map 9 C1. 313 80
38. 24 hours daily.

Seeblick
Rykestrasse 14.
442 92 26.
10am–2am Mon–Fri.

Tantalus
Knaackstrasse 26.
442 88 58. 1pm–
late Mon–Fri, 11am–late
Sat–Sun.

Telecafé
Alexanderplatz (TV Tower).
Map 8 D2. 242 33
33. 10am–1am daily.

Voltaire
Stuttgarter Platz 14.
324 50 28.
24 hours daily.

COFFEE BARS AND TEA ROOMS

Barcomi's
Bergmannstrasse 21.
Map 13 A5. 694 81
38. 9am–midnight
Mon–Sat, 10am–mid-
night Sun.

Barcomi's Deli
Sophienstrasse 21
(second courtyard).
Map 7 B1. 28 59
83 63. 9am–10pm
Mon–Sat, 10am–10pm Sun.

Mittendrin
Sophienstrasse 9.
Map 7 B1. 28 49 77
40. noon–11pm
Wed–Thu, noon–1am
Fri–Sat, noon–5pm Sun.

Tadschikische Teestube
Am Festungsgraben 1.
Map 7 A3, 16 E2.
201 06 95. 5pm–
midnight Mon–Fri, 3pm–
midnight Sat–Sun.

TTT – Tee, Tea, Thé
Goltzstrasse 2.
Map 11 A4. 21 75 22
40. daily 8:30am–
midnight Mon–Sat,
10am–midnight Sun.

Bars and Wine Bars

TRYING TO MAKE a clear distinction between wine bars, bars, pubs and *Bierstuben* or giving a precise definition for the word *Kneipe* is practically impossible. However, regardless of the nuances behind all these names, they do share some basic characteristics: they are places where drinking is the primary activity, although eating is sometimes possible; they are usually open from late afternoon or early evening but do not close till late at night or even till morning, if the atmosphere is lively.

KNEIPEN

IN GENERAL TERMS, a *Kneipe* means a cosy sort of place which serves beer (although other drinks are available, too) and where you can have something to eat. The typical *Alberliner Kneipe* is a dark room with panelled oak walls, a big bar and buffet with snacks such as *Buletten* (made from pork), *Soleier* (pickled eggs), *Rollmöpse* (marinated herring) and a selection of cold meats, black pudding (blood sausage) and patés. This kind of traditional pub can still be found in the less affluent districts of Berlin – in Moabit, Kreuzberg and in Prenzlauer Berg, for example, but they are not as common in the city centre. Among the most popular are **Metzer Eck** in Prenzlauer Berg, **Zur Kneipe** and **Ranke 2**, as well as several *Kneipen* in Mitte around the Nikolaiviertel, including **Zum Nussbaum**.

Each *Kneipe* has its own character. More and more of them are choosing modern and inventive interiors, often specializing in less traditional kinds of food: Italian, French or Oriental. Whatever the blend, however, a relaxed atmosphere and a big choice of alcoholic beverages seem to be common features. One of the best *Kneipen* is **Obst & Gemüse** (Fruit & Vegetables), which, despite its name, does not serve any fruit or vegetables. In Savignyplatz, you might want to visit **Dicke Wirtin**, where you can try a hearty *Eintopf* (a hearty soup-type stew). The majority of these fashionable places are situated in Kreuzberg and in Prenzlauer Berg – especially around Kollwitzplatz, which is liberally dotted with all sorts of bars and pubs.

A bit of a curiosity, **Ku'dorf** is a huge complex of 18 pubs in the western part of the centre, but the beer is inexpensive and the food is decent.

BIERGARTEN

WHAT DISTINGUISHES a *Biergarten* from other hostelries is that it is an outdoor venue only open during the summer months, and usually located somewhere scenic, maybe in a park or by a lake. In addition to the usual food and drinks, it completes the outdoor experience with a barbecue. The **Loretta im Garten** provides a much welcome breath of fresh air in the centre of Berlin; or if you are exploring Prenzlauer Berg, try **Pfefferberg** or the nearby **Prater**. After enjoying the views or, for the more active, the watersports at Wannsee, the **Loretta am Wannsee** is a pleasant place to end the day.

WINE BARS

BERLIN WINE BARS tend to have a Mediterranean feel to them. Interiors are often quite rustic in style, but there are exceptions. They open from early evening and stay open late. As for food, menus feature predominantly Italian, Spanish and French cuisine, while the bar serves a huge selection of wines by the glass, bottle or carafe. **Enoteca Reale** – a wine bar with an established reputation, features Italian food and wine, as does **Il Calice**. If you are visiting Prenzlauer Berg you might want to try **Weinstein** which offers French and Spanish food and wine. By way of contrast, at **Lutter & Wegener** in Mitte you can match German-Austrian food with appropriate, native wines, although they too serve a wide variety of wines from vineyards all over Europe.

BARS

A BERLIN BAR IS a good place to finish your evening, and the dedicated barfly is spoiled for choice. You should not count on food but you can drink till late, as most bars do not open until 8pm or later. Although there is no strict dress code, scruffy clothes are not really appropriate. **Galerie Bremer**'s stylish interiors were designed by Hans Scharoun, its drinks are served by well-groomed bar staff and soft jazz plays in the background. A less self-consciously cool atmosphere is created at **Champussy** by a concoction of champagne and live music. You might step in to **Cut** to try one of its huge range of cocktails in a pre-war movie setting. Don't forget to visit some of the hotel bars which are among the best late-night venues in the city. Two worthy of mention are **Harry's New York Bar** (the later the better), in the Hotel Esplanade and **Sam's Bar** in the Hotel Palace.

GAY AND LESBIAN BARS

BERLIN HAS A unique tradition of nightlife for homosexuals, dating back to the 1920s when its cabarets and bars, especially around Nollendorfplatz, were the most outrageous in Europe. Today that hardcore legacy remains, but there are also bars to suit every taste. Some, like **Café Seidenfaden** or **Amsterdam** are for women only. **Roses** is exclusively for men, while **WMF/Gay MF** is mixed during the week, but for men only on Sundays. Most, like **Sundström**, are frequented by both gays and lesbians. The friendly attitude of bars such as **Lenz** or **So 36** means they are popular with both gay and straight visitors alike.

DIRECTORY

KNEIPEN

Le Bateau
Europa-Center
(cellar bar).
Map 10 E1.
261 36 09.

Dicke Wirtin
Carmerstrasse 9.
Map 3 C5.
312 49 52.

**Gerichtslaube mit
Bierschenke und
Ratsherren-Stube**
Poststrasse 28.
Map 7 C3.
241 56 97.

Ku'dorf
Joachimstaler Strasse 15
(in Metropolhaus).
Map 10 D2.
883 66 66.

Meilenstein
Oranienburger Strasse 7.
Map 7 B2, 16 F1.
282 89 95.

Metzer Eck
Metzer Strasse 33.
442 76 52.

Mutter
Hohenstaufenstrasse 4.
Map 11 A3.
216 49 90.

Oberwasser
Zionskirchstrasse 6.
448 37 19.

Obst & Gemüse
Oranienburger
Strasse 48.
Map 6 F1.
282 96 47.

Ranke 2
Rankestrasse 2.
Map 10 E1.
883 88 82.

Slumberland
Goltzstrasse 24.
Map 11 A3.
216 53 49.

Titanic
Winsstrasse 30.
442 03 40.

Zum Nussbaum
Am Nussbaum 3.
Map 7 C3.
242 30 95.

**Zum
Patzenhofer**
Meinekestrasse 26.
Map 10 D1.
882 11 35.

**Zur
Kneipe**
Rankestrasse 9.
Map 10 D2.
883 82 55.

BIERGARTEN

**Loretta
am Wannsee**
Kronprinzessinnen-
weg 260.
803 51 56.

**Loretta
im Garten**
Lietzenburger Strasse 87.
Map 9 C2.
882 33 54.

Pfefferberg
Schönhauser Allee 176.
44 38 31 13.

Prater
Kastanienallee 7–9.
Map 1 A5, 1 B3.
448 56 88.

WINE BARS

Il Calice
Giesebrechstrasse 19.
Map 9 A2.
324 23 08.

**Enoteca
Reale**
Gottschedstrasse 2.
461 74 33.

**Lutter
& Wegener**
Charlottenstrasse 56.
Map 7 A4, 16 D4.
202 95 40.

**Risto
Vinoteca
Cristallo**
Knesebeckstrasse 3.
Map 3 C5.
312 61 17.

BARS

**Bar am
Lützowplatz**
Lützowplatz 7.
Map 11 A1.
262 68 07.

b-flat
Rosenthaler Strasse 13.
Map 7 B1.
280 63 49.

**Blue Note
Bar**
Courbièrestrasse 13.
Map 11 A2.
214 12 37.

Champussy
Uhlandstrasse 171.
Map 9 C2.
881 22 20.

Cut
Knesebeckstrasse 16.
Map 9 C5.
313 35 11.

Distillery
Eisenacher Strasse 64.
Map 11 A5.
784 62 44.

Dr Jazz
Alte Schönhauser
Strasse 13.
Map 7 C1.
28 38 98 48.

Ferry's
Grolmannstrasse 52.
Map 3 C5.

**Galerie
Bremer**
Fasanenstrasse 37.
Map 9 C2.
881 49 08.

**Green
Door**
Winterfeldtstrasse 50.
215 25 15.

Haifischbar
Arndtstrasse 25.
Map 13 A5.
691 13 52.

Weinstein
Lychener Strasse 33.
441 18 42.

BARS

**Bar am
Lützowplatz**
Lützowplatz 7.
Map 11 A1.
262 68 07.

**Harry's New
York Bar**
Lützowufer 15 (in Hotel
Esplanade). **Map** 11 A1.
25 47 80.

**La Casa del
Habano (cigar bar)**
Fasanenstrasse 9–10.
Map 10 D1.
31 10 36 46.

Öxle-Bar
Mulackstrasse 29/30.
Map 7 C1.
28 38 72 40.

Sam's Bar
Budapester Strasse 42
(in Hotel Palace).
Map 10 E1.
2502 1030.

Zur weissen Maus
Ludwigkirchplatz 12.
Map 9 C3.
882 22 64.

GAY AND LESBIAN BARS

Amsterdam
Gleimstrasse 24.
448 07 92.

Café Seidenfaden
Dircksenstrasse 47.
Map 7 C3.
283 27 83.

Lenz
Eisenacher Strasse 3.
Map 11 A2.
217 78 20.

Roses
Oranienstrasse 187.
Map 14 E2.
615 65 70.

So 36
Oranienstrasse 190.
Map 13 B1, 14 D1.
61 40 13 06.

Sundström
Mehringdamm 61.
Map 12 F4.
392 44 14.

WMF/Gay MF
Johannisstrasse 20.
Map 6F2, 7A2.
28 38 88 50.

SHOPPING IN BERLIN

WITH A SHOPPING CENTRE in every district, each selling a wide variety of merchandise, Berlin is a place where almost anything can be bought, so long as you know where to look. The most popular places are Kurfürstendamm and Friedrichstrasse, but the smaller shops in Wedding, Friedrichshain, Schöneberg and the Tiergarten are also worth a visit. Small boutiques selling flamboyant Berlin-style clothes crop up in unexpected courtyards, while the top fashion houses offer the latest in European elegance. Early on Saturday morning is often the best time to visit the city's various markets, the most popular of which – with their colourful stalls full of hats, bags and belts – can be found on Museum Island and at the Tiergarten. The Galeries Lafayette, KaDeWe and any of the city's numerous bookshops all make ideal venues for a pleasant afternoon's window shopping.

Inside the modern, multi-level Europa-Center (see p144)

OPENING HOURS

THE MAJORITY of shops are open Monday to Friday from 10am to 8pm (10am to 4pm on Saturday), but some department stores open as early as 9am, and some smaller shops open in the afternoons only. Generally, there are no lunch-breaks unless the shop is a one-person business. During the six weeks before Christmas, shops stay open until 8pm on Saturdays and the local transport authority, the Berliner Verkehrs-Betriebe, or BVG *(see pp290–91)*, runs a useful service for shoppers. You can leave your bags in a special Weihnachtsgeschenke-Bus (Christmas-gift bus) and shop without dragging all your purchases around with you.

DEPARTMENT STORES

KAUFHAUS DES WESTENS, better known as **KaDeWe** at Wittenbergplatz *(see p149)*, is undoubtedly the biggest and the best department store in Berlin.

Only products of the highest quality are sold in these luxurious halls, where virtually everything you need is on sale – from unusual perfumes and elegant underwear to *haute couture*, all sold in a system of shops-within-shops. The food hall on the sixth floor is legendary for its restaurant overlooking Tauentzienstrasse.

Galeries Lafayette on Friedrichstrasse is nothing less than a slice of Paris placed in the heart of Berlin. Perfumes, domestic accessories and clothing attract an enormous clientele, many of whom also visit the food counter which offers a wide range of French specialities. An extraordinary glass cone rises through the middle of the store, reflecting the interiors of the shops.

Another very popular store is **Wertheim** on the Ku'damm.

A typical street-side stall, brimming with souvenirs for visitors

Although its range of goods is not as broad the range at Galeries Lafayette, there is still an enormous choice and the top floor restaurant offers excellent views over the city.

SHOPPING CENTRES

IN ADDITION TO the two biggest shopping districts in town – Ku'damm and Friedrichstrasse – new shopping

The well-stocked toy department of KaDeWe (see p149)

Elegantly displayed china and table linens

centres are constantly being built, usually conveniently situated close to S-Bahn stations. These massive three-level structures, resembling huge arcaded passageways, contain an enormous number of shops, ranging from supermarkets and chemists to bars, high-street fashion and bookshops. Like most of the shops in Berlin they stay open until 8pm during the week. They also do business on Sundays. One of the newest shopping centres is the **Potsdamer Platz Arkaden**. Built in October 1998 it is now very popular both as a shopping mall and a meeting place. It is visited by thousands of tourists and Berliners every day.

Of a similar character, although built on a slightly smaller scale, is **Galleria** on Schlossstrasse in Steglitz. Here, under one roof, you can browse through an extraordinary selection of goods. **Gesundbrunnencenter** is the biggest shopping passage in Berlin, and has countless stalls and tables offering every kind of bargain. A large number of bars also makes this a popular place to meet friends for a beer or a coffee.

SEASONAL SALES

ALL SHOPS IN BERLIN empty their racks and shelves in the sale, or *Schlussverkauf*, which takes place twice a year. At the end of January, before the new year's collections are displayed in shop windows, you can buy winter clothes for as little as 50 per cent of their original price. During the summer sales (*Sommerschlussverkauf*), which take place at the end of July, you can find similarly-reduced summer outfits. Goods bought in a sale are officially non-returnable, but if you are really keen to take an item back, there is no harm in at least trying to negotiate with the shop assistant.

A number of shops sell a variety of articles marketed as "second season" items. These are always new articles, albeit stocked for the previous season, and they are offered at often generously-reduced prices. You will also find that various shops specialize in top-brand jeans, selling them at much-reduced rates owing to what are often very minor defects. These represent excellent value for money.

HOW TO PAY

WHEN IT COMES to paying for goods you may find that small shops still insist on cash, but otherwise Eurocheques are an acceptable form of payment everywhere. Most department stores will also accept credit cards, but you will need your PIN number to use an EC card.

SHOPPING GUIDE

IF YOU ARE PLANNING to do some serious shopping in Berlin, and are worried about getting lost among the many possibilities, you may want to use the services of a "shopping guide". These are specialists who will tell you what is currently on offer in both the big department stores and in the smaller boutiques.

A stand offering cosmetics for sale in Galeries Lafayette *(see p65)*

Clothes and Accessories

THERE ARE MANY SHOPPING centres in Berlin, and nearly every district has its own high street where residents do their shopping. If it's luxury, elegance and a wide variety of goods you are after, however, then head for the shops on Kurfürstendamm, Friedrichstrasse and Potsdamer Platz. This is where all the major fashion houses and perfume makers have their shops, right in the heart of the city. Alternatively, if you want to explore the smaller boutiques of some lesser-known designers, make your way to Hackescher Markt in the Mitte district, or to Prenzlauer Berg.

WOMEN'S FASHIONS

THE MOST FAMOUS fashion houses are on the Ku'damm (Kurfürstendamm) and its side streets, particularly in the area around the quietly elegant Fasanenstrasse. Among the many famous names doing business here are **Yves Saint Laurent**, **Max Mara**, **Sonja Rykiel**, **Gianni Versace**, **Horn Modehaus**, **ESCADA**, **Chanel** and **Gucci**. Simplicity is the order of the day in the **Jil Sander** shop, making it the ideal place to buy a straightforward dress with exquisite accessories, while the **Boutique Prada** is famous for its light green colour scheme. Gucci manages two shops in the area, one in Fasanenstrasse and another in the fashionable Quartier 206 on Friedrichstrasse. The latter shares the street with many other fashion houses that specialize in women's clothes: **Donna Karan** and **DKNY**, **Strenesse**, **Strenesse Blue** and **ETRO**, to name a few.

MEN'S FASHIONS

FOR THE FULL RANGE of the latest in fashion for men, Kurfürstendamm is the place to shop, for this is where retailers sell clothing straight from Europe's best-known fashion houses. **Selbach** on the Ku'damm is certainly worth a visit with its choice of the best designer labels around. Clothes by Giorgio Armani, Helmut Lang, Dries van Noten and Gianfranco Ferré can all be found here. Also very popular is **Mientus**, which has a second outlet on Wilmersdorfer Strasse.

CHILDREN'S CLOTHING

SHOPS SELLING children' clothes can generally satisfy any taste, depending on how much you are willing to spend. **Babissimo**, which specializes in younger children, offers clothes for up to 6-year-olds, as well as children's furniture, prams and other essentials for baby-care. **Boom** has a wide range of clothes for children up to 14, while **Cinderella** on the Ku'damm offers *haute couture* for all ages, including Armani Junior, Pinco Pallino, Simonetta, DKNY, Miss Blumarine and Young Versace. Similar in style is **Elephant's Knot**, which also sells an array of top designer labels. The needs of children whose parents have a more restricted budget can be met in **H&M Kinder**, which sells fashionable items at relatively moderate prices.

YOUNG DESIGNERS

A NUMBER OF GALLERIES, studios and boutiques specialize in the so-called Berlin style, the collections on sale usually consisting of short-series items that are produced in strictly limited numbers. At one time it was possible to find shops like this across the whole of the city, but now they are concentrated mainly in the northern part of the Mitte area, where a unique fashion centre has now been firmly established. **NIX** offers timeless clothes made from heavy, dark fabrics and cut in classical fashion, while **Stephanie Schenk** offers high-quality knitted goods.

A great selection of clothing by 19 very different designers is on offer in **Tagebau** in Rosenthaler Strasse 19, where just about every kind of item can be bought, from evening dresses and luxury wedding gowns to elegant hats and other fashion accessories.

Among the other shops in Mitte, **Fishbelly** on Sophienstrasse is noted for its unique range of erotic underwear, designed by Jutta Teschner. At **Molotow**, in Kreuzberg, the choice is more classical than the trendy name might suggest. Another very popular place to buy clothes is the **Nardini Collection**, which is located in Charlottenburg.

SHOES AND ACCESSORIES

ONE OF THE largest shoe shops in Berlin is **Schuhtick**, which has three branches in the city, but the highest quality can be found in the **Budapester Schuhe** chain. Classical English shoes are on sale in **Schuhatelier Dietrich & Seiberth**, where the shop's own brand stands among a variety of well-established names.

Penthesileia on Tucholskystrasse offers an amusing range of handbags, which come in all kinds of shapes and sizes. If it's a hat you are after, then you need go no further than **Hut Up**, in the Heckmannhöfen. All kinds are headgear are available here, from typical Russian *shlapas* to party hats with Rastafarian dreadlocks.

PERFUMES

ALL OF THE LARGE department stores, including **KaDeWe** and **Galeries Lafayette**, offer a sizeable selection of the best-known perfumes, but there are also a number of specialist shops dotted around the city. The **Douglas** chain, which has numerous outlets, has a wide range of perfumes at very reasonable prices. **Quartier 206** has a good selection of the better-known perfumes, but if you are looking for something unusual, then **DK One** on the Kurfürstendamm is the place to visit. It offers a wide choice of natural products, many of which would make the perfect gift: Japanese aromatic candles, nail polish of various shocking colours, tomato

shower gel, henna for tattoos and sculptures made of soap are just a few of the many quirky items on offer. The **Body Shop** group is becoming popular in Berlin.

Natural perfumes of all kinds can be bought here, and its policy of no animal testing is popular with customers. It also encourages the return of its containers for recycling.

DIRECTORY

WOMEN'S FASHION

Boutique Prada
Kurfürstendamm 189.
Map 10 D1.
884 80 70.

Chanel
Fasanenstrasse 30.
Map 9 C3.
885 13 24.

Donna Karan
Friedrichstrasse 71.
Map 6 F3.
20 94 60 10.

DKNY
Friedrichstrasse 71.
Map 6 F3.
20 94 60 20.

ESCADA
Kurfürstendamm 186/187.
Map 10 D1.
881 16 36.

ETRO
Friedrichstrasse 71.
Map 6 F3.
20 94 61 20.

Gianni Versace
Kurfürstendamm 185.
Map 10 D1.
885 74 60.

Gucci
Fasanenstrasse 73.
Map 9 C2.
885 63 00.

Friedrichstrasse 73.
Map 6 F3.
201 70 20.

Horn Modehaus
Kurfürstendamm 213.
Map 9 A2.
881 40 55.

Jil Sander
Kurfürstendamm 185.
Map 10 D1.
886 70 20.

Max Mara
Kurfürstendamm 178.
Map 10 D1.
885 25 45.

Sonja Rykiel
Kurfürstendamm 186.
Map 9 A2.
882 17 74.

Strenesse & Strenesse Blue
Friedrichstrasse 71.
Map 6 F3.
20 94 60 35.

Yves Saint Laurent
Kurfürstendamm 52.
Map 9 A2.
883 39 18.

MEN'S FASHIONS

Mientus
Wilmersdorfer Strasse 73.
Map 2 F3, 3 A5, 9 A1.

Kurfürstendamm 52.
Map 9 A2.
323 90 77.

Selbach
Kurfürstendamm 195.
Map 9 A2.
883 25 26.

CHILDREN'S CLOTHING

Babissimo
Schlüterstrasse 42.
Map 9 B2.
885 27 87.

Boom
Uhlandstrasse 170.
Map 9 C1.
883 72 12.

Cinderella
Kurfürstendamm 195.
Map 10 D1.
881 28 63.

Elephant's Knot
Meinekestrasse 3.
Map 10 D2.
883 38 97.

H&M Kinder
Schlossstrasse 1 (Steglitz).
Map 2 E3, E4.

YOUNG DESIGNERS

Fishbelly
Sophienstrasse 7a.
28 04 51 80.

Molotow
Gneisenaustrasse 112.
Map 13 A4.
693 08 18.

Nardini Collection
Schlüterstrasse 70.
Map 9 B1.
313 14 64.

NIX
Oranienburger Strasse 32.
Map 7 A2.
281 80 44.

Stephanie Schenk
Gipsstrasse 9.
Map 7 B1.
28 39 07 85.

Tagebau
Rosenthaler Strasse 19.
Map 7 B1.
28 39 08 90.

SHOES AND ACCESSORIES

Budapester Schuhe
Kurfürstendamm 199.
Map 10 D1.

Bleibtreustrasse 24.
Map 9 B1.

Friedrichstrasse 81.
Map 6 F3.
Central Switchboard
881 70 01.

Hut Up
Oranienburger Strasse 32.
Map 7 A2.
28 38 61 05.

Penthesileia
Tucholskystrasse 31.
Map 7 A2, 16 D1.
282 11 52.

Schuhatelier Dietrich & Seiberth
Gipsstrasse 14.
Map 7 B1.
281 48 97.

Schuhtick
Savignyplatz 11.
Map 9 C1.
315 93 80.

Tauentzienstrasse 5.
Map 10 E1.
214 09 80.

Alexanderplatz.
Map 8 D2.
242 40 12.

PERFUMES

Body Shop
Hardenbergerstrasse
(in the main hall of Zoologischer Garten railway station).
Map 10 D1.

DK One
Kurfürstendamm 56.
Map 9 A2.
32 79 01 23.

Douglas
Kurfürstendamm 216.
Map 10 D1.
881 25 34.

Galeries Lafayette Parfümerie
Franzözische Strasse 23.
Map 6 F4.
20 94 82 94.

KaDeWe Parfümerie
Tauentzienstrasse 21–24.
Map 10 E1.
21 21 22 53.

Quartier 206
Friedrichstrasse 71.
Map 6 F3.
20 94 68 00

Gifts and Souvenirs

U NLIKE LONDON, PARIS OR ROME, where whole industries are devoted to providing mementos for travellers and tourists, Berlin doesn't have a great variety of typical souvenirs. But this doesn't mean you won't be able to find an interesting gift – a browse through any of the major markets or a trip along one of the main shopping thoroughfares should be sufficient for you to buy whatever you need. Posters and records are easy to find, but if you're looking for something elegant, then a piece of china made by Königliche Porzellan-Manufaktur Berlin might be a good idea. For a child, a teddy bear is always an option, particularly in this city, where it is part of the official insignia. For hand-made jewellery or contemporary art, head for Strasse des 17 Juni during one of its Sunday markets *(see p256)*.

BOOKS AND RECORDS

T HE BEST PLACES to buy books on art are the shops at major museums, where you will also find a good selection of cards, posters and general souvenirs. The best of these are in **Hamburger Bahnhof** *(see pp110–11)*, **Gemälde-galerie** *(see pp122–25)*, **Sammlung Berggruen** *(see p151)*, **Schloss Char-lottenburg** *(see pp154–5)* and **Altes Museum** *(see p75)*.

The **Bücherbogen** chain offers a huge choice of books and has several outlets in the city; the one under the S-Bahn bridge near Savignyplatz has the largest stock. Other good stores include **Autorenbuch-handlung** or, if you want to combine shopping and art appreciation, **Artificium** has a gallery attached. The biggest stores also have sections on Berlin art such as the huge **Hugendubel**, which sells CDs as well as books, and **Kiepert**.

For English-language books or papers, **British Bookshop** and **Buchexpress** are the places to go with their choice of both English and American literature. **Prinz Eisenherz** also has a good selection of gay literature. In all of these shops the staff are very helpful and will gladly assist you in finding what you want.

Music lovers should head for **Artificium** in Schloss-strasse, **City Music** near the Ku'damm or any of the **WOM** (World of Music) stores which offer a wide variety of CDs. For Latin American rhythms sound out **Canzone** in the S-Bahn 593 Arcade, and for something avant-garde don't miss **Gelbe Musik** on Schaper-strasse. If you happen to be short of funds there is always the option of flicking through the second-hand CDs on offer at the Sunday antique market on Strasse des 17 Juni *(see p256)*. The market is always crammed with souvenirs and is a great hunting-ground for collectors of old vinyl records.

TOYS

Y OU WON'T HAVE to travel far to buy a typical Berlin teddy bear – you can find them in stores all over the city, especially the gift shops in the Nikolaiviertel. If you're after a wider variety of toys, then **KaDeWe** (Kaufhaus des Westens) is the place to go. Like all the major department stores, KaDeWe offers a whole range of toys for children of all ages, but its teddy bear section is second to none in Berlin. From the highly portable half-inch bear to the life-size 2-metre model, every kind of bear you can imagine is on sale here, so you shouldn't be disappointed. Also, the store can arrange a delivery to your home, so if your child has always dreamed of having an enormous teddy bear, this is a perfect opportunity to fulfil the dream.

Small manufacturers still make old-style wooden toys, from dolls' house furniture to traditional jigsaw puzzles, and these make excellent gifts to take home. **Heidi's Spiel-zeugladen** on Kantstrasse, **Johanna Petzoldt** on Sophienstrasse and **Spielen** on Hufelandstrasse are the best places to go for souvenirs of this kind. Train lovers hoping to extend their tracks and build more depots and stations should visit **Michas Bahnhof** on Nürnberger Strasse, the city's top provider of model train set accessories. An amazing range of goods is available here.

As an old Prussian capital, Berlin is also a good place to look for Germanic lead soldiers; the best places to look are **Berliner Zinnfiguren Kabinett** and **Zinnsoldaten**. While most of the soldiers available are designed for children, collecting them is a popular hobby among adults, and the rarities often fetch very high prices.

FLOWERS

I T IS VERY EASY to find a nice bouquet in Berlin. Flower shops stand on nearly every street corner and the majority of them are open for business on Sundays. **Blumenwiese** on Friedrichstrasse is famous for its bouquets of exotic flowers which are always arranged and wrapped with real artistry. Similarly, **Blumen-Koch** in Wilmersdorf offers an amazing selection of beautiful and colourful plants. However, if you want to arrange a surprise delivery then **Fleurop** on Kurfürsten-damm will send a bouquet of flowers to a given address.

CHINA AND CERAMICS

T HE HISTORY of European china started in Germany in 1708. The alchemist Böttger, while searching for the secret of making gold, discovered instead how to make Chinese-style porcelain. Berlin soon became a major producer. **KPM (Königliche Porzellan-Manufaktur Berlin)** *(see p158)* is still in operation, and its products will satisfy even the most choosy of porcelain collectors. Plenty of newly made china is available, but if you are looking for something older, then an afternoon could be spent in some of the city's antique shops *(see pp256–7)*. Currently manufactured pieces can be bought in the KPM factory shop or in the elegant salon on the ground-floor of the Kempinski hotel *(see p222)*. Those who prefer Meissen porcelain will be able to find it in several shops along the Ku'damm.

While porcelain is expensive, an equally precious gift can be made of a ceramic dish or breakfast set, traditionally manufactured in Thuringia. With their characteristic blue and white patterns, a wide choice of exquisite Thuringian ceramics can be found in **Bürgel-Haus** on Friedrichstrasse.

SPECIALIST SHOPS

I F YOU ARE determined to find something unique, or even quirky, you might want to visit some of the interesting specialist shops – like **Knopf Paul**, which specializes in extraordinary buttons, or **Bären-Luftballons**, which offers a delightful variety of colourful and amusing balloons. There are also a number of shops which specialize in teas and tea-time accessories. **King's Teagarden** and **TeeHaus** offer the best selection in this field.

Smart letter paper and good pens can be bought in **Papeterie**, but if you're still stuck for ideas, there's no harm in browsing through the specialist departments in KaDeWe *(see Toys)* where there's always something guaranteed to catch the eye.

DIRECTORY

BOOKS AND RECORDS

Artificium
Rosenthalerstrasse 40/41.
Map 7 B1.
30 87 22 80.

Schlossstrasse 101.
Map 7 B1.
797 36 12.

Autorenbuch-handlung
Carmerstrasse 10.
Map 3 C5.
313 01 51.

British Bookshop
Mauerstrasse 83–84.
Map 6 F5.
238 46 80.

Buchexpress
Habelschwerdter Allee 4.
831 40 04.

Bücherbogen
Savignyplatz.
Map 9 C1.
31 86 95 11.

Kochstrasse 19.
Map 12 F1.
251 13 45.

Canzone
Savignyplatz.
Map 9 C1.
312 40 27.

City Music
Kurfürstendamm 11.
Map 10 D1.
88 55 01 30.

Gelbe Musik
Schaperstrasse 11.
Map 10 D2.
211 39 62.

Gemäldegalerie
Matthäikirchplatz 8.
Map 5 C5.
20 90 55 55.

Hamburger Bahnhof
Invalidenstrasse 50/51.
Map 6 D1.
397 83 40.

Hugendubel
Tauentzienstrasse 13.
Map 10 E1.
21 40 60.

Kiepert
Hardenbergstrasse 4–5.
Map 3 C5.
31 18 80.

Prinz Eisenherz
Bleibtreustrasse 52.
Map 9 C1.
313 99 36.

Sammlung Berggruen
Schlossstrasse 1.
Map 2 E3.
326 958-0.

WOM
Augsburger Strasse 35–41.
Map 10 D1.
885 72 40.

TOYS

Berliner Zinn-figuren Kabinett
Knesebeckstrasse 88.
Map 3 C5. 313 08 02.

Heidi's Spielzeugladen
Kantstrasse 61.
Map 2 F5.
323 75 56.

Johanna Petzoldt
Sophienstrasse 9.
Map 7 B1.
282 67 54.

KaDeWe
Tauentzienstrasse 21.
Map 10 E1.
212 10.

Michas Bahnhof
Nürnberger Strasse 42.
Map 10 E2, 10 F2.
218 66 11.

Zinnsoldaten
Skalitzer Strasse 81.
618 38 15.
By appointment only.

FLOWERS

Blumenwiese
Friedrichstrasse 151.
Map 6 F3, 15 C2.
20 16 50 67.

Blumen-Koch
Westfälische Strasse 38.
Map 9 A4.
896 69 00.

Fleurop
Kurfürstendamm 69.
Map 9 A2.
881 91 23.

Müllerstrasse 151
(near Leopoldplatz).
453 80 05.

CHINA AND CERAMICS

Bürgel-Haus
Friedrichstrasse 154.
Map 6 F3, 15 C3.
204 45 19.

KPM
Wegelystrasse 1.
39 00 92 15.

Kurfürstendamm 27.
Map 10 D1.
886 72 10.

SPECIALIST SHOPS

Bären-Luftballons
Kurfürstenstrasse 31/32.
Map 9 C1.
261 92 99.

Kings Teagarden
Kurfürstendamm 217.
Map 10 D1.
883 70 59.

Knopf Paul
Zossener Strasse 10.
Map 13 A4.
692 12 12.

Papeterie
Uhlandstrasse 28.
Map 9 C2.
881 63 63.

TeeHaus
Krumme Strasse 35.
Map 3 A5.
31 50 98 82.

Antiques and Objets d'Art

THE ANTIQUE AND ART MARKETS in Berlin are booming. New galleries are opening all the time, particularly in the eastern areas of town. Spandauer Vorstadt is full of antique shops and contemporary art galleries, but the northern part of Mitte (the area around East of the Centre) is the focus of the Berlin art market. Constantly raising their standards, the galleries attract numerous art dealers and collectors, while non-commercial exhibitions organized by art societies like NGbK, NBK and Kunst-Werke add to the creative atmosphere. As for the antique trade, a walk through any of the city's main thoroughfares should show that it is active in just about every district.

AUCTION HOUSES

BERLIN'S OLDEST and most prestigious auction houses are **Gerda Bassenge** and **Villa Grisebach**, both of which organize sales at the start of the year and in the autumn. Bassenge specializes in graphic art, and a month before each sale an auction of books and autographs is held. A photographic auction takes place a few days after the main sale of graphic art. The prices are usually higher at Grisebach which deals mainly in 19th-century paintings. Expressionists and modern classics often go under the hammer here. Another good auctioneer is **Kunst-Auktionen Leon Spik** on Ku'damm; top London auction house **Christie's** has facilities on Fasanenstrasse.

GALLERIES

IF YOU ARE pressed for time, Spandauer Vorstadt in the northern part of Mitte might be the place to go. Since the fall of the Berlin Wall, some 30 galleries have been established in the Linienstrasse, August-strasse, Sophienstrasse and Gipsstrasse areas. Among these are **Arndt & Partner** and **Eigen & Art**, both on August-strasse, **Contemporary Fine Arts**, **Gebauer**, **Max Hetzler**, **Mehdi Chouakri**, **Shift** and **Wohnmaschine**. **Wiens Laden & Verlag** and **Neuger-riemenschneider** are both on Linienstrasse. So-called "open days" take place three or four times a year when all the galleries open at the same time to exhibit the new collections. One is always in early

October, when the Art Forum Berlin fair is held, providing a chance to spot the changing trends in contemporary art.

The galleries near Kurfürsten-damm, such as **Brusberg**, offer high-quality art in a quieter atmosphere. Other galleries include **Hartmann & Noé** and **Fine Art Rafael Vostell**, both on Knesebeckstrasse, as well as **Anselm Dreher**, **Barbara Weiss**, **Franck & Schulte** and **Poll**.

ANTIQUE SHOPS

ANTIQUE SHOPS can be found in every district of Berlin. Near Kurfürstendamm and around Ludwigkirchplatz there are a number of high-class shops offering expensive *objets d'art*, from Chinese furniture in **Alte Asiatische Kunst** to Secession trinkets in **ART 1900** and glass from different periods in the **Galeries Splinter**.

Furniture specialists can be found in Suarezstrasse in Charlottenburg, where original Thonets can be bought as well as modern steel items by well-known designers. For a slightly lower grade of antique, the best place to go is Berg-mannstrasse in Kreuzberg. In its mildly Oriental atmosphere you can often find valuable pieces among masses of junk. **Das Zweite Büro** in Zossener Strasse specializes in trading old desks, cupboards and filing cabinets, which don't come cheap, but the quality of the merchandise is excellent. Standing opposite Das Zweite Büro is **Radio Art** with its extensive collection of old radios and record players.

Some other interesting shops to try are **Antiklampen**, **Bleibtreu Antik**, **Chinaantik** and **Lakeside Antiques**. There's a real market atmosphere in the arcades of the S-Bahn railway bridge near Friedrichstrasse where a host of street traders sell all kinds of nick-nacks, from clothes and books to cutlery and domestic accessories.

FLEA MARKETS

MANY BERLINERS spend their Saturday and Sunday mornings at flea markets, and after a coffee go for a walk in the Tiergarten or take a stroll to a museum. Trödelund Kunstmarkt, on Strasse des 17 Juni near Tiergarten S-Bahn station, is the most popular market in town. It is divided into two parts, and the antique section deals with books and magazines as well as pricey rarities. If you have the time and patience to sift through the enormous amount on offer, you are likely to find some great bargains. Arts and crafts trading takes place on the other side of Charlotten-burger Brücke, and the goods on offer range from leather items and ceramics to colourful silk clothes and jewellery. Shops from all over Berlin are usually represented here.

From **Berliner Kunst-und Nostalgiemarkt an der Museumsinsel**, it is only a few steps to the museums. The stalls along Kupfergraben stand opposite the Pergamon- and Altes Museum, and art objects, books, records and other antiques are always on display around the Zeughaus.

The flea market operating in the car park near the Fehr-belliner Platz U-Bahn station opens at the weekends at 8am. If you are interested in going, you would do well to get there as early as possible as it is full of experienced collectors who only need a few minutes to spot something valuable. Another flea market can be found on Arkonaplatz, in the centre of a residential district in the eastern part of the town. If you are after memorabilia from the former GDR, you should try the stalls around the Brandenburg Gate. However, the redevelopment of Pariser Platz means they may have to move elsewhere.

Another great market is the **Treptower Hallentrödel** on Eichenstrasse, which offers everything under one roof. Old telephones and army boots can be found beside bathroom accessories and piles of very cheap books (5 for DM 4). The hall itself, a former bus depot, is worth visiting for its interesting architecture alone.

Other good flea markets to visit include **Antik & Trödelmarkt am Ostbahnhof, Boxhagener Platz** and **Kiezmarkt am Moritzplatz.**

Berliner Stadtrèinigungsbetriebe is an organization responsible for disposing of rubbish, and a number of "BSR" shops sell old furniture which is still in good condition. They are ideal places to pick up a bargain, although you are often in competition with small traders.

Food Products

FOOD SPECIALITIES FROM ALL OVER the world can be found in Berlin, a fact which is due partly to the city's own lack of traditional cuisine. Gone are the days when local fare was restricted to pork shank with cabbage, cutlets, *Currywurst* and potatoes. Today the side-streets and thoroughfares are teeming with the shops and restaurants of many nationalities – Italian, Greek, Turkish, Spanish and French as well as Mexican, American, Japanese, Chinese and Thai. As befits any major European capital, the food is of the highest quality, and there are more and more shops providing organic products, from vegetables and wholemeal bread to various wines and beers.

PATISSERIES AND SWEET SHOPS

BERLINERS CERTAINLY have a sweet tooth for there are plenty of patisseries and sweet shops all over the city, and a wide range of cakes is available. A typical speciality is a doughnut known simply as a *Berliner*, but the majority of places offer a whole range of cakes along with French pastries and fruits. **Buchwald** is renowned for producing some of the best cakes in town, mainly to take away, but there are also a number of patisseries, or *Konditoreien*. Among the best of these are **Café Kranzler**, **Café Möhring Konditorei** and **Opernpalais**. Delicacies from Vienna can be bought in **Wiener Konditorei Caffeehaus**, while **Leysieffer** shops, with their exquisite chocolates and pralines, are a temptation for chocoholics. Visitors with a sweet tooth should also try the large stores: **KaDeWe's Feinschmecker Etage** and **Galeries Lafayette's Gourmet** departments both have a wonderful range of confectioneries.

CHEESES

THE LARGEST SELECTION of cheeses in Berlin can be found at the **Galeries Lafayette** which has a particularly broad choice from France. **KaDeWe**'s cheese department also offers a wide variety, while **Maître Philipe** sells only select cheeses from small producers. You won't find any fridges here but the whole shop is air-conditioned and the aroma whets the appetite. Italian cheese can be bought in **Südwind** on Akazienstrasse, together with Italian wines and oils, and **Grand Vignoble, Wein & Delicatessen** specializes in French products, mainly wines and cheeses. **Fuchs & Rabe**, **Lindner** and **Salumeria** are also a must for cheese lovers.

WINES

BETWEEN THEM, **KaDeWe** and **Galeries Lafayette** have the biggest wine cellars, while smaller businesses usually specialize in wines from a particular region. **Der Rioja-Weinspezialist**, for example, sells only wines from northern Spain. **Vineyard** deals only in American and Australian wines, while **Vendemmia** specializes in Tuscan wines. A big selection of German wines is available at **Viniculture**.

MEATS, COLD CUTS AND FISH

BERLINERS EAT QUITE a lot of meat and meat products – the latter in particular are real German specialities. So if you are not vegetarian you should try something from the bewildering range of sausages and meat rolls. As well as the well-stocked departments in **KaDeWe** and **Galeries Lafayette**, small shops also offer excellent quality products. **Fleischerei Bachhuber** is good, and **Alternative Fleischerei** specializes in chemical- and hormone-free meats, while a broad selection of fish (both fresh- and saltwater) and game is offered in **KaDeWe's** delicatessen. **Rogacki** is another good fishmonger and in **Ochlummermeyer** you can always find good quality cold meats.

FOOD HALLS

THE OLD 19TH-CENTURY food halls are not as important today as they were before World War II, when they were the chief source of produce. The biggest of them all was on Alexanderplatz. The place used to teem with people 24 hours a day, but the hall wasn't rebuilt after sustaining damage during World War II. The GDR authorities had no use for such a large food hall, and with the advent of supermarkets, there was no need for it.

Today there are only three food halls in operation; **Arminiushalle** in Moabit, the **Markthalle am Marheinekeplatz** and **Eisenbahnhalle**, both in Kreuzberg. All of these are usually open all day six days per week – Monday to Saturday. Typically, Berliners use the food halls to pick up the one or two specialty items they can't find in the supermarkets. Shopping in these halls is a good opportunity to try traditional German *Currywurst*: the outlets in these food halls are regarded as the best in town.

MARKETS

MARKETS OFFER an additional way of shopping for food. They take place twice a week, and one of the best is the **Winterfeldtmarkt** which takes place on Wednesdays and Saturdays from 7am till 2pm. On Saturdays the opening hours are extended if the crowd is big, which it often is. You can buy everything from high quality fruits, through vegetables and cheeses from all over the world to clothing and domestic accessories. Fast-food outlets offer falafel or grilled sausages, and the place is surrounded by bars and cafés full of clients and traders' relaxing with a glass of beer. The atmosphere and range of goods on offer is truly international.

Türken Markt am Maybachufer is a big Turkish market which opens on Tuesdays and Fridays until 6:30pm. It is popular with Turks living in Kreuzberg and Neukölln. The stalls offer all kinds of Turkish specialities. There are also markets in the city centre on Wittenbergplatz – **Wochenmarkt Wittenbergplatz** on Tuesdays and Fridays, Winterfeldtmarkt on Wednesdays and Saturdays and the **Bauernmarkt Wittenbergplatz** on Thursdays. In fact, Thursday is the day when Wittenbergplatz is invaded by farmers from all over the region offering a variety of products.

You won't find any exotic fruits at these, but if you have had enough of tasteless supermarket tomatoes and apples then they should provide a good alternative. Depending on the season, you can buy pickled gherkins (*Salzgurken*) from the Spreewald, asparagus from the Beelitz region and delicious, sweet aromatic strawberries.

DIRECTORY

DEPARTMENT STORES WITH FOOD HALLS

Feinschmecker Etage at KaDeWe
Tauentzienstrasse 21.
Map 10 E2.
212 10.

Gourmet in Galeries Lafayette
Friedrichstrasse 23.
Map 6 F4.
20 94 80.

PATISSERIES AND SWEET SHOPS

Buchwald
Bartningallee 29.
Map 4 F3.
391 59 31.

Café Kranzler
Kurfürstendamm 18–19.
Map 10 D1.
885 77 20.

Café Möhring Konditorei
Gendarmenmarkt.
Map 7 A4, 16 D4.
203 09 22 40.

Konditorei Am Hagenplatz
Hagenplatz 3.
826 16 38.

Leysieffer
Kurfürstendamm 218.
Map 10 D1.
885 74 80.

Hotel Adlon
Unter den Linden 77.
Map 6 E3, 15 A3.
22 67 98 65.

Opernpalais
Unter den Linden 5.
Map 7 A3, 16 E3.
20 26 83.

Wiener Konditorei Caffeehaus
Hohenzollerndamm 92.
89 59 69 20.

Reichsstrasse 81.
304 55 35.

CHEESES

Fuchs & Rabe
Ludwigkirchstrasse 3.
Map 9 C2.
882 39 84.

Schlossstrasse 119,
Steglitz.
Map 2 E3, 2 E4.
792 81 68.

Grand Vignoble, Wein & Delicatessen
Joachim-Friedrich-Strasse 37.
893 59 82.

Lindner
Olivaer Platz 17
(near Ku'damm).
Map 9 B2.
881 35 53.

Maître Philipe
Emser Strasse 42.
Map 9 B3, 9C3.
88 68 36 10.

Salumeria
Windscheidstrasse 20.
Map 2 E5.
324 33 18.

Südwind
Akazienstrasse 7.
Map 11 A5.
782 04 39.

WINES

Der Rioja-Weinspezialist
Akazienstrasse 13.
782 25 78.

Vendemmia
Akazienstrasse 20.
784 27 28.

Vineyard
Windscheidstrasse 19.
32 70 20 73.

Viniculture
Grolmanstrasse 44–45.
883 81 74.

MEATS, COLD CUTS AND FISH

Alternative Fleischerei
Körtestrasse 20.
Map 13 C4.
691 64 86.

Fleischerei Bachhuber
Güntzelstrasse 47.
Map 9 C4.
873 21 15.

Rogacki
Wilmersdorfer Strasse 145–146.
Map 2 F4.
343 82 50.

Schlemmermeyer
Schlossstrasse 6
Map 2 E3.
793 31 38

FOOD HALLS

Arminiushalle
Arminiusstrasse.
Map 4 E1.
8am–6:30pm
Mon–Sat.

Eisenbahnhalle
Pücklerstrasse.
Map 14 E2.
8am–6:30pm
Mon–Sat.

Markthalle am Marheinekeplatz
Marheinekeplatz.
Map 13 A5.
8am–6:30pm
Mon–Sat.

MARKETS

Bauernmarkt Wittenbergplatz
Wittenbergplatz.
Map 10 F1.
10am–8pm Thu.

Winterfeldtmarkt
Wittenbergplatz.
Map 11 A3.
7am–2pm Wed & Sat.

Türken Markt am Maybachufer
Maybachufer.
Map 14 E3, F4.
noon–6:30pm
Tue & Fri.

Wochenmarkt Wittenbergplatz
Wittenbergplatz.
Map 10 F2.
8am–2pm Tue & Fri.

ENTERTAINMENT IN BERLIN

With so much on offer, from classical drama and cabaret to variety theatre and an eclectic nightclub scene, it is possible to indulge just about any taste in Berlin. During the summer months many bars and restaurants set up outdoor tables, and the area around Unter den Linden, the Kurfürstendamm, Kreuzberg and Prenzlauer Berg in particular, seems to turn into one large social arena. The city really comes into its own at night, when its clubs, all-night cafés and cocktail bars give you

Flute player in costume

the chance to dance till dawn. The city has many night-life centres, each with a slightly different character. Prenzlauer Berg is best for mainstream bars, cafés and clubs, while Friedrichshain is more exclusive, and Kreuzberg has a vibrant gay scene. The Mitte district (*see* East of the Centre) offers a true mixture, its opera house and classical theatre surrounded by lively and inexpensive bars. On a Sunday, a quiet trip down the river or along the canals offers a pleasant way to unwind.

Claudio Abbado conducting the Berlin Philharmonic Orchestra

PRACTICAL INFORMATION

There are so many things going on in Berlin that it can be difficult to find what you're looking for. The Information Centre offers basic information *(see p279)*, but for greater detail you can buy a copy of the listings magazines *Tip* or *Zitty* which offer the widest range of suggestions. Information on festivals, sports events, cinema programmes, theatre schedules, cabarets and concerts can be found on the following websites: *Berlinonline* and *Berlin.de*.

But if you've only just arrived in town and haven't made it yet to an internet café or a kiosk, the chances are the bar you're sitting in, or your hotel foyer, has leaflets on the wall to point you in the right direction. And there is no end of posters around town telling you what's on offer.

GUIDES

You won't be short of cultural guides in Berlin. The fortnightly listings magazines *Tip* and *Zitty*, which cover the widest choice of events, are issued on Wednesdays, while the daily newspaper *Berliner Morgenpost* has a supplement "*bm Live*" which is available each Friday. The Thursday supplement to *Tagesspiegel* is called *Ticket*, and *Taz* publishes cinema programmes every other Thursday in *Cinemataz*. All of these can be bought at news kiosks.

Berlin Programm provides details of the month ahead and *Berlin Magazin*, issued by Berlin Tourismus Marketing GmbH, contains quarterly information. The free magazines *Partysan* and *Flyer* are full of news about nightclubs and discos and they should be available in restaurants.

If you want general information about the whole range of cultural events on offer, including current exhibitions in galleries and museums, then turn to the monthly *Kunstkalender* which is available in most bookshops, museums and galleries.

TICKETS

Tickets can usually be bought two weeks before an event, and you can buy them directly at theatre box

Prokoviev's *The Love of Three Oranges* staged at the Komische Oper

The Love Parade, a festival of techno music

offices or make a telephone booking. Reserved tickets have to be picked up and paid for at least half an hour before a show. Students, pensioners and the disabled are entitled to a 50 per cent discount, but you will need to present appropriate documentation. You can also pre-book tickets at special outlets all over Berlin but they charge a 20 per cent commission. All the major theatres and concert halls have special wheelchair access, but the number of places for the disabled is limited; make it clear when buying a ticket that you need an appropriate place. Tickets to some theatres include a pass for public transport.

If a performance has sold out, you can always try to find tickets just before the show, for some of the pre-booked tickets may not have been collected. One agency which specializes in these last-minute purchases is called **Hekticket Theaterkassen**. You can buy tickets on the day, even an hour before a performance. If someone has already returned their ticket, you might be able to buy it at a 50 per cent discount.

Other agencies to contact for tickets are **Fullhouse Service** on Budapester Strasse, and **Box Office**, with two convenient locations.

INFORMATION FOR THE DISABLED

IN ALL THE GUIDES to theatres and concert halls the availability of wheelchair access is noted by a distinctive blue sign. The majority of the bigger theatres, halls and opera houses have special places for wheelchairs and seats reserved for people with walking difficulties. When buying a ticket you must specify your need as the number of places is limited.

If you are disabled you should be able to commute without restriction on public transport, as the majority of U- and S-Bahn stations have lifts, and they are clearly marked on maps of the underground. Many buses now have special ramps and facilities for wheelchairs, but if you experience any difficulty members of the BVG staff will always help.

PUBLIC TRANSPORT AT NIGHT

THE LAST U-BAHN TRAINS run at around 1am, but buses and trams continue running every half an hour, making

Cinema Zoo Palast, where many cinema festivals are held

Berlin's night-time transport one of the most efficient in Germany. Bus and tram time-tables are linked, and there are two major interchange points: one on Hardenberg-platz, near the Zoo railway station, and the other on Hackescher Markt. On Friday and Saturday nights you can also use lines 1 and 9 of the U-Bahn which operate every 15 minutes. Some S-Bahn lines also work at night over the weekend. Every ticket office and information point in town has brochures with all the relevant details about night-time public transport.

Afternoon with the children in the Museumsdorf Düppel *(see p172)*

(see p172)

DIRECTORY

TICKET AGENTS

Hekticket Theaterkassen
Hardenbergstrasse 29a.
Map 10 D1.
☎ 23 09 93 0.

Rathausstrasse 1.
Map 8 D2.
☎ 24 31 24 31.

Fullhouse Service
Budapester Strasse 48.
Map 10 E1.
☎ 262 05 15.

Box Office
Nollendorfplatz 7.
Map 11 A2.
☎ 215 54 63.

Kurt-Schumacher-Platz 1.
☎ 496 22 23.

Theatres

THANKS TO REINHARDT AND BRECHT, Berlin became a landmark in the European theatre scene in the 1920s, and its success continues to this day. During the years of Nazi rule, many people working in the business were killed or forced to emigrate as the stage became a propaganda machine, but after World War II a revival spread through Berlin's theatres. At the heart of this revival were Bertolt Brecht and his Berliner Ensemble, and Peter Stein who ran the Schaubühne.

MODERN HISTORY

FOLLOWING THE construction of the Berlin Wall, the number of venues doubled as each part of the divided city worked to build its own theatres. The Volksbühne in the East had its equivalent in the West called the Freie Volksbühne, and the eastern acting school, the Academy, was matched by a second Academy in the west.

The economic difficulties caused by the reunification of Germany forced a number of places to shut down, but the theatres of East Berlin managed to survive. In the west, the Freie Volksbühne and the Schiller-Theater (the largest stage in Germany) had to close, but the Volksbühne, under Frank Castorf, and the Deutsches Theater, led by Thomas Langhoff, continued to do well. Independent theatres have fared equally well in both parts of the city.

The theatre season runs from September to July, with its peak in May during Berliner Theatertreffen (Berlin Theatre Forum), when many other German theatre groups are invited to stage their plays. There are also a number of youth theatres which produce the work of young writers, and these follow the seasons of the major venues.

Repertoires are published in the listings magazines *Tip* and *Zitty*, and also displayed on yellow posters in U-Bahn stations and thoughout Berlin. Leaflets are available in many restaurants around the city.

MAJOR STAGES

THE **Deutsches Theater** and its small hall **Kammerspiele** on Schumannstrasse is a top-class theatre and offers a varied repertoire of productions with very professional modern stagings. From the Greek classics to the modern classics and contemporary plays, the Deutches Theater has successfully staged them all. Tickets for these plays can be difficult to obtain, but it is worth persevering.

At **Volksbühne** you can see interesting performances of classical plays in modern settings, as well as adaptations of books or films or pieces written by young writers. Concerts, lectures and dance evenings are organized in the Red and Green Salon of the theatre, and with so much going on the Volksbühne now seems more of a cultural centre with a multimedia character than just a stage.

Although it was particularly important for German theatre in the 1970s and 80s, **Schaubühne am Lehniner Platz** is no longer as popular as it was, which is a shame, for production values don't get any higher than this. The close attention to detail – on everything from the sets and scenery to the choice of music and the editing of the printed programme – is extraordinary, and distinguishes it from the other theatres in town; every performance is an event.

The **Berliner Ensemble** (or BE for short) has been managed by such influential dramatists as Bertolt Brecht from 1949 and then Heiner Müller in 1970. The spectacles created by these two are still performed today. The whole theatre is magnificent, and it has some superb architecture including the stage; after each performance you can meet the actors in the canteen in the courtyard, behind the building. Another venue well worth visiting is the **Hebbel-Theater** – an ambitious place with a programme that includes contemporary plays from all over the world and works of modern dance.

Other major venues include the **Maxim Gorki Theater**, the **Renaissance-Theater** and the **Schlosspark Theater**.

SMALL STAGES AND ALTERNATIVE THEATRE

THERE ARE a number of alternative theatres in Berlin, each enthusiastically playing the works of what are generally lesser known authors. **Theater am Halleschen Ufer** is devoted to avant-garde theatre and dance and is considered to be the city's best alternative stage. The smaller boulevard theatres, like **Theater am Kurfürstendamm**, **Komödie am Kurfürstendamm** or **Berlins Volkstheater Hansa**, offer different, lighter programmes.

Among other small theatres are **Bat-Studiotheater** and **Kleines Theater**. There are many other notable venues, including **Theater zum Westlichen Stadthirschen**, **Hackesches-Hoftheater**, **Theater 89**, **Theater Zerbrochene Fenster**, **Theater Kreatur**, and the **Vagantenbühne**.

MUSICALS, REVIEWS AND CABARETS

THERE ARE THREE main musical theatres in Berlin, in addition to the many small venues which fit musicals into their more general repertoire. **Friedrichstadtpalast**, in the eastern part of the city, stages many of the new major shows as well as classical musicals, and a smaller stage is reserved for cabaret. The **Theater des Westens** in Charlottenburg is more traditional, while the **Stella Musical Theater Berlin am Potsdamer Platz** is a modern theatre established in the newly built city on Potsdamer Platz in 1999.

As for cabaret, there are probably as many acts in Berlin today as there were in the 1920s. They are usually performed by small itinerant groups which rely on the hospitality of theatres for a venue.

Distel, in Friedrichstrasse, continues its success from GDR times, and **Stachelschweine** celebrates its popularity in western Berlin.

There are many more venues for musicals, reviews and cabarets. Among these are **Bar jeder Vernunft**, **Chamäleon Variété**, **Dr Seltsam Kabarett**, **Musical-Zelt**, **Scheinbar**, **Wintergarten Varieté** and **Wühlmäuse**.

TICKETS

IT IS USUALLY POSSIBLE to pre-book tickets two weeks before a performance. You can buy them directly from the box office of the theatre or by telephone booking. There are also ticket vendors all over town, but they usually charge a 15–22 per cent commission. Even if the theatre or concert has been sold out,

there is still a chance of buying something just before the performance, provided that not all pre-booked tickets have been collected.

Hekticket Theaterkassen specializes in this kind of last-minute ticket. If you are lucky enough to pick up a ticket on the day of performance, you may find it has been returned and reduced to half its former price.

DIRECTORY

MAJOR STAGES

Berliner Ensemble
Bertold-Brecht-Platz 1.
Map 6 F2, 15 C1.
28 408 155.

Deutsches Theater
Schumannstrasse 13.
Map 6 E2, 16 F1.
28 44 12 25.

Kammerspiele
Schumannstrasse 13a.
Map 6 E2, 15 A1.
28 44 12 26.

Hebbel-Theater
Stresemannstrasse 29.
Map 12 F2.
25 90 04 27.

Maxim Gorki Theater
Am Festungsgraben 21.
Map 7 A3, 16 E2.
20 22 11 15.

Renaissance-Theater
Hardenbergstrasse 6.
Map 3 C5.
312 42 02.

Schaubühne am Lehniner Platz
Kurfürstendamm 153.
89 00 23.

Schlosspark Theater
Schlossstrasse 48
Map 2 E4.
793 15 15.

Volksbühne
Rosa-Luxemburg-Platz.
Map 8 D1.
247 67 72.

SMALL STAGES AND ALTERNATIVE THEATRE

Bat-Studiotheater
Belforter Strasse 15.
442 76 13.

Hackesches-Hoftheater
Rosenthaler Strasse 40.
Map 7 B2.
283 25 87.

Berlins Volkstheater Hansa
Alt-Moabit 48.
391 44 60.

Kleines Theater
Südwestkorso 64.
821 30 30.

Komödie am Kurfürstendamm
Kurfürstendamm 206.
Map 9 C2.
47 99 74 40.

Sophiensäle
Sophienstrasse 18.
Map 7 B1.
283 52 66.

Theater 89
Torstrasse 216.
Map 6 F1.
282 46 56.

Theater am Halleschen Ufer
Hallesches Ufer 32.
Map 12 F2.
251 06 55.

Theater am Kurfürstendamm
Kurfürstendamm 206.
Map 9 C2.
47 99 74 40.

Theater Kreatur
Tempelhofer Ufer 10.
Map 12 F2.
251 31 16.

Theater Zerbrochene Fenster
Fidicinstrasse 2.
Map 12 F5.
691 29 32.

Theater zum Westlichen Stadthirschen
Kreuzbergstrasse 37.
Map 12 D4.
785 70 33.

Vagantenbühne
Kantstrasse 12a.
Map 10 D1.
312 45 29.

MUSICALS, REVIEWS & CABARETS

Bar jeder Vernunft
Schaperstrasse 24.
Map 10 D2.
26 55 06 96.

Chamäleon Variété
Rosenthaler Strasse 40–41.
Map 7 B2.
282 71 18.

Distel
Friedrichstrasse 101.
Map 6 F2, 15 C1.
204 47 04.

Friedrichstadtpalast
Friedrichstrasse 107.
Map 6 F2, 15 C1.
23 26 23 26.

Dr Seltsam Kabarett
Johannisstrasse 2 (behind Friedrichstadtpalast).
Map 6 F2.
282 37 97.

Scheinbar
Monumentenstrasse 9.
Map 11 C5.
784 55 39.

Stachelschweine
Europa-Center.
Map 10 E1.
261 47 95.

Stella Musical Theater Berlin am Potsdamer Platz
Marlene-Dietrich-Platz 1.
(0180) 544 44.

Theater des Westens
Kantstrasse 12.
Map 2 E5, 9 A1, 10 D1.
88 22 888.

Wintergarten Varieté
Potsdamer Strasse 96.
Map 11 C2.
23 0882 30.

Wühlmäuse
Nürnberger Strasse/ Lietzenburger Strasse.
Map 10 E2.
80 60 29 29.

TICKETS

Hekticket Theaterkassen
Hardenbergstrasse 29.
Map 10 D1.
23 09 93 0.

Rathausstrasse 1.
Map 7 C3.
24 31 24 31.

Cinema

BERLIN HAS ALWAYS BEEN THE CAPITAL of German cinema, and it is likely to remain so. In November 1895, exactly two months after the Lumière Brothers presented their first moving pictures in France, brothers Emil and Max Skladanowsky showed a series of short films to a spellbound German public. Wintergarten Varieté-theater was the place where you could go to see those famous pioneering films of kangaroos fighting, acrobats tumbling and children performing folk dances. By 1918 there were already some 251 cinemas with 82,796 seats available in Berlin, and by 1925 the number of people involved in the film industry had reached 47,600. The history of UFA (Universal Film AG), established in 1917, is intimately linked to that of Berlin, for the company has its two studios here.

BIG SCREENS AND BIG FILMS

THE MAJORITY of cinemas can be found in the western part of town, around Breitscheidplatz, near the Ku'damm and Tauentzienstrasse, and this is where the big American and German blockbusters are shown. After the fall of the Berlin Wall, many new multiplex cinemas were built, the biggest being the 19-screen **CinemaxX Potsdamer Platz**. Mainstream Anglo-American movies are dubbed, but you can also see films in their original language here.

Next door to CinemaxX is the Berlin **Imax** cinema – the biggest screen in Germany. It can only show films that are shot with an Imax camera, but the spectacle is always breathtaking. Its huge curved screen is 27m (89 ft) in diameter and covers approximately 1000 sq m (10,750 sq ft). There are three other areas of Berlin that are known as cinema centres; East of the City, in Friedrichshain and in Prenzlauer Berg.

The **International** on Karl-Marx-Allee is typical of cinemas built in the communist era. It was built in 1963 and may be of interest to anyone curious about the days of the GDR, but it's pretty austere and only has 551 seats. Another venue on Karl-Marx-Allee is the **UFA-Palast Kosmos**. It is now a multiplex with ten screens, but it was originally very small; only the exterior provides hints of its GDR-era origins.

STUDIO CINEMAS

THERE ARE PLENTY of small studio cinemas scattered across town, and it is in these that new independent films and retrospectives of particular actors and directors are shown. Cinemas like **Hackesche Höfe Kino** or **Central**, situated near Hackescher Markt, offer a pleasant break from the bustle of city life, and most have bars of their own. The café at Hackesche Höfe Kino offers light snacks and a wonderful 5th-floor view over the neighbourhood.

The **Arsenal**, on Welserstrasse, belongs to the Freunde der Deutschen Kinemathek (Friends of German Cinema), and is ideal for lovers of German film for this is where you can see all the national classics. The venue has a detailed monthly programme which includes four screenings per day, many of which come with a small introductory lecture. Copies of the programme are distributed in bars all over town, but if you're interested in taking a look you'd better hurry, for the cinema will soon be moving to the new Haus der Deutschen Kinemathek (The House of German Cinema) in Sony's headquarters near Potsdamer Platz *(see p126)*. The quality of the programme will remain the same, but the old cinema will be missed.

If you're interested in original language movies, **Cinéma Paris** in Charlottenburg is the place to go for French films, while the **Odeon** in Schöneberg specializes in English and American films.

OPEN-AIR CINEMA

OPEN-AIR cinemas start operating as soon as the weather allows. The biggest is **Waldbühne** – a concert hall with seating for an audience of 20,000. Others can be found in Hasenheide, Künstler Haus Bethanien garden, in Friedrichshain or in UFA-Fabrik, and all of them show current first-run films as well as established classics. Screenings start at around 9pm, which is when it starts to grow dark during summer.

NON-COMMERCIAL FILMS

ALTHOUGH MOST people go to the cinema nowadays to see the latest blockbuster movie, it is still possible to track down venues which show documentaries and other non-commercial films. Cinemas like **Landesbildstelle Berlin** on Wikingerufer specialize in these. It mainly presents films about Berlin, and while admission is often free the showing-times are irregular. The **Zeughauskino**, which is shut until 2002 for rebuilding work, will also specialize in non-commercial films. It used to co-ordinate its repertoire with exhibitions in the Deutsches Historisches Museum (the German Historical Museum), as well as showing its own series of documentaries. Once it re-opens it should resume this joint programme. The **Museum für Völkerkunde** in Dahlem *(see p170)* also organizes film showings, usually in conjunction with exhibitions of non-European culture. As at Zeughaus, a ticket is reasonably priced.

PRICES

CINEMA TICKETS usually cost between DM11–15 and students and senior citizens don't always receive a discount. Many cinemas declare Tuesday or Wednesday as Cinema Day, when tickets are

DM2–4 cheaper. Some cinemas also organize so-called "Blue Mondays" when ticket prices are reduced to as little as DM7.

In most cinemas there are usually three shows per evening, the first starting at 6pm, the last at around 10pm. All cinemas accept telephone bookings, but you have to turn up to pay for your ticket at least half an hour before a show, otherwise it may go to somebody else. The majority of ticket offices don't take credit cards, so it's important to have cash in hand.

Twenty minutes of commercials tend to precede the screenings of most films, although some venues use this time to show short films by up-and-coming directors.

THE FILM BUSINESS

IF YOU'RE INTERESTED in the business of film production then you will want to visit Studio UFA in Babelsberg, Potsdam. A must for all cinema fans, the **Studiotour Babelsberg** allows you to see a live film crew working on a current production *(see p197)*. You will also get a chance to see some classic film sets – some going back to the days of Marlene Dietrich – as well as samples of the latest technical wizardry. Memorabilia from the Warner Brothers studios can be seen at the **Warner Bros Studio Store** near Tauentzienstrasse, but if you prefer to mix your love of film with a bite to eat, then a trip to Planet Hollywood in Friedrichstrasse may be in order. The restaurant is part of a chain set up by Hollywood cinema stars Sylvester Stallone, Arnold Schwarzenegger and Bruce Willis.

Books in many different languages about cinema and film can be found in **Bücherbogen** under the arcade of the S-Bahn railway bridge at Savignyplatz.

DIRECTORY

BIG SCREENS AND BIG FILMS

CinemaxX Potsdamer Platz
Potsdamer Strasse 5.
Map 6 D5.
44 31 63 16.

Imax
Marlene-Dietrich-Platz 4.
443 16 131.

International
Karl-Marx-Allee 33
(corner of Schillingstrasse).
Map 8 E3.
24 75 60 11.

UFA-Palast Kosmos
Karl-Marx-Allee 131a.
Map 8 E3.
42 28 40.

STUDIO CINEMAS

Arsenal
Welserstrasse 25.
Map 10 F2.
219 00 10.

Central
Rosenthaler Strasse 39.
Map 7 B1.
30 50 09 77.

Cinéma Paris
Kurfürstendamm 211.
Map 9 A2, 10 D1.
881 31 19.

Hackesche Höfe Kino
Kurfürstendamm 211.
Map 9 C2.
283 46 03.

Odeon
Hauptstrasse 116.
Map 11 B5.
78 70 40 19.

OPEN-AIR CINEMA

Waldbühne
Gockenturmstrasse 1.
23 08 82 30 (tickets).

NON-COMMERCIAL FILMS

Landesbildstelle Berlin
Wikingerufer 7.
Map 4 D2.
39 84 90.

Museum für Völkerkunde
Lansstrasse 8.
830 14 38.
until 2002.

Zeughauskino
Unter den Linden 2.
Map 7 B3.
20 30 40.

THE FILM BUSINESS

Bücherbogen am Savignyplatz
Stadtbahnbogen 585.
31 86 95 16.

Studiotour Babelsberg
August-Bebel-Str. 26–53, Potsdam.
(0331) 721 27 55.

Warner Bros Studio Store
Tauentzienstrasse 9.
Map 10 E1.
254 54 0.

FAMOUS FILMS ABOUT BERLIN

Berlin Alexanderplatz
Germany 1931, directed by Phillip Jutzi, based on Alexander Döblin's book.

Berlin Alexanderplatz
GDR 1980, directed by Rainer Werner Fassbinder.

Berlin, Chamissoplatz
GDR 1980, directed by Rudolf Thome.

Berlin – Ecke Schönhauser
GDR 1957, directed by Gerhard Klein.

Berliner Ballade (Berlin Ballad)
American Occupied Zone 1948, directed by Robert Stemmle.

Berlin, die Symphonie einer Grossstadt (Berlin, Symphony of a Great City)
Germany 1927, directed by Walter Ruttmann.

Coming Out
GDR 1988/1989, directed by Heiner Carow.

Der Himmel über Berlin (The Sky Above Berlin)
GDR /France 1987, directed by Wim Wenders.

Die Legende von Paul und Paula (The Legend of Paul and Paula)
GDR 1973, directed by Heiner Carow.

Eins, zwei, drei (One, two, three)
USA 1961, directed by Billy Wilder.

Kuhle Wampe
Germany 1932, directed by Slatan Dudow, script by Bertolt Brecht.

Menschen am Sonntag (Men on Sunday)
Germany 1930, directed by Robert Siodmak and Edgar G Ulmer.

Lola rennt (Run, Lola, Run)
Germany 1998, directed by Tom Tykwer.

Classical Music

BERLIN HAS one of the world's finest orchestras (the Berlin Philharmonic Orchestra) as well as one of the most beautiful concert halls (the Philharmonie). The Berlin Philharmonic has long been pre-eminent among the city's three symphonic orchestras, all of which perform regularly in Berlin. There are three major opera houses to choose from and a smaller one for lovers of the avant-garde. Apart from regular concerts the city offers many festivals, two of the most popular being the Musik-Biennale and the Open Air Festival on Gendarmenmarkt. Smaller concerts are organized year-round in the city's many churches, halls and palaces.

CONCERT HALLS

THE **Philharmonie** is one of Europe's grandest concert halls, with excellent acoustics. The Berlin Philharmonic Orchestra itself was founded in 1882 by a group of 54 ambitious musicians, and it achieved great popularity under the conductor Herbert von Karajan, who stayed at the helm from 1954 through to 1989. The orchestra was taken over by Claudio Abbado, a worthy successor, and from 2002 will be directed by Sir Simon Rattle, an acclaimed British conductor. Tickets for popular programmes quickly sell out, but the more obscure concerts will usually have some seats available. It is easier to obtain tickets when other orchestras such as the Berlin Symphony Orchestra and the Berlin Radio Symphony Orchestra are playing in the Philharmonie.

Chamber orchestras perform special chamber pieces in the smaller **Kammermusiksaal** attached to the bigger hall.

Konzerthaus Berlin, known as the Schauspielhaus (see p65), is another important venue for classical music. The building was restored after World War II and now contains a large concert hall and a smaller room for chamber music. It is one of the best places to hear classical music in elegant surroundings. Two unconventional places that also sometimes put on musical concerts are the **Hochschule der Künste** on Hardenbergerstrasse and the **Staatsbibliothek** (State Library) on Potsdamer Strasse.

Many churches in Berlin also open their doors for concerts throughout the year. For a guide all these events, look up the listings magazines *Tip* or *Zitty* (see p260).

OPERA

AMONG BERLIN'S three major opera houses, the **Staatsoper Unter den Linden** (see p63), now under the leadership of Daniel Barenboim, is a gem. In this beautiful building, painstakingly restored according to Knobelsdorff's original design, performances take place in the Grosser Saal and the Apollo-Saal. The repertoire includes the traditional German classics, Italian opera and to a lesser extent, contemporary pieces.

Komische Oper (see p68), managed by Harry Kupfer, is known for its broad range of lighter opera. Its operas usually have a long run, so you can nearly always find tickets. The ballet produced here is particularly innovative.

Deutsche Oper Berlin on Bismarckstrasse is the only one of the three main opera houses to be a modern building. The interior is a rather plain 1960s style, but the repertoire includes all kinds of music from different periods ranging from major Italian operas and Mozart, to Wagner and Saint Saëns. There is often an exhibition organized in the foyer so the waiting time passes quickly.

A fourth opera house is the **Neuköllner Oper** in the Neukölln district. Less-famous than the others, it is known for its unconventional approach.

CONTEMPORARY MUSIC

THE BERLIN organization **Initiative Neue Music Berlin e.V.** publishes a bulletin every two months containing information about current performances of contemporary music. It always includes **BKA** near Mehringdamm with its **Unerhörte Music** series. The **Akademie der Künste** and **Sender Freies Berlin (SFB)** initiated a project designed to promote contemporary music; it is called *Insel Music* and one of its achievements is a series of concerts organized each November in the Haus des Rundfunks.

FESTIVALS

THE **Berliner Festwochen** takes place throughout the month of September, and every year there is a different theme. Each festival promises a range of exhibitions, theatrical events and concerts, and the most famous orchestras and soloists come to take part each year.

Every other year in March you can also experience the **Musik-Biennale Berlin**, where contemporary music dominates. Numerous world premieres are made here, both of music by new names and that of established composers.

A real treat for opera lovers is the summer festival of opera – Classic Open Air – which is organized on an open stage on Gendarmenmarkt, specially built for the occasion. Another musical feast well worth volunteering for is the Bach-Tage festival, a charming showcase of Baroque music, which takes place every year in July.

OPEN AIR CONCERTS

THERE ARE TWO open stages in Berlin and during the summer months a number of classical concerts are staged. **Waldbühne**, located near the Olympia Stadion, has seating for 20,000, and is the venue for concerts by European youth orchestras. The atmosphere is relaxed and informal, very often with children running around while their parents eat and drink during the shows. After sunset, when the crowds light the candles they have brought for the occasion, the atmosphere becomes quite magical.

After a long period of closure for restoration, the **Parkbühne Wuhlheide** stage is finally open. Although the concerts organized here are every bit as good as the ones held in Waldbühne, the audiences tend to be smaller.

MUSIC IN PALACES AND NOTED BUILDINGS

DURING MUSIC FESTIVALS, recitals are often held in beautiful historic buildings, and a concert in the Berliner Dom *(see p77)*, the Eichen-gallerie in Schloss Charlotten-burg *(see pp154–5)* or Schloss Friedrichsfelde *(see p166)* can be an unforgettable

experience. The **Hochschule der Künste** *(see Concert Halls)* has very good acoustics, but if you prefer a more modern environment, try one of the rooms in **Staatsbibliothek** *(see Concert Halls)* or the concert hall in the **Akademie der Künste** *(see Contem-porary Music).* Occasionally classical concerts are also held in venues that are normally reserved for popular music.

VARIOUS

THE **Musikinstrumenten-Museum** offers concerts on selected Sunday mornings, and as a part of the Alte Musik Live scheme you can listen to the music of old masters played on their original instruments. A special booklet covering all the museum's events is published twice a year and

is available from all theatres, concert halls and music shops.

The **Kulturkaufhaus Duss-mann** shop offers the widest range of music in Berlin, with a stock of over 50,000 titles, and competent staff always ready to help. They also organize numerous small concerts around town, the details of which can be found in a programme available at the check-out. **Gelbe Musik** on Schaperstrasse is also more than a shop; it has a gallery specializing in contemporary music and co-ordinates many concerts and recitals. **Schöne Künste Exkursionen** organizes walks around the city under the theme of Musikstadt Berlin; these take place on Saturday and set off from Bebelplatz, at the back of the opera building on Unter den Linden.

DIRECTORY

CONCERT HALLS

Hochschule der Künste
Hardenbergstrasse 33.
Map 4 E3.
(31 85 23 74.

Kammermusiksaal
Herbert-von-Karajan-Str. 1.
Map 6 D5.
(254 88 132.

Konzerthaus Berlin
(Schauspielhaus)
Gendarmenmarkt 2.
Map 7 A4, 16 D4.
(203 09 21 01/02.

Philharmonie
Herbert-von-Karajan-Strasse 1.
Map 6 D5.
(254 88 132.

Staatsbibliothek
Potsdamer Strasse 33.
(26 60.

OPERA

Deutsche Oper Berlin
Bismarckstrasse 34–37.
Map 3 A4.
(343 84 01.

Komische Oper
Behrenstrasse 55–57.
Map 6 F4, 15 C3.
(47 99 74 00.

Neuköllner Oper
Karl-Marx-Str. 131–133,
Neukölln.
Map 14 F5.
(68 89 07 77.

Staatsoper Unter den Linden
Unter den Linden 7.
Map 7 A3, 16 D3.
(20 35 45 55.

CONTEMPORARY MUSIC

Akademie der Künste
Hanseatenweg 10.
Map 4 F3.
(390 76 0.

Initiative Neue Musik Berlin e. V.
Klosterstrasse 68–70.
Map 8 D3.
(242 45 34.

Sender Freies Berlin (SFB)
Masurenallee 8–14.
Haus des Rundfunks.
Map 1 B5.
(30 31 0.

Unerhörte Musik (BKA)
Mehringdamm 34.
Map 12 F3, 12 F4.
(251 01 12.

FESTIVALS

Musik-Biennale Berlin
Berliner Festspiele GmbH
Budapester Strasse 50.
Map 10 E1.
(254 89 100.

Berliner Festwochen
Berliner Festspiele GmbH
Budapester Strasse 50.
Map 10 E1. (254 89 100.

OUTDOOR CONCERTS

Parkbühne Wuhlheide
An der Wuhlheide.
(53 07 91 90.

Waldbühne
Glockenturmstrasse 1.
(23 08 82 30.

VARIOUS

Gelbe Musik
Schaperstrasse 11.
Map 10 D2.
(211 39 62.

Kulturkaufhaus Dussmann
Friedrichstrasse 90.
(202 50.

Musikinstrument-en-Museum
Tiergartenstrasse 1.
Map 6 D5.
(20 90 55 55.

Schöne Künste Exkursionen
(782 12 02.

TICKETS

Box Office
Nollendorfplatz 7.
(215 54 63.

Kurt-Schumacher-Platz 1.
(496 22 23.

Bahnhofstrasse 83,
Köpenick.
(65 07 06 00.

Concert & theaterkasse city
Knesebeckstrasse 10.
(0800 719 27 10.

Fulhouse Service
Budapester Strasse 48.
Map 10 E1.
(262 05 15.

Rock, Jazz and World Music

To MUSIC LOVERS Berlin can mean anything from techno to the Berlin Philharmonic Orchestra, for the city has a thriving and multi-faceted music industry. Between its classical and ultra-modern extremes the full spectrum of musical taste is catered for, from bar-room blues to rock n' roll and international pop. Whether it's a major event by a world-famous band or a small-scale evening of jazz improvization, you needn't look far to find what you want. The biggest events take place in sports halls and stadiums, but most of the action can be found in discos, bars and the city's various clubs *(see pp270-71)*. There are also a number of cultural centres where you can stop by to listen to modern music. The best way to find something for yourself is to get hold of a copy of the listings magazines *Zitty* or *Tip*, and look out for flyers and leaflet in bars.

BIG CONCERTS

BERLIN IS ALWAYS high up on the list when major pop, rock or jazz bands go on tour. While people flock from all over the country to attend these events, there are a number of smaller events which attract an equally devoted audience. Since the closure of the huge Deutsch-landhalle, the big events take place in **Max-Schmeling-Hall** and the **Velodrom** *(see p273)*. For the really big crowds, events are usually held at the **Olympia Stadion** *(see p176)* which has seating for 100,000. The **Waldbühne** next door has a capacity of 20,000 and hosts both classical orchestras and rock bands. **Parkbühne Wuhlheide** is another equally flexible venue. For detailed information about what's on and where, consult the listings magazines *Zitty* and *Tip* or the websites BerlinOnline and Berlin.de.

OTHER MUSICAL EVENTS

THERE ARE PLENTY of smaller venues in Berlin where concerts are held. Among them are the **Loft** in Metropol on Nollendorfplatz, nearby **Café Swing**, and the famous **SO 36** in Kreuzberg. Schöneberg was notorious in the 1980s for its punk rock scene, but while those days are over, there are still plenty of exciting things on offer today. One of the most popular places in town is **Tempodrom**, which

will soon be moving to its new building (check listings magazines for details).

Columbiahalle, which is located near Columbiadamm, is a well-known location for medium-size events, and so is the **Knaack Club**, a multi-sited venue on Greifswalder Strasse. If you are looking for particularly atmospheric concerts, try the **Passion-kirche**, a church in Kreuzberg. For a whole range of cultural events the **Palais Podewils** *(see p97)* is the place to go. Everything is on offer here from theatrical performances to dance and evenings of jazz improvization – and all in a truly modern style.

Concerts and plays are also organized at the popular **Arena** in Treptow – a very large music hall, dating from the 1920s, which used to be a local bus depot.

JAZZ

JAZZ lovers from all over the world descend on Berlin for the **Jazzfest Berlin**, and its accompanying **Total Music Meeting**, both of which are held each year. The former is more traditional, but the latter is devoted to modern experimental work. "Jazz across the Border" takes place in July; its a festival at which all kinds of borders are crossed, not least those of musical inhibition.

As far as regular clubs are concerned, jazz is still very popular in Berlin, in spite of the pull of its perhaps better

known electronic and techno discotheques. The **A Trane** and **b-flat** are classical bars where you listen to small bands just about every day, and **Flöz**, on the ground floor and basement of a place in Nassauische Strasse, is famous of its excellent acoustics.

Another great venue is **Quasimodo** on Kantstrasse, but its concerts only start after 10pm when performances at Theater des Westens have finished; the vibrations would otherwise disturb the neighbouring audience. The acoustics at Quasimodo are also excellent, which is perhaps just as well as little can be seen through the clouds of cigarette smoke. Two other venues which fit evenings of jazz into their otherwise varied programmes are **Kalkscheune** on Johannisstrasse and **Palais Podewils** on Klostestrasse. Another good venue for enjoying jazz is **Bilderbuch**, on Akazienstrasse.

Apart from the typical, classical jazz clubs, jazz can also be heard in many of the city's smaller bars, like **Schlot** on Kastanienallee or **Harlem** in Prenzlauer Berg. If it's a mixture of soul, rap and jazz you want then head for the **Junction Bar** in Kreuzberg. The **Blue Note** is also a good address in Nollendorfplatz, particularly on Saturdays, while the nearby **pipapo** is a worthy choice on Sunday. The **Badenscher Hof Jazzclub** on Badensche Strasse is another great place for jazz.

WORLD MUSIC

AS A BROADLY cosmopolitan town with an increasingly multi-national population, Berlin is home to a wide variety of music. The SFB4 MultiKulti radio station and Weltmusikfestival Heimak-länge were established here in 1988, and the presence of music from all parts of the world is never that far away.

The **Haus der Kulturen der Welt** on John-Foster-Dulles-Allee is an institution set up by the Berlin Upper Chamber to support this cosmopolitanism, and its main aim is to make non-European cultures more accessible to Germany. As music is one of the best ways of bridging cross-cultural differences, the Haus der Kulturen der Welt organizes all kinds of concerts at its own **Café Global** – one of the best Saturday evening venues for listening to and dancing to music from all over the world. Details of the bands on offer can be found in a booklet which should be available in bookshops and restaurants around town.

A similar organization is the **Werkstatt der Kulturen** on Wissmannstrasse which has been staging all kinds of cultural events for some years now. These include regular concerts and music festivals. Between them, the Haus der

Kulturen der Welt and the Werkstatt are the most reliable providers of world music in town, but you can also find a number of bars and clubs that specialize in the music of one particular nation. Details of these can be found in the listings magazines *Zitty* and *Tip*, and on flyers all over town.

Latin American discos are becoming ever more popular throughout Berlin – **El Barrio** in Tiergarten is one of the city's most popular and best.

Irish music is also well represented in the city, and all you have to do is visit a few pubs. Live music is played in **The Dubliner** on Mondays, Wednesdays and weekends. However, if it's Russian ballads you want then head for the ever popular **Chagall**.

TICKETS

THE PRICE OF TICKETS for major pop concerts can be astronomical, particularly if you want to secure a good seat. At the other extreme, you should be able to get into smaller clubs for between DM10 and 20, but again, if a famous person or band is playing you will have to pay a good deal more. Often you will find the ticket price includes a drink at the bar.

Tickets for major events are likely to sell out quickly and should be booked well in advance; there are numerous ticket offices in the busier parts of town (*see p261*).

If you just want to spend the night at a club you should have no trouble buying a ticket at the door.

DIRECTORY

BIG CONCERTS

Waldbühne
Glockenturmstrasse 1.
Map 1 A4.
23 08 82 30.

Parkbühne Wuhlheide
An der Wuhlheide.
53 07 91 44.

OTHER MUSIC EVENTS

Arena
Einemstrasse 4.
Map 11 A2.
533 73 33.

Café Swing
Nollendorfplatz 3–4.
Map 11 A2.
216 61 37.

Columbiahalle
Columbiadamm 13–21.
698 09.

Knaack Club
Greifswalder Strasse 224.
442 70 61.

Loft (Metropol)
Nollendorfplatz 5.
Map 11 A2.
217 36 80.

Palais Podewils
Klostestrasse 68–70.
Map 8 D3.
24 74 97 77.

Passionskirche
Marheineckeplatz
Map 13 A5.
69 40 12 41.

SO 36
Oranienstrasse 190.
Map 14 E2.
61 40 13 06.

Tempodrom
Am Ostbahnhof, Strasse der Pariser Kommune 8–10.
61 28 42 35.

JAZZ

A Trane
Bleibtreustrasse 1.
Map 3 C5.
313 25 50.

Badenscher Hof Jazzclub
Badensche Strasse 29.
Map 10 D5.
861 00 80.

Rosenthaler Strasse 13.
Map 7 B1.
283 31 23.

Bilderbuch
Akazienstrasse 28.

Map 11 A5.
78 70 60 57.

Blue Note
Courbierestrasse 13.
Map 11 A2.
218 72 48.

Flöz
Nassauische Strasse 37.
Map 9 C5.
861 10 00.

Musik-Café Harlem
Rodebergstrasse 37.
444 56 54.

Jazzfest Berlin
Budapester Strasse 50.
Map 10 E1.
25 48 92 54 .

Junction Bar
Gneisenaustrasse 18.
694 66 02.

Kalkscheune
Johannisstrasse 2.
Map 6 F2.
28 39 00 65.

Palais Podewils
Klostestrasse 68–70.
Map 8 D3.
247 49 6.

pipapo
Grossgörschenstrasse 40.
Map 11 C4.
216 15 43.

Quasimodo
Katzlerstrasse 12a.
312 80 86.

Schlot
Kastanienallee 29.
Map 1 A4.
448 21 60.

Total Music Meeting
Lübecker Strasse 19.
394 17 56.

WORLD MUSIC

Chagall
Kollwitzstrasse 2.
441 58 81.

Haus der Kulturen der Welt & Café Global
John-Foster-Dulles-Allee 10.
Map 5 C3.
39 78 71 75.

El Barrio
Potsdamer Strasse 84.
Map 11 B3.
262 18 53.

The Dubliner
Gleimstrasse 33–35.
261 77 00.

Werkstatt der Kulturen
Wissmannstrasse 32.
Map 14 E5.
622 20 24.

Classical and Modern Dance

WITH SO MUCH ON OFFER in the arts, Berlin is a place where you can spend the early evening watching a ballet or musical, and later go out dancing yourself. The three opera houses have interesting ballet programmes built into their repertoires, and these are performed largely by resident dance companies. The city also attracts international ballet groups, not only during the May and August festivals but throughout the year. These productions are usually held in the Hebbel-Theater on Stresemannstrasse, although in recent years the Tanzfabrik in Kreuzberg has become a centre of contemporary dance. Berlin also has a thriving techno scene, which spills out on to the streets for the annual Love Parade, and a plethora of dance clubs.

CLASSICAL BALLET

ALL THREE BALLET groups working within Berlin's opera houses regularly stage new performances which appeal to a wide variety of audiences. To provide a balance, ballet evenings are often arranged to combine elements of classical and ballet with modern choreography. Recently the Komische Oper (see p68) has turned towards a more modern repertoire, while the Staatsoper Unter den Linden (see p63) focuses on classical work, such as Swan Lake with its traditional choreography.

MODERN DANCE

THE Hebbel-Theater is the customary venue that welcomes foreign avant-garde dance companies. In return for its hospitality, its own productions are staged in co-operation with other dance groups all over the world. Together with Theater am Halleschen Ufer, it organizes the dance festival called "Tanz", which takes place every August. As the seating capacity for both theatres is limited, buying a ticket can be difficult; it is worth booking tickets well in advance.

The Sophiensäle, a theatre now mainly used for drama, also features contemporary and avant-garde dance companies from time to time. Tanzfabrik, based on Möckernstrasse in Kreuzberg, is an excellent stage for all kinds of modern dance, and it also organizes dance workshops as well as popular body-work courses.

The International Choreographic Theatre of Johann Kresnik, in the Volksbühne on Rosa-Luxemburg-Platz (see p263), has earned a great reputation, with many outstanding performances of their productions of Frida Kahlo, Hotel Lux and Malinche.

TANGO

YOU CAN DANCE the tango in Berlin every day of the week. A full schedule could incorporate the Fliegendes Theater on Monday, Kalkscheune on Tuesday, the Red Salon on Wednesday and the Grüner Salon on Thursday (both at Volksbühne) and Friday at the Walzerlinksgestrickt. And for the grand finale on Saturday you can always head for one of the many dance schools. But if that still hasn't satisfied your appetite, Saturday lessons can even be extended to Sunday to prepare yourself for the week ahead.

TECHNO

AMONG ITS MANY artistic claims, Berlin is also the techno capital of Europe, with over a million devotees celebrating the genre at the annual Love Parade. The festival is held at the beginning of July and most of the action takes place around the Tiergarten, but even over the following weekend, after the event has ended, streets all over Berlin are still packed with people dancing. Parties and discos are organized throughout Berlin, and the areas around clubs turn into meeting areas where people exchange news about what's going on elsewhere in the city.

The Love Parade lasts only one weekend, but techno fans can spoil themselves all year round at any of countless clubs, most of which stay open through the night until noon the following day. Tresor is at the very heart of it all; situated in the old vault of a defunct department store (Wertheim on Leipziger Platz). This is where the best DJs in town can now be heard.

Few clubs specialize in a particular kind of music, but most reserve certain days of the week for different styles. Find out where the latest techno outfits can be heard – a good way to start is to get hold of a copy of the free publications Flyer or Party-san, both of which are distributed widely in bars.

The clubs Matrix, Ostgut, Stellwerk and Im Eimer are guaranteed to provide what you're after, and so too is the special techno-room known as Subground, which is located in the subways of Pfefferberg. Techno dominates the menu here, but Subground also caters for music lovers of all kinds.

DISCOS AND OTHER CLUBS

IF IT'S A GOOD old-fashioned disco you're looking for, with happy tunes and a little less of the techno, then Big Eden is the place to go. It was famous before the fall of the Wall and now it's the number one disco in Berlin; movie stars and politicians rub shoulders with the locals and tourists here. For a crowded house with 2000 Watts for 2000 people, head for the Loft (see p268) which is always packed, but if you're no longer a teenager and fancy a bit of retro then a night at the Tränenpalast could be the choice; it's based in the pavilion that served as the former passport control between East and West Berlin (*see p39*). The **Privat Club** is known for arranging a good disco or two, aside from its customary repertoire of jazz.

During the summer, you can dance to pop music in the open air at **Golgatha** in Kreuzberg's Viktoriapark, or in **Die Insel**, a café built on an island in Treptow.

Fou Na Na is one of the best places in town for soul music, salsa and funk, but if it's purely Latin-American rhythms you want, then **Salsa** (*see p269*), **Havanna**, **La Charanga** and **Taba** are the best places to go. The **Akba-Lounge** is another good choice of venue.

Many smaller bars have a space for itchy feet. Lovers of soul and reggae should head for **Fat Cat** or **Lumumba Tanzcafé**, while pop music can be heard in the **Mitte Bar**. For something a little more intimate, the romantic atmosphere of **Sophienclub** might be worth a try.

There are also a few places where you can waltz and experience the ambience of the old dance halls. Among the oldest are **Clärchens Ballhaus** and **Tanzpalast**, which are often frequented by single people.

GAY AND LESBIAN CLUBS

BERLIN GENERALLY maintains a tolerant attitude to people with different sexual orientations. A big day for the gay community is the gigantic parade on Christopher Street Day, which takes place annually at the end of June. On a daily basis, homosexual men and women meet in their own clubs and discos, or during special evenings organized by places normally frequented by heterosexuals. The city's most popular gay discos are **SchwuZ** on Mehringdamm, **Connection** on Fuggerstrasse and **Broken Heart** on Mierendorffstrasse. Gay-only discos are held regularly in Stellwerk (*see Techno*) and other clubs around town.

For lesbians the best clubs are **Die Zwei-Am Wasserturm** and **So 36**, which also admits gay men.

DIRECTORY

MODERN DANCE

Hebbel-Theater
Stresemannstrasse 29.
Map 12 F2.
(25 90 04 27.

Sophiensäle
Sophienstrasse 18.
Map 7 B1.
(283 52 66.

Tanzfabrik
Möckernstrasse 68.
Map 12 E4.
(786 58 61.

Theater am Halleschen Ufer
Hallesches Ufer 32.
Map 12 E2, 12 F2.
(251 06 55.

TANGO

Fliegendes Theater
Hasenheide 54.
Map 13 C5.
(692 21 00.

Kalkscheune
Johannisstrasse 2.
Map 6 F2.
(28 39 00 65.

Walzerlinksgestrickt
Am Tempelhofer Berg 7d.
Map 12 F5.
(69 50 50 00.

TECHNO

Im Eimer
Rosenthaler Strasse 68.
Map 7 B1.

Ostgut
Mühlenstrasse 26–30.

Matrix
Warschauer Platz 18.

Pfefferberg
Schönhauser Allee 176.
(44 38 31 15.

Stellwerk
Danneckerstrasse 1
Friedrichshain.

Tresor
Leipziger Strasse 126a.
Map 6 F5.

DISCOS AND OTHER CLUBS

Akba-Lounge
Sredzkistrasse 64.
(441 14 63.

Big Eden
Kurfürstendamm 202.
Map 9 C2.
(882 61 20.

Clärchens Ballhaus
Augustastrasse 24.
Map 7 A1, 7 B1.
(282 92 95.

Die Insel
Alt Treptow 6.
(53 60 80 20.

Fat Cat
Gormannstrasse 19.
Map 7 C1.
(28 38 92 78.

Fou Na Na
Bachstrasse (S-Bahnbogen 475). **Map** 4 E3.
(391 24 42.

Golgatha
Dudenstrasse 48–64.
Map 12 D5, 12 E5.
(785 24 53.

Havanna
Hauptstrasse 30.
Map 11 A5.

La Charanga
Brüsseler Strasse 3.
(45 49 01 36.

Lumumba Tanzcafé
Steinstrasse 12.
Map 7 C1.
(28 38 54 65

Mitte Bar
Oranienburger Strasse 46.
Map 6 F1.
(283 38 37.

Privat Club
Markthalle Pücklerstrasse 34.
Map 14 F2.
(611 33 02.

Sophienclub
Sophienstrasse 6.
Map 7 B1.
(282 45 52.

Taba
Chausseestrasse 106.
Map 6 F1.
(282 67 95.

Tanzpalast
Kantstrasse 162.
Map 10 D1.
(883 83 64.

Tränenpalast
Reichstagufer 17.
Map 6 D2, 6 F3.
(20 61 00 11.

GAY & LESBIAN DISCOS

Broken Heart
Mierendorffstrasse 21.
Map 2 F2.
(34 50 10 19.

Connection
Fuggerstrasse 33.
Map 10 F2.
(218 14 32.

Die Zwei – Am Wasserturm
Spandauer Damm.
Map 1 A2.
(302 52 60.

SchwuZ
Mehringdamm 61.
Map 12 F4.
(693 70 25.

So 36
Oranienstrasse 190.
Map 14 E2.
(61 40 13 06.

Sport and Recreation

Berlin is a sports-loving town, and every year the major sports events attract a growing number of fans and competitors. The Berlin Marathon, run in September, is now the third largest in the world, its 42-km (26-mile) distance tackled by runners, roller-skaters and the disabled alike. The cup final of the Bundesliga, the German football league, takes place in May in the Olympia Stadion. Crowds of each team's supporters converge on the city a few days before the game, and after the match they all join a huge party for the winners along the Ku'damm. The world tennis élite battle it out during the German Open championship every April.

CYCLING

The flat terrain, numerous parks and countless special routes for cyclists – which reach a total of 850 km (530 miles) – make Berlin a cycle-friendly city. Outside rush hour you can take your bike on S- or U-Bahn trains, which provide easy access to the three most popular routes – along the Havel river, around the Grunewald forest, and around the Müggelsee.

There are many places all over Berlin where you can rent a bike for DM10–20 per day (see p293), provided you leave a deposit, either as cash or a cheque. The best hotels in town also hire out their own bikes for guests. The route from the historic centre of Mitte to the Ku'damm via Tiergarten can be an unforgettable experience.

In January those lovers of two wheels meet during Berliner Sechs-Tage-Rennen in the newly built **Velodrom** on Paul-Heyse-Strasse. You might have some problems buying a ticket as the event is very popular, so give them a call beforehand. For information concerning routes, events, tours, or anything you may need to know about cycling in Berlin, contact the **ADFC (Allgemeiner Deutscher Fahrrad-Club)**.

GOLF

Just about every sporting discipline is catered for in Berlin, and golfing is no exception. The Driving Range golf club is situated in the centre of the town on Chausseestrasse, and during spring and summer it is open from noon until sunset. Entrance to the course is free, but you have to leave a deposit on hiring golf clubs. A bucket of 30 balls costs only DM3. Golf coaching is available either for individuals or in a group.

There are two golf courses within Berlin: the **Golf und Landclub Berlin-Wannsee**, which has a large 18-hole course and a smaller one with 9 holes, and **Berliner Golfclub-Gatow** which only has a 9-hole course. There are a total of 15 golf clubs around Berlin, most of which have excellent restaurants and are situated close to hotels.

SWIMMING POOLS

Public swimming facilities in Berlin are extremely clean and you can always swim there safely. Some of the best places to try are on the Havel river and the city's lakes. Swimming on natural beaches is free, but there are no changing rooms or toilet facilities.

Berlin also has a number of artificial beaches which are all manned by lifeguards. The best known is the **Strandbad Wannsee**, which was built in the 1920s and remains very popular today. Another excellent spot is the **Strandbad Müggelsee**, which also has an area for nude bathing. The entrance fee to these beaches is similar to that of swimming pools – usually around DM6.

One of the most beautiful swimming pool complexes is **Olympia Stadion** (see p176) which was a venue for the 1936 Berlin Olympic Games. A special pool for diving has a 10-m (33-ft) tower with a lift. Alternatively, you can simply sunbathe on the steps and admire the view.

The three most beautiful swimming pools are situated in Mitte, Neukölln and Wilmersdorf. **Stadtbad Mitte**, on Gartenstrasse, is a painstakingly restored building which dates from the 1930s. It has a 50-m (164-ft) pool designed for sporting events as well as recreational swimming. **Stadtbad Charlottenburg**, on the other hand, offers a smaller pool which is more appropriate for relaxation than serious swimming; it is also beautifully decorated with Secessionist paintings. But if it's a swim in luxurious surroundings you want, then take a dive at the **Stadtbad Neukölln**; the extraordinary decorative mosaics, frescos, and marble-and-bronze ornamentation is enough to make you forget why you came here in the first place.

A good day out for the whole family can be had at **"blub" Badeparadies**, situated on Buschkrugallee in the southern part of town. More than simply a pool, this is an aquapark with a 120-m (394-ft) long slide, a wave-pool and diving boards, as well as several saunas.

BADMINTON, SQUASH AND TENNIS

You won't have to travel far in Berlin to find facilities to play badminton, squash or tennis as numerous courts are scattered all over town, from local parks to sophisticated sports centres. It is customary to bring your own sports shoes, but rackets are almost always available to rent.

The entrance fee in most cases includes the use of a sauna. **Fit-Fun Squash und Fitness Center** has 14 courts for squash, and at **Sportoase** there are 18 badminton courts in addition to 8 squash courts. **Tennis & Squash City** offers an opportunity to play tennis on any of its five courts. Other addresses can be found in the telephone directory.

OTHER SPORTS

EVERY WEEKEND in August, John-Foster-Dulles-Allee in Tiergarten is closed to traffic to become a genuine paradise for rollerblade and in-line skaters. If you fancy trying this yourself, there are plenty of shops in the area offering skates and safety equipment at reasonable rates.

If you fancy a boat trip, rowing boats are available for hire at many places along the banks of the lakes. In the Tiergarten you can rent them near Café am Neuen See and around Schlachtensee; the price is usually somewhere around DM15–20 per hour.

FITNESS

THERE ARE ALWAYS new gyms opening and others closing down in Berlin, so your best bet is to check the telephone directory for the most up-to-date listings. At many gyms you can buy a daily card, rather than becoming a member. But if your visit to Berlin is a long one, it may be worth joining. **Jopp-Frauen-**

Fitness-Berlin is one of the best options for women; it has five studios across the city and they are all large and well equipped. The main one is situated on Tauentzienstrasse and has a pleasant terrace overlooking town. A one-day ticket costs DM45 and a carnet, valid for 10 days, can be bought for DM250.

SPECTATOR SPORTS

AS A RULE, Berlin's sports teams tend to be among the country's best, and rank highly in each of their respective leagues. Football matches of Hertha BSC take place in the Olympia Stadion and tickets are usually available at approximately DM12–35.

Alba Berlin is among the top basketball teams in Germany, and its matches in **Max-Schmeling-Halle** can be attended by up to 8,500 fans. For international events it's best to pre-book tickets well in advance, and these can vary between DM20 and 100, depending on the match. Berlin has two very good hockey teams: Berlin-Capitals

and Eisbären Berlin – both of whose matches always sell out of tickets very quickly.

HORSE RACING

LOVERS OF HORSE RACING have two tracks to choose from in Berlin. **Trabrennbahn** in Mariendorf is open all year and the races held there are strictly commercial. **Galopprennbahn Hoppegarten**, on the other hand, has a more approachable feel.

MARATHON

MARATHON RUNNING isn't everyone's cup of tea, but when you see the enormous crowds gathered to run the **Berlin-Marathon** in August, you may well wish you were one of the pack.

The route is one of the fastest in the world, attracting top sponsors and athletes alike; the world record was broken here in 1998. Thousands of viewers gather en route to cheer the runners, rollers and disabled athletes – the latter having their own group which starts before the others.

DIRECTORY

CYCLING

ADFC
Brunnenstrasse 28.
448 47 24.

Velodrom
Paul-Heyse-Strasse.
44 30 44 30.

GOLF

Berliner Golfclub-Gatow
Kladower Damm 182–288
Gatow.
365 77 25.

Golf und Landclub Berlin-Wannsee
Golfweg 22.
806 70 60.

SWIMMING

"blub" Badeparadies
Buschkrugallee 64.
609 06 0.

Stadtbad Charlottenburg
Krumme Strasse 9–10.
34 30 32 14.

Stadtbad Mitte
Gartenstrasse 5.
Plan 7 A1.
30 88 09 10.

Stadtbad Neukölln
Ganghoferstrasse 3.
68 24 98 12.

Strandbad Müggelsee
Fürstenwalder Damm 838.
648 77 11.

Strandbad Wannsee
Wannseebadweg 25.
803 54 50.

BADMINTON, SQUASH, TENNIS

FitFun Squash und Fitness Center
Uhlandstrasse 194.
312 50 82.

Sportoase
Stromstrasse 11–17.
Plan 4 F1, 4 F2.
394 50 94.

Tennis & Squash City
Brandenburgische Strasse 53.
Map 9 A3, 9 B5.
873 90 97.

MARATHON

Berlin-Marathon
Informations Bureau
Waldschulallee 34.
302 53 70.

SPECTATOR SPORTS

Max-Schmeling-Halle
Am Falkplatz.
44 30 44 30.

FITNESS

Jopp-Frauen-Fitness-Berlin
Tauentzienstrasse 13.
Map 10 E1.
235 17 00
(central switchboard).

Karl-Liebknecht-Strasse 13.
Map 7 C2.

Schlossstrasse 126.
Map 2 E3, 2 E4.

HORSE RACING

Galopprennbahn Hoppegarten
Goetheallee 1.
(03342) 389 30.
4–10pm Sat-Sun.

Trabrennbahn Mariendorf
Mariendorfer Damm 222,
Tempelhof.
740 12 12.
6:30pm Wed, 1:30pm Sun.

CHILDREN IN BERLIN

WHEN IT COMES to entertainment, people of all ages are catered for in Berlin, and children are no exception. There are numerous shops, theatres and cinemas to keep them occupied, not to mention circuses and zoological gardens. Additionally, there is the Deutsches Technikmuseum

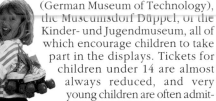
One of Berlin's young roller skaters

(German Museum of Technology), the Museumsdorf Düppel, or the Kinder- und Jugendmuseum, all of which encourage children to take part in the displays. Tickets for children under 14 are almost always reduced, and very young children are often admitted for free. Restaurants often have special areas for toddlers.

The Potsdam train, always a favourite among children

INFORMATION

BERLIN IS VERY welcoming to its younger visitors. Families with children are entitled to public transport discounts, and children can travel free or at a reduced rate, depending on their age. For detailed information on the discounts and opportunities for children, contact the **Berlin Tourismus Marketing GmbH**. From this organization you can obtain the so-called Ferienpass, valid for the whole summer, which entitles the holder to all kinds of reductions around town. For girls there is a special pocket diary on offer, called Berta, which has much information and advice about current events.

ZOOLOGICAL GARDENS

ONE OF BERLIN'S zoological gardens can be visited the moment you arrive in town, as it is located opposite the Zoo railway station. The **Zoologischer Garten** offers extensive parkland and many animal enclosures, as well as an excellent aquarium with the biggest collection of aquatic fauna in the world.

The second zoo, **Tierpark Berlin** in Friedrichsfelde, isn't quite so convenient but it is much bigger and can still be reached by U-Bahn. Covering a wide area around Schloss Friedrichsfelde, the Tierpark is the largest park in Europe.

Apart from these zoological gardens, a lot of the parks in Berlin contain mini-zoos where many different kinds of animals can be seen. In a garden behind the Märkisches Museum, for example, you can see a family of bears.

As well as the more exotic animals, however, it is also possible to see the familiar favourites. Small children will love the **Kinderbauernhof Görlitzer Bauernhof**, which has a collection of domestic animals. Here geese, pigs and rabbits run happily around the Görlitzer Park.

MUSEUMS

GENERALLY SPEAKING, Berlin's museums are well set up for children. Perhaps the most entertaining is the **Deutsches Technikmuseum** (see pp 138–9) where children can take part in all kinds of interesting experiments. The **Museum für Völkerkunde** (see p170)

also prepares special exhibitions for children. On some days you can take part in a game with Mexican papier-mâché dolls, on others you can participate in a Japanese ceremonial bath. A visit to the **Museumsdorf Düppel** is an excellent way to show a child the workings of a medieval village. The Museum für Naturkunde (see p109) is another fun place for children, particularly the dinosaur sections and the dioramas of animals in their natural habitats. The **Kindermuseum Labyrinth** is another favourite.

Two other great places to go are the **Puppentheatermuseum**, and the **Teddy Museum Berlin**, whose collection has now reached several thousand. The puppet museum is always lively, and offers a chance for children to take part in minor performances. For more information about museum events try to get hold of the brochure Museumpädagogischer Dienst. Exhibitions and events change regularly, but you are bound to find something of interest.

Children admiring Neptune's Fountain by the Town Hall

A visit to the medieval village at Museumsdorf Düppel

THEATRES

ESTABLISHED IN 1969, **Grips Theater** is probably the most interesting theatre for children and teenagers. Its independent and ambitious programme attracts many spectators and one of its performances, *Linie 1*, was made into a film. Other venues worth trying are the **carrousel-Theater an der Parkaue**, **Theater o.N.**, **Zaubertheater Igor Jedlin** and the **Puppentheater Berlin**. Another option is to go to one of the city's many circuses, all of which prepare their programmes with children in mind.

SPORTS

ICE-SKATING IN WINTER and roller-skating in summer are popular in Berlin, and football and swimming are popular year-round. You can swim in rivers, lakes and swimming pools (Hotline **Berliner Bäderbetriebe** offers useful information) but "blub" Badeparadies *(see p273)* is the best place for children. Each district has its own ice-skating rink, but the **Eisstadion Berlin Wilmersdorf** is outstanding with its 400-m (1,312-ft) run and large ice-hockey rink. **FEZ Wuhlheide** offers a special daily programme for kids.

OTHER ENTERTAINMENT

AN ASCENT OF the Fernsehturm (television tower) at Alexanderplatz *(see p98)* is a great way to treat a child, with cake and juice waiting in its rotating café, perhaps for afternoon tea. A lift in the Funkturm (radio tower) in the Messegelände *(see p175)* offers an excellent view of the city, from a slightly lower height. Another great view can be had from the giant Ferris wheel in Rummel am Plänterwald. From April to October you can ride on a mountain railway, visit the hall of mirrors, or have a ride on a carousel – and the **Berliner Gruselkabinett** (Room of Fear) is enough to frighten anybody.

For an out-of-the-ordinary experience, you can't go wrong at either the **Zeiss-Planetarium** or the **Planetarium am Insulaner**. A programme of wonderful shows allows you to explore the known universe and have a good look at the stars.

DIRECTORY

INFORMATION

Berlin Tourismus Marketing GmbH
Am Karlsbad 11.
(264 74 80.

ZOOLOGICAL GARDENS

Kinderbauernhof Görlitzer Bauernhof
Wiener Strasse 59
(in Görlitzer Park).
(611 74 24.

Tierpark Berlin
Am Tierpark 125,
Lichtenberg.
(51 53 10.

Zoologischer Garten
Hardenbergplatz 9,
Charlottenburg.
(25 40 10.

MUSEUMS

Kindermuseum Labyrinth
Osloer Strasse 12.
(494 53 48.
○ 9am–1pm Mon–Fri, also 2–6pm Tue–Fri, 1–6pm Sat, 11am–6pm Sun.

Museumsdorf Düppel
Clauertstrasse 11.
(802 66 71 or 802 33 10.
○ Apr–Oct: 3–7pm Thu, 10am–5pm Sun and holidays .

Puppentheater-Museum Berlin
Karl-Marx-Strasse 135.
(687 81 32.
○ 9am–1pm & 3–5pm Mon–Fri, 11am–5pm Sun.

Teddy Museum Berlin
Kurfürstendamm 147.
(893 39 65.
○ 3–6pm Wed–Fri.

THEATRES

carrousel-Theater an der Parkaue
Parkaue 29.
(55 77 52 52.

Grips Theater
Altonaer Strasse 22.
(39 74 74 77.

Puppentheater Berlin
Haubachstrasse 26.
(342 19 50.

Theater o.N.
Kollwitzstrasse 53.
(440 92 14.

Zaubertheater Igor Jedlin
Roscherstrasse 7.
(323 77 77.

SPORTS

Berliner Bäderbetriebe
((01803) 10 20 20.

Eisstadion Berlin Wilmersdorf
Fritz-Wildung-Strasse 9.
(824 10 12.

FEZ Wuhlheide
Ander Wuhlheide,
Köpenick.
(53 07 15 04.

OTHER ENTERTAINMENT

Berliner Gruselkabinett
Schöneberger Strasse 23a.
Map 12 E1.
(26 55 55 46.

Planetarium am Insulaner
Münsterdamm 90.
(790 09 30.

Zeiss-Planetarium
Prenzlauer Allee 80.
(42 18 45 12.

SURVIVAL GUIDE

PRACTICAL INFORMATION

BERLIN IS A tourist-friendly city, so you shouldn't have too much difficulty getting around. Many Germans speak English and Berliners as a rule are welcoming to newcomers. Cash machines, telephones and parking meters all have clear instructions, and public transport is of the highest standard *(see pp292–3).* For reduced fares on public transport, buy

Berlin tourist information sign

yourself a daily or weekly travel card, or a Welcome Card which also gives you reduced access to many museums. There are plenty of information centres in the busiest areas of town, and a number of different listings magazines and brochures are available for tourists. If you have access to the internet, BerlinOnline will point you in the right direction.

Entrance ticket for some of Berlin's historic buildings

MUSEUMS AND HISTORIC BUILDINGS

THERE ARE OVER 150 museums and galleries in Berlin, but exhibitions change and collections move continually. This guide covers the most important places, but plenty of information is also available on lesser-known museums and galleries. A tourist information office could be your first port of call, but better still is the museum information centre itself, run by **Museumpädagogischer Dienst Berlin**. Details of current and forthcoming exhibitions can be picked up here, including

information on seasonal events, like the bi-annual Lange Nacht der Museen, when museums stay open until midnight. A good information line is the **Info-Telefon der Staatlichen Museen zu Berlin** and there are also information centres devoted to the Pergamonmuseum and the Sanssouci complex in Potsdam. Contact the **Besucherbetreuung der Schlösser und Gärten Potsdam-Sanssouci** for more details.

Museums and historic buildings are usually open Tuesday to Sunday, from 10am to 5pm (sometimes 6pm). Some museums, however, close on another day instead of Mondays. For reduced entrance prices, you may want to get hold of the Museums-Pass, which allows three days' unlimited access to the major museums. This pass is sold in the **Europa-Center** and **Brandenburg Gate** information centres. It can be used at all the national museums, including the whole Museum

Island complex, the Kulturforum, Museumszentrum Dahlem and four additional institutions in Charlottenburg (Ägyptisches Museum, Galerie der Romantik, Sammlung Berggruen, Museum für Vor- und Frühgeschichte). In this case, the Museums-Pass is like a one-day ticket, allowing you to visit all the sites in the same complex.

Another option is the Welcome Card. This entitles you to free public transport for three days within Berlin and Potsdam, and a discount on many museums. Each Welcome Card is valid for one adult and up to three children.

OPENING HOURS

OFFICES IN BERLIN usually open from 9am until 6pm, with an hour's lunch break, but many people in the east of the city still work to the old timetable of 8am till 4 or 5pm. Smaller shops open from 9:30 or 10am until 8pm, and on Saturdays most shops close at 4pm. The majority of shops are also open on Sundays in the period leading up to Christmas, and opening hours are extended during the week. Bank hours are 9am until 3pm (Monday and Wednesday), 6pm (Tuesday and Thursday) and 1pm (Friday).

TOURIST INFORMATION

THERE ARE MANY excellent tourist information centres in Berlin. The two biggest are at the **Europa-Center** and the **Brandenburg Gate**, but others can be found at **Tegel Airport**, in the KaDeWe department store

A modern rickshaw providing alternative transport on Berlin's streets

(see p149) and in a branch of Dresdner-Bank on Unter den Linden. The **Potsdam Information** office is in the centre of Potsdam, on Friedrich-Ebert-Strasse.

For additional up-to-the-minute news, you can also turn to the Internet; **Berlin-Online**, which is managed by **Berlin Tourismus Marketing** is a very reliable source of information for tourists.

ENTERTAINMENT

THE THREE BEST magazines devoted to cultural events are *Zitty, Tip* and *Berlin-Programm*, all of which cover the major (as well as minor) concerts, exhibitions and lectures held throughout Berlin. The very latest news can also be obtained from tourist information centres and the Internet, the most popular site being Berlin-Online. There are many ticket offices all over town where you can pre-book tickets *(see p261)*, some of them offering excellent bargain deals. On-the-day tickets can often be bought at half price.

Popular listings magazines

Guided bus tour offering an overview of Berlin and its environs

GUIDED TOURS

THERE ARE MANY bus tours available in Berlin, each of which, in 3 or 4 hours, introduces you to the city's chief historic buildings. A single ticket usually allows you to get off at any stage and rejoin the tour at different stops. However, if you want to save some money, the public transport bus No. 100 follows a similar route *(see p295)*. If you would rather go on foot, walking tours are also possible – these provide a more intimate tour of the city, stopping at all the major landmarks and museums. Organized trips to buildings just nearing completion can also be arranged. For information on these and other tours, visit the red Info-Box, currently on the corner of Leipziger and Postdamer Platz. If you are in Potsdam you can ride a train around town, starting outside the Kutscherhaus Inn in Sanssouci.

DISABLED VISITORS

NOT ALL OF BERLIN'S streets and shops have been altered to cater for the disabled, but the majority of theatres and galleries do have the required facilities. Detailed information can be obtained from the **Informations-und Beratungsgruppe für Behinderte** on Landesamt für Zentrale Soziale Aufgaben. Three other organizations to turn to are the **Berliner Behindertenverband**, **Service-Ring-Berlin** and **Movado**. Give them a call if you want to hire a wheelchair, a special bus, or someone to help you for the day.

Additional Information

A typical kiosk selling newspapers, drinks and cigarettes

VISAS AND CUSTOMS

A VALID PASSPORT IS necessary for all visitors to Germany. Visas are not required for citizens of EU countries. A list, available from all German embassies, specifies other countries whose nationals do not need a visa for visits of less than 90 days. Non-EU citizens wishing to stay in Germany for longer than three months will need a special visa, available from German consulates. These are generally difficult to obtain and preference is given to people on business trips or to students taking up scholarships.

On arrival in Germany, you will not be charged duty on personal articles. As in other European countries, no drugs or weapons may be brought across the border. The amount of cigarettes and alcohol allowed in or out of the country is restricted. Adults resident outside the EU can bring up to 200 cigarettes (50 cigars, or 250g of tobacco), and one litre of spirits (or two litres of wine).

Antique pump

VAT REFUND

I F YOU BUY non-edible goods in Berlin you are entitled to a VAT refund *(Mehrwersteuer)*, unless you are a citizen of another EU country. Individual shops differ on the minimum taxable amount, but it is usually somewhere around DM100. If you enter a shop with a Tax-Free sign outside, ask for a special form or Tax-Free cheque (you will need to present your passport). This form must be stamped when you go through Customs – but do be prepared to show your goods, which must still be in their original packing (you won't be able to claim a refund on anything that has been opened or which has been used). The tax is refunded either at the border or sent to the address on the envelope containing the cheque. Make sure you leave the right details with Customs staff – chasing old claims is a time-consuming and often fruitless task.

A Welcome Card with a small information brochure

INFORMATION FOR YOUNG PEOPLE

B EFORE YOU ARRIVE in Berlin it is worth getting hold of an ISIC card (or International Student Identity Card). This entitles you to a 50 per cent reduction in some museums, and to occasional discounts on theatre, plane and rail tickets. For similar reasons you might want to have a GO25 or EURO<26 card, both of which entitle you to a variety of reductions. These cards are only valid in Europe, but can earn you up to 300,000 different discounts.

A selection of Berlin's most popular daily newspapers

NEWSPAPERS

N EWSPAPERS CAN BE bought in shops all over Berlin, but mostly they are sold by the city's numerous street vendors. In the evenings you will also find them on sale in bars and cafés. The most popular titles are the *Berliner Zeitung, Der Tagesspiegel*, the *Berliner Morgenpost* and *BZ*. Foreign language papers can be found all over the city, especially at airport and railway kiosks. Some of the major department stores also sell newspapers and magazines. A whole range of English-language books and newspapers is available at the British Bookshop at Mauerstrasse No. 83–4 in Mitte.

Theatre ticket office and an old-fashioned post with posters

TELEVISION AND RADIO

Y OU MAY find yourself spoiled for choice when it comes to television channels in Germany. Apart from the national ARD and ZDF there are many regional and private channels (Berlin has its own, alongside RTL, RTL2, SAT1 and PRO7). You can also pick up special interest channels, like DSF for sport and VIVA or VIVA2 for music. In addition to these there is even an option for Turkish programmes in Berlin, and thanks to cable and satellite television you can easily tune into foreign programmes in English, American, French and many other languages. In hotels the channels mainly cover the news, music and sport. For radio news in English, you can tune into Info-Radio (93.1 MHz), the BBC World Service (90.2 MHz), or the very popular SFB4 Multi-Kulti (106.8 MHz), which transmits in a number of different languages.

TIME

G ERMANY IS IN the Central-European time zone, which means that Berlin is one hour ahead of Greenwich Mean Time; six hours ahead of US Eastern Standard Time, and 11 hours behind Australian Eastern Standard Time.

ELECTRICAL EQUIPMENT

M OST ELECTRICAL sockets carry 220V, although in bathrooms the voltage may be slightly lower for safety reasons. Plugs are all of the standard continental type, with two round pins. A European travel adaptor (buy it before you leave home), will allow you to use electric appliances.

EMBASSIES AND CONSULATES

U NTIL THE UNIFICATION of Germany, many countries had an Embassy in Eastern Berlin and a Consulate in the West. Currently, because of the government's move from Bonn to Berlin, many countries have employed top architects to build luxurious embassies in the central part of the town; as a result, the addresses listed here are liable to change. If you are in any doubt, check at a tourist information point or in the telephone directory.

PUBLIC CONVENIENCES

T HERE ARE PLENTY of public toilets in Berlin, but you can also use the facilities in museums, stores and cafés. In some places the convenience comes with a charge, usually around 50 pfennigs. Men's toilets are marked by the word *"Herren"* or a triangle with the vertex pointing downwards; ladies', by the word *"Damen"* or *"Frauen"*, or a triangle with its vertex pointing upwards.

A refurbished antique public convenience in Kreuzberg

Security and Health

Berlin police insignia

GONE ARE THE DAYS when demonstrations were held against the influx of foreign nationals, for Berlin is now a broadly cosmopolitan city. Nevertheless, as with all major European destinations, you should always be careful with your wallet, particularly on public transport during rush hours. If you do run into trouble, or simply need advice, you can always get help from the police. For minor health problems, which don't require a doctor, advice from a competent chemist is often sufficient.

Policeman   Policewoman

PERSONAL PROPERTY

UNFORTUNATELY, TOURISTS are more frequently targeted by thieves than any other group, which is why all valuables should be kept in a hotel safe. Major robberies are rare in Berlin, but pickpockets are active, particularly on the U-Bahn. If you are travelling by car, don't leave sound equipment or luggage in open view, and try to use a parking lot or hotel garage when possible. Zoo railway station is notorious for its drug pushers, so be careful there late at night. Like most big cities around the world, few of the S- and U-Bahn stations are pleasant after dark, but these are often patrolled by guards with dogs – if you need assistance, don't hesitate to turn to them. There are also panic buttons installed on each platform, to be used in the event of emergency.

Before you set off for Berlin, it is advisable to buy insurance, and, if you are unlucky enough to be the victim of street crime, you must report it to the police straight away. Remember to obtain a statement confirming what was stolen – you will need this when it comes to making your insurance claim.

If you spot a fire, phone the **Fire Brigade**, or *Feuerwehr*, or use one of the bright-red public fire alarms placed strategically around Berlin.

A public fire alarm

LOST PROPERTY

THERE IS ONE central bureau for lost property in Berlin (the **Zentrales Fundbüro**), and this is where anything left in public is deposited. It is worth noting, however, that the BVG (Berliner Verkehrs-Betriebe) has its own office (the **Fundbüro der BVG**) so that's where you should go if you think that you've left something on a bus or tram or in the U-Bahn. Some items left on S-Bahn trains may also be sent to the **Fundbüro der Deutschen Bahn AG**.

WOMEN TRAVELLING ON THEIR OWN

IN BERLIN IT IS quite normal for women to go to theatres, bars and restaurants on their own. You won't find yourself in danger during the day, but some basic precautions should be taken late at night, when it is preferable to avoid empty platforms or S-Bahn and U-Bahn trains. Night buses are a much safer option, and if something should go wrong the driver can always call the **police** with his radio. The safest, and

Police boats patrolling the water 24-hours a day

One of a popular chain of chemists in Berlin's city centre

most expensive, way to travel is by taxi. If you are determined to walk alone in a park or in one of the quieter districts, is is best to do so during daylight hours only. For all kinds of advice there is a **Confidential Help-Line for Women**.

MEDICAL CARE AND INSURANCE

CITIZENS OF THE EU do not have to buy special insurance to cover emergency treatment, but non-EU visitors should do so. In case of sudden illness you can call an

Symbol for *Apotheke*
(pharmacy)

ambulance, but if the state of the patient allows, then drive them to the nearest Emergency Room. If the complaint is minor, a chemist should be able to help. Chemists, such as **Bären-Apotheke**, usually keep the same hours as other shops, but there are always a few places open overnight. There is a special telephone line offering **Information about Chemists**, but in an emergency you can always call the police. Other telephone helplines include a

Narcotics Emergencies service, as well as an **Emergency Poison Help-Line**, and a **Confidential Help-Line for Spiritual and Religious Support**. Most foreign embassies will be able to tell you which doctors are able to speak your language.

German police van, a common sight around the city

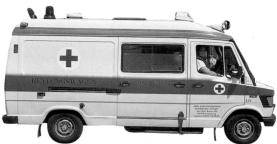

Rettungswagen or ambulance bearing the red cross

DIRECTORY

EMERGENCY SERVICES

Fire Brigade and Ambulance
[112.

Police
[110.

DRK-Rettungsdienst (German Red Cross)
[85 00 55.

Ambulance
[31 00 31.

Narcotics Emergencies
[192 37.

Emergency Poison Help-Line
[192 40.

Confidential Help-Line for Women
[615 42 43.

Confidential Help-Line for Religious Support (Telefon-Seelsorge)
[0800 111 02 22.

CHEMISTS

Information about Chemists
[0 11 41.

Bären-Apotheke
[40 91 11 12.

LOST PROPERTY

Zentrales Fundbüro
Platz der Luftbrücke 6.
[69 95.

Fundbüro der BVG
Alexanderplatz.
[25 63 13 22.

Fundbüro der Deutschen Bahn AG
Mittelstrasse 20.
[29 72 96 12.

Banking and Local Currency

Reise Bank
Logo of ReiseBank

Only a few years ago, some credit cards, like VISA, were far less popular in Germany than they were in other countries, but recently things have started to change. Now, on the whole, tourists have few problems using credit cards at German banks. There are plenty of cash machines available, as well as numerous banks and Bureaux de Change for exchanging foreign currencies.

CHANGING MONEY

There are no restrictions on the amount of cash you can bring into Germany, but most visitors use travellers' cheques or debit cards for safety.

Cash can be exchanged at banks and Bureaux de Change (*Wechselstuben*). The major banks, such as **Berliner Bank** and **ReiseBank**, usually have similar rates of exchange, but some charge a commission; be sure to ask how much before commencing your transaction. Banks have limited office hours, so try to get to one immediately on arrival at the airport or station.

Bureaux de Change are often located close to railway stations and other places frequented by tourists. **Thomas Cook Foreign Exchange** and **American Express** are among the best known places for exchanging travellers' cheques. Other Bureaux de Change can be found near the Bahnhof Zoo railway station on Joachimstaler Strasse, between Hardenbergstrasse and Kurfürstendamm.

You can also exchange cash at hotel reception desks, but this should be a last resort as their rates tend to be poor.

A typical cash machine

TRAVELLERS' CHEQUES

Travellers' cheques are a secure method of carrying money, with the advantage that you can change as much or as little as you need. Keep your receipts separate from the cheques themselves for added security. It may be convenient to carry cheques denominated in German marks.

At many of the larger hotels you can pay for your room with travellers' cheques. For most other purchases, however, it is easier to use cash.

DEBIT AND CREDIT CARDS

Credit cards can be used in most larger hotels, shops and restaurants. A sign on the door should tell you which cards are accepted – **VISA**, **American Express**, **Euro-MasterCard** and **Diner's Club** are most frequently used. Some restaurants or cafés require a minimum purchase to use a credit card – a figure usually around DM50. If you're only ordering a snack, check that you have

---

DIRECTORY

BANKS AND BUREAUX DE CHANGE

American Express
Bayreuther Strasse 37.
📞 21 47 62 92.

Friedrichstrasse 172.
📞 20 17 400.

Berliner Bank
Tegel Airport.
📞 417 78 10.
🕐 8am–10pm.

ReiseBank
Bahnhof Zoo.
📞 881 71 17.
🕐 7:30am–10pm Mon–Sat, 8am–9pm Sun.

Ostbahnhof
📞 296 43 93 or 426 70 29.
🕐 7am–7:30pm Mon–Fri, 8am–noon, 12:30pm–4pm Sat & Sun.

Thomas Cook Foreign Exchange
Friedrichstrasse 56.
📞 20 16 59 16.

LOST CARDS AND CHEQUES

American Express
📞 (069) 97 97 10 00.

EuroCard
📞 (069) 74 09 87.

Euro-MasterCard
📞 (069) 33 19 10.

Diner's Club
📞 (05921) 86 12 34.

VISA
📞 (0800) 814 91 00.

One of the city's many Bureaux de Change

some cash just in case your card is not accepted.

In the centre of Berlin it is easy to find cash machines, but many of them accept only the **EuroCard**. Others display the symbols of compatible cards, too. Compare the symbol on your card with those displayed to see if it will work.

If your cheques or card go missing, contact the bank or card issuer immediately.

CURRENCY

THE GERMAN MARK or Deutsch Mark (DM) will remain as the German currency until the year 2002. After that, as the next phase in the European Monetary Union, the Euro will be used as the standard currency. The Euro is already available as an alternative currency, but very few businesses accept it yet.

Bank Notes
German bank notes come in the following denominations: 5, 10, 20, 50, 100, 200, 500, 1000 and 2000 Marks. Five-Mark bank notes are rare, and 1000- and 2000-Mark notes can be very difficult to change. The notes differ in size: as a rule, the larger the bank note, the higher the monetary value.

DM 5

DM 10

DM 20

DM 50

DM 100

DM 200

DM 500

10 Pfennig

DM 1

DM 2

DM 5

5 Pfennig

2 Pfennig

1 Pfennig

Coins
Coins fall into the following denominations: 1, 2, 5, 10, 20 and 50 Pfennigs plus 1, 2 and 5 Marks. 1-, 2-, 5- and 10-Pfennig coins are copper coloured, while the rest are silver. For local calls from public phones, use 10-Pfennig coins.

Communications

Logo for Deutsche Telekom

THE POSTAL AND telecommunications services in Germany are both very efficient. You may have to wait a minute or two at the post office, but letters addressed within the country are usually delivered within 24 hours. Making a telephone call certainly shouldn't be difficult: public telephones stand on just about every street corner, and many restaurants and cafés have phone booths of their own. U-Bahn and S-Bahn stations always have a telephone or two, and often a mailbox to post your letters.

A typical Deutsche Telekom public telephone booth in Berlin

USING THE TELEPHONE

THERE ARE VARIOUS types of public phone booths in Berlin, all of which are owned by Deutsche Telekom. The oldest is the coin-operated telephone, which requires a minimum of 30 pfennigs to make a call. The 10-pfennig piece is the smallest coin it accepts, and if you insert a large number of coins it will give you back whatever coins you haven't used.

Telephone cards are far more convenient to use, and these are sold at all post offices. When using a card-operated

telephone, your credits are displayed on a panel beside the receiver, so you should have plenty of warning before your card runs out and you need to buy a new one.

There are also a few public phones which accept credit cards. Most of these are in the busy centre of town. As with a phone card, all you have to do is place your credit card in the phone, which will then ask you for your PIN (personal identification number).

Many public phones have their own numbers and accept incoming calls, so you can be called back if your card or

money runs out. Every public phone should also have a set of phone directories.

Charges depend on the type of call (local or international) and the time of day. Early mornings, evenings and weekends have the cheapest rates.

Making telephone calls from your hotel room is usually the least economical option.

USING A COIN TELEPHONE

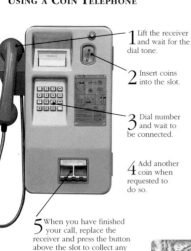

1 Lift the receiver and wait for the dial tone.

2 Insert coins into the slot.

3 Dial number and wait to be connected.

4 Add another coin when requested to do so.

5 When you have finished your call, replace the receiver and press the button above the slot to collect any unused coins.

USING A CARD TELEPHONE

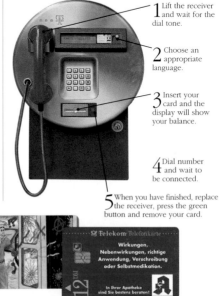

1 Lift the receiver and wait for the dial tone.

2 Choose an appropriate language.

3 Insert your card and the display will show your balance.

4 Dial number and wait to be connected.

5 When you have finished, replace the receiver, press the green button and remove your card.

One of many telephone cards available, complete with instructions

Entrance to the post office (Deutsche Post) on Budapester Strasse

POSTAL SERVICES

GERMAN POST OFFICES are difficult to miss with their distinctive yellow Deutsche Post signs. Mailboxes, too, are an eye-catching yellow.

As in other European countries, you can send registered letters, parcels, telegrams and money orders from the post office. In addition to stamps, a number of products are sold here, too, including telephone cards and the usual variety of postal stationery. Local postcards are also available, as are limited-edition German stamps.

German postage stamps

SENDING A LETTER

STAMPS FOR LETTERS and cards can be bought at the post office, but sometimes they are sold together with cards, and there are also special stamp machines around town. When posting a letter, always check the signs on the mailbox. Some boxes are divided, with one side accepting only mail destined within Berlin.

POST OFFICES

POST OFFICES IN Berlin usually open from 8am until 6pm during the week, and until noon on Saturdays. Branches with extended hours, including Sundays, can be found at the airports and major railway stations. Poste restante letters can be collected from **Budapester Strasse** post office, which is open until midnight, every single day. Two other major post office branches are at **Flughafen Tegel** and **Bahnhof Friedrichstrasse.**

A rare antique mailbox, predating the contemporary yellow boxes

Information about collection times

Slot for local letters

Slot for other letters

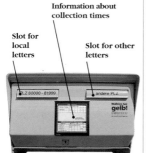

Typical Berlin-style mailbox found on street corners

Operating instructions

Buttons for different kinds of stamp

Slot for collecting stamps

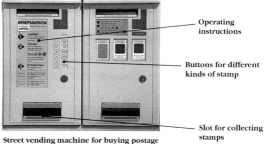

Street vending machine for buying postage stamps as well as telephone cards

IMPORTANT NUMBERS

- Germany country code 49.
- Berlin area code 030.
- Potsdam area code 0331.
- National directory inquiries 11 8 33.
- International directory inquiries 11 8 34.
- Operator 1 11 41.
- Police 110.

- To make an international call, dial 00, wait for the dialling tone, then dial the country code, area code and number, omitting the initial 0. Country codes: UK 44; Eire 353; Canada and US 1; Australia 61; South Africa 27; New Zealand 64.

GETTING TO BERLIN

BERLIN LIES at the heart of Europe and has excellent rail and air links with the rest of the continent. Its three airports receive regular flights from major European cities as well as North America, the

A Lufthansa aeroplane

Middle East and Southeast Asia. Likewise Lufthansa, the German national carrier, offers flights to destinations around the world. The railway network is as good as

anywhere in Europe, and takes you right to the centre of Berlin. One of the cheapest ways to travel to the city is by international coach, although this is usually the slowest form of transport. If you are travelling by car, the *Autobahn* (motorway) leads to the Berliner Ring (Berlin Circular Road), from where a number of exits are signposted to the city centre.

Airport information signs, directing passengers to various services

ARRIVING BY AIR

ALTHOUGH BERLIN receives numerous flights from destinations in Europe, Asia and North America, Frankfurt is still Germany's chief intercontinental airport. All this will change with the expansion of Berlin's second airport at Schönefeld, which currently handles mainly Asian and chartered flights. For the time being, however, Tegel Airport is Berlin's busiest terminal with its endless traffic from Europe and North America.

The most frequent flights are made by **Lufthansa** (the German national carrier), **American Airlines** and **British Airways**, but the airport is also used by Air France, Alitalia, KLM, Polish Airlines LOT, Iberia and many

others. For flight information either telephone the airport directly or contact your individual carrier. Otherwise, most travel agents should be able to supply you with details of arrivals and departures.

A third airport lies near the centre of Berlin at Tempelhof, but this caters for domestic and private flights only.

TICKETS

WHEN PLANNING your trip to Berlin, it is worth shopping around for a ticket, as there are various deals on offer. It is hard to choose between the airlines, as each company offers good deals and discounts throughout the year; children, young people and senior citizens can sometimes fly at reduced rates.

Bear in mind that prices vary depending on when you book your ticket. By far the best option is the APEX return which has to be booked several weeks in advance. As a rule, the earlier you book the ticket, the cheaper the fare. However, a lot of companies sell flights on the Internet, and,

Destinations listings on the departures board

if you are willing to travel at short notice, you can occasionally find a last-minute bargain.

TEGEL AIRPORT

TEGEL AIRPORT is located conveniently within Berlin, only 5 miles (8 km) from the city centre. It has one terminal, designed for maximum convenience. In the main hall you can find an information point, a bank with Bureau de Change and a post office, as well as a number of shops for gifts, souvenirs and newspapers.

The city centre can be reached easily by bus or taxi, both of which stop in front of the main hall. Bus No. 109 stops at Bahnhof Zoologischer

Tegel Airport, the main international airport serving Berlin

The busy main hall at Tegel Airport

Garten and several other places in the centre before terminating at Budapester Strasse. Bus No. 128 links the airport with U-Bahn Kurt-Schumacher-Platz, while No. X9 takes you to Kurfürstenstrasse. TXL buses are a little more expensive, but they take you quickly to Unter den Linden. A journey by bus from the airport to the centre of Berlin usually takes between 25 and 30 minutes.

Taxi ranks are located in front of the lower exit leading from the arrivals hall and on the inner square at the back of the main hall. A taxi from the airport to the city centre is not very expensive; the journey to Bahnhof Zoologischer Garten costs around DM25-30 and takes about 15 minutes.

SCHÖNEFELD AIRPORT

LOCATED ABOUT 12 miles (20 km) south of the city centre, Schönefeld Airport

used to be the main airport of East Berlin. Bus No. 171 can take you from the airport to Flughafen Berlin Schönefeld railway station, from where you can catch the S-Bahn 9 or S-Bahn 45 train (or any of the long-distance trains which stop there) straight to the city centre. Another option is to take bus No. 171 to Rudow U-Bahn station. A taxi ride from Schönefeld to the centre of Berlin is quite expensive.

TEMPELHOF AIRPORT

THE OLDEST AIRPORT in Berlin, Tempelhof is also the least busy of the three. It is located close to the city centre, at the border of Kreuzberg and Tempelhof. The easiest way to get from Tempelhof Airport to the centre of Berlin is by U-Bahn train from Platz der Luftbrücke station. Otherwise, bus No. 119 will take you to Kurfürstendamm.

DIRECTORY

AIRPORTS

Tegel Airport
☎ (01805) 00 01 86.

Schönefeld Airport
☎ (01805) 00 01 86.

Tempelhof Airport
☎ (01805) 00 01 86.

AIRLINES

Lufthansa
Kurfürstendamm 220.
☎ 88 75 38 00.

American Airlines
c/o British Airways.
☎ (01803) 24 23 24.

British Airways
Europa-Center.
☎ 25 40 00-0.

Airport check-in counter for First-Class passengers

TEGEL AIRPORT

Tegel Airport is relatively small and easy to use. A series of circular corridors leads to the departure gates. Shops and other services are situated in the main hall on two levels.

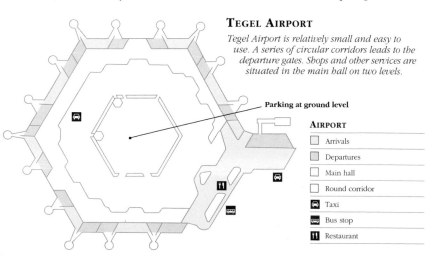

Parking at ground level

AIRPORT

☐	Arrivals
☐	Departures
☐	Main hall
☐	Round corridor
🚗	Taxi
🚌	Bus stop
🍴	Restaurant

Leaflets offering special deals on
international train travel

TRAVELLING BY TRAIN

THE STANDARDS of European
public transport are generally very high, particularly in
central Europe, so whichever
rail link you take to Berlin your
journey is bound to be comfortable. The city has excellent
connections with most major
German and European cities.
There are direct
lines between
Berlin and Zürich,
Brussels, Prague,
Amsterdam, Paris,
and Warsaw.
Besides these
lines, there are
many convenient
international routes
to choose from, via
other German cities.

If you are thinking of staying in Germany for quite a
while, and are keen to travel
around a lot by train, one of
the cheapest options is an
InterRail card. This can be
bought by persons of any
age, from any European
country, Morocco or
Turkey, and gives the
traveller unlimited access
to transport in a selection
of European countries.
North American visitors can
enquire into Eurail cards,
available through travel
agents. The prices differ
depending on your age and
the number of countries you
want to visit; the younger the
visitor, and the more limited
number of countries you wish
to visit, the cheaper the card.

At various times of the year,
but especially in summer,
there are often special deals
offering discounted travel.
Among these are weekend
tickets and family tickets. It
pays to visit the information
desk and ask about the different fares currently on offer.

What promises to be the
biggest railway station in Berlin
is currently under construction near the Lehrter Bahnhof
S-Bahn station,
but for the time
being the major-
ity of Germany's
long-distance
trains arrive at
Bahnhof Zoo
(Zoo station) – a
small-scale station
in which it is
impossible to get
lost. The trains stop on platforms from which you descend
to reach the main hall. This
hall contains a small shopping
precinct with a restaurant, a
left-luggage office, a bank
(see p284), a hotel reservation
point and a car rental kiosk.

Deutsche Bahn railway workers
wearing navy uniform jackets

One downside to the station
is the number of drug pushers,
pickpockets and other strange
characters who tend to hang
around. Police patrols make
sure that the area is safe for
travellers, but be careful here,
particularly late at night.

Bahnhof Zoo is situated in
the centre of old West Berlin
and has excellent connections
with the other districts via five
U-Bahn and three S-Bahn lines.
There is also a taxi rank located outside the station and a
number of bus stops, for both
day and night buses.

The best place to obtain
information about public
transport is the BVG pavilion
on Hardenbergerplatz (see
p295). You can also buy
tickets from the pavilion.

Some trains coming from
destinations in the south or
east arrive in **Ostbahnhof**
(the former Hauptbahnhof), a
convenient station where you
can easily exchange money,
send a letter and use the
tourist information office.
Ostbahnhof is linked to other
districts in Berlin via S-Bahn.

Some international trains
arriving in Berlin from eastern
destinations only come as far
as **Bahnhof Berlin Lichtenberg**, but from there you can
get to the Alexanderplatz or
Bahnhof Zoo by S-Bahn trains
5, 7 or 75 or U-Bahn train 5.

Always remember that the
ticket for your journey to
Berlin is also valid on all
S-Bahn connections to other
stations, providing you use it
immediately on arrival. For
details of train times and
destinations telephone the
Railway Information line.

DB

Logo of Deutsche Bahn
(German Railways)

Main hall of Zoo railway station (Bahnhof Zoo)

Coach Travel

WHEREVER YOU CAN travel by train, the chances are you can also travel by coach, and Germany is no exception. On international routes, the fast network of *Autobahnen* (motorways) enables coaches to nearly match the speed of the trains. Some try to raise the level of comfort by showing videos and serving light refreshments; but coaches generally are less roomy and less comfortable than trains. It often a question of cost. Coach travel is nearly always cheaper than rail travel.

After you have visited Berlin, you may decide to take a coach trip to another German city or further afield. If so, the place to go is the **Zentral-Omnibus-bahnhof**, situated near the Funkturm between Masurenallee and Messedamm. This is the city's largest long-distance coach station, and you will find connections to towns all over Germany, as well as links to other major European cities. Some coach companies, on overnight journeys, offer more comfortable sleeper seats for a small extra charge.

Information signs for passengers at a railway station

Travelling by Car

BERLIN is surrounded by a circular *Autobahn* or motorway (the Berliner Ring), which is linked to *Autobahnen* leading to Dresden, Nürnberg, Munich, Hannover, Hamburg

One of the many express coaches available in Berlin

and beyond. Numerous exits from the ring road are sign-posted into the city centre, but the road is so long that it is sometimes quicker to cut through town to get to wherever you're going (although not during rush hour).

While driving around the city, keep an eye on your speed; the police are extremely vigilant at doing speed checks. Less experienced drivers may feel a little uneasy on the *Autobahn* (motorway) as German drivers tend to zoom along at speeds reaching 125 mph (200 km/h). Keep to the right, unless you are overtaking. Always remember to check your side- and rear-view mirrors before switching to a left-hand lane. If you want to overtake, make sure there's nobody coming up behind. The speed at which fast cars come up behind you can be surprising. On some stretches of the *Autobahn*, speed limits are imposed depending on weather and road conditions.

Driving licences from all European countries are valid in Germany. Visitors from other countries need an international licence. You must also carry your passport and the standard documentation (including insurance certificate or "green card") while driving. These will certainly be needed if you intend to hire a car. There are several places to

rent vehicles around the city, including the major train stations and airports.

As in most countries, German law is tough on drinking and driving. In the event of an accident, or being pulled over by the police, you may find yourself in serious trouble if alcohol is found in your bloodstream. It is better not to take the risk in the first place, and abstain from drinking.

Typical road signs indicating the *Autobahn* and sights within Berlin

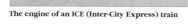

The engine of an ICE (Inter-City Express) train

GETTING AROUND BERLIN

BERLIN ISN'T the easiest of cities to move around in, largely because of the endless work being done to the roads. Building sites are scattered all over the city, and the number of parking spaces is still inadequate, so congestion is bad and driving should be avoided if possible. The centre of town (Mitte) can easily be seen on foot, but more peripheral areas

Taxi rank sign

should be reached by public transport. The U and S Bahn are by far the quickest way to travel, but the buses are very reliable – and if you happen to get a double-decker, they are excellent for sightseeing. Cyclists are exemely well catered for, so you may well want to hire a bike; there are many cycling routes around the city and further afield.

Lights at a pedestrian crossing

BERLIN ON FOOT

GERMAN DRIVERS are generally careful and watch out for pedestrians, but it always pays to be vigilant. Cyclists travelling at speed can be dangerous as many cycle routes run along the pavements (sidewalks), only marked by a line

or by a different colour. You may not be aware of a cyclist coming up behind you, so be warned; you can easily be hit, or at least scolded for being in the wrong lane.

When walking in Berlin one thing worth remembering is that street numbers increase along one side of the street and then "turn round" at the end and continue on the other side. Only along Unter den Linden do the street numbers increase equally on both sides, with odd and even numbers separated. If you are looking for a particular address, always make a note of where the street ends – although finding the right house is also made much easier by the street signs on every corner. These include the name of the street, as well as the numbers within that particular block.

Disabled tourists should get in contact with **Telebus-Zentrale** for transport details.

DRIVING

ALTHOUGH CONGESTION is often quite bad in the centre of town, driving around Berlin is not as difficult as it is in some European capitals, for the town doesn't have a typical old centre with narrow, winding streets. You can drive to Unter den Linden and Museum Island along the wide boulevards with few delays.

Local drivers are usually very careful and don't break speed limits or enter junctions on yellow lights; you are legally allowed to turn right on a red light if there is also a green arrow showing.

You won't have a problem hiring a car in Berlin, as long as you show your passport and a valid driving licence; a credit card is the preferred method of payment. There are many international hire companies with offices at the airports, railway stations and

Various old-fashioned local street signs in Berlin

Stopping and parking prohibited from Monday to Friday

Parking permitted during working hours and Saturday mornings only with a ticket

Parking Meter

Parking meters are used on most streets. You have to pay for parking between 9am and 7pm on weekdays and 9am and 2pm on Saturdays. It cost DM 1 for 30 minutes and meters accept 1-, 2- and 5-Mark coins.

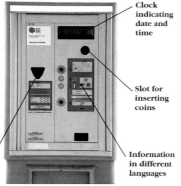

Clock indicating date and time

Slot for inserting coins

Information in different languages

Ticket is dispensed here

Some of the best known and most reliable car hire companies

the city centre, some of which require the driver to be over 21 years of age. **Hertz** and **AVIS** are two of the most reliable – and if you experience any trouble on the road, you should telephone **ADAC Auto Assistance**.

Taxis are also a very reliable and convenient method of transport around Berlin, three of the best companies being **Funk Taxi Berlin**, **Würfelfunk** and **Spree Funk**.

German road sign indicating various locations

PARKING

F INDING A PARKING place won't always be easy, especially during lunchtime, but with a bit of luck you should be able to leave your car, free of charge, in the middle lane of the Ku'damm or in Alexanderplatz. There are also parking meters situated on just about every street corner, and many multistorey car parks around West Berlin. Parking your car illegally certainly is not worth the risk; Berlin traffic wardens are constantly on the prowl, and apart from giving you a ticket, they can arrange to have your vehicle towed away. Retrieving an impounded car from the police is expensive and can be very inconvenient as these places are usually located out of town.

When using a parking meter, always check its time limit. These vary from area to area, so you may have to return after an hour or two to feed more money in the meter.

CYCLING

C YCLING IS VERY popular in Berlin, so most of the main roads have separate cycling lanes and even special traffic lights at intersections. Many offices, schools and banks have bicycle racks outside, but make sure your bike is securely locked and don't leave it there for too long.

You can also take your bike on S-Bahn trains, but you must enter the carriage by a marked door and leave your bike in a designated place. There are various places around town where you can hire a bike; one of the most reliable is **Fahrradstation**, with several outlets in the city.

A cycling lane between the pavement and the main road

DIRECTORY

CAR RENTAL

AVIS
(23 09 370.
((06171) 68 18 00
(International booking).

Hertz
(261 10 55.

BICYCLE RENTAL

Fahrradstation
Hackesche Höfe/Rosenthaler Strasse 40/41.
◯ 10am–7pm Mon–Fri, 10am–4pm Sat. (28 38 48 48.
Station Friedrichstrasse
◯ 10am–7pm Mon–Fri, 10am– 4pm Sat & Sun.
(20 45 45 00.

ROAD ASSISTANCE

ADAC Auto Assistance
((01802) 22 22 22.

DISABLED VISITORS

Telebus-Zentrale (Special bus)
Esplanade 17
◯ 9am–6pm Mon–Fri.
(41 02 00.

TAXI

Funk Taxi Berlin
(690 22.

Würfelfunk
(210 101.

Spree Funk
(44 33 22.

Buses, Trams and Taxis

Travelling by bus in Berlin can be something of a trial during rush hour, but at other times of the day it is highly recommended. Most of the major roads have special bus lanes so buses are punctual even when the main roads are getting congested. A double-decker bus is worth taking if you're new in town and want to have a good look round. Trams are another option in the eastern part of the centre; like the buses and S-Bahn lines they are part of BVG and accept the same tickets.

BVG pavilion on Hardenbergplatz provides transport information

TICKETS

THE WHOLE OF Berlin is divided into three travel zones: A, B and C. Zone A covers the city centre, Zone B the outskirts of town, while Zone C includes Potsdam and its environs. Travel between the zones is very simple, with tickets for each combination of zones. The most expensive option is to travel by buying single tickets, which come in two kinds, the normal ticket (*Normaltarif*) and the cheaper ticket (*Kurzstrecke*). The former is valid for two hours and gives you access to all methods of public transport, including S- and U-Bahn trains, with as many changes as you need, while the latter can only be used for three stops on trains and six stops on buses. Single

Three-day Welcome Card

tickets can be bought from ticket offices at U- or S-Bahn stations, or from the bus driver. You must validate your ticket before you start your journey by inserting it in a red machine (*Entwerter*) found on the train platforms or in the bus, where it will be punched with the date and time. Children under 14 years old are entitled to a discount (*Ermässigungstarif*) and those under 6 can travel for free. No fee is charged for bringing a pram or a dog on board.

At most stations there are machines selling tickets and cards. The One-Day Ticket (*Tageskarte*) is valid from the moment it is punched until 3 o'clock the following morning, and the One-Day Group Ticket (*Kleingruppenkarte*) allows five people to travel on one ticket. Weekly cards (*7-Tage-Karte*) are valid for seven days until midnight and are transferable. The three-day Welcome Card is another good option, giving unlimited travel in Berlin and Potsdam. Cheap tickets are also made available on special occasions. During the Love Parade (*see p49*), for example, people are allowed to use all kinds of transport at a cheaper rate for two days.

During the Love Parade (*see p49*)

Tram Stop
Every tram stop displays the appropriate tram numbers, timetables and maps. Buses sometimes also use the stops and are listed accordingly.

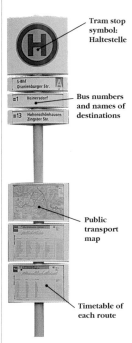

Tram stop symbol: **Haltestelle**

Bus numbers and names of destinations

Public transport map

Timetable of each route

For information about tickets and public transport in general, telephone **BVG Information (BVG-Kundendienst)** or the **Ticket Information** line – or the **U-Bahnhof Turmstrasse** for information about trains. If you think you may have mislaid something on a bus or a tram, give the **BVG Lost Property** number a call.

TRAVELLING BY BUS

ALL BUS ROUTES have a detailed timetable on display at each stop. Apart from its number, a bus will also have its destination on show, and it is important to pay attention to this as many buses shorten their routes outside rush hour. In the more modern buses you have to press a button to open the door. Until 8pm you can use all the doors to enter the bus, but after 8pm you should

A typical double decker bus

only use the front door near the driver; you will have to show him or her your ticket. The driver usually calls out the next stop, which may also be displayed electronically. Outside the city centre, however, the electronic display is something of a rarity. When travelling in the suburbs (and in the city centre outside rush hour) you need to press the *"Halt"* ("Stop") button as necessary, since most stops are made "on request" only.

TYPES OF BUS SERVICE

THERE ARE SEVERAL different bus services operating in Berlin. Buses run frequently throughout the week, but somewhat less often on Saturdays and Sundays. Apart from the regular buses, marked by three-digit numbers, there are also some slightly more expensive "express" buses. These carry a two digit number preceded by an X, amd stop less frequently than other services. The regular daytime bus services start to wind down at around 11pm, but their place is taken by a very reliable network of night buses. These are marked by the letter N and require special tickets which can be bought from the driver.

ROUTE 100

THIS SPECIAL ROUTE is served mainly by double-deckers and incorporates the most attractive parts of town. The buses operate between Bahnhof Zoo and Prenzlauer Berg, passing most of the city's interesting historic sites. Using a one-day ticket you can get off at any bus stop and visit Museum Island, Unter den Linden, the Brandenburg Gate, the Reichstag, the Tiergarten or Kaiser-Wilhelm-Gadächtniskirche. An extremely useful map and leaflet with descriptions (in German and English) of the route can be obtained from the **BVG Pavilion** on Hardenbergerplatz.

TRAMS

TRAMS OPERATE mainly within the area of former East Berlin; only one route was extended to Wedding. They can always be relied upon to depart on time as they never have traffic jams to deal with. A tram ticket can also be used on buses and S-Bahn trains.

TAXIS

TAXIS ARE A comfortable but expensive way of getting around Berlin. Regardless of the make of car, all taxis are of the same cream colour and have a big TAXI sign on the roof. You can easily hail one on the street or arrange a cab by phone *(see p293)*. You can also get a taxi at a taxi rank, though these are quite rare. If the taxi rank is empty, you can use the rank telephone to

Modern tram operating in the former East Berlin quarter

call a cab directly, as each car has its own phone. The fare is calculated by a meter on the driver's dashboard. The cheapest fares are charged on weekdays in the centre of town (night-time and weekend rates are higher). There is also a special rate called the *Winketarif:* if you flag down a taxi at night and ask for a very short lift, the ride will only cost you 5DM. It is generally a good idea to find out the name and telephone number of the taxi company nearest to your hotel.

DIRECTORY

USEFUL NUMBERS

BVG Information (BVG-Kundendienst)
📞 194 49.

Ticket Information
Bahnhof Alexanderplatz.
📞 29 72 06 48.
🕐 8am–9pm Mon–Fri,
9am–6pm Sat & Sun.

U-Bahnhof Turmstrasse
🕐 6:30am–8:30pm Mon–Fri,
9am–3:30pm Sat.

BVG Pavillon
Hardenbergplatz.
📞 256 31 67.
🕐 6:30am–8:30pm daily.

BVG Lost Property
Alexanderplatz.
📞 25 63 13 22.
🌐 www.bvg.de

A typical Berlin bus stop during rush hour

U-Bahn and S-Bahn

U-Bahn information sign

WHILE IN THEORY Berlin has two separate train networks – the U-Bahn and S-Bahn systems – in practical terms there is not much difference between them, and commuters use the same tickets for both. Strictly speaking, the U-Bahn operates as a metro system, with trains running underground, while the S-Bahn is a longer-distance commuter service. In practice however, there is a great deal of overlap between the two systems, and many stations have both S- and U-Bahn platforms. The U-Bahn is owned by BVG and the S-Bahn by the independent S-Bahn GmbH.

U-Bahn display board with U-Bahn platform *(Gleis)*, and destination

only valid for three stops. Vending machines stand at the entrance to each station, selling single tickets, returns, and one- and seven-day travel cards. The red machines that punch your ticket are usually behind the vending machines at the entrance to each platform. You may notice that there are no gates to stop free-riders trying their luck on the trains, but attempting to travel free of charge is a rather risky business in Berlin. Trains are patrolled by ticket inspectors who always work in plain clothes. They go on their rounds as soon as the train starts moving, and tend not to accept any excuses; fines for not having a ticket are high.

Trains arriving and departing at a station on U-Bahn line 6

U-BAHN

THE U-BAHN network is very dense, with numerous stations very close together, many of them on lines which do not connect. During rush hours trains are very frequent, usually arriving every minute or two. There are ten U-Bahn lines in all, although one of them (number 15) has enough branches to count as several, while number 12 is little more than a connection between lines 1 and 2. Most of the service closes down between midnight and 5am, but lines U1 and U9 offer an overnight service during the weekends.

S-BAHN

TRAIN ROUTES ARE usually a bit longer on the S-Bahn, which doesn't have as dense a network as the U-Bahn. As many as five lines go along the same route between Ost- and Westkreuz, but the stations are spaced much further apart than U-Bahn

stops, and trains run every ten or 20 minutes. There are a total of 15 S-Bahn lines, all running well beyond the confines of the city.

TICKETS

TICKETS FOR S- and U-Bahn trains are the same as the tickets used on local buses and trams. The *Kurzstrecke* (short stretch) single ticket is also acceptable, although it is

SIGNS

THERE'S NO MISTAKING a U-Bahn station with its large rectangular sign and trademark white U on a black background; similarly for S-Bahn stations, which have a round sign with a large white S on a green background. On metro maps each line is marked by a different colour. The direction of the train is noted by the displays which always give the final destination of the train. White ovals or circles on the map indicate where you can change to another line. All stations have maps of the local area as well as maps

Buying an S-Bahn ticket from a machine on the platform

An S-Bahn line 5 train heading out to Pichelsberg

of the entire metro system. Maps of the network are also on view in the train carriages. When embarking, always check both the line number and the final destination of the train as it is very easy to confuse your direction.

Older-style carriages have manually-opened doors which will close behind you automatically. Newer ones are fully automatic. A station attendant on each platform is responsible for co-ordinating departures. When you hear *"Zurück bleiben!"* you must not enter the train as this means it is ready to depart. During the journey the next station is often announced inside the carriage – on more modern trains information about your journey is given on an electronic screen.

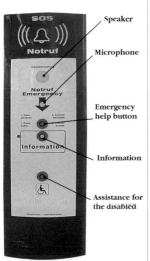

Speaker

Microphone

Emergency help button

Information

Assistance for the disabled

Information and emergency help point for the S-Bahn and U-Bahn

JOURNEY BY U- AND S-BAHN

1 Find the station you want on a map and see which line runs there. Do not forget to make a note of the final destination of the line so you can be sure of travelling in the right direction.

Map of U- and S-Bahn lines
(see inside back cover)

2 Find the button showing the type of ticket you require. After making your selection, the price is displayed and you can insert your coins in the slot.

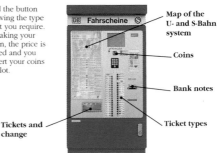

Map of the U- and S-Bahn system

Coins

Bank notes

Tickets and change

Ticket types

3 A ticket from the machine looks different from one bought at the counter, but it will always contain information about its type and price.

Weekly travel card (left) and one–day travel card

4 After entering the station you must validate your ticket in one of the red stamping machines located on the platform.

Ticket

Colour-coded sign of various S-Bahn stations

5 Follow the signs to the appropriate platform and choose the correct side by checking the destinations of departing trains.

An information board indicating the destinations of departing trains

S3	Westkreuz
S5	Pichelsberg
S7	Potsdam Stadt
S9	Westkreuz
S75	Pichelsberg

U U2 U5 U8

Sign indicating where to wait for these U-Bahn lines

6 After leaving a train, proceed to the exit marked by the *Ausgang* sign. If there are several exits from the station additional signs will tell you the names of the streets outside.

Ausgang ↑
Am Weidendamm
Reichstagufer

A typical exit sign

Getting Around by Boat

T HE RIVER ROUTES of Berlin may not be as dense as those of Amsterdam or Venice, but the Spree and the Havel offer more than just a pleasure cruise in the sun. An extensive system of canals and lakes links the city centre with Potsdam, Spandau, Charlotten-burg and the area of Müggelsee. All kinds of transport are available, from rowing boats to catamarans and barges.

A ship's bell

Timetable and routes of various boats near the Nikolaiviertel

One of many tourist boats on the Spree river

GETTING AROUND BERLIN ON THE WATER

O NE OF THE MOST relaxing ways to spend the after-noon in Berlin is to take a leisurely three- or four-hour journey by boat along the Spree river and the Landwehr-kanal. There is no shortage of companies offering this kind of trip. Four of the most reliable are **Reederei Bruno Winkler**, **Stern und Kreis**, **Reederei Hartmut Triebler** and **Reederei Riedel**. Each has its own dock, but the routes they follow are similar. You can admire the historic buildings of Mitte as the boat passes by the Berliner Dom along Museum Island, before heading off to the new government district and the Reichstag. You should have a good view of the Haus der Kulturen der Welt and the new city in Moabit shortly before entering the Landwehr-kanal. This runs alongside the Zoological Garden and new city buildings on Potsdamer Platz, and passes through Kreuzberg on its way to the junction with the Spree at Oberbaumbrücke. Most of the boats available along this

route have closed lower decks and open upper decks, with a bar serving snacks and drinks. All the sights are ex-plained by a guide along the way; the commentary is usually in German, but some companies can arrange for an English speaker.

TRIPS ALONG THE SPREE AND HAVEL RIVERS

I F YOU WANT TO try something a little more adventurous there are longer trips to choose from, some of which cover the

western lakes as well as the city centre. A particularly nice route takes you along the Spree, past the Mitte district, to Treptow, Charlottenburg and Spandau. From here you can carry on along the Havel river to the Grunewald and the Wannsee, then take a trip past Pfaueninsel to Potsdam. To do this, enquire at Stern und Kreis. Companies Reederei Bruno Winkler, and Reederei Hartmut Triebler offer similar trips starting at Spandau and Charlottenburg.

Other options include a trip from Tegel port to Spandau and Wannsee, or a journey from Treptow to Köpenick. If you really want to, you can cover the whole of Berlin by boat, starting from Tegel in the north and finishing at Köpenick in the southeast, all within five or six hours.

Boat moored along the river in the summer

One of the larger boats available on the Spree

DIRECTORY

TOUR BOAT COMPANIES

Reederei Bruno Winkler
Mierendorffstrasse 16.
[C] 349 95 95.

Reederei Hartmut Triebler
Bratringweg 29.
[C] 371 16 71.

Reederei Riedel
Planufer 78.
[C] 691 37 82, 693 46 46,
or 694 21 91.

Stern und Kreis
Schiffahrt GmbH Berlin
Puschkinallee 16/17.
[C] 53 63 60 0.
[W] www.STERNundKREIS.de

Weisse Flotte Potsdam
Lange Brücke.
[C] (0331) 275 92 10.

LONGER JOURNEYS AROUND BERLIN

FOR EVEN LONGER TOURS, you may decide to take a whole day exploring the rivers, canals and lakes of Berlin. From Treptow you can take a boat to Woltersdorf which takes you through the charming lakeland area of Müggelsee. This region really is one of Berlin's greatest

A sight-seeing boat negotiating a lock on a canal

treasures, and is ideal for anyone searching for a quiet place to relax. There are many man-made beaches to choose from, as well as summer gardens and cafés - and a large white fleet of ships to show you around the area. Müggelsee is best visited on a warm summer's day when you can easily spend a few hours on one of its beaches.

Another adventurous idea is to take a voyage along the Teltowkanal from Treptow to Potsdam, from where **Weisse Flotte Potsdam** can take you not only to Wannsee and the other familiar routes around town, but also to Caputh, Werder and to many other sites to the south and west of Potsdam. For the absolute die-hards of the waterways, there is still one other option, which is to

Reederei Riedel company logo

take a boat all the way to Szczecin in Poland. You will need to allow a whole day to reach Szczecin, so be prepared to stay the night there as well. Perhaps the best idea is to leave your boat at the docks, spend a restful day exploring the city, and return by coach to Berlin.

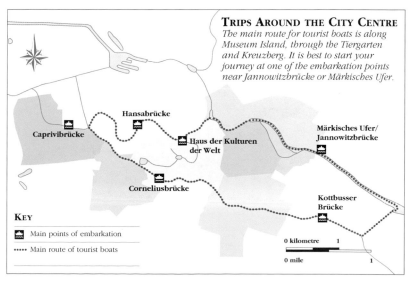

TRIPS AROUND THE CITY CENTRE

The main route for tourist boats is along Museum Island, through the Tiergarten and Kreuzberg. It is best to start your journey at one of the embarkation points near Jannowitzbrücke or Märkisches Ufer.

Hansabrücke

Caprivibrücke

Haus der Kulturen der Welt

Märkisches Ufer/ Jannowitzbrücke

Corneliusbrücke

Kottbusser Brücke

KEY

🔲 Main points of embarkation

••••• Main route of tourist boats

0 kilometre 1

0 mile 1

STREET FINDER

MAP REFERENCES given for historic buildings, hotels, restaurants, bars, shops and entertainment venues refer to the maps included in this section of the guidebook. A complete index of street names and all places of interest can be found on the following pages. The key map below shows the area of Berlin covered by the *Street Finder*. The maps include all the major sightseeing areas, historic attractions, railway stations, bus stations and the suburban stations of the U-Bahn and S-Bahn, as well as the ferry embarkation points. The names of the streets and squares in the index and maps are given in German. The word Strasse (Str.) indicates a street, Platz a square, Brücke a bridge and Bahnhof a railway station.

Gendarmen-markt lit up at night

KEY

▢ Major sight	🅿 Parking	→ One-way street
▢ Place of interest	🚊 Tram stop	― Pedestrianized street
▢ Other building	✚ Hospital with emergency room	═ Autobahn (motorway)
Ⓢ S-Bahn station	🚓 Police station	**SCALE OF MAP PP 1–14**
Ⓤ U-Bahn station	✝ Church	0 metres 250 **1:16 500**
🚆 Railway station	✡ Synagogue	0 yards 250
🚌 Bus station	⊠ Post office	**SCALE OF MAP PP 15–16**
🚌 Bus terminus	═ Railway line	0 metres 150 **1:11 350**
		0 yards 150

Palm house in the Botanischer Garten

Rococo Chinesisches Teehaus in Park Sanssouci, Potsdam

UNTER DEN LINDEN

KARL-MARX-ALLEE

LEIPZIGER STRASSE

POTSDAMER STRASSE

TEMPELHOFER DAMM

Modern business centre of
Potsdamer Platz

Street Finder Index

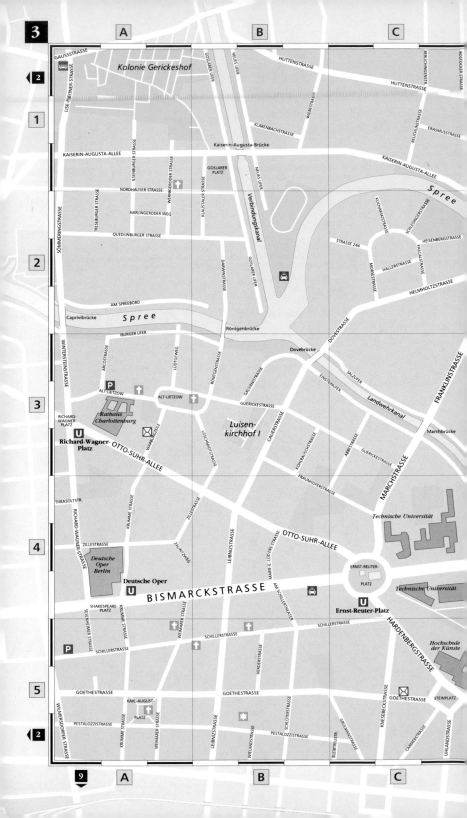

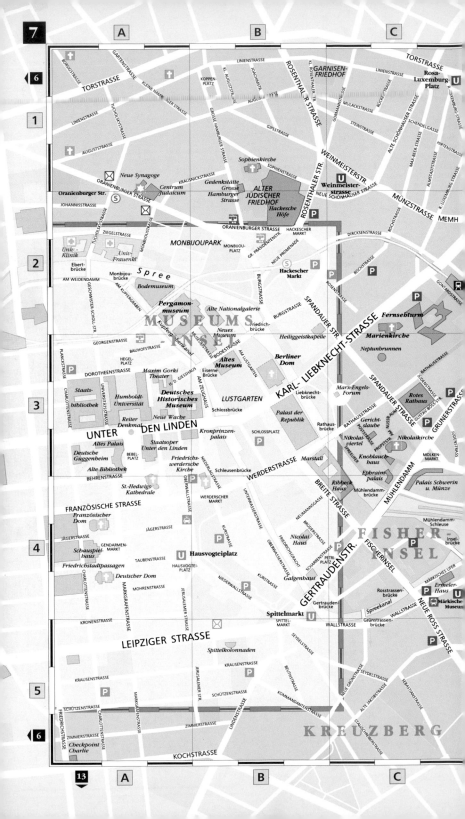

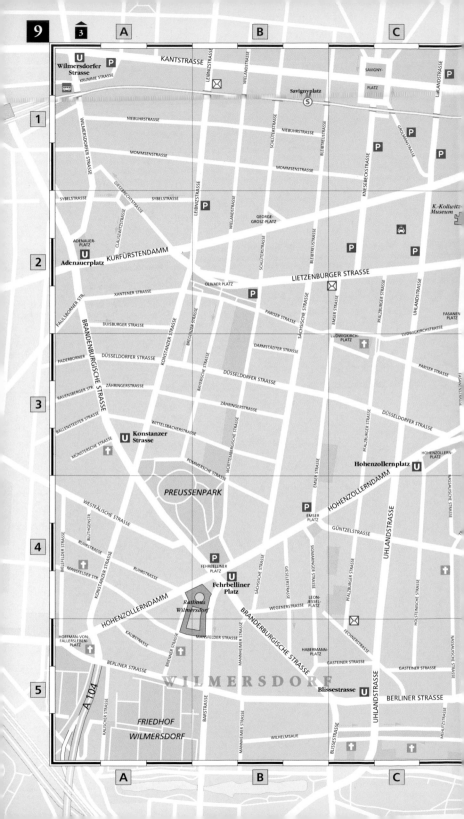

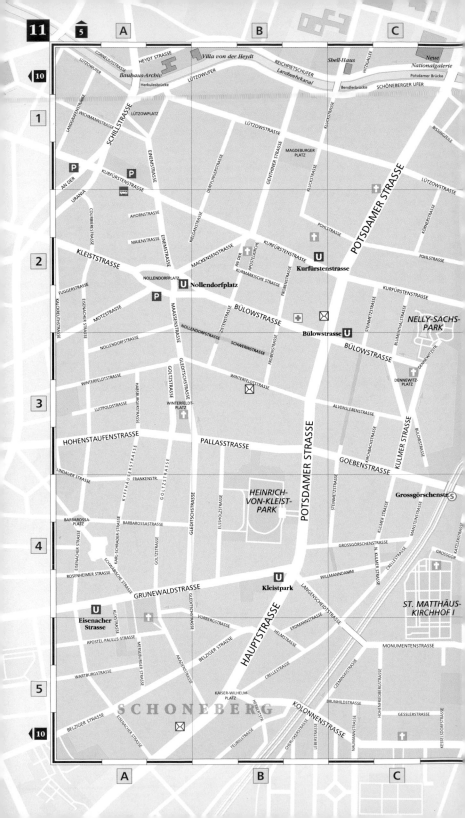

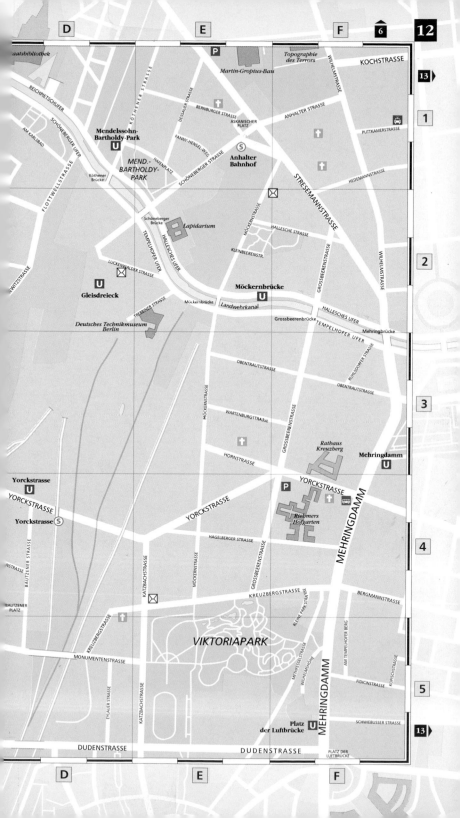

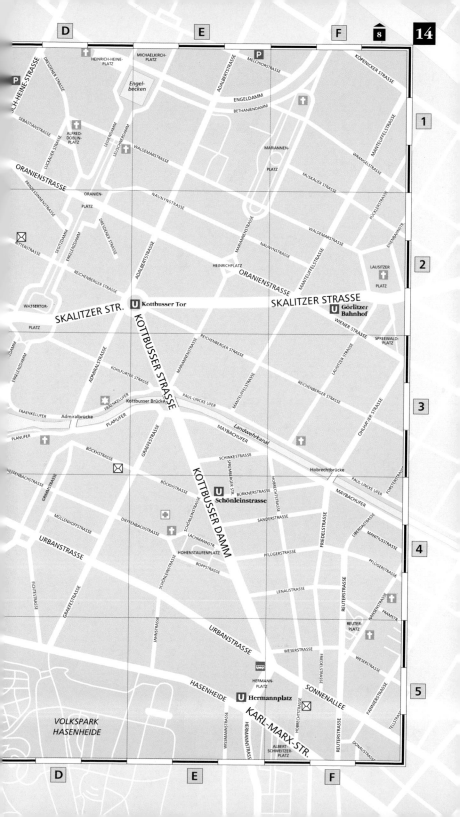

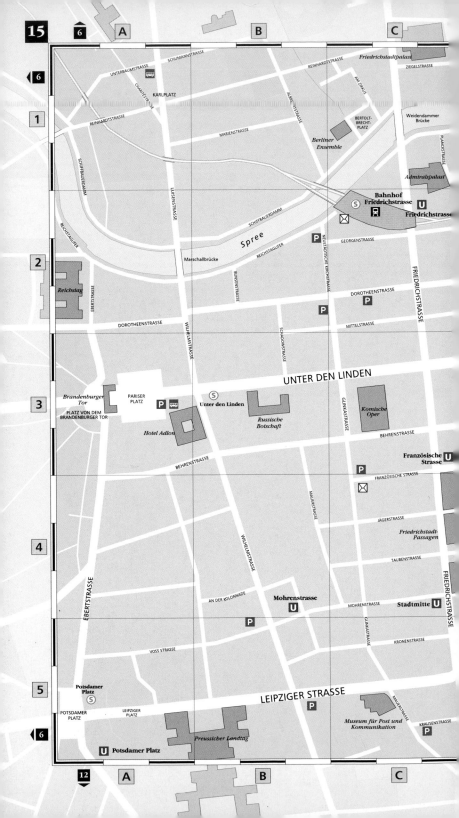

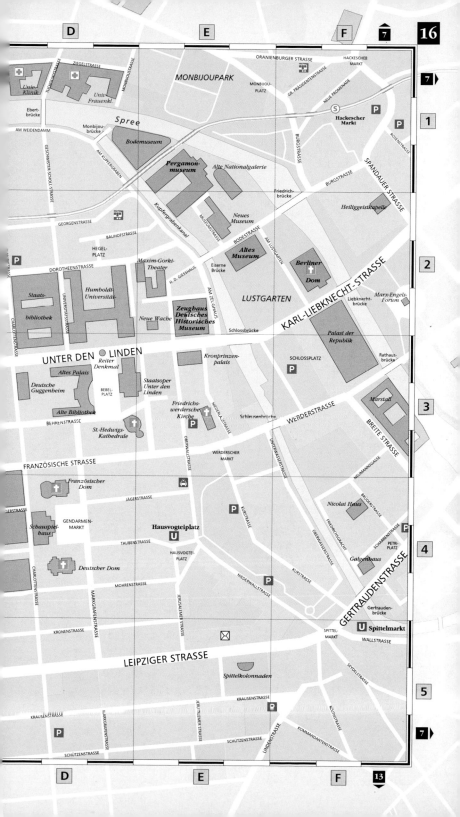

Index
Page numbers in bold type refer to main entries

Acknowledgements

DORLING KINDERSLEY would like to thank the following people whose contributions and assistance have made the preparation of this book possible.

MANAGING ART EDITOR
Kate Poole

EDITORIAL DIRECTOR
Vivien Crump

ART DIRECTOR
Gillian Allan

CONSULTANT
Gordon McLachlan

FACT CHECKERS
Paul Otto Schulz, Margaret Schulz-Wenzel

TRANSLATORS
Magda Hannay, Anna Johnson, Ian Wisniewski

PROOFREADER
Stewart Wild

INDEXER
Hilary Bird

DESIGN AND EDITORIAL ASSISTANCE
Gillian Andrews, Brigitte Arora, Arwen Burnett, Jessica Hughes, Andrew Szudek

DTP
Samantha Borland, Lee Redmond

ADDITIONAL ILLUSTRATIONS
Paweł Pasternak

SPECIAL ASSISTANCE
DORLING KINDERSLEY would like to thank the staff at the featured museums, shops, hotels, restaurants and other organizations in Berlin for their invaluable help. Special thanks go to the following for providing photographs and pictures: Heidrun Klein of the Bildarchiv Preussischer Kulturbesitz; Frau Betzker and Ingrid Jager of the Bröhan Museum; Margit Billeb of the Centrum Judaicum; Brucke-Museum; Deutsche Press Agency (DPA); Renate Forster of the Deutsches Technikmuseum Berlin; Andrei Holland-Moritz of Forschung- und Gedenkstätte Normannenstrasse (Stasi-Museum); Matthias Richter of Konzerthaus Berlin and the Berlin Symphony Orchestra; Georg Kolbe Museum; Carl Kamarz of Stiftung Preussische Schlösser und Gärten Berlin and the Berlin and Potsdam Palaces; Thomas Wellmann of the Museum of the City of Berlin; Hamburger Bahnhof; Annette Jäckel of DeragHotels for providing photographs of the interiors of DeragHotel Grosser Kurfürst; Reinhard Friedrich; Hans-Jürgen Dyck of Haus am Checkpoint Charlie; Gaby Hofmann of Komische Oper Berlin; Gesine Steiner of Museum für Naturkunde; Ute Grallert of Deutsches Historisches Museum; Elke Pfeil of the Brecht-Weigel-Museum; Ingrid Flindell of the Käthe-Kollwitz-Museum; Sylvia U Moller of Villa Kastania; Manuel Volsk of the Savoy Hotel; Sabine Rogge of the Grand Hotel Esplanade Berlin; Claude Borrmann of the Hotel Palace Berlin; Gerald Uhligow of the Einstein Café; Hotel Adlon; Hotel Brandenburger Hof and Restaurant Die Quadriga; Hotel Kempinski; Rockendorf's Restaurant; The Westin Grand Hotel.

PHOTOGRAPHY PERMISSIONS
DORLING KINDERSLEY would like to thank the following for their kind permission to photograph at their establishments: Margaret Hilmer of the Berliner Dom; Kaiser-Wilhelm-Gedächtniskirche; Galeries Lafayette; KaDeWe; Frau Schneider of BVG (Berlin Underground system); Deutsche Bundesbahn for allowing photography of the Zoo railway station; Dorotheenstädtischer Friedhof for allowing photographs of the tombs; Flughafen Schönefeld for allowing photography of the airfield; Annie Silbert of the Zoologischer Garten Berlin for allowing photography of the animals and attractions; Hilton Hotel; Carlos Beck of the Sorat Art'otel, Berlin; Manuel Volsk of the Savoy Hotel, Berlin; Sabine Rogge of the Grand Hotel Esplanade; Claude Borrmann of the Hotel Palace Berlin; Gerald Uhligow of the Einstein Café; the Olive restaurant; the Bamberger Reiter restaurant; Sklepo for allowing photography of its interiors and porcelain.

Particular thanks to Hans-Gunter Harms, chef at the Hilton Hotel, for preparing the dishes for photography; Manfred Duhatschko for preparing cakes and desserts; Hilton Hotel for allowing photography of the interiors and the preparation of the food.
Count Lehmann of Senatsverwaltung für Bauen, Wohnen und Verkehr for providing cartographic information as well as copyright for the use of maps.

Picture Credits

t=top; tl= top left; tc=top centre; tr= top right; cla=centre left above; ca= centre above; cra= centre right above; cl=centre left; c=centre; cr=centre right; clb=center left below; cb= center below; crb=centre right below; bl=bottom left; bc=bottom centre; br=bottom right; b=bottom

Every effort has been made to trace the copyright holders and we apologize in advance for any unintentional omissions. We would be pleased to insert the appropriate acknowledgements in subsequent editions of this publication.

The publisher is grateful to the following individuals, companies and picture libraries for their permission to reproduce their photographs.

ANA E BRUNO 228t; ADLON 229d.

BILDARCHIV PREUSSISCHER KULTURBESITZ 9c, 20–21c, 29tr, 30tr, 30br, 32tr, 32br, 33t, 33b, 54cb, 67b, 80ca, 82tl, 82b, 83tl, 85b, 115cra, 118tl, 118tr, 122cb, 123clb, 126t, 152cra, 156t, 157cl, 159tl, 170tr, 170b; Jorg P Anders 20tc, 20cl, 21t, 29cl, 30cl, 73cra, 114c, 114b, 117t, 122tl, 122tr, 122ca, 122b, 123t, 123cr, 123b, 124t, 124ca, 124b, 125t, 125cb, 125cb, 179b; Hans-Joachim Bartsch 118cla, 118c, 120tl, 121cr; Margarete Busing 32c; Ingrid Geske-Heiden 30tl, 75tr, 121b; Klaus Goken 60t, 31crb, 78t, 80b, 81b; Dietmar Katz 41b; Johannes Laurentius 75b; Erich Lessing 72t, 80t, 81cb; Jürgen Liepe 31cra, 75cla, 80cb, 82t, 83b, 118b, 158b; Saturia Linke 32tl; Georg Niedermeiser 80t, 81ca; Arne Psille 118c, 119t, 119b, 120c, 121t, 120b; Steinkopf 114tr; G Stenzel 83tr; Jens Ziehe 110t, 111c; Jürgen Zimmermann 29tl; BRANDENBURGER HOF 212br; BRIDGEMAN ART LIBRARY 47c, 167b; BRECHT-WEIGEL-GEDENKSTÄTTE 46t, 109b; BRÖHAN-MUSEUM 159cb.

CENTRUM JUDAICUM 102t.

DERAGHOTEL GROSSER KURFÜRST 213br; DEUTSCHES HISTORISCHES MUSEUM (Zeughaus) 8–9, 22cb, 22bl, 23tr, 23b, 23clb, 24–25b, 25tr, 26tl, 26cr, 26cb, 26dp, 27tr, 27bl, 46br, 47cra, 58tl, 58tr, 58ca, 58cb, 58br, 59t, 59ca, 59cb, 59b; DEUTSCHES TECHNIKMUSEUM BERLIN 31bl, 132; DIE QUADRIGA 228clb; DEUTSCHE PRESS AGENCY (DPA) 46ca, 46cb, 46bl, 47t, 47crb, 47b, 48tc, 48cla, 48b, 50t, 50b, 51t, 67t, 145br, 191b.

GEORG KOLBE MUSEUM 175tr; GRAND HOTEL ESPLANADE 208b.

HAMBURGER BAHNHOF 110ca, 110cb, 110b, 111t, 111cra, 111crb, 111b; HAUS AM CHECKPOINT CHARLIE 39br; HOTEL ADLON 68t, 213tl; HOTEL KEMPINSKI 212bl; HOTEL PALACE 211tr, 212tr; HAYDER ADAM 231br.

KÄTHE-KOLLWITZ-MUSEUM 148b; KOMISCHE OPER MONIKA RITTERSHAUS 49b, 68b; KONZERTHAUS BERLIN 65t.

MEYER NILS 27crb, 38tr; MUSEUM FÜR NATURKUNDE 109t.

PHILHARMONIE 115t.

ROCKENDORF'S RESTAURANT 229tr.

STADTMUSEUM BERLIN 21tr, 22t, 24cla, 129tr; Hans-Joachim Bartsch 16, 17b, 18c, 19tl, 19br, 25br, 85t; Christel Lehmann 18tl, 18cb; Peter Straube 88b, 90tr; STASI-MUSEUM 166cr; STIFTUNG PREUSSISCHE SCHLÖSSER UND GÄRTEN BERLIN 14t, 19c, 154t, 154c, 155ca, 155c, 155b, 180clb, 186tl, 186cla, 186clb, 186br, 187cra, 187br, 187bl, 190t, 192cla, 192b, 193cra, 193crb, 193bl, 193br.

VILLA KASTANIA 209b, 212clb.

THE WESTIN GRAND 210b; WOJCIK PAWEŁ 233bl.

DORLING KINDERSLEY SPECIAL EDITIONS

Dorling Kindersley books can be purchased in bulk quantities at discounted prices for use in promotions or as premiums. We are also able to offer special editions and personalized jackets, corporate imprints, and excerpts from all of our books, tailored specifically to meet your own needs. To find out more, please contact:

(in the United Kingdom) – SPECIAL SALES, DORLING KINDERSLEY LIMITED, 9 HENRIETTA STREET, COVENT GARDEN, LONDON WC2E 8PS; TEL. 020 7753 5572;

(in the United States) – SPECIAL MARKETS DEPARTMENT, DORLING KINDERSLEY PUBLISHING, INC., 95 MADISON AVENUE, NEW YORK, NY 10016; TEL. 212 213 4800.

Phrasebook

IN AN EMERGENCY

Where is the telephone?	Wo ist das Telefon?	voh ist duss tel-e-fone?
Help!	Hilfe!	hilf-uh
Please call a doctor	Bitte rufen Sie einen Arzt	bitt-uh roof'n zee ine-en artst
Please call the police	Bitte rufen Sie die Polizei	bitt-uh roof'n zee dee poli-tsy
Please call the fire brigade	Bitte rufen Sie die Feuerwehr	bitt-uh roof'n zee dee foyer-vayr
Stop!	Halt!	hult

COMMUNICATION ESSENTIALS

Yes	Ja	yah
No	Nein	nine
Please	Bitte	bitt-uh
Thank you	Danke	dunk-uh
Excuse me	Verzeihung	fair-tsy-hoong
Hello (good day)	Guten Tag	goot-en tahk
Goodbye	Auf Wiedersehen	owf-veed-er-zay-ern
Good evening	Guten Abend	goot'n ahb'nt
Good night	Gute Nacht	goot-uh nukht
Until tomorrow	Bis morgen	biss morg'n
See you	Tschüss	chooss
What is that?	Was ist das?	voss ist duss
Why?	Warum?	var-room
Where?	Wo?	voh
When?	Wann?	vunn
today	heute	hoyt-uh
tomorrow	morgen	morg'n
month	Monat	mohn-aht
night	Nacht	nukht
afternoon	Nachmittag	nahkh-mit-tahk
morning	Morgen	morg'n
year	Jahr	yar
there	dort	dort
here	hier	hear
week	Woche	vokh-uh
yesterday	gestern	gest'n
evening	Abend	ahb'nt

USEFUL PHRASES

How are you? (informal)	Wie geht's?	vee gayts
Fine, thanks	Danke, es geht mir gut	dunk-uh, es gayt meer goot
Until later	Bis später	biss shpay-ter
Where is/are?	Wo ist/sind...?	voh ist/sind
How far is it to...?	Wie weit ist es...?	vee vite ist ess
Do you speak English?	Sprechen Sie Englisch?	shpresh'n zee eng-glish
I don't understand	Ich verstehe nicht	ish fair-shtay-uh nisht
Could you speak more slowly?	Könnten Sie langsamer sprechen?	kurnt-en zee lung-zam-er shpresh'n

USEFUL WORDS

large	gross	grohss
small	klein	kline
hot	heiss	hyce
cold	kalt	kult
good	gut	goot
bad	böse/schlecht	burss-uh/shlesht
open	geöffnet	g'urff-nett
closed	geschlossen	g'shloss'n
left	links	links
right	rechts	reshts
straight ahead	geradeaus	g'rah-der-owss

MAKING A TELEPHONE CALL

I would like to make a phone call	Ich möchte telefonieren	ish mer-shtuh tel-e-fon-eer'n
I'll try again later	Ich versuche noch ein mal später	ish fair-zookh-uh nokh ine-mull shpay-ter
Can I leave a message?	Kann ich eine Nachricht hinterlassen?	kan ish ine-uh nakh-risht hint-er-lahss-en
answer phone	Anrufbeantworter	an-roof-be-ahnt-vort-er
telephone card	Telefonkarte	tel-e-fohn-kart-uh
receiver	Hörer	hur-er
mobile	Handi	han-dee
engaged (busy)	besetzt	b'zetst
wrong number	Falsche Verbindung	falsh-uh fair-bin-doong

SIGHT-SEEING

library	Bibliothek	bib-leo-tek
entrance ticket	Eintrittskarte	ine-tritz-kart-uh
cemetery	Friedhof	freed-hofe
train station	Bahnhof	barn-hofe
gallery	Galerie	gall-er-ree
information	Auskunft	owss-koonft
church	Kirche	keersh-uh
garden	Garten	gart'n
palace/castle	Palast/Schloss	pallast/shloss
place (square)	Platz	plats
bus stop	Haltestelle	hal-te-shtel-uh
national holiday	Nationalfeiertag	nats-yon-ahl-fire-tahk
theatre	Theater	tay-aht-er
free admission	Eintritt frei	ine-tritt fry

SHOPPING

Do you have/ Is there...?	Gibt es...?	geept ess
How much does it cost?	Was kostet das?	voss kost't duss
When do you open/ close?	Wann öffnen Sie? schliessen Sie?	vunn off'n zee shlees'n zee
this	das	duss
expensive	teuer	toy-er
cheap	preiswert	price-vurt
size	Grösse	gruhs-uh
number	Nummer	noom-er
colour	Farbe	farb-uh
brown	braun	brown
black	schwarz	shvarts
red	rot	roht
blue	blau	blau
green	grün	groon
yellow	gelb	gelp

TYPES OF SHOP

antique shop	Antiquariat	antik-var-yat
chemist (pharmacy)	Apotheke	appo-tay-kuh
bank	Bank	bunk
market	Markt	markt
travel agency	Reisebüro	rye-zer-boo-roe
department store	Warenhaus	vahr'n-hows
chemist's, drugstore	Drogerie	droog-er-ree
hairdresser	Friseur	freezz-er
newspaper kiosk	Zeitungskiosk	tsytoongs-kee-osk
bookshop	Buchhandlung	bookh-hant-loong

bakery	Bäckerei	beck-er-**eye**
post office	Post	posst
shop/store	Geschäft/Laden	gush-**eft/lard**'n
film processing shop	Photogeschäft	fo-to-gush-**eft**
self-service shop	Selbstbedienungs-laden	selpst-bed-**ee**-nungs-lard'n
shoe shop	Schuhladen	shoo-lard'n
clothes shop	Kleiderladen, Boutique	klyder-lard'n boo-**teek**-uh
food shop	Lebensmittel-geschäft	lay-bens-mittel-gush-eft
glass, porcelain	Glas, Porzellan	**glars, Port-sellahn**

STAYING IN A HOTEL

Do you have any vacancies?	Haben Sie noch Zimmer frei?	harb'n zee nokh **tsimm**-er-fry
with twin beds?	mit zwei Betten?	mitt tsvy bett'n
with a double bed?	mit einem Doppelbett?	mitt ine'm **dopp**'l-bet
with a bath?	mit Bad?	mitt **bart**
with a shower?	mit Dusche?	mitt **doosh**-uh
I have a reservation	Ich habe eine Reservierung	ish **harb**-uh ine-uh rez-er-**veer**-oong
key	Schlüssel	shlooss'l
porter	Pförtner	**pfert**-ner

EATING OUT

Do you have a table for...?	Haben Sie einen Tisch für...?	harb'n zee tish foor
I would like to reserve a table	Ich möchte eine Reservierung machen	ish **mer**-shtuh ine-uh rezer-**veer**-oong makh'n
I'm a vegetarian	Ich bin Vegetarier	ish bin vegg-er-**tah**-ree-er
Waiter!	Herr Ober!	hair **oh**-bare!
The bill (check), please	Die Rechnung, bitte	dee **resh**-noong bitt-uh
breakfast	Frühstück	**froo**-shtock
lunch	Mittagessen	**mit**-targ-ess'n
dinner	Abendessen	**arb**'nt-ess'n
bottle	Flasche	**flush**-uh
dish of the day	Tagesgericht	**tahg**-es-gur-isht
main dish	Hauptgericht	**howpt**-gur-isht
dessert	Nachtisch	**nahkh**-tish
cup	Tasse	**tass**-uh
wine list	Weinkarte	vine-kart-uh
tankard	Krug	khroog
glass	Glas	**glars**
spoon	Löffel	**lerff**'l
teaspoon	Teelöffel	tay-**lerff**'l
tip	Trinkgeld	**trink**-gelt
knife	Messer	**mess**-er
starter (appetizer)	Vorspeise	**for**-shpize-uh
the bill	Rechnung	**resh**-noong
plate	Teller	**tell**-er
fork	Gabel	**gahb**'l

MENU DECODER

Aal	**arl**	eel
Apfel	**upf**'l	apple
Apfelschorle	**upf**'l-shoorl-uh	apple juice with sparkling mineral water
Apfelsine	**upf**'l-seen-uh	orange
Aprikose	upri-**kawz**-uh	apricot
Artischocke	arti-**shokh**-uh	artichoke
Aubergine (eggplant)	or-ber-jeen-uh	aubergine
Banane	bar-**narn**-uh	banana
Beefsteack	**beef**-stayk	steak
Bier	beer	beer

Bockwurst	**bokh**-voorst	a type of sausage
Bohnensuppe	burn-en-zoop-uh	bean soup
Branntwein	brant-vine	spirits
Bratkartoffeln	brat-kar-toff'ln	fried potatoes
Bratwurst	brat-voorst	fried sausage
Brötchen	bret-tchen	bread roll
Brot	brot	bread
Brühe	bruh-uh	broth
Butter	**boot**-ter	butter
Champignon	**shum**-pin-yong	mushroom
Currywurst	**kha**-ree-voorst	sausage with curry sauce
Dill	**dill**	dill
Ei	**eye**	egg
Eis	**ice**	ice/ ice cream
Ente	**ent**-uh	duck
Erdbeeren	ayrt-**beer**'n	strawberries
Fisch	**fish**	fish
Forelle	for-**ell**-uh	trout
Frikadelle	Frika-**dayl**-uh	rissole/hamburger
Gans	ganns	goose
Garnele	**gar**-nayl-uh	prawn/shrimp
gebraten	g'**braat**'n	fried
gegrillt	g'**grilt**	grilled
gekocht	g'**kokh**t	boiled
geräuchert	g'**rowk**-ert	smoked
Geflügel	g'**floog**'l	poultry
Gemüse	g'**mooz**-uh	vegetables
Grütze	**grurt**-ser	groats, gruel
Gulasch	**goo**-lush	goulash
Gurke	**goork**-uh	gherkin
Hammelbraten	hamm'l-**braat**'n	roast mutton
Hähnchen	**haynsh**'n	chicken
Hering	**hair**-ing	herring
Himbeeren	him-**beer**'n	raspberries
Honig	**hoe**-nikh	honey
Kaffee	kaf-**fay**	coffee
Kalbfleisch	kalp-flysh	veal
Kaninchen	ka-**neensh**'n	rabbit
Karpfen	**karpf**'n	carp
Kartoffelpüree	kar-**toff**'l-poor-ay	mashed potatoes
Käse	**kayz**-uh	cheese
Kaviar	**kar**-vee-ar	caviar
Knoblauch	k'**nob**-lowkh	garlic
Knödel	k'**nerd**'l	noodle
Kohl	**koal**	cabbage
Kopfsalat	**kopf**-zal-aat	lettuce
Krebs	**krayps**	crab
Kuchen	**kookh**'n	cake
Lachs	**lahkhs**	salmon
Leber	**lay**-ber	liver
mariniert	mari-neert	marinated
Marmelade	marmer-**lard**-uh	marmalade, jam
Meerrettich	may-re-tish	horseradish
Milch	**milsh**	milk
Mineralwasser	minn-er-**arl**-vuss-er	mineral water
Möhre	**mer**-uh	carrot
Nuss	**nooss**	nut
Öl	**crl**	oil
Olive	o-**leev**-uh	olive
Petersilie	payt-er-**zee**-li-uh	parsley
Pfeffer	**pfeff**-er	pepper
Pfirsich	**pfir**-zish	peach
Pflaumen	**pflow**-men	plum
Pommes frites	pomm-**fritt**	chips/ French fries
Quark	kvark	soft cheese
Radieschen	ra-**deesh**'n	radish
Rinderbraten	**rind**-er-brat'n	joint of beef
Rinderroulade	**rind**-er-roo-lard-uh	beef olive
Rindfleisch	**rint**-flysh	beef
Rippchen	**rip**-sh'n	cured pork rib
Rotkohl	roht-koal	red cabbage
Rüben	rhoob'n	turnip
Rührei	**rhoo**-er-eye	scrambled eggs
Saft	**zuft**	juice
Salat	zal-aat	salad

Salz	zults	salt
Salzkartoffeln	zults-kar-toff'l	boiled potatoes
Sauerkirschen	zow-er-keersh'n	cherries
Sauerkraut	zow-er-krowt	sauerkraut
Sekt	zekt	sparkling wine
Senf	zenf	mustard
scharf	sharf	spicy
Schaschlik	shash-lik	kebab
Schlagsahne	shlahgg-zarn-uh	whipped cream
Schnittlauch	shnit-lowhkh	chives
Schnitzel	shnitz'l	veal or pork cutlet
Schweinefleisch	shvine-flysh	pork
Spargel	shparg'l	asparagus
Spiegelei	shpeeg'l-eye	fried egg
Spinat	shpin-art	spinach
Tee	tay	tea
Tomate	tom-art-uh	tomato
Wassermelone	vuss-er-me-lohn-uh	watermelon
Wein	vine	wine
Weintrauben	vine-trowb'n	grapes
Wiener Würstchen	veen-er voorst-sh'n	frankfurter
Zander	tsan-der	pike-perch
Zitrone	tsi-trohn-uh	lemon
Zucker	tsook-er	sugar
Zwieback	tsvee-bak	rusk
Zwiebel	tsveeb'l	onion

NUMBERS

0	null	nool
1	eins	eye'ns
2	zwei	tsvy
3	drei	dry
4	vier	feer
5	fünf	foonf
6	sechs	zex
7	sieben	zeeb'n
8	acht	uhkht
9	neun	noyn
10	zehn	tsayn
11	elf	elf
12	zwölf	tserlf
13	dreizehn	dry-tsayn
14	vierzehn	feer-tsayn
15	fünfzehn	foonf-tsayn
16	sechzehn	zex-tsayn

17	siebzehn	zeep-tsayn
18	achtzehn	uhkht-tsayn
19	neunzehn	noyn-tsayn
20	zwanzig	tsvunn-tsig
21	einundzwanzig	ine-oont-tsvunn-tsig
30	dreissig	dry-sig
40	vierzig	feer-sig
50	fünfzig	foonf-tsig
60	sechzig	zex-tsig
70	siebzig	zeep-tsig
80	achtzig	uhkht-tsig
90	neunzig	noyn-tsig
100	hundert	hoond't
1000	tausend	towz'nt
1 000 000	eine Million	ine-uh mill-yon

TIME

one minute	eine Minute	ine-uh min-oot-uh
one hour	eine Stunde	ine-uh shtoond-uh
half an hour	eine halbe Stunde	ine-uh hullb-uh shtoond-uh
Monday	Montag	mohn-targ
Tuesday	Dienstag	deens-targ
Wednesday	Mittwoch	mitt-vokh
Thursday	Donnerstag	donn-ers-targ
Friday	Freitag	fry-targ
Saturday	Samstag/ Sonnabend	zums-targ zonn-ah-bent
Sunday	Sonntag	zon-targ
January	Januar	yan-ooar
February	Februar	fay-brooar
March	März	mairts
April	April	april
May	Mai	my
June	Juni	yoo-ni
July	Juli	yoo-lee
August	August	ow-goost
September	September	zep-tem-ber
October	Oktober	ok-toh-ber
November	November	no-vem-ber
December	Dezember	day-tsem-ber
spring	Frühling	froo-ling
summer	Sommer	zomm-er
autumn (fall)	Herbst	hairpst
winter	Winter	vint-er